The GREGG REFERENCE MANUAL

A QUICK GUIDE TO KEY PARAGRAPHS

D0044880

FIFTH EDITION

The GREGG REFERENCE MANUAL

William A. Sabin

PUBLISHER, BUSINESS AND OFFICE EDUCATION
GREGG DIVISION, McGRAW-HILL BOOK COMPANY

Gregg Division / McGraw-Hill Book Company

New York   St. Louis   Dallas   San Francisco   Auckland
Bogotá   Düsseldorf   Johannesburg   London   Madrid   Mexico
Montreal   New Delhi   Panama   Paris   São Paulo
Singapore   Sydney   Tokyo   Toronto

Sponsoring Editor: *Joseph Tinervia*
Senior Editing Manager: *Elizabeth Huffman*
Editing Supervisor: *Gloria Schlein*
Production Manager: *Gary Whitcraft*
Design Supervisor: *Edwin Fisher*
Designer: *Betty Binns*

THE GREGG REFERENCE MANUAL, Fifth Edition

Formerly published under the title Reference Manual for
Stenographers and Typists.

    5 6 7 8 9 0   WCBP   7 8 6 5 4 3 2 1 0 9

Library of Congress Cataloging in Publication Data

Sabin, William A
    The Gregg reference manual.

    Fourth ed., by R. E. Gavin and W. A. Sabin, published
under title: Reference manual for stenographers and
typists.
    Bibliography: p.
    Includes index.
    1. Authorship—Handbooks, manuals, etc. I. Gavin,
Ruth E., date.   Reference manual for stenographers and
typists. II. Title.
PN147.S23   1977   808'.042   76-53730
ISBN 0-07-054387-9 (Text ed.)
ISBN 0-07-054389-5 (Miniature ed.)
ISBN 0-07-054388-7

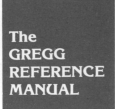

The GREGG REFERENCE MANUAL

PREFACE

The Gregg Reference Manual is intended for anyone who writes, transcribes, or types. It presents the basic rules that apply in virtually every piece of business writing, as well as the fine points that occur infrequently but cause trouble when they do. It offers an abundance of examples and illustrations so that you can quickly find a model on which to pattern a solution to a specific problem. It also provides the rationale underlying specific rules so that you can manipulate the principles of style with intelligence and taste.

Features of the New Edition. *The Gregg Reference Manual* has been expanded by about 50 pages in this edition to ensure that users will find a definitive answer to virtually every problem that is likely to occur in ordinary written communications. Among the new topics covered in this edition is *metrication:* ¶¶537–538 deal with metric measurements and the style of metric abbreviations; various paragraphs in Section 13 deal with metric sizes of stationery and envelopes. Also a topic of primary concern in this edition is the matter of *sexism* in our language: ¶¶808–809 discuss the generic use of terms like *businessman* and *chairman* and how to avoid them; ¶837 discusses ways to avoid feminine suffixes like *ess* and *ette;* ¶¶1050–1053 discuss ways to avoid the generic pronoun *he* when the antecedent is a noun of common gender (like *parent* or *teacher*) or an indefinite pronoun (like *everyone* or *anyone*); ¶1350 discusses alternatives to the common salutation *Gentlemen.*

Along with this expansion in coverage *The Gregg Reference Manual* has been updated to reflect the significant changes in style that have occurred since the last edition was published. The manual acknowledges, for example, such trends as dropping the comma before terms like *Jr., Sr.,* and *Inc.* or dropping the period after abbreviations of measurements (like *ft, oz,* and *lb*). The manual also offers up-to-date answers to such questions as these: (1) how to address a woman when you are not sure which title of respect she prefers; or (2) how to address a person (like *C. V. O'Brien* or *Marion Nichols*) when you are not sure of the person's gender.

To enhance the effectiveness of the manual as a reference tool, many new illustrations, models, and examples have been added in this edition. Note, too, that each section of the manual begins with a detailed list of the topics covered in that section. These lists will make it easier for you to grasp the organization and coverage of each section; they also provide you with a new way to look things up.

Available for use with *The Gregg Reference Manual* is an all-new, 64-page set of worksheets designed specifically to build three critical editing skills. First of all, the *Worksheets for The Gregg Reference Man-*

ual will familiarize you with the wide range of potential problems you are likely to encounter in any material that you write, transcribe, or type. Second, these worksheets will direct you to the key rules in each section of *The Gregg Reference Manual* so that later on, when you encounter similar problems in your own work, you'll know where to look. Third, they will sharpen your ability to apply the rules correctly under many different circumstances.

An Overview of the Organization and the Coverage. This edition of *The Gregg Reference Manual* consists of 18 sections, organized as follows:

Part One (Sections 1–11) deals with grammar, usage, and the chief aspects of style—punctuation, capitalization, numbers, abbreviations, plurals and possessives, spelling, compound words, and word division.

Part Two (Sections 12–15) deals with techniques and procedures for producing all kinds of written communications in business—letters, memos, reports, manuscripts, and tabular matter.

Part Three (Sections 16–18) provides three appendixes for fast reference: a listing of model forms of address, a glossary of grammatical terms, and a bibliography of useful reference works.

While a reference manual is not intended to be read from cover to cover, an hour or two devoted at the outset to scanning the manual will enhance its usefulness later on as specific problems occur. The following comments provide a brief orientation to the manual and highlight features of each section that warrant special attention.

Section 1 (¶¶101–199) deals with the major marks of punctuation—the period, the question mark, the exclamation point, the comma, the semicolon, and the colon. As you scan Section 1, give especially close attention to the rules on the comma and the semicolon, since they treat punctuation problems that commonly occur in all business writing. In particular, note ¶¶122–125, which provide a new overview of commas used to *set off* and commas used to *separate*. Also note paragraphs such as ¶132, which provides an extensive list of model sentences for all the varied applications of the basic rule.

Section 2 (¶¶201–299) deals with the other marks of punctuation—the dash, parentheses, quotation marks, the underscore, the apostrophe, ellipsis marks, the asterisk, the diagonal, and brackets. Of special note are the model sentences provided for quotation marks (particularly those in ¶¶257–258) and the rules in ¶299, which indicate the typewriter spacing to be used with all marks of punctuation.

Section 3 (¶¶301–362) covers capitalization. Give particular attention to the introduction and the basic rules (¶¶301–310). If you grasp the function of capitalization, you will not only have a better perspective on all the specific rules that follow but also be better equipped to resolve capitalization problems on your own.

Section 4 (¶¶401–468) discusses number style. For an explanation of the concepts that underlie all aspects of number style, read the introduction and the basic rules (¶¶401–406). If you understand the functional difference between expressing numbers in figures and in words, you can solve many specific style questions without having to refer to the manual.

Section 5 (¶¶501–547) deals with abbreviations. Study the basic rules (¶¶501–514) and give special attention to the rules for abbreviating customary measurements (¶¶535–536) and metric measurements (¶¶537–538). Also note the new or expanded lists of common abbreviations provided in ¶¶541, 543, and 544.

Section 6 (¶¶601–650) covers plurals and possessives. Because of the frequency with which these forms occur, give special attention to the basic rules that govern their formation and usage.

Section 7 (¶¶701–718) provides a number of spelling guides that could help you reduce your dependence on the dictionary. For fast assistance on words that look alike or sound alike, consult ¶717, which provides a 12-page guide to these troublesome combinations. To avoid spelling errors, consult ¶718 for a 3-page list of words commonly misspelled.

Section 8 (¶¶801–838) deals with all kinds of compound words and provides guides as to whether they should be spaced, solid, or hyphenated. Note in particular ¶¶813–829 on compound adjectives; these paragraphs offer an extensive series of patterns and examples to clarify the applications of the basic rule.

Section 9 (¶¶901–922) discusses word division in terms of a few absolute rules and a number of preferred practices. In addition, Section 9 offers several hints on determining correct syllabication without reference to a dictionary.

Section 10 (¶¶1001–1084) offers a compact survey of all the rules of grammar that you are likely to need. The coverage ranges from subject-verb agreement to proper sentence structure, with special attention given to problems involving verbs, pronouns, adjectives, adverbs, prepositions, and the use of negatives.

Section 11 (¶1101) deals with problems of usage. Individual entries are provided for a wide range of troublesome words and phrases and are listed alphabetically for fast reference.

Section 12 (¶¶1201–1231) provides a useful summary of proper dictation, transcription, and typing techniques.

Section 13 (¶¶1301–1399) is a key unit for anyone who writes or types letters and memos. Substantially revamped and expanded for this edition, it provides extensive styling notes on every element in a letter—from the letterhead to the postscript. It also discusses letter styles, punctuation patterns, and effective placement, with the aid of extensive illustrations and tables; it treats the preparation of envelopes and gives up-to-date instructions on how to handle addresses; and it provides special guides on memos and social-business correspondence.

Section 14 (¶¶1401–1433) provides guides and illustrations on the preparation of reports, manuscripts, footnotes, and bibliographies. Note in particular ¶1418, which offers a series of easy-to-follow patterns for constructing footnotes.

Section 15 (¶¶1501–1514) offers detailed guidelines and sample layouts for the arrangement of tabular matter.

Section 16 (¶1601) lists the correct forms of address and appropriate salutations for government officials, members of the armed services, religious dignitaries, and education officials.

Section 17 (¶1701) provides an alphabetized glossary of grammatical terms for the user who wants to quickly check the meaning of a particular term or who wants a fast review of grammatical terminology as a whole.

Section 18 (¶1801) offers a recommended bibliography of reference books that are useful on any office bookshelf.

The foregoing notes are only a preliminary guide to what you can discover more effectively firsthand. As you make your own survey of the text, you will want to single out the key rules that deserve further study; these are the rules that deal with everyday situations, the rules you need to have at your command. You may also want to develop a passing acquaintance with the fine points of style. It is sufficient simply to know that such rules exist; then, when you need them, you will know where to find them. Finally, you will want to take note of special word lists, sentence patterns, and illustrations that could be useful to you later on. If you find out now what aids the manual provides, you will know what kind of help you can count on in the future. And what is more important, you will be able to find what you are looking for faster.

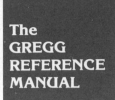

HOW TO LOOK THINGS UP

Suppose you were writing to someone in another department:

> I understand you are doing a confidential study of the Bronson matter. May I please get an advance copy of your report [At this point you hesitate. Should this sentence end with a period or a question mark?]

This is the kind of problem that continually comes up in any type of written communication. How do you find a fast answer to such questions? In this manual there are several ways to proceed.

Using the Index. The surest approach, perhaps, is to check the detailed index at the back of the manual (11 pages, with over 1,600 entries). For example, any of the following entries will lead you to the right punctuation for the problem sentence above:

Periods, **101–109**   Question marks, **110–118**   Request, punctuation
. . .   . . .   of, **103**
  at end of requests, **103**   at end of requests, **103, 113**

In each entry the boldface number refers to the proper rule, ¶103. (If you look up ¶103, you will find that a question mark is the right punctuation for the sentence in question.)

In almost all of the index entries, references are made to specific rule numbers so that you can find what you are looking for fast. In a few cases, where a page reference will provide a more precise location (for example, when a rule runs on for several pages), a page number is given in lightface type. Suppose you were confronted with this problem:

> If you compare the performance records of Catano, Harris, and Williams, you won't find much difference (*between/among*) them.

The index will show the following entries:

  among–between, 214   **OR**   *between–among,* 214

The rule on page 214 indicates that *between* is correct in this situation.

Using a Fast-Skim Approach. Many users of reference manuals have little patience with detailed indexes; they would rather open the book and skim through the pages until they find what they are looking for. If you are the kind of person who prefers this approach, you will find the brief topical index on the inside front cover especially helpful, since indicates the key paragraphs for each major topic. Moreover, at the start of each section you will find a detailed list of all the topics covered in that section. This list will help you quickly focus on the rule or rules that pertain to your problem. Extensive cross-references have also been provided throughout the manual so that you can quickly locate related rules that could prove helpful. Suppose the following problem came up:

> The only point still at issue is whether or not new *Federal* [or is it *federal?*] legislation is required.

The index on the inside front cover indicates that ¶¶301–362 deal with the topic of capitalization. A fast skim of the outline preceding ¶301 will turn up the entry *Names of Government Bodies* (¶¶325–330). If you turn to that set of rules, you will find in ¶328 that *federal* is the proper form.

Playing the Numbers. There is still a third way to find the answer to a specific problem—and this is an approach that will grow in appeal as you become familiar with the organization and the content of the manual. From a fast inspection of the rule numbers, you will observe that they all carry a section number as a prefix. Thus Section 3 (on capitalization) has a "300" series of rules—from 301 to 362; Section 4 (on number style) has a "400" series—from 401 to 468; and so on. Once you become familiar with the section numbers and the section titles, you can find your way around fairly quickly, without reference to either index. For example, you are about to write the following sentence:

> 43 percent of the questionnaires have now been returned. [Or should it be, "*Forty-three* percent of the questionnaires . . ."?]

If you know that matters of number style are treated in Section 4, you can quickly turn to the "400" series of rules, where a fast skim of the outline of topics at the start of the section will lead you to the answer in ¶421. (*Forty-three percent* is the right answer in this instance.)

A familiarity with the section numbers and section titles can also save you time when you are using the index. If your index entry lists several different paragraph numbers, you can often anticipate what the paragraphs will deal with. For example, if you want to know whether to type 5 *lb* or 5 *lbs* on a purchase order and you check the index, you might encounter the following entry:

> Weights, **429–430, 535–538, 621**

If you know that Section 6 deals with plurals, you will try ¶621 first.

Looking Up Specific Words. Many of the problems that arise deal with specific words. For this reason the index provides as many entries for such words as space will permit. For example, in the following sentence, should *therefore* be set off by commas or not?

> It is(,) *therefore*(,) essential that operations be curtailed.

A check of the index will show the following entry:

> *therefore,* **122, 138–142**

A reading of the rules in ¶141 will indicate that no commas should be used in this sentence. If you asked the same question about another specific word and did not find it listed as a separate entry in the index, your best approach would be to check the index under "Comma" and investigate the most promising references or make a direct scan of the comma rules in Section 1 until you find the answer you are looking for.

If you are having difficulty with words that look alike and sound alike—*jibe* and *gibe* or *affect* and *effect*—turn directly to ¶717. For other troublesome words and phrases, consult ¶1101.

The
GREGG
REFERENCE
MANUAL

CONTENTS

Part 1: Grammar, Usage, and Style

Part 2: Techniques and Procedures

Part 3: References and Resources

The five brief essays that follow deal with a number of specific points of style that cause the greatest difficulty for writers, transcribers, and typists. However, these essays also attempt to deal with the broad concept of style itself—the art of tailoring one's use of language to fit the situation.

Mastering Number Style:
One (or 1?) Approach

Several years ago, while making a presentation on the subject of style, I asked the audience to select the preferable form in each of the following pairs of examples:

$87,525	OR	eighty-seven thousand five hundred and twenty-five dollars
$700 billion	OR	$700,000,000,000
4:30 p.m., January 19	OR	half after four o'clock, on the nineteenth of January

No one could see any use for the forms in the second column. Those in the first column were far easier to read and simpler to write and were clearly to be preferred in business writing. However, after some discussion, we tended to agree that Tiffany's had had the right idea in a recent ad, where beneath a picture of an elegant diamond necklace was the legend "Eighty-seven thousand five hundred and twenty-five dollars." Somehow, we felt, if they were going to charge that elegant a price, the least they could do was spell it out. Moreover, we tended to agree that a liberal in fiscal matters might readily dismiss the federal debt as "only $700 billion," whereas a fiscal conservative who wanted to emphasize the enormity of the amount might well have written "The federal debt now stands at $700,000,000,000" and thereby have forced upon us a sense of the magnitude of the amount by making us calculate it for ourselves. Finally, we agreed that we would much rather be married at "half after four, on January nineteenth in the year of Our Lord . . ." than at "4:30 p.m., January 19."*

These, admittedly, are extreme examples of occasions on which an unusual number style could be justified, but they tend to throw light on the more customary style for expressing numbers and on the notion of

---

* One dissenter indicated that she simply wanted to get married and didn't much care how the invitations read.

style in general. At the very least, these examples suggest that style should not be thought of as a rigid set of rules but rather as a set of principles for adjusting one's means of expression to fit a particular set of circumstances. We express our style in clothes through a varied wardrobe that suits the needs not only of everyday situations but of formal and informal occasions as well. It is the impoverished man who meets every situation with the same set of clothes. By the same token, it is an impoverished writer who meets all situations with a rigid set of rules. The writer of the Tiffany ad, who chose words instead of figures to express an amount of money, in this instance had some true sense of how to vary style for best effect.

Manipulating principles of style for specific effect ought not to be a random, hit-or-miss exercise but should proceed from some coherent notion about style itself. In the case of numbers, an intelligent control of number style proceeds from an awareness of the difference in effect that results from using figures or words to express numbers.

Figures are big (like capital letters); when used in a sentence, they stand out clearly from the surrounding tissue of words. As a result, they are easier to grasp on first reading, and they are easier to locate for subsequent reference. Thus whenever quick comprehension and fast reference are important (and this is true of most business writing), figures are to be preferred to words.

But the very characteristics of figures that make them preferable to words can be disadvantageous in certain circumstances. Figures stand out so sharply against a background of words that they achieve a special prominence and obtain a special emphasis. Not all numbers warrant that kind of emphasis, however, and in such cases words are preferable to figures. Keep in mind, too, that figures have the same conciseness and the same informality of an abbreviation. Thus the more formal the occasion, the more likely one is to spell numbers out (as in the wedding announcement cited on page xi).

Given these basic differences between using figures and using words, it is quite clear why figures are preferred in ordinary business letters. These are typically straightforward communications that pass between business firms and their suppliers or their customers, containing frequent references to price quotations, quantities, shipping dates, credit terms, and the like. Frequently, these numbers represent data that has to be extracted from the letter and processed in some way: they may have to be checked against other numbers or included in some computation or simply transferred to another document. The advantage of figures to words in these ordinary cases is so clear that the point does not need to be argued.

But there is another kind of business writing in which the writer is not typically dealing with the workaday transactions of his business. It may be a special promotion campaign with an air of elegance and formality; it may be a carefully constructed letter with special stylistic objectives in mind; or it may be a special report which involves community relations and will have a wider distribution than the normal technical business report. This kind of writing tends to occur more often at the executive level, and it tends to occur in the more creative departments of a business (such as sales promotion, advertising, public relations, and customer relations). In this kind of writing, numbers don't occur very frequently; when they do, they are usually expressed in words.

As if in response to the different needs posed by these two kinds of writing, there are two basic number styles in use today. Both use figures and words but in different proportions. The *figure style* uses figures for all numbers above 10, whether exact or approximate; the *word style* spells out all numbers up through 100 and all numbers above 100 that can be expressed in one or two words (such as *twenty-five hundred*).

As a practical matter, your job may require you to use only the figure style. However, since the figure style itself involves the use of words to some extent, you will find it easier to master the ins and outs of the figure style if you grasp the basic difference between using words and figures to express numbers. Given this basic understanding of number style, you will be better able to decide how to proceed in specific situations without having to consult a style manual each time.

In any case, keep the following ideas in mind:

1. There are no absolute rights and wrongs in number style—only varying sets of stylistic conventions that people follow in one set of circumstances or another. There are, however, effective differences in using words or figures, and you should take these differences into account.

2. Before deciding on which number style to follow for a given piece of writing, first determine the basic objective of the material. If the material is intended to communicate information as simply and as briefly as possible, use the *figure style*. If the material is of a formal nature or aspires to a certain level of literary elegance, use the *word style*.

3. Having decided on a basic style, *be consistent in context*. When related numbers occur together in the same context and according to the rules some should go in figures and some should go in words, treat these related numbers all the same way.

4. Treat approximate numbers exactly the same way you would treat an exact number. If you would write *50 orders,* then you should also write *about 50 orders.* (If the figure 50 looks too emphatic to you when used in an approximation, the chances are that you should be using the word style—and not just for approximate numbers but throughout.)

5. In areas where the style could go either way (for example, *the 4th of June* vs. *the fourth of June* or *9 o'clock* vs. *nine o'clock*), decide in accordance with your basic style. Thus if you are following the figure style, you will automatically choose *the 4th of June* and *9 o'clock.*

6. In expressions involving *ages, periods of time,* and *measurements,* use figures whenever these numbers have technical significance or serve as measurements or deserve special emphasis; otherwise, use words. (For example, *you receive these benefits at 65, the note will be due in 3 months, the parcel weighs over 2 pounds;* but *my father will be sixty-five next week, that happened three months ago, I hope to lose another two pounds this week.*)

7. In general, always use figures in dates (*June 6*) and in expressions of money (*$6*), except for reasons of formality or special effect (as in the wedding announcement or the Tiffany ad). Also use figures in percentages, proportions, ratios, scores, and with abbreviations and symbols.

8. In general, always use words for numbers at the beginning of a sentence, for most ordinals (*the third time, the twentieth anniversary*), and for fractions standing alone (*one-third of our sales*).

All manuals of style (including this one) include many more than eight rules. They give exceptions and fine points beyond those summarized above. Yet for all practical purposes these eight rules—and the philosophy that underlies them—will cover almost every common situation. Just remember that the conventions of number style were meant to be applied, not as an absolute set of dogmas, but as a flexible set of principles that help to fit the form to the occasion. When manipulated with intelligence and taste, these principles of style can do much to enhance and support your broader purposes in writing.

A Fresh Look at Capitalization

The rules on capitalization give most people fits. First of all, there are a seemingly endless number of specific rules to master; second, the authorities themselves don't agree on the rules; and third, the actual practices of writers often diverge from the contradictory recommendations of the authorities.

A frequent solution is to pretend that disagreements on capitalization style don't exist; instead, writers, transcribers, and typists are given one fixed set of rules to be applied under all circumstances. Yet all too many people never do remember the full complement of rules, and those they do remember they apply mechanically without comprehension. As a result, they never get to see that capitalization can be a powerful instrument of style if it is shrewdly and knowingly used.

To understand the basic function of capitalization, you should know that capitalization gives importance, emphasis, and distinction to everything it touches. That's why we capitalize the first word of every sentence—to signify emphatically that a new sentence has begun. That's why we capitalize proper nouns like *Marianne* and *California* and *April*—to indicate distinctively that these are the official names of particular people, places, or things. Moreover, when we take a word that normally occurs as a common noun and capitalize it, we are loading into that word the special significance that a proper noun possesses. The *fourth of July,* for example, is just another day in the year; when it signifies a national holiday, it becomes the *Fourth of July.* In exactly the same way, the *white house* that stands at 1600 Pennsylvania Avenue becomes the *White House* when we think of it, not as one of many white houses, but as the residence of the *President,* who is himself something special compared to the *president* of a business firm.

This process of giving special significance to a common noun and transforming it into a proper noun explains why we capitalize names coined from common nouns—for example, the *Windy City,* the *First Lady,* the *Sunflower State,* the *Stars and Stripes, Mother's Day,* and the *Industrial Revolution.* And it also explains why manufacturers who coin trade names try to register them whenever possible. As long as they can get legal protection for these names, they are entitled to capitalize them. The owners of such trade names as *Coke, Kleenex, Photostat, Dacron,* and *Xerox* are likely to take legal action against anyone who uses such words generically. They are determined to protect their rights zealously because they don't want to lose the distinctive forcefulness that a capitalized noun possesses. In this respect they demonstrate an understanding of the function of capitalization that few of us can compete with.

Once it becomes clear that capitalization is a process of loading special significance into words, it's easier to understand why capitalization practices vary so widely. Individual writers will assign importance to words from their own vantage points. The closer they are to the term in question, the more inclined they will be to capitalize it. Thus it is quite possible that what is important to me (and therefore worthy of capitalization) may not be important to you and thus will not be capitalized.

One could cite any number of examples to prove the point. A retail merchant will take out full-page ads so that he can exclaim in print about his *Year-End Clearance Sale.* The rest of us can respect his right to capitalize the phrase, but we are under no obligation to share his enthusiasm for what is, after all, just another *year-end clearance sale.* In legal agreements, as another example, it's customary to load such terms as *buyer* and *seller* with the significance of proper nouns and thus write, "The *Buyer* agrees, moreover, to pay the *Seller* . . ."; in all other contexts, however, this kind of emphasis would not be warranted.

When it is understood that it is appropriate to capitalize a given term in some contexts but not necessarily in all contexts, a lot of the agony about capitalization disappears. Instead of trying to decide whether *Federal Government* or *federal government* is correct, you should recognize that both forms are valid and that depending on the context and the importance you want to attach to the term, one form will be more appropriate to your purpose than another. If you are a federal employee, you are very likely to write *Federal Government* under all circumstances, out of respect for the organization that employs you. If you are not a government employee, you are more likely to write *federal government* under ordinary circumstances. If, however, you are writing to someone connected with the federal government or you are writing a report or document in which the federal government is strongly personified, you will probably choose the capitalized form.

By the same token, you need not agonize over the proper way to treat terms like *advertising department, finance committee,* and *board of directors.* These are well-established generic terms as well as the official names of actual units within an organization. Thus you are likely to capitalize these terms if they refer to units within your own organization, because you would be expected to assign a good deal of importance to such things. But you wouldn't have to capitalize these terms when referring to someone else's organization unless for reasons of courtesy or flattery you wanted to indicate that you considered that organization important. (For example, "I would like to apply for a job as copywriter in your Advertising Department.") Moreover, when writing to outsiders, you should keep in mind whether or not they would assign the same importance you do to units within your organization. In an interoffice memo you would no doubt write, "David Walsh has been appointed to the Board of Directors"; in a news release intended for a general audience, you would more likely write, "David Walsh has been appointed to the board of directors of the Wilmington Corporation."

This switch in form from one context to another will appear surprising only to those who assume that one form is intrinsically right and the other intrinsically wrong. Actually, there are many more familiar instances of this kind of flexibility. We normally write the names of seasons in lowercase (e.g., *spring*), but when the season is meant to be personified, we switch to uppercase (*Spring*). The words *earth*, *sun*, and *moon* are normally expressed in lowercase, but when these terms are used in the same context with proper names like *Mars* and *Venus*, they also become capitalized. Or we write that we are taking courses in *history* and *art*, but once these terms become part of the official names of courses, we write *History 101* and *Art 5C*.

Once you come to view capitalization as a flexible instrument of style, you should be able to cope more easily with ambiguous or conflicting rules. For example, one of the most troublesome rules concerns whether or not to capitalize titles when they follow a person's name or are used in place of the name. According to most authorities, only the titles of "high-ranking" officials and dignitaries should be capitalized when they follow or replace a person's name. But how high is high? Where does one draw the line? You can easily become confused at this point because the authorities as well as individual writers have drawn the line at various places. So it helps to understand that the answer to how high is high will depend on where you stand in relation to the person named. At the international level, probably all of us would be willing to bestow initial caps on the *Queen of England*, the *Premier of France*, the *Pope*, the *Secretary General of the United Nations*, and people of similar eminence. At the national level in this country, we would all agree on honoring with caps the *President*, the *Vice President*, Cabinet members (such as the *Attorney General* and the *Secretary of Defense*), the heads of federal agencies and bureaus (such as the *Director* or the *Commissioner*), but probably not lower-ranking officials in the national government. (However, if you worked in Washington and were closer to those lower-ranking people, you might very well draw the line so as to include at least some of them.) At the state level, we would probably all agree to honor the *Governor* and even the *Lieutenant Governor*, but most of us would probably refer to the *attorney general* of the state in lowercase (unless, of course, we worked for the state government or had dealings with the official in question, in which case we would write the *Attorney General*). Because most people who write style manuals are removed from the local levels of government, they rarely sanction the use of caps for the titles of local officials; but anyone who works for the local government or on the local newspaper or has direct dealings with these officials will assign to the titles of these officials a good deal more importance than the writers of style manuals typically do. Indeed, if I were writing to the mayor of my town or to someone in the mayor's office, I would refer to the *Mayor*. But if I discuss this official with you in writing, I would refer to the *mayor;* in this context it would be bestowing excessive importance on this person to capitalize the title.

What about titles of high-ranking officials in your own organization? They certainly are important to you, even if not to the outside world. Such titles are usually capped in formal minutes of a meeting or in formal documents (such as a company charter or a set of bylaws). In ordinary written communications, however, these titles are not—as a matter of taste—usually capitalized, for capitalization would confer an excessive importance on a person who is neither a public official nor a prominent dignitary. But those who insist on paying this gesture of respect and honor to their top executives have the right to do it if they want to. (And in some companies this gesture is demanded.)

In the final analysis, the important thing is for you to establish an appropriate capitalization style for a given context—and having established that style, to follow it consistently within that context, even though you might well adopt a different style in another context. Though others may disagree with your specific applications of the rules, no one can fault you if you have brought both sense and sensitivity to your use of capitalization.

The Comma Trauma

Consider the poor comma, a plodding workhorse in the fields of prose—exceedingly useful but like most workhorses overworked. Because it can do so many things, a number of writers dispense commas to cure their ailing prose the way doctors dispense aspirin: according to this prescription, you take two at frequent intervals and hope the problem will go away. Other writers, having written, stand back to admire their handiwork as if it were a well-risen cake—and for the final touch they sprinkle commas down upon it like so much confectioners' sugar. And one writer I know, when pushed to desperation, will type several rows of commas at the bottom of her letter and urge you to insert them in the copy above wherever you think it appropriate.

It's too bad that commas induce a trauma in so many writers. Despite the seemingly endless set of rules that describe their varied powers, commas have only two basic functions: they either separate or set off. Separating requires only one comma; setting off requires two.

The separating functions of the comma, for the most part, are easy to spot and not hard to master. A separating comma is used:

1. To separate the two main clauses in a compound sentence when they are joined by *and, but, or,* or *nor.*

2. To separate three or more items in a series (*Tom, Dick, and Harry*)—unless all the items are joined by *and* or *or* (*Bob and Carol and Ted and Alice*).

3. To signify the omission of *and* between adjectives of equal rank (as in *a quiet, unassuming personality*).

4. To separate the digits of numbers into groups of thousands (*30,000*).

Writers get into trouble here mostly as a result of separating things that should not be separated—for example, a subject and a verb (*Bob, Carol, Ted, and Alice decided to see a movie*) or an adjective and a noun (*a quiet, unassuming personality*). Yet this is not where the comma trauma begins to set in.

The real crunch comes with the commas that set off. These are the commas that are intended to set off words, phrases, or clauses that (1) provide additional but nonessential information or (2) are out of their normal order in the sentence or (3) manage, in one way or another, to disrupt the flow of the sentence from subject to verb to object or complement. What makes it so difficult for people to use these commas correctly is that they have a hard time analyzing the difference between an expression used as an essential element in one context and as a nonessential element in another.

Consider the following example. I would venture that most people have been taught to punctuate the sentence exactly as it is given here:

It is, therefore, essential that we audit all accounts at once.

To be specific, they have probably been taught that *therefore* is always nonessential when it occurs within a sentence and that it must therefore always be set off by commas. What they probably have not been taught is that commas that set off (unlike commas that separate) usually signal the way a sentence should sound when spoken aloud. For example, if I were to read the foregoing sentence aloud the way it has been punctuated, I would pause slightly at the sign of the first comma and then let my voice drop on the word *therefore:*

IT IS, therefore, ESSENTIAL . . .

Now if this is the reading that is desired, then the use of commas around *therefore* is quite correct. Yet I would venture that most people would read the sentence this way:

It is THEREFORE essential . . .

letting the voice rise on *therefore* to give it the special emphasis it demands. If this is the desired reading, then commas would be altogether wrong in this sentence, for they would induce a "nonessential" inflection in the voice where none is wanted.

If people have been mechanically inserting commas around *therefore* and similar words where commas do not belong, it is because they have not been encouraged to listen to the way the sentences are supposed to sound. Certainly once you become aware of the differences in inflection and phrasing that accompany essential and nonessential elements, it becomes a lot easier for you to distinguish between them and to insert or omit commas accordingly. Given this kind of approach, sentences like the following pair are simple to cope with.

Please let me know *if I have remembered everything correctly.*
He said he would meet us at three, *if I remember correctly.*

Although it would be possible, by means of a structural analysis, to establish why the first *if* clause is essential and why the second is not, you would do well to be guided by the inflection implied in each sentence. In the first instance, the voice arcs as it bridges the gap between *Please let me know* and *if I have remembered everything correctly.* In the second instance, the inflectional arc embraces only the first part of the sentence, *He said he would meet us at three;* then comes a slight pause followed by the *if* clause, which is uttered in a much lower register, almost as if it were an afterthought.

As you gain confidence in your ability to detect the inflectional patterns characteristic of essential and nonessential expressions, you should have no difficulty in picking your way through a variety of constructions like these:

I must report, *nevertheless,* that his work is unsatisfactory.
I must *nevertheless* report that his work is unsatisfactory.

The location, *I must admit,* is quite attractive.
The location is one *I must admit* I find attractive.

There are, *of course,* other possible answers to the problem.
It is *of course* your prerogative to change your mind.

This awareness of inflectional patterns is especially helpful when it comes to coping with appositives, a frustrating area in which the use or omission of commas often seems illogical. When the appositive expression is truly nonessential, as in:

Ed Brown, *the president of Apex,* would like to meet you.

the customary pause and the characteristic drop in voice are there. And when the appositive expression is essential, as in phrases like *the year 1980* and *the term "recommend,"* you can hear the single inflectional arc that embraces each group of words in one closely knit unit. You can also hear the same continuous arc in the phrase *my wife Marie.* By all that is logical, the name *Marie* should be set off by commas because it is not needed to establish which of my wives I'm speaking about; unlike an Arabian sheik, I have only one wife. Yet according to today's standards, *my wife Marie* is considered good form. Although not essential to the meaning, the name *Marie* is treated as if it were essential because of what style manuals call "a very close relationship with the preceding words." Although it is difficult, if not impossible, to state in concrete terms what constitutes "a very close relationship," you can tell by the sound when it exists. There is a subtle but very real difference in the phrases *my sister Florence* and *my sister, Florence Stern.* Once the second name is added, there tends to be a slight pause after *sister* and the voice tends to drop while uttering the full name. Yet it is not safe to conclude that adding the second name accounts for the difference in the inflection, for when one speaks of *the composer John Cage* or *the author John Fowles,* one hears the same inflectional pattern as in *my wife Marie* or *the year 1980.* So in the case of appositives, it is wise to be wary of simple generalizations and to listen attentively in each case to the way the expression ought to sound.

In stressing, as I have, the significance of inflection and phrasing as a guide to the use of commas, I do not mean to suggest that one can punctuate by sound alone and can safely ignore structure and meaning. What I am suggesting is that in a number of cases, such as those I have cited, an awareness of the sound of sentences can help you grasp relationships that might otherwise be obscure.

There are many other problems involving the comma that should be discussed here, but someone else (Ogden Nash, perhaps) will have to take over . . .

And now if you'll excuse me comma
I must lie down and have my trauma . . . . ,

The Plight of the Compound Adjective— Or, Where Have All the Hyphens Gone?

The hyphen, it grieves me to report, is in trouble. Indeed, unless concerted action is taken at once, the hyphen is likely to become as extinct as the apostrophe in *ladies aid.* The problem can be traced to two dangerous attitudes that are afoot these days. One is revolutionary in tone; its motto: "Compound adjectives, unite! You have nothing to lose but your hyphens." The other attitude reflects the view of the silent majority. These are the people who don't pretend to know how to cope with the "hyphen" mess; they just earnestly wish the whole problem would quickly disappear. It may now be too late to reverse the long-range trend. For the present, however, the hyphen exists—and anyone who expects to write or transcribe with any degree of proficiency needs to come to terms with the noble beast. Here, then, is a last-ditch effort to make sense out of an ever-changing and possibly fast-disappearing (but not-soon-to-be-forgotten) aspect of style.

As a general rule, the English language depends largely on word order to make the relationships between words clear. When word order alone is not sufficient to establish these relationships, we typically resort to punctuation. It is in this context that the hyphen has a service to offer. The function of the hyphen is to help the reader grasp clusters of words—or even parts of words—as a unit. When a word has to be divided at the end of a line, the hyphen signifies the connection between parts. Whenever two or more words function as a unit but cannot (for one reason or another) be written either as a solid word or as separate words, the hyphen clearly establishes the relationship between these words and prevents a lapse in comprehension.

If hyphens are typically required in compound adjectives, it is because there is something "abnormal" about the word order of such expressions. Other kinds of modifiers, by contrast, do not require hyphens. For example, if I write about "a *long, hard* winter," I am actually referring to a winter *that will be long and hard;* so I need a comma—not a hyphen—to establish the fact that *long* and *hard* modify *winter* independently. If I write about a "*long opening* paragraph," the word order makes it clear that *opening* modifies *paragraph* and that *long* modifies the two words together; so no punctuation is needed to establish the fact that I'm speaking about "*an opening paragraph that is long.*"

However, if I write about "a long-term loan," an entirely different relationship is established between the elements in the modifier. I am not speaking of a *loan* that is *long* and *term,* nor am I referring to a *term loan* that is *long.* I am speaking about a loan "that is to run for a *long term* of years." The words *long-term* (unlike *long, hard* or *long opening*) have an internal relationship all their own; it is only as an integral unit that these two words can modify a noun. Thus a hyphen is inserted to establish this fact clearly.

For a better understanding of the internal relationship that exists between the elements in a compound adjective, one has to go back to its origins. A compound adjective is actually a compressed version of an adjective phrase or clause. For example, if I describe a product as carrying "a *money-back* guarantee," I am actually talking about "a guarantee *to give you your money back if you are not satisfied with the product.*" Or if I refer to a "*take-charge* kind of guy," I am really speaking of "the kind of guy *who always takes charge of any situation he finds himself in.*" One can easily see from these examples why compound adjectives are so popular, for these expressions are usually a good deal crisper and livelier than the phrases or clauses they represent. These examples give further evidence of why a hyphen is needed. In each case we have zeroed in on a couple of words, we have wrenched them out of context and out of their normal order in a descriptive phrase or clause, and we have inserted them before a noun as if they were an ordinary adjective—a role these two words were never originally designed to play. Deprived of all the other words that would clearly establish the relationship between them, these elements require a hyphen to hold them together.

The two factors of compression and dislocation are all the justification one needs to hyphenate a compound adjective. However, there are often additional clues to the need for a hyphen. In the process of becoming a compound adjective, the individual words frequently undergo a change in form: "a contract for *two years*" becomes "a *two-year* contract"; "a blonde with *blue eyes*" becomes "a *blue-eyed* blonde." Sometimes the words are put in inverted order: "lands *owned* by the *government*" becomes "*government-owned* lands." Sometimes the elements undergo both a change in form *and* in word order: "an employee *who works hard*" becomes "a *hard-working* employee"; "bonds *exempt from taxation*" becomes "*tax-exempt* bonds." The change in form or the inversion in word order is an additional signal that you are in the presence of a compound adjective and ought to hyphenate it.

I f the compound adjective is so simple to understand in theory, why is it so difficult to handle in practice? A good deal of the problem can be traced to that neat rule, "Hyphenate compound adjectives when they precede the noun but not when they follow the noun." It is indeed a very neat rule but not a very precise one. Let's take it apart and put it back together.

It is quite true that compound adjectives should be hyphenated when they occur *before* a noun—for the most part. There's the catch—"for the most part." The exceptions seem to occur in such a random, hit-and-miss, now-and-then, flip-a-coin, make-it-up-as-you-go-along fashion that one begins to lose respect for the rule. Yet there is a very definite pattern to the exceptions. Keep in mind that the hyphen serves to hold a cluster of words together as a unit. If, through some other means, these words make themselves clearly recognizable as a unit, the hyphen is superfluous and can be omitted. There are at least three such situations where a hyphen is unnecessary: when the compound modifier is a proper name, when it is a well-recognized foreign expression, and when it is a well-established compound noun serving as a compound adjective. Let's look at some samples.

If I speak of "a *Madison Avenue* agency," the capital *M* and *A* virtually guarantee that the expression will be quickly grasped as a unit. And if I talk about "a *bona fide* contract," the reader will recognize this Latin expression as a unit without the help of a hyphen. By the same token, terms like *social security, life insurance,* and *high school* are so well established as compound nouns that when they are used as adjectives, we immediately grasp such expressions as a unit, without the support of any punctuation.

If no hyphen is needed in "*social security* benefits," one may well ask why a hyphen is required in "*short-term* benefits." After all, words like *short term* and *long range* are adjective-noun combinations that closely resemble *social security, life insurance,* and *high school.* Why hyphenate some and not others? The reason is this: Words like *short term, long range,* and *high level* don't have any standing as compound nouns in their own right; they do not represent a concept or an institution (as terms like *social security* and *life insurance* do). Therefore, these words require a hyphen to hold them together when they occur before a noun.

Once you grasp the difference between *social security* and *short-term* as compound adjectives, you can use these two expressions as touchstones in deciding how to handle other adjective-noun combinations. With a principle like this in hand, you don't have to engage in profound analysis to resolve the "hyphen" problem. Consider a random list of examples such as these:

a *red letter* day	a *white collar* worker
a *civil service* test	a *real estate* agent
mass production techniques	*word processing* equipment
long distance calls	*high level* decisions

The expressions *civil service, mass production, real estate,* and *word processing* all resemble *social security,* since they stand for well-known concepts or institutions; therefore, as compound adjectives they can all be written without hyphens. However, *red-letter, long-distance, white-collar,* and *high-level* are much more like *short-term* and should have a hyphen.

So much for compound adjectives before the noun. When they occur *after* the noun, according to the traditional rule, they should not be hyphenated. Yet this traditional formulation is somewhat misleading. If we aren't supposed to hyphenate a "compound adjective" when it follows a noun, it's for the simple reason that the words in question no longer function as a compound adjective—they are playing a normal role in a normal order. It's one thing to use hyphens in the expression "an *up-to-date* report," for a prepositional phrase doesn't normally belong before a noun. However, if I said "This report is *up to date,*" there would be no more justification for hyphenating here than there would be if I said, "This report is *in good shape.*" Both expressions—*in good shape* and *up to date*—are prepositional phrases playing a normal role in the predicate.

However, if the expression still exhibits an abnormal form or inverted word order in the predicate, it is still a compound adjective—and it must still be hyphenated. For example, whether I speak of "*tax-exempt* items" or say "these items are *tax-exempt,*" the hyphen must be inserted because regardless of where it appears—*before* or *after* the noun—the expression is a compressed version of the phrase "exempt from taxation."

There are at least four kinds of compound adjectives that must always be hyphenated *after* as well as *before* the noun (because of inverted word order or change of form). These compound adjectives consist of the following patterns:

noun + adjective (*duty-free*)
noun + participle (*interest-bearing*)
adjective + participle (*soft-spoken*)
adjective + noun + ed (*old-fashioned*)

Once you learn to recognize these four patterns, you can safely assume that any compound adjective that fits one of these patterns must always be hyphenated, no matter where it falls in a sentence.*

It does no good to pretend that compound adjectives are an easy thing to master. They aren't. And for that very reason writers and transcribers

---

* There is only one worm in this rosy apple: some of the words that fit these patterns are now acceptably spelled as one word.

who have to cope with these expressions need more guidance than they get from a simple "hyphenate before but not after" kind of rule. In the final analysis, what becomes of the hyphen over the long run is of little consequence. What does matter is that we express ourselves with precision, verve, and grace. If the hyphen can help us toward that end, why not make use of it?

The Semicolon; and Other Myths

In certain circles that I move in, the fastest way I know to start a quarrel is to attack the semicolon. If I knocked my friends' politics or sneered at their religious beliefs, they would simply smile. But attack their views on the semicolon and they reach for a bread knife. Why this particular mark of punctuation should excite such intense passion escapes me. The semicolon has always been a neurotic creature, continually undergoing an identity crisis. After all, it is half comma and half period, and from its name you would think it is half a colon. It is hardly any wonder, then, that a lot of people are half crazy trying to determine "who" the semicolon really is and what its mission in life is supposed to be.

In the course of this brief essay, I hope to explore a few of the myths that have grown up over the years about the semicolon and some other marks of punctuation.

Myth No. 1: If either clause in a compound sentence contains an internal comma, use a semicolon (not a comma) before the coordinating conjunction that connects the clauses. According to this line of reasoning, it is all right to use a comma in a compound sentence like this:

> The regional meeting in Salem has been canceled, but all other meetings will go on as scheduled.

However, if I use commas for a lesser purpose within either clause (for example, by inserting *Oregon* after *Salem* and setting it off with commas), then the comma before the conjunction must be upgraded to a semicolon.

> The regional meeting in Salem, Oregon, has been canceled; but all other meetings will go on as scheduled.

It is harsh, I concede, to dismiss this rule as a myth when it has been taught for years in various classes and various texts. But the unhappy fact is that outside those classes and those texts, almost no one punctuates that way anymore. The trouble with using a semicolon in such sentences is that it creates a break that is too strong for the occasion. It closes down the action of the sentence at a point where the writer would like it to keep on going. So contemporary writers see nothing wrong with using commas simultaneously to separate clauses and to perform lesser functions within the clauses—unless, of course, total confusion or misreading is likely to result. But in most cases it doesn't. In the following sentence, commas are used both *within* clauses and *between* clauses without any loss of clarity and also without any loss of verbal momentum.

> On March 19, 1979, I wrote to your credit manager, Mr. Lopez, but I have not yet heard from him.

This simultaneous use of commas within and between clauses may look offensive to anyone accustomed to the traditional rule. The fact remains that we have been using commas for both purposes in *complex* sentences all along, and it has never occasioned any comment.

Although I wrote to your credit manager, Mr. Lopez, on March 19, 1979, I have not yet heard from him.

It should be clearly understood that the use of a semicolon before the conjunction in a compound sentence is not wrong. If you want a strong break at that point, the semicolon can and should be used. But you ought to know that the reason for using it is the special effect it creates—and not the presence of internal commas. For example:

I have tried again and again to explain to George why the transaction had to be kept secret from him; but he won't believe me.

Myth No. 2: Always use a semicolon before an enumeration or an explanation introduced by *for example, namely,* **or** *that is.* In many cases this rule is quite true, but in other cases either a colon or a comma is better suited to the occasion. Let's look at some examples.

There are several things you could do to save your business (?) namely, try to get a loan from the bank, find yourself a partner with good business judgment, or pray that your competitor goes out of business before you do.

If you put a semicolon before *namely,* you will close the action down just when the sentence is starting to get somewhere. Because the first part of the sentence creates an air of anticipation, because it implicitly promises to reveal several ways of saving the business, you need—not a mark that closes the action down—but one that supports the air of anticipation. Enter the colon.

The colon is one of the underrated stars in the firmament of punctuation. It would be more widely used, perhaps, if its sound effects were better understood. The colon is the mark of anticipation. It is a blare of trumpets before the grand entrance; it is the roll of drums before the dive off the 100-foot tower. It marks the end of the buildup and gets you ready for "the real thing." Thus:

There are several things you can do to save your business: namely, try to get a loan . . .

Consider this example, however:

Always express numbers in figures when they are accompanied by abbreviations; for example, 4 *p.m., 8 ft.*

The first part of this sample sentence expresses a self-contained thought. If the sentence ended right there, the reader would not be left up in the air. The examples that follow are unexpected, unanticipated, added on almost as an afterthought. We're glad to have them, but they aren't anything we were counting on. The semicolon here is quite appropriate; it momentarily closes down the action of the sentence after the main point is expressed.

In other situations a comma may be the best mark to use before *namely, for example,* or *that is.* Consider this sentence as an example:

Do not use quotation marks to enclose an *indirect quotation*, that is, a restatement of a person's exact words.

In this case, a semicolon would be inappropriate before *that is* because it would close off the action just as we were about to get a definition of a term within the main clause. Moreover, a colon would be inappropriate because it would imply that the sentence up to that point was a buildup for what follows—and that is not true in this case. Here all that is needed is a simple comma to preserve the close relationship between the term *indirect quotation* and the explanatory expression that follows it.

Myth No. 3: When a polite request is phrased as a question, end it with a period. This is another statement that does not, unfortunately, always hold true. In fact, once a period is used at the end of some requests, they no longer sound very polite. I once posted the following note in my home: "Will you please close the door." My children knew this was not really a polite request but a firm parental command. When they chose to ignore it, I amended the sign to read, "Will you please close the door!" (I was relying on the exclamation point to carry the full force of my exasperation.) That approach failed too, so I tried a new tack in diplomacy, amending the sign once again: "Will you please close the door?" My children now knew they had broken my spirit. They now sensed in the sign a pleading note, a petitioning tone, the begging of a favor. They also knew that now I was asking them a real yes-or-no question (or at least I was creating the illusion of asking). Then, in the paradoxical way that children have, once they knew they had the chance to say no, they began to answer my question with tacit affirmations, tugging the door after them on the way out or kicking it shut behind them on the way in.

My problems with my kids are, of course, my own, but learning how to express and punctuate polite requests tends to be a problem for all of us. Consider, for a moment, the wording of those three signs, alike in all respects except for the final mark of punctuation. The version that ends with a period is really a quiet but nonetheless firm demand. There is no element of a question in it at all. The voice rises in an arc and then flattens out at the end on a note of resolution. In the version that ends with an exclamation point, the voice rises in a higher arc and resounds with greater intensity and force of feeling, but it, too, comes down at the end—this time with something of a bang. In the final version, the one with the question mark, the voice starts on an upward curve and then trails off, still on an upward note. Three different readings of the same words, each with a different impact on the reader—all evoked by three different punctuation marks at the end.

Once you become sensitive to the effects produced by these marks of punctuation, handling polite requests becomes quite simple. All you have to do is say the sentence aloud and listen to the sound of your own voice. If you end the sentence with your voice on an upward note, you know that a question mark is the right punctuation to use. If your voice comes down at the end, you know that you need a period. (And if you really feel forceful about it, you probably want an exclamation point.)

If there is any potential danger in so simple a rule, it is this: we sometimes express our requests orally as flat assertions ("Will you please do this for me.") when, as a matter of good taste and good manners, we ought to be asking a question ("Will you please do this for me?").

Now it is true that in the normal course of events we all make demands on one another, and though we tack on a "Will you please" for the sake of politeness, these are still demands, not questions. As long as your reader is not likely to consider them presumptuous, it is appropriate to punctuate these demands with periods:

> Will you please sign both copies of the contract and return the original to me.
>
> May I suggest that you confirm the departure time for your flight before you leave for the airport.
>
> Will you please give my best regards to your family.

As opposed to these routine demands, there is the kind of polite request that asks the reader for a special favor. Here, if you really want to be polite, you will punctuate your request as a question so as to give your reader the chance to say no.

> May I please see you sometime next week?
>
> May I please get an advance copy of the confidential report you are doing?
>
> Will you please acknowledge all my correspondence for me while I'm away?

In these cases you are asking for things that the reader may be unable or unwilling to grant; therefore, you ought to pose these requests as questions. (If you try reading them as statements, you will observe how quickly they change into peremptory demands.) Suppose, however, that these requests were addressed to your subordinates. Under those conditions you would have the right to expect your reader to make the time to see you, to supply you with an advance copy of the confidential report, and to handle your mail for you; therefore, you would be justified in ending these sentences with periods. But even when you have this authority over your reader, you ought to consider the alternative of asking. The inspired public official who replaced the "Keep Off the Grass" signs with a simple "PLEASE?" understood people and how they like to be talked to. If a question mark will get faster results or establish a nicer tone, why not use it?

There are other myths that one could discuss, but these three are sufficient to permit me to make one central point. Mastery over the rules of punctuation depends to a considerable extent on cultivating a sensitivity to the way a sentence moves and the way it sounds.

Punctuating by ear has come to be frowned on—and with much justification—for it has come to mean punctuating solely by feeling, by instinct, by intuition, without much regard for (or knowledge of) the structure of the language and the function of punctuation. Yet the solution, it seems to me, is not to abandon the technique of punctuating by ear but to cultivate it, to develop in yourself a disciplined sense of the relationship between the sound and the structure and the mechanics of language. Many authorities on language, if pressed, have to concede that they often consider first whether a thing sounds right or looks right; only then do they utter a pronouncement as to why it is right. If they rely on their ears for this kind of assurance, then why shouldn't you provide yourself with the same skill?

1

PUNCTUATION: MAJOR MARKS

THE PERIOD

THE QUESTION MARK

THE EXCLAMATION POINT

THE COMMA

THE SEMICOLON

THE COLON

Punctuation marks are the mechanical means for making the meaning of a sentence easily understood. They indicate the proper relationships between words, phrases, and clauses when word order alone is not sufficient to indicate these relationships.

One important caution about punctuation. If you find it particularly hard to determine the appropriate punctuation for a sentence you have written, the chances are that the sentence is improperly constructed. To be on the safe side, recast your thought in a form you can handle with confidence. In any event, do not try to save a badly constructed sentence by means of punctuation.

Section 1 deals with the three marks of terminal punctuation (the period, the question mark, and the exclamation point) plus the three major marks of internal punctuation (the comma, the semicolon, and the colon). All other marks of punctuation are covered in Section 2.

The Period

At the End of a Statement or Command

101 Use a period to mark the end of a sentence that makes a statement or expresses a command.

> I was very happy to read about your promotion.
> I question the wisdom of Jones's recommendation.
> Be sure to insist on quick service when you order from Lyons Inc.

102 Use a period to mark the end of an *elliptical* (condensed) expression that represents a complete statement or command. These elliptical expressions often occur as answers to questions or as transitional phrases.

> Yes. By all means. No.
> Now, to answer your closing question.

NOTE: Do not confuse elliptical expressions with sentence fragments. An elliptical expression represents a complete sentence. A sentence fragment is a word, phrase, or clause that is incorrectly treated as a separate sentence when in fact it ought to be incorporated with adjacent words to make up a complete sentence.

> Great news! The shipment arrived yesterday. After we had waited for six weeks. (*Great news* is an elliptical expression; it represents a complete sentence, *I have great news. After we had waited for six weeks* is a sentence fragment, incorrectly treated as a sentence in its own right; this dependent clause should be linked with the main clause that precedes it.)
> REVISED: Great news! The shipment arrived yesterday, after we had waited for six weeks.

At the End of a Polite Request or Command

103 Requests, suggestions, and commands are often phrased as questions out of politeness. Use a period to end this kind of sentence if you expect your reader to respond *by acting* rather than by giving you a yes-or-no answer.

(*Continued on page 4.*)

Will you please let us have your decision as soon as possible.

Would you kindly send my order to this address.

May I suggest that you call in advance to be sure of prompt service.

If you would like a free ticket to the exhibition, would you please send us your name and address.

If your reader might think your request presumptuous when presented as a statement, use a question mark instead. The question mark offers your reader a chance to say no to your request and preserves the politeness of the situation.

May I have an appointment to see you next week?

May I make a suggestion?

Will you please handle the production reports for me while I'm away?

NOTE: If you are not sure whether to use a question mark or a period, reword the sentence so that it is clearly a question or a statement; then punctuate accordingly. For example, the sentence directly above could be revised as follows:

Would you be willing to handle the production reports for me while I'm away?

I would appreciate your handling the production reports for me while I'm away.

At the End of an Indirect Question

104 Use a period to mark the end of an indirect question. (See also ¶¶115–116).

Our marketing director has asked when the sales figures will be ready.

The only question I have is whether the job will be completed on schedule.

Who the new vice president will be has not yet been decided.

The problem is clear; the question is what to do about it.

With Decimals

105 Use a period (without space before or after it) to separate a whole number from a decimal fraction; for example, *$5.50, 33.33 percent.*

In Outlines and Displayed Lists

106 Use periods after numbers or letters that enumerate items in an outline or a displayed list—unless the numbers or letters are enclosed in parentheses. (See ¶¶107, 223 for illustrations.)

NOTE: Ordinarily, leave two spaces after the period that follows a number or letter in an enumeration. However, if the list consists entirely of one-line items typed single-spaced, then leave only one space after the period. (See also ¶1409e.)

107 Use periods after independent clauses, dependent clauses, or long phrases that are displayed on separate lines in a list. No periods are needed after short phrases unless the phrases are essential to the grammatical completeness of the statement introducing the list.

Please order the following items:

1. Paper clips
2. Rubber bands
3. Staples

BUT: Capitalize the first word of:

a. Every sentence.
b. Direct quotations.
c. Items displayed in a list.

With Headings

108　**a.** Use a period after a *run-in* heading (one that is immediately followed by text matter on the same line) unless some other mark of punctuation, such as a question mark, is required.

b. Omit the period if the heading is *free-standing* (displayed on a line by itself). (However, retain a question mark or an exclamation point with a free-standing head if the wording requires it.)

OVERVIEW OF THE OFFICE WORK FLOW

The Three Clerical Systems

　　　Sales System. When orders come into the office from customers, they are forwarded immediately to the Sales Department, where clerks . . .

NOTE: A period follows a run-in expression like *Table 3*, even though the heading as a whole is free-standing.

　　Table 3. Equipment Acquisition Schedule

A Few Don'ts

109　Don't use a period:

a. After letters used to designate persons or things (for example, *Miss A, Class B, Grade C, Brand X*). **EXCEPTION:** Use a period when the letter is the actual initial of a person's last name (for example, *Mr. A.* for *Mr. Adams*).

b. After contractions (for example, *cont'd;* see ¶505).

c. After ordinals expressed in figures (*1st, 2d, 3d, 4th*).

d. After roman numerals (for example, *Volume I, Henry Ford II*). **EXCEPTION:** Periods follow roman numerals in an outline. (See ¶223.)

- *Periods with abbreviations: see ¶¶506–510.*
- *Periods with dashes: see ¶¶213, 214, 215a.*
- *Periods with parentheses: see ¶¶224c, 225a, 225c, 226c.*
- *Periods with quotation marks: see ¶¶247, 252, 253, 257, 258.*
- *Three spaced periods (ellipsis marks): see ¶¶274–280, 291.*
- *Typewriter spacing with periods: see ¶299.*

The Question Mark

To Indicate Direct Questions

110　Use a question mark at the end of a direct question. (See ¶¶104, 115, 116 for the punctuation of indirect questions.)

　　Where are the records for Frasier Inc.?　　　Why not see your dealer today?

NOTE: Be sure to place the question mark at the *end* of the question.

　　How do you account for this entry: "Paid to E. M. Johnson, *$300*"?
　　(**NOT:** How do you account for this entry? "Paid to E. M. Johnson, $300.")

111　Use a question mark at the end of an *elliptical* (condensed) *question*, that is, a word or phrase that represents a complete question.

(*Continued on page 6.*)

Jean has told me that you are still opposed to the plan. Why? (The complete question is, "Why are you still opposed to the plan?")

NOTE: Punctuate complete and elliptical questions separately, according to your meaning.

When will the job be finished? In a week or two? (**NOT:** When will the job be finished in a week or two?)

Where shall we meet? At the airport? (As punctuated, the writer allows for the possibility of meeting elsewhere.)

Where shall we meet at the airport? (As punctuated, the writer simply wants to pinpoint a more precise location within the airport.)

112 Use a question mark at the end of a sentence that is phrased like a statement but spoken with the rising intonation of a question.

They still doubt his ability?   These figures are correct?

113 A request, suggestion, or command phrased as a question out of politeness may not require a question mark. (See ¶103.)

To Indicate Questions Within Sentences

114 When a short direct question falls *within a sentence*, set the question off with commas and put a question mark at the end of the sentence.

You have the authority, *do you not*, to make this decision yourself?

When a short direct question falls *at the end of a sentence*, use a comma before it and a question mark after.

I can count on your support, *can't I?*

115 When a direct question comes *at the end of a larger sentence*, it starts with a capital letter and is preceded by a comma or a colon. The question mark that ends the question also serves to mark the end of the sentence.

The important question is, What profit can we expect?

This is the important question: What profit can we expect? (Use a colon if the introductory matter is an independent clause.)

BUT: We now come to the important question of what profit we can expect. (Indirect question; no special punctuation or capitalization is needed.)

116 When a direct question comes *at the beginning of a larger sentence*, it should be followed by a question mark (for emphasis) or simply a comma.

How *can we* achieve these goals? is the next question. (Leave one space after a question mark within a sentence.)

OR: How *can we* achieve these goals, is the next question.

BUT: How *we can* achieve these goals is the next question. (Indirect question; no special punctuation is needed.)

NOTE: See how a simple shift in word order above converts a direct question to an indirect question. When the verb precedes the subject (as in *How can we*), the question is direct. When the verb follows the subject (as in *How we can*), the question is indirect.

117 A series of brief questions at the end of a sentence may be separated by commas or (for emphasis) by question marks. Do not capitalize the individual questions.

> Can you estimate the cost of the roofing, the tile work, and the painting?
> OR: Can you estimate the cost of the roofing? the tile work? the painting?

NOTE: Do not confuse these brief questions (which are all related to a common subject and verb) with a series of independent questions. Each independent question must start with a capital and end with a question mark.

> Consider the following points: Is the plan adequate? Is it financially feasible? Is it acceptable to management?

Independent questions in a series are often elliptical (condensed) expressions. (See ¶111.)

> Has Walter's loan been approved? *When? By whom? For what amount?* (In other words: *When* was the loan approved? *By whom* was the loan approved? *For what amount* was the loan approved?)
> (NOT: Has Walter's loan been approved, when, by whom, and for what amount?)

To Express Doubt

118 A question mark enclosed in parentheses may be used to express doubt or uncertainty about a word or phrase within a sentence.

> She was graduated from Oberlin in 1974(?).

NOTE: When dates are already enclosed within parentheses, question marks may be inserted as necessary to indicate doubt.

> the explorer Verrazzano (1485?–1528?)

- *Question marks with dashes: see ¶¶214, 215a.*
- *Question marks with parentheses: see ¶¶224d, 225a, 225d, 226c.*
- *Question marks with quotation marks: see ¶¶249, 252, 254, 257, 258.*
- *Typewriter spacing with question marks: see ¶299.*

The Exclamation Point

The exclamation point is most often found in advertising copy and sales correspondence. However, it should be avoided wherever possible.

NOTE: If your typewriter does not carry the exclamation point as a standard character, you can construct it by typing the apostrophe, backspacing once, and then typing the period. On manual machines it is not necessary to backspace if the space bar is held down while both characters are typed.

To Express Strong Feeling

119 Use an exclamation point at the end of a sentence (or an elliptical expression that stands for a sentence) to indicate enthusiasm, surprise, disbelief, urgency, or strong feeling.

(Continued on page 8.)

Yes! Dresses, jackets, and coats are selling at 50 percent off!

No! It can't be true! How could it have happened! Fantastic!

NOTE: The exclamation point may be enclosed in parentheses and placed directly after a word that the writer wants to emphasize.

Did you know that Erskine's is selling genuine(!) mink coats for $500?

120 **a.** A single word may be followed by an exclamation point to express intense feeling. The sentence that follows it is punctuated as usual.

Congratulations! We were delighted to read about your promotion.

b. When such words are repeated for emphasis, an exclamation point follows each repetition.

Hurry! Hurry! Our sale ends this week.

c. When exclamations are mild, a comma or a period is sufficient.

Well, well, don't let it get you down. No. There's no use in vain regrets.

With *Oh* and *O*

121 The exclamation *oh* may be followed by either an exclamation point or a comma, depending on the emphasis desired. It is capitalized only when it starts a sentence. The capitalized *O*, the sign of direct address, is not usually followed by any punctuation.

Oh! I didn't expect that! O Lord, help me!

Oh, what's the use? O America, where are you headed?

- *Exclamation point with dashes: see ¶¶214, 215a.*
- *Exclamation point with parentheses: see ¶¶224d, 225a, 225d, 226c.*
- *Exclamation point with quotation marks: see ¶¶249, 252, 254, 257, 258.*

The Comma

The comma has two primary functions: it *sets off* nonessential expressions that interrupt the flow of thought from subject to verb to object or complement, and it *separates* elements within a sentence to clarify their relationship to one another. It takes only a single comma to "separate," but it typically requires two commas to "set off."

¶¶122–125 present an overview of the rules governing the use of the comma. For a more detailed treatment of the specific rules, see ¶¶126–175.

Basic Rules for Commas That Set Off

122 Use commas to set off *nonessential expressions*—words, phrases, and clauses that are not necessary for the meaning or the structural completeness of the sentence.

IMPORTANT NOTE: In many sentences you can tell whether an expression is nonessential or essential by trying to omit the expression. If you can leave it out without affecting the meaning or the structural completeness of the sentence, the expression is nonessential and should be set off by commas.

> NONESSENTIAL: I would like to hire Frances Klein, *who has already had two years' experience as a management consultant.*
>
> ESSENTIAL: I would like to hire someone *who has already had two years' experience as a management consultant.* (Without the *who* clause, the meaning of the sentence would be incomplete.)
>
> NONESSENTIAL: There is, *no doubt,* a reasonable explanation for his behavior at the board meeting.
>
> ESSENTIAL: There is *no doubt* about her honesty. (Without *no doubt* the structure of the sentence would be incomplete.)

However, in other sentences the only way you can tell whether an expression is nonessential or essential is by the way you would say it aloud. If your voice tends to *drop* as you utter the expression, it is nonessential; if your voice tends to *rise,* the expression is essential.

> NONESSENTIAL: We have decided, *therefore,* to proceed with the construction of the new building.
>
> ESSENTIAL: We have *therefore* decided to proceed with the construction of the new building.

■ *For additional examples see ¶141, note.*

a. Interrupting words, phrases, and clauses are set off by commas when they break the flow of a sentence from subject to verb to object or complement. (See also ¶¶144–147.)

> We will hold the package for your arrival or, *if you prefer,* forward it to your office. (When this is read aloud, note how the voice drops on the nonessential expression *if you prefer.*)
>
> It is true, *isn't it,* that you offered to buy the property?
>
> I could use, *say,* eight cases if you have them.
>
> Franklin Hardware, *rather than Flynn & Son,* has been given the contract.
>
> BUT: Franklin Hardware has been given the contract *rather than Flynn & Son.* (The phrase is not set off when it does not interrupt.)

b. Afterthoughts—words, phrases, or clauses loosely added onto the end of a sentence—are set off by a comma. (See also ¶144.)

> Send us your check as soon as you can, *please.*
>
> Grant promised to share expenses with us, *if I remember correctly.*
>
> It is not too late to place an order, *is it?*

c. Transitional expressions (like *however, therefore, on the other hand*) and independent comments (like *obviously, in my opinion, of course*) are set off with commas when they interrupt the flow of the sentence. They are not set off, however, when they are used to emphasize the meaning (the voice goes up in such cases). In the following examples, consider how the voice drops when the expression is nonessential and how it rises when the expression is essential.

> NONESSENTIAL: I must report, *nevertheless,* that his work is unsatisfactory.
>
> ESSENTIAL: I must *nevertheless* report that his work is unsatisfactory.

(*Continued on page 10.*)

NONESSENTIAL: It is, *of course,* your prerogative to change your mind. (Here the voice rises on *is* and drops on *of course.*)

ESSENTIAL: It is *of course* your prerogative to change your mind. (Here the voice rises on *of course.*)

- *See also ¶¶138–143.*

d. Descriptive expressions that *follow* the words they refer to are set off when they provide additional but nonessential information. (See also ¶¶148–153.)

NONESSENTIAL: Her latest book, *Management Case Studies,* was published last month. (*Her latest* indicates which book is meant; the title gives additional but nonessential information.)

ESSENTIAL: The book *Management Case Studies* was published last month. (Here the title is essential to indicate which book.)

NONESSENTIAL: We have all read your letter of June 4, *in which you propose a different schedule of payments.* (The date indicates which letter; the *in which* clause gives additional information. See also ¶152.)

ESSENTIAL: We have all read the letter *in which you propose a different schedule of payments.* (Here the *in which* clause is needed to indicate which letter is being referred to.)

e. Use commas to set off the year in complete dates (July 21, *1977,* . . .), abbreviations that follow a person's name (Ethel Harris, *Ph.D.,* will speak . . .), and names of states or countries following city names (Orem, *Utah,* . . .). In personal names and company names the trend is not to set off elements like *Jr., Sr., III, Inc.,* or *Ltd.* (for example, *Roy Daly Jr.* and *Ibex Inc.*); however, individual preferences should be respected when known. (See also ¶¶154–161.)

Basic Rules for Commas That Separate

123 Use a single comma:

a. To separate the two main clauses in a compound sentence when they are joined by *and, but, or,* or *nor.* (See also ¶¶126–129.)

The reorganization has not been formally announced, *but* the details are widely known.

b. To separate three or more items in a series—unless all the items are joined by *and* or *or.* (See also ¶¶162–167.)

It takes time, effort, *and* a good deal of money.

BUT: It takes time *and* effort *and* a good deal of money.

c. To separate two or more adjectives that both modify the same noun. (See also ¶¶168–171.)

We need to mount an *exciting, hard-hitting* ad campaign.

d. To separate the digits of numbers into groups of thousands. (See ¶461.)

Sales projections for the Southern Region next year range between $900,000 and $1,000,000.

e. To indicate the omission of key words or to clarify meaning when the word order is unusual. (See also ¶¶172–175.)

Half the purchase price is due on delivery of the goods; the balance, in three months. (The comma here signifies the omission of *is due.*)

What will happen, we don't know. (The comma separates the object, *What will happen,* from the subject, *we,* which follows.)

124 Use a single comma after *introductory elements*—items that begin a sentence and come before the subject and verb of the main clause.

When I return to the office, I will get back in touch with you. (Introductory dependent clause.)

Established in 1936, the firm grew from a small manufacturer of plastics to a multinational corporation. (Introductory participial phrase.)

To find the answer, divide by 36. (Introductory infinitive phrase.)

Yes, we can have the typewriter repaired by Monday. (Introductory word.)

a. Use a comma after an *introductory request or command.*

Look, we've been through tougher situations before.

You see, the previous campaigns never did pan out.

Please remember, all expense accounts must be on my desk by Friday.

BUT: *Please remember that all . . .* (With the addition of *that, please remember* becomes the main verb and is no longer an introductory element.)

b. Commas are not needed after *ordinary introductory adverbs* or *short introductory phrases* that answer such questions as:

WHEN: tomorrow, yesterday, recently, early next week, in the morning, soon, in five years, in 1978

HOW OFTEN: occasionally, often, frequently, once in a while

WHERE: here, in this case, at the meeting

WHY: for that reason, because of this situation

However, commas are used after introductory adverbs and phrases:

(1) When they function as *transitional expressions* (such as *well, therefore, however, for example, in the first place*), which provide a transition in meaning from the previous sentence.

(2) When they function as *independent comments* (such as *in my opinion, by all means, obviously, of course*), which express the writer's attitude toward the meaning of the sentence. (See also ¶¶138–143.)

In the morning things may look better. (Short prepositional phrase telling *when;* no comma needed.)

In the first place, they don't have sufficient capital. (Transitional expression; followed by comma.)

In my opinion, we ought to look for another candidate. (Independent comment; followed by comma.)

Recently we had a request for school enrollment trends. (Introductory adverb telling *when;* no comma needed.)

Consequently, we will have to cancel the agreement. (Transitional expression; followed by comma.)

Obviously, the request will have to be referred elsewhere. (Independent comment; followed by comma.)

NOTE: Many writers use commas after *all* introductory elements to avoid having to analyze each situation.

125 Separating commas are often improperly used in sentences. In the following examples the diagonal marks indicate points at which single commas *should not* be used.

a. Do not separate a subject and its verb.

Her coauthor on the book/is Mr. Schatzkin.
but: Her coauthor on the book, *I believe,* is Mr. Schatzkin. (Use *two* commas to set off an interrupting expression.)
Whether further price increases are necessary/remains to be seen. (Noun clause as subject.)
but: *Whatever was done, was done* in good faith. (In special cases like this, a comma may be required for clarity. See also ¶174.)

b. Do not separate a verb and its object or complement.

Our research staff *will undertake/a* comprehensive *study* of the problem. (Verb and object.)
Frank Bednar *said/that her promotion would be approved.* (Noun clause as object.)
but: Frank Bednar *said, "Her promotion will be approved."* (A comma ordinarily follows a verb when the object is a direct quotation. See also ¶256.)
or: The question before us *is, What alternatives are there to further tax increases?* (A comma also follows a verb when the object or complement is a direct question. See also ¶115.)
He *has been/controller* for the last twelve years. (Verb and complement.)
She *is/honest, hard-working, and extremely capable.* (Verb and complement.)

c. Do not separate an adjective and a noun.

We need a person who is willing to put in long, *hard/hours.* (Adjective and noun.)

d. Do not separate a noun and a prepositional phrase that follows.

The board of directors/of the Fastex Corporation will announce its decision this Friday.
but: The board of directors, *of necessity,* must turn down the merger at this time. (Use *two* commas to set off an interrupting expression.)

e. Do not separate a coordinating conjunction (*and, but, or,* or *nor*) and the following word.

You can read it now *or/when* you get home tonight.
but: You can read it now or, *if you prefer,* when you get home tonight. (Use two commas to set off an interrupting expression.)

f. Do not separate *two* items joined by a coordinating conjunction.

The letters on the Gray case/and those concerning Mr. Pendleton should be shown to Mrs. Almquist. (Two subjects.)
I *have read the report/and find it well done.* (Two predicates. See also ¶127.)
We hope *that you will visit our store soon/and that you will find the styles you like.* (Two objects of the verb *hope.*)
He may go on to graduate school at *Stanford/or Harvard.* (Two objects of the preposition *at.*)
but: *Frank Albano will handle the tickets, and Edna Hoehn will be responsible for publicity.* (A comma separates two independent clauses joined by a coordinating conjunction. See ¶126.)

The following rules (¶¶126–137) deal with the punctuation of clauses and phrases in sentences.

With Clauses in Compound Sentences

126 **a.** When a compound sentence consists of two independent clauses joined by a coordinating conjunction (*and, but, or,* or *nor*), place a separating comma before the conjunction. (See also ¶129.)

> Mr. Arakelian spoke for twenty minutes, *and* then he answered questions.
> **BUT:** Mr. Arakelian spoke for twenty minutes *and* then answered questions. (See ¶127*a, b.*)
> Take this message to Mrs. Lavigne, *and* please wait for her answer. (See ¶127*c.*)
> Either our costs have to be reduced, *or* our prices have to be raised.
> Not only can we take on the project at once, *but* we can also quote you a competitive price.

b. When a compound sentence consists of *three* or more independent clauses, punctuate this series of clauses like any other series. (See also ¶162.)

> Ted can do the typing, Pam can handle the art, *and* Sue and I can do the rest.

127 Do not confuse a *compound sentence* with a simple sentence containing a *compound predicate.*

a. A *compound sentence* contains at least two independent clauses, and each clause contains a subject and a predicate.

> *Ella was graduated in May,* and *she began working for a bank in June.*

b. A sentence may contain one subject with a *compound predicate,* that is, two predicates connected by a coordinating conjunction. In such sentences no comma separates the two predicates.

> *Ella was graduated in May* and *began working for a bank in June.* (When *she* is omitted from the example in *a* above, the sentence is no longer a compound sentence. It is now a simple sentence with a compound predicate.)
> Mr. Fong not only *criticized the report* but also *recommended that it be revised.* (Compound predicate; no comma before *but.*)
> Mr. Fong not only *criticized the report,* but *he also recommended that it be revised.* (Compound sentence; comma before *but.*)

c. When one or both verbs are in the imperative and the subject is not expressed, treat the sentence as a compound sentence and use a comma between the clauses. (See ¶129.)

> *Send* this letter to Mrs. Tyminski, and *please attach* a copy of Invoice 43011.
> *Please sign* both copies of the contract, and *return* the original copy to us.
> You may take as much time as you need to reach a decision, but *don't overlook* the advantages of acting promptly.

d. When nonessential elements precede the second part of a compound predicate, they are treated as interrupting expressions and are set off by two commas. When these same expressions precede the second clause of a compound sentence, they are treated as introductory expressions and are followed by one comma.

(Continued on page 14.)

I can meet with you on Wednesday or, *if that is not a good day for you,* on Thursday. (Interrupting expression.)

I can meet with you on Wednesday, or *if that is not a good day for you,* I can make some time on Thursday. (Introductory expression.)

Ms. Holtz strode to the platform and, *speaking in a loud voice,* called the meeting to order. (Interrupting expression.)

Ms. Holtz strode to the platform, and *speaking in a loud voice,* she called the meeting to order. (Introductory expression.)

- *See also ¶¶131c, 136a, 142.*

128 Do not use a comma between two independent clauses that are not joined by a coordinating conjunction (*and, but, or,* or *nor*). This error of punctuation is known as a *comma splice* and produces a *run-on sentence.* Use a semicolon, a colon, or a dash (whichever is appropriate), or start a new sentence.

Mark top-priority letters "Rush"; transcribe them first.

OR: Mark top-priority letters "Rush." Transcribe them first.

129 If the two clauses of a compound sentence are short, the comma may be omitted before the conjunction.

Their prices are low and their service is very efficient.

Please initial these forms and return them by Monday.

With Clauses in Complex Sentences

A complex sentence contains one independent clause and one or more dependent clauses. *After, although, as, because, before, if, since, unless, when,* and *while* are among the words most frequently used to introduce dependent clauses. (See ¶132 for a longer list.)

130 Introductory Dependent Clauses

a. When a dependent clause *precedes* the independent clause, separate the clauses with a comma.

Before we can make a decision, we must have all the facts.

When a child is tired and pale, the cause is often lack of nutritious food.

After we have studied all aspects of the complaint, we will make a recommendation.

BUT: *Only after we have studied all aspects of the complaint* will we make a recommendation. (No comma follows the introductory clause when the word order in the main clause is abnormal. Compare the abnormal *will we make* here with the normal *we will make* in the example above.)

If, however, they had watched their investments more closely, do you think they could have avoided bankruptcy?

When you read the Weissberg study, look at Appendix 2 first.

b. Be sure to recognize an introductory dependent clause, even if some of the essential words are omitted from the clause. (Such constructions are known as *elliptical clauses.*)

Whenever possible, he leaves his office by six. (Whenever it is possible, . . .)

If so, I will call you tomorrow. (If that is so, . . .)

Should you be late, just call to let me know. (If you should be late, . . .)

c. Use a comma after an introductory clause when it serves as the *object* of a sentence (but not when it serves as the *subject*).

Whomever you nominate, I will support. (Introductory clause as object.)

Whomever you nominate will have my support. (Introductory clause as subject.)

That the department must be reorganized, I no longer question. (Introductory clause as object.)

That the department must be reorganized is no longer questioned. (Introductory clause as subject.)

d. Sentences like those illustrated above are often introduced by an expression such as *he said that, she believes that,* or *they know that.* In such cases use the same punctuation as prescribed in ¶130a, b, and c.

Doctors will tell you that *when a child is tired and pale,* the cause is often lack of nutritious food.

Harry says that *whenever possible,* he leaves his office by six.

Everyone knows that *whomever you nominate* will have my support.

Liz believes that *before we can make a decision,* we must have all the facts. (A separating comma follows the dependent clause, just as if the sentence began with the word *Before.* No comma precedes the dependent clause because it is considered introductory, not interrupting.)

but: He said that, *as you may already know,* he was planning to take early retirement. (Two commas are needed to set off an interrupting dependent clause. See also ¶131c.)

131   Dependent Clauses Elsewhere in the Sentence

When a dependent clause *follows* the main clause or *falls within* the main clause, commas are used or omitted depending on whether the dependent clause is essential (restrictive) or nonessential (nonrestrictive).

a. An *essential* clause is necessary to the meaning of the sentence. Because it *cannot be omitted,* it should not be set off by commas.

Political leaders *who are responsive to the wishes of their constituents* will support the bill. (Tells which political leaders.)

This ruling applies to everyone *who works in the plant.* (Tells which persons.)

The airport limousine arrived *before I was ready to leave.* (Tells when.)

The fact *that he arrived on time today* is some sign of improvement. (Tells which fact.)

Greg said *that he would wait.* (Tells what was said.)

Give this letter to *whoever is at the front desk.* (Tells which person.)

b. A *nonessential* clause provides additional descriptive or explanatory detail. Because it *can be omitted* without changing the meaning of the sentence, it should be set off by commas.

He stopped off in Chicago to see his mother, *who is a prominent lawyer.* (Simply adds information about his mother.)

Green's first book, *which sold a million copies,* is now out of print. (Gives additional information about Green's book but is not needed to establish *which* book is meant; this is Green's *first* book.)

(Continued on page 16.)

The airport limousine arrived at ten, *before I was ready to leave.* (Gives additional information but is not essential to establish *when* the limousine arrived.)

Jim's last suggestion, *that we send Torres to the meeting in Miami next month,* is a good one. (Gives additional information but is not essential to establish *which* suggestion.)

c. A dependent clause occurring within a sentence must always be set off by commas when it *interrupts* the flow of the sentence.

I can set up the meeting for tomorrow or, *if that is inconvenient,* for Friday.

Please include each customer's full address and, *whenever possible,* the account number. (The complete dependent clause is *whenever it is possible.*)

Mr. Gifford, *when asked about his alleged participation in the price-rigging scheme,* refused to comment.

She is the kind of person who, *if you understand her,* will be a devoted employee.

If, *when you have tried our product,* you are not satisfied with it, please return it for a full refund of the purchase price.

BUT: He said that *when he had the time,* he would help us with the report. (See ¶130d for dependent clauses following *he said that, she knows that,* and similar expressions.)

132 The following list presents the words and phrases most commonly used to introduce dependent clauses. For most of these expressions two sentences are given: one containing an essential clause and one a nonessential clause. In a few cases only one type of clause is possible. If you cannot decide whether a clause is essential or nonessential (and therefore whether commas are required or not), compare it with the related sentences below.

After. ESSENTIAL: The telegram came *after you left last evening.* (Tells when.) NONESSENTIAL: The telegram came this morning, *after the decision had been made.* (The phrase *this morning* clearly tells when; the *after* clause provides additional but nonessential information.)

All of which. ALWAYS NONESSENTIAL: The rumors, *all of which were unfounded,* brought about the defeat of the candidate.

Although, even though, and **though.** ALWAYS NONESSENTIAL: She has typed her letter of resignation, *although I do not believe she will submit it.* (Clause of concession.)

As. ESSENTIAL: The results of the mailing are *as you predicted they would be.* NONESSENTIAL: The results of the mailing are disappointing, *as you predicted they would be.* (See page 213 for a usage note on *as.*)

As . . . as. ALWAYS ESSENTIAL: He talked *as* persuasively at the meeting *as* he did over the telephone.

As if and **as though.** ESSENTIAL: The man walked *as if* (or *as though*) *he were pursued by bees.* (Tells how he walked.) NONESSENTIAL: The man walked fast, *as if* (or *as though*) *he were pursued by bees.* (The adverb *fast* tells how he walked; the *as if* clause provides additional but nonessential information.)

As soon as. ESSENTIAL: We will fill your order *as soon as we receive new stock.* NONESSENTIAL: We will fill your order next week, *as soon as we receive new stock.*

At, by, for, in, and **to which.** ESSENTIAL: I went to the floor *to which I had been directed.* NONESSENTIAL: I went to the tenth floor, *to which I had been directed.*

Because. *Essential* or *nonessential,* depending on closeness of relation.
ESSENTIAL: She left *because she had another appointment.* (Here the reason expressed by the *because* clause is essential to complete the meaning.)
NONESSENTIAL: I need to have two copies of the final report by 5:30 tomorrow, *because I am leaving for Chicago on a 7:30 flight.* (Here the meaning of the main clause is complete; the reason expressed in the *because* clause offers additional but nonessential information.)

Before. ESSENTIAL: The shipment was sent *before your letter was received.*
NONESSENTIAL: The shipment was sent on Tuesday, *before your letter was received.* (Tuesday tells when; the *before* clause provides additional but nonessential information.)

Even though. See *Although.*

For. ALWAYS NONESSENTIAL: He read the book, *for he was interested in psychology.* (A comma should always precede *for* as a conjunction to prevent misreading *for* as a preposition.)

If. ESSENTIAL: Let us hear from you *if you are interested.*
NONESSENTIAL: She promised to write from Toronto, *if I remember correctly.* (Clause added loosely.)

In order that. *Essential* or *nonessential,* depending on closeness of relation.
ESSENTIAL: Please notify your instructor promptly *in order that a makeup examination may be scheduled.*
NONESSENTIAL: Please notify your instructor promptly if you will be unable to attend the examination on Friday, *in order that a makeup examination may be scheduled.*

No matter what (why, how, etc.**).** ALWAYS NONESSENTIAL: The order cannot be ready by Monday, *no matter what the manager says.*

None of which. ALWAYS NONESSENTIAL: We received five boxes of samples, *none of which have been opened.*

None of whom. ALWAYS NONESSENTIAL: We have interviewed ten applicants, *none of whom were satisfactory.*

Since. ESSENTIAL: We have taken no applications *since we received your instructions.*
NONESSENTIAL: We are taking no more applications, *since our lists are now closed.* (Clause of reason.)

So . . . as. ALWAYS ESSENTIAL: The second copy was not *so clear as the first one.*

So that. *Essential* or *nonessential,* depending on closeness of relation.
ESSENTIAL: Examine all shipments *so that any damage may be detected promptly.*
NONESSENTIAL: Examine all shipments as soon as they arrive, *so that any damage may be detected promptly.*

So . . . that. ALWAYS ESSENTIAL: The costs ran *so high that we could not make a profit on the job.*

Some of whom. ALWAYS NONESSENTIAL: The agency has sent us five applicants, *some of whom seem promising.*

Than. ALWAYS ESSENTIAL: The employees seem to be more disturbed by the rumor *than they care to admit.*

That. Used in referring to things; also to persons when a class or type is meant.
ALWAYS ESSENTIAL: This is the house *that he owns today.* She is the kind of candidate *that I prefer.* (See also ¶1062.)

Though. See *Although.*

Unless. ESSENTIAL: The item will be discontinued *unless customers begin to show an interest in it.*
NONESSENTIAL: I plan to reorganize the files, *unless you have other work for me.* (Clause added loosely as an afterthought.)

(Continued on page 18.)

Until. ALWAYS ESSENTIAL: I will continue to work *until my children are out of school.*

When. ESSENTIAL: The changeover will be made *when Mr. Ruiz returns from his vacation.*
NONESSENTIAL: The changeover will be made next Monday, *when Mr. Ruiz returns from his vacation.* (*Monday* tells when; the *when* clause provides additional but nonessential information.)

Where. ESSENTIAL: I plan to visit the town *where I used to live.*
NONESSENTIAL: I plan to stop off in Detroit, *where I used to live.*

Whereas. ALWAYS NONESSENTIAL: The figures for last year include large cities only, *whereas those for this year include rural areas as well.* (Clause of contrast.)

Which. Used in referring to animals, things, and ideas. Always use *which* (instead of *that*) to introduce nonessential clauses: The bay, *which was full of small sailing craft,* was very rough. *Which* may also be used to introduce essential clauses. (See ¶1062*b*, note.)

While. ESSENTIAL: The union decided not to strike *while negotiations were still going on.* (*While* meaning "during the time that.")
NONESSENTIAL: The workers at the Apex Company struck, *while those at the Powers Company remained at work.* (*While* meaning "whereas.")

Who. ESSENTIAL: All students *who are members of the Backpackers Club* will be excused at two o'clock today.
NONESSENTIAL: John Behnke, *who is a member of the Backpackers Club,* will be excused at two o'clock today.

Whom. ESSENTIAL: This package is for the friend *whom I am visiting.*
NONESSENTIAL: This package is for my cousin Amy, *whom I am visiting.*

Whose. ESSENTIAL: The prize will be awarded to the employee *whose suggestion yields the greatest cost savings.*
NONESSENTIAL: The prize was awarded to Joyce Bruno, *whose suggestion produced the greatest cost savings.*

With Clauses in Compound-Complex Sentences

133 A compound-complex sentence typically consists of two independent clauses (joined by *and, but, or,* or *nor*) and one or more dependent clauses. To punctuate a sentence of this kind, first place a separating comma before the conjunction that joins the two main parts. Then consider each half of the sentence alone and provide additional punctuation as necessary.

Peter Conboy, Eastwood's treasurer, promised to call me as soon as he arrived in town, but I have not yet heard from him.

On May 8, 1976, the merger was first proposed, but Roy Fox, *who was then Allied's chief executive officer,* refused to make a firm commitment.

I thought their offices were in Canton, Ohio, but *when my letter came back undelivered,* I realized they must be in Canton, Massachusetts. (No comma precedes *when* because the *when* clause is considered an introductory expression, not an interrupting expression. See also ¶127*d*.)

NOTE: If a misreading is likely or a stronger break is desired, use a semicolon rather than a comma to separate the two main clauses. (See ¶177.)

134 When a sentence starts with a dependent clause that applies to both independent clauses that follow, no comma separates the independent clauses. (A comma would make the introductory dependent clause seem to apply only to the first independent clause.)

> If you want to become an executive, you must understand accounting *and* you must know your product. (The *if* clause applies equally to the two independent clauses; hence no comma before *and*.)
>
> BUT: If you want to become an executive, you must understand accounting, *but* don't think your preparation ends there.

With Participial, Infinitive, and Prepositional Phrases

135 Introductory Phrases

a. Use a comma after an *introductory participial phrase.*

> *Speaking in a loud voice,* Ms. Califano called the meeting to order.
> *Pleased by the unusual service,* the woman has become a steady customer.
> *Having made the correction,* I now feel sure the total is correct.

NOTE: Watch out for phrases that look like introductory participial phrases but actually represent the subject of the sentence or part of the predicate. Do not put a comma after these elements.

> *Looking for examples of good acknowledgment letters in our files* has taken me longer than I had hoped. (Gerund phrase as subject.)
>
> BUT: *Looking for examples of good acknowledgment letters in our files,* I found four you can use. (Participial phrase used as an introductory element.)
>
> *Following Mrs. Fahnstock's speech* was a presentation by Ms. Paley. (With normal word order, the sentence would read, "A presentation by Ms. Paley was *following Mrs. Fahnstock's speech.*" The introductory phrase is actually part of the predicate.)
>
> BUT: *Following Mrs. Fahnstock's speech,* Ms. Paley made her presentation. (Participial phrase used as an introductory element.)

b. Use a comma after an *introductory infinitive phrase* unless the phrase is the subject of the sentence. (Infinitive phrases are introduced by the word *to.*)

> *To get the best results from your dishwasher,* follow these directions.
>
> *To have displayed the goods more effectively,* he should have consulted a lighting specialist.
>
> BUT: *To have displayed the goods more effectively* would have been an expensive project. (Infinitive phrase used as subject.)

c. In general, use a comma after all *introductory prepositional phrases.* A comma may be omitted after a *short* prepositional phrase if (1) the phrase does not contain a verb form, (2) the phrase is not a transitional expression or an independent comment, or (3) there is no sacrifice in clarity or desired emphasis. (Many writers use a comma after all introductory prepositional phrases to avoid having to analyze each situation.)

> *In response to the many requests of our customers,* we are opening a suburban branch. (Comma required after a long phrase.)
>
> *On Monday morning* the mail is always late. (No comma required after a short phrase.)

(Continued on page 20.)

In 1976 our entire inventory was destroyed by fire. (No comma required after a short phrase.)

BUT: In 1976, 384 cases of potential lung infections were reported. (Comma required to separate two numbers. See ¶456.)

At the time you called, I was tied up in a meeting. (Comma required after a short phrase containing a verb form.)

In preparing your report, be sure to include last year's figures. (Comma required after a short phrase containing a verb form.)

In addition, a 3 percent city sales tax must be imposed on these orders. (Comma required after short phrase used as a transitional expression. See ¶¶138*a*, 139.)

In my opinion, your ads are misleading as they now appear. (Comma required after short phrase used as an independent comment. See ¶¶138*b*, 139.)

CONFUSING: After all you have gone through a great deal.

CLEAR: *After all,* you have gone through a great deal. (Comma required after a short phrase to prevent misreading.)

In legal documents, amounts of money are often expressed both in words and figures. (Comma used to give desired emphasis to the introductory phrase.)

NOTE: Omit the comma after an introductory prepositional phrase if the word order in the rest of the sentence is abnormal.

From these modest beginnings grew a multinational industrial empire. (Normal word order: A multinational industrial empire grew from these modest beginnings.)

In the office where I last worked were two supervisors who constantly gave me contradictory instructions. (Omit the comma after the introductory phrase when the verb in the main clause immediately follows.)

BUT: *In the office where I last worked,* there were two supervisors who constantly gave me contradictory instructions.

136   Phrases at the Beginning of a Clause

a. When a participial, infinitive, or prepositional phrase occurs *at the beginning of a clause within the sentence,* insert or omit the comma following, just as if the phrase were an introductory element at the beginning of the sentence. (See ¶135.)

I was invited to attend the monthly planning meeting last week, and *seizing the opportunity,* I presented an overview of our medium-range plans. (A separating comma follows the participial phrase just as if the sentence began with the word *Seizing.* No comma precedes the phrase because the phrase is considered introductory, not interrupting. See also ¶127*d*.)

The salesclerk explained that *to get the best results from your dishwasher,* you should follow the directions.

We would like to announce that *in response to the many requests of our customers,* we are opening a suburban branch.

Last year we had a number of thefts, and *in 1976* our entire inventory was destroyed by fire. (No comma is needed after a short introductory prepositional phrase.)

b. If the phrase interrupts the flow of the sentence, set it off with two commas.

He was a man who, *in the best tradition of the company,* did what the job demanded.

If, *in the interest of time,* you decide to fly to Detroit, I'll be glad to help you make your plane reservations.

137 Phrases Elsewhere in the Sentence

When a participial, infinitive, or prepositional phrase occurs *at some point other than the beginning of a sentence or the beginning of a clause,* commas are omitted or used depending on whether the phrase is essential or nonessential.

a. An *essential* participial, infinitive, or prepositional phrase is necessary to the meaning of the sentence and cannot be omitted. Therefore, do not use commas to set it off.

> The instructions *printed in italics* are the most important. (Participial.)
> The time *to place your order* is now! (Infinitive.)
> The copy *with the signatures* should be retained. (Prepositional.)

b. A *nonessential* participial, infinitive, or prepositional phrase provides additional information but is not needed to complete the meaning of the sentence. Set off such phrases with commas.

> Our entire collection of dining room furniture, *created by one of Denmark's outstanding designers,* will be on sale throughout this month. (Participial.)
> I found worn brake linings, *to mention only one defect.* (Infinitive.)
> She has extraordinary talents, *in my opinion.* (Prepositional.)

c. A phrase occurring within a sentence must always be set off by commas when it *interrupts* the flow of the sentence.

> The commission, *after hearing arguments on the proposed new tax rate structure,* will consider amendments to the tax law.
> The company, *in its attempt to place more women in high-level management positions,* is undertaking a special recruitment program.

The following rules (¶¶138–161) deal with the various uses of commas to set off nonessential expressions. See also ¶¶201–202 and ¶¶218–219 for the use of dashes and parentheses to set off these expressions.

With Transitional Expressions and Independent Comments

138 a. Use commas to set off *transitional expressions.* These nonessential words and phrases are called *transitional* because they help the reader mentally relate the preceding thought with the idea now being introduced. They express the notion of:

ADDITION: also, besides, furthermore, in addition, moreover, too (see ¶143), what is more

CONSEQUENCE: accordingly, as a result, consequently, hence (see ¶139b), otherwise, so (see ¶179), then (see ¶139b), therefore, thus (see ¶139b)

SUMMARIZING: after all, all in all, all things considered, briefly, by and large, in any case (event), in brief, in conclusion, in short, in summary, in the final analysis, in the long run, on balance, on the whole, to sum up, ultimately

GENERALIZING: as a rule, as usual, for the most part, generally (speaking), in general, ordinarily, usually

RESTATEMENT: in essence, in other words, namely, that is, that is to say

(Continued on page 22.)

CONTRAST AND COMPARISON:	by contrast, by the same token, conversely, instead, likewise, on one hand, on the contrary, on the other hand, rather, similarly, yet (see ¶179)
CONCESSION:	anyway, at any rate, be that as it may, even so, however, in any case (event), nevertheless, still, this fact notwithstanding
SEQUENCE:	afterward, at first, at the same time, finally, first, first of all, for now, for the time being, in conclusion, in the first place, in time, in turn, later on, meanwhile, next, second, then (see ¶139*b*), to begin with
DIVERSION:	by the by, by the way, incidentally
ILLUSTRATION:	for example, for instance, for one thing

b. Use commas to set off *independent comments,* that is, nonessential words or phrases that express the writer's attitude toward the meaning of the sentence. By means of these independent comments, the writer indicates that what he is about to say carries his wholehearted endorsement (*indeed, by all means*) or deserves only his lukewarm support (*apparently, presumably*) or hardly requires saying (*as you already know, clearly, obviously*) or represents only his personal views (*in my opinion, personally*) or arouses some emotion in him (*unfortunately, happily*) or presents his honest position (*frankly, actually, to tell the truth*). Such terms modify the meaning of the sentence as a whole (rather than a particular word within the sentence).

AFFIRMATION:	by all means, indeed, of course, yes
DENIAL:	no
REGRET:	alas, unfortunately
PLEASURE:	fortunately, happily
QUALIFICATION:	ideally, if necessary, if possible, literally, strictly speaking, theoretically
PERSONAL VIEWPOINT:	according to her, as I see it, in my opinion, personally
ASSERTION OF CANDOR:	actually, frankly, in reality, to be honest, to say the least, to tell the truth
ASSERTION OF FACT:	as a matter of fact, as it happens, as you know, believe it or not, certainly, clearly, doubtless, in fact, naturally, needless to say, obviously, without doubt
WEAK ASSERTION:	apparently, perhaps, presumably

139 At the Beginning of a Sentence

a. When the words and phrases listed in ¶138*a* and *b* appear at the beginning of a sentence, they should be followed by a comma unless they are used as essential elements.

NONESSENTIAL: *After all,* you have done more for him than he had any right to expect.
ESSENTIAL: *After all* you have done for him, he has no right to expect more.

NONESSENTIAL: *However,* you look at the letter yourself and see whether you interpret it as I do.
ESSENTIAL: *However* you look at the letter, there is only one possible interpretation.

NONESSENTIAL: *Obviously,* the guest of honor was quite moved by the welcome he received.

ESSENTIAL: *Obviously* moved by the welcome he received, the guest of honor spoke with an emotion-choked voice. (Here *obviously* modifies *moved.* In the preceding sentence, *obviously* modifies the meaning of the sentence as a whole.)

b. When *hence, then,* or *thus* occurs at the beginning of a sentence, the comma following is omitted unless the connective requires special emphasis or a nonessential element occurs at that point.

Thus we have decided to move our plant to South Carolina.
Then you can draw up the contract.
BUT: *Then,* when the terms are agreed on, you can draw up the contract.

▪ *See also ¶142a, note.*

c. When an introductory transitional expression or independent comment is incorporated into the flow of the sentence without any intervening pause, the comma may be omitted.

Of course we can do it.   *Perhaps* she will write.
No doubt they will call.   *Indeed* I will.

140 At the End of a Sentence

Use one comma to set off a transitional expression or an independent comment at the end of a sentence. However, be sure to distinguish between nonessential and essential elements.

NONESSENTIAL: We shall take all appropriate measures, *of course.*

ESSENTIAL: We shall take all appropriate measures as a matter *of course.*

141 Within the Sentence

Use two commas to set off a transitional expression or an independent comment when it occurs as a nonessential element *within the sentence.*

It is generally understood, *however,* that she will accept the position.
You, *too,* will be pleased with the materials used in our products.

If, however, the expression is used as an essential element, omit the commas.

NONESSENTIAL: Let me say, *to begin with,* that I have always thought highly of him.

ESSENTIAL: If you want to improve your English, you ought *to begin with* a good review of grammar.

NOTE: In many sentences the only way you can tell whether an expression is nonessential or essential is by the way you say it. If your voice tends to *drop* as you utter the expression, it is nonessential and should be set off by commas.

It is understood, *nevertheless,* that she will accept the position.
He is willing, *certainly,* to do the job over.
It is important, *therefore,* that we check the files at once.

(Continued on page 24.)

If your voice tends to *rise* as you utter the expression, it is essential and should not be set off by commas.

It is *nevertheless* understood that she will accept the position.

He is *certainly* willing to do the job over.

It is *therefore* important that we check the files at once.

If commas are inserted in the previous example, the entire reading of the sentence will be changed. The voice will rise on the word *is* and drop on *therefore*. (If this is the inflection intended, then commas around *therefore* are appropriate.)

It is, *therefore*, important that we check the files at once.

142 At the Beginning of a Clause

a. When a transitional expression or independent comment occurs *at the beginning of the second independent clause* in a compound sentence and is *preceded by a semicolon*, use one comma following the expression.

I never met her formally; *however*, I know her by sight.

My schedule on Friday has eased up considerably; *therefore*, I can see you any time after two.

NOTE: When *hence, then*, or *thus* appears at the beginning of an independent clause, the comma following is omitted unless the connective requires special emphasis or a nonessential element occurs at that point.

Melt the butter over high heat; *then* add the egg.

BUT: Melt the butter over high heat; *then*, when the foam has subsided, add the egg.

b. When the expression occurs *at the beginning of the second independent clause* in a compound sentence and is *preceded by a comma and a coordinating conjunction*, use one comma following the expression. (See also ¶127*d*.)

The job seemed to have no future, and *to tell the truth*, the salary was pretty low.

In the first place, I think the budget for the project is unrealistic, and *in the second place*, the deadlines are almost impossible to meet.

NOTE: If the expression is a simple adverb like *therefore* or *consequently*, the comma following the expression is usually omitted.

The matter must be resolved by Friday, and *therefore* our preliminary conference must be held no later than Thursday.

c. If the expression occurs *at the beginning of a dependent clause*, either treat the expression as nonessential (and set it off with two commas) or treat it as essential (and omit the commas).

If, *moreover*, they do not meet the next interim deadline, we have the right to cancel the contract.

If *indeed* they are interested in settling the dispute, why don't they agree to submit the issues to arbitration?

He is a man who, *in my opinion*, will make a fine marketing director.

She is a woman who *no doubt* knows how to run a department smoothly and effectively.

The situation is so serious that, *strictly speaking,* bankruptcy is the only solution.

The situation is so serious that *perhaps* bankruptcy may be the only solution.

143 With the Adverb *Too*

a. When the adverb *too* (in the sense of "also") occurs at the end of a clause or a sentence, the comma preceding is omitted.

If you want to bring your wife along *too,* I'll make the necessary arrangements.

You should try to improve your math *too.*

b. When *too* (in the sense of "also") occurs elsewhere in the sentence, particularly between subject and verb, set it off with two commas.

You, *too,* can save by shopping at Feder's.

c. When *too* is used as an adverb meaning "excessively," it is never set off with commas.

I will be *too* busy to participate in the session.

The package arrived *too* late to be delivered.

With Interruptions and Afterthoughts

144   Use commas to set off words, phrases, or clauses that interrupt the flow of a sentence or that are loosely added at the end as an afterthought.

She has received, *so I was told,* a letter of commendation from the mayor.

The exhibit contained only modern art, *if I remember correctly.*

Our lighting equipment, *you must admit,* is most inadequate.

His record is outstanding, *particularly in the field of electronics.*

This book is as well written as, *though less exciting than,* her other books.

This course of action is the wisest, *if not the most expedient,* one under the circumstances.

▪ *See also ¶¶131c, 136b, 137c.*

CAUTION: When enclosing an interrupting expression with two commas, be sure the commas are inserted accurately.

WRONG: That is the best, *though not the cheapest method,* of rebuilding your garage.

RIGHT: That is the best, *though not the cheapest,* method of rebuilding your garage.

WRONG: Glen has a deep interest in, *as well as a great fondness,* for oriental art.

RIGHT: Glen has a deep interest in, *as well as a great fondness for,* oriental art.

With Direct Address

145   Names and titles used in direct address must be set off by commas.

You cannot deny, *Ms. Monroe,* that you made that statement.

No, *sir,* I did not see him.

I look forward to your visit, *Jane.*

With Additional Considerations

146 A phrase introduced by *as well as, in addition to, besides, accompanied by, together with, plus,* or a similar expression should be set off by commas when it falls between the subject and the verb.

> Our executives, *as well as our staff,* acclaimed the decision.

When the phrase occurs elsewhere in the sentence, commas may be omitted if the phrase is closely related to the preceding words.

> The decision was acclaimed by our executives *as well as* our staff.
>
> **BUT:** She is leaving for Atlanta on Friday morning, *together with her assistant and two marketing consultants.*

With Contrasting Expressions

147 Contrasting expressions should be set off by commas. (Such expressions often begin with *but* or *not.*)

> The Sanchezes are willing to sell, *but only on their terms.*
>
> He had changed his methods, *not his objectives,* we noticed.
>
> The more money we invested in the business, *the worse the situation became.*
>
> **BUT:** The sooner the better. (The comma may be omitted when the contrasting expressions are short.)
>
> Paula, *rather than Al,* has been chosen for the job.

NOTE: When such phrases fit smoothly into the flow of the sentence, no commas are required.

> They have chosen Paula *rather than Al.*
>
> It was a busy *but enjoyable* trip.

The following rules (¶¶148–153) deal with descriptive expressions that immediately follow the words to which they refer. When nonessential, these expressions are set off by commas; when essential, they remain unpunctuated.

With Identifying, Appositive, or Explanatory Expressions

148 Use commas to set off expressions that provide additional but *nonessential* information about a noun or pronoun immediately preceding. (Such expressions serve to further identify or explain the word they refer to.)

> Mr. De Groot, *our president,* is retiring on Monday, *June 30.* (Phrases such as *our president* and *June 30* are appositives.)
>
> Etymology, *that is, the study of the history of words,* is her latest interest. (See also ¶¶181–183 for other punctuation with *that is, namely,* and *for example.*)
>
> His first book, *written while he was still in graduate school,* launched a successful writing career.
>
> Our first thought, *to run to the nearest exit,* would have resulted in panic.
>
> Ms. Ballantine, *who has been a senior copywriter for three years,* will be the new head of our advertising department.
>
> Everyone in our family likes outdoor sports, *such as tennis and skiing.*

NOTE: In some cases, other marks of punctuation may be preferable in place of commas.

> **CONFUSING:** Mr. Newcombe, *my boss*, and I will discuss this problem next week. (Does *my boss* refer to Mr. Newcombe, or are there three people involved?)
> **CLEAR:** Mr. Newcombe (my boss) and I will be discussing this problem next week. (Use parentheses or dashes instead of commas when an appositive expression could be misread as an item in a series.)
>
> There are two factors to be considered, *sales and collections.* (A colon or a dash could be used in place of the comma. See ¶¶189, 201.)
> **BUT:** There are three factors to be considered: sales, collections, and inventories. (When the explanatory expression consists of a series of *three* or more items and comes at the end of the sentence, use a colon or dash. See ¶¶189, 201.)
> **OR:** These three factors—sales, collections, and inventories—should be considered. (When the explanatory series comes within the sentence, set it off with dashes or parentheses. See ¶¶183, 202, 219.)

149 When the expression is *essential* to the completeness of the sentence, do not set it off. (In the following examples, the expression is needed to identify which particular item is meant. If the expression were omitted, the sentence would be incomplete.)

> The year *1976* marked the two hundredth anniversary of this country.
> The word *accommodate* is often misspelled.
> The poet *Richard Wilbur* will give a reading at the college tomorrow night.
> The statement "*I don't remember*" was frequently heard in court yesterday.
> The impulse *to get away from it all* is very common.
> The notes *in green ink* were made by Mrs. Long.
> The person *who takes over as general manager* will need everyone's support.
> Everyone in our family likes *such* outdoor sports *as tennis and skiing.*

NOTE: Compare the following set of examples.

> Her article *"Color and Design"* was published in June. (The title is essential; it identifies *which* article.)
> Her latest article, *"Color and Design,"* was published in June. (Nonessential; the word *latest* already indicates which article.)
> Her latest article *on color and design* was published in June. (Without commas, this means she has earlier articles on the same subject.)
> Her latest article, *on color and design,* was published in June. (With commas, this means her earlier articles were on other subjects.)

150 A number of expressions are treated as essential simply because of a very close relationship with the preceding words. (If read aloud, the combined phrase sounds like one unit, without any intervening pause.)

> Mary *herself* made all the arrangements for the conference.
> We *managers* need better lines of communication with our employees.
> *My husband John* will accompany me to the national conference. (Strictly speaking, *John* should be set off by commas since the name is not needed to indicate *which* husband. However, commas are omitted in expressions like these because they are read as a unit.)

(*Continued on page 28.*)

My brother Paul may join us as well.
BUT: My brother, *Paul Engstrom,* may join us.
The composer *Stephen Sondheim* has many Broadway hits to his credit.
BUT: My favorite composer, *Stephen Sondheim,* has many Broadway hits . . .

151 When *or* introduces a word or a phrase that identifies or explains the preceding word, set off the explanatory expression with commas.

First, determine whether the clauses are coordinate, *or of equal rank.*

However, if *or* introduces an alternative thought, the expression is essential and should not be set off by commas.

First, determine whether the clauses are coordinate *or noncoordinate.*

152 When a business letter is referred to by date, any related phrases or clauses that follow are usually nonessential.

Thank you for your letter of May 8, *in which you reported receiving damaged shipments.* (The date is sufficient to identify which letter is meant; the *in which* clause simply provides additional but nonessential information.)

However, no comma is needed after the date if the following phrase is short and closely related.

Thank you for your letter of May 8 *about the damaged shipment.*

With Residence and Business Connections

153 Use commas to set off a *long phrase* denoting a person's residence or business connections.

Miss Lee, *of the Hansford Company in Clarksville, Tennessee,* will be in town next Thursday.
Miss Lee *of Clarksville, Tennessee,* will be in town next Thursday. (Omit the comma before *of* to avoid too many breaks in a short phrase. The state name must always be set off by commas when it follows a city name.)
Miss Lee *of the Hansford Company* will be in town next Thursday. (Short phrase; no commas.)
Miss Lee *of Clarksville* will be in town next Thursday. (Short phrase; no commas.)

The following rules (¶¶154–161) deal with the "nonessential" treatment of certain elements in dates, personal names, company names, and addresses. Because these elements cannot truly be called nonessential, the established tradition of setting them off with commas has in many cases begun to change.

In Dates

154 Use two commas to set off the year when it follows the month and day.

Since May 1, *1977,* I have been working for an architectural firm.
The July 21, *1978,* issue of *Newsweek* was the source of that quotation.

NOTE: Some writers omit the comma following the year.

155 The growing trend is to omit the commas when only the month and year are given.

> In *September 1977* the first signs of mismanagement were detected.
>
> (**OLDER STYLE:** In *September, 1977,* the first signs of mismanagement were detected.)
>
> The article first appeared in the *April 1976* issue of *Esquire.* (To avoid the fragmented look of "the April, 1976, issue," do not set off the year in commas when the month-year phrase serves as an adjective.)

- *See ¶410 for additional examples involving dates.*

With *Jr., Sr.,* Etc.

156 In personal names ending with *Jr., Sr.,* or roman or arabic numerals, the growing trend is to omit commas with these elements. However, always respect an individual's preference when you know what it is.

> Lawrence B. Kelly Jr. Henry Ford II
> Frederick Vargas Sr. David Weild 3d
>
> Harold Van Voorhis *Jr.'s* promotion will be announced tomorrow.

NOTE: When a person prefers to use commas in his name, observe the following style:

> John Di Angelo, Jr. (Use one comma when the name is displayed on a line by itself.)
>
> John Di Angelo, Jr., vice president of . . . (Use two commas when other copy follows.)
>
> John Di Angelo, Jr.'s resignation (Drop the second comma when a possessive ending is attached.)

157 Abbreviations like *Esq.* and those that stand for academic degrees or religious orders are set off by two commas.

> Address the letter to Helen E. Parsekian, *Esq.,* in New York.
> Roger Farrier, *LL.D.,* will address the Elizabethan Club on Wednesday.
> The Reverend James Hanley, *S.J.,* will serve as moderator of the panel.

158 When a personal name is given in inverted order, set off the inverted portion with commas.

> McCaughan, James W., Jr.

With *Inc.* and *Ltd.*

159 The growing trend is to omit the commas with *Inc., Ltd.,* and similar expressions in company names. However, always follow a company's preference when you know what it is. (See also ¶1328.)

> *Time Inc.*   *Field Hats, Ltd.*
>
> Time *Inc.* has expanded its operations beyond magazine publishing.
> Field Hats, *Ltd.,* should be notified about this mistake.

(Continued on page 30.)

NOTE: When commas are to be used in a company name, follow this style:

McGraw-Hill, Inc. (Use one comma when the name is displayed on a line by itself.)

McGraw-Hill, Inc., announces the publication of . . . (Use two commas when other copy follows.)

McGraw-Hill, Inc.'s annual statement (Drop the second comma after a possessive ending.)

■ *See ¶163 for the use of commas with other parts of a company name.*

In Geographical References and Addresses

160 Use two commas to set off the name of a state, country, county, or the equivalent when it directly follows the name of a city.

You can fly from Miami, *Florida*, to Bogotá, *Colombia*, in under four hours.
Show your address as Verona, *Essex County*, *New Jersey*, on the application.
I attended the Carbondale, *Pennsylvania*, public schools.
OR: I attended the Carbondale (*Pennsylvania*) public schools. (Parentheses are clearer than commas when a city-state expression serves as an adjective.)
Washington, *D.C.'s* reputation for good restaurants is not exaggerated. (Omit the second comma after a possessive ending.)

161 When expressing complete addresses, follow this style:

IN SENTENCES: During the month of August you can send material directly to me at 402 Woodbury Road, Pasadena, CA 91104, or you can ask my secretary to forward it. (Note that a comma follows the ZIP Code but does not precede it.)

IN DISPLAYED BLOCKS: 402 Woodbury Road
Pasadena, CA 91104

The following rules (¶¶162–175) deal with various uses of separating commas: to separate items in a series, to separate adjectives that precede a noun, and to clarify meaning in sentences with unusual word order or omitted words.

In a Series

162 When three or more items are listed in a series and the last item is preceded by *and, or,* or *nor,* place a comma before the conjunction as well as between the other items. (See also ¶126*b*.)

Study the rules for the use of the comma, the semicolon, *and* the colon.
The consensus is that your report is well written, that your facts are accurate, *and* that your conclusions are sound.
The show will appeal equally to women and men, adults and children, *and* sophisticates and innocents. (See the entry for *and* in Section 11.)

163 For a series in a company name, always follow the style preferred by the particular firm.

Merrill Lynch, Pierce, Fenner & Smith Incorporated
Hart Schaffner & Marx

If you do not have the company's letterhead or some other reliable resource at hand, follow the standard rule on commas in a series (¶162).

> Our prime supplier is *Ames, Koslow, Milke, and Company.*

164 When an expression such as *and so on* or *etc.* closes a series, use a comma before and after the expression (unless, of course, the expression falls at the end of a sentence).

> Our sale of suits, coats, hats, *and so on,* starts tomorrow.
> Tomorrow morning we will start our sale of suits, coats, hats, *etc.*

▪ *See page 216 for a usage note on* etc.

165 Do not insert a comma after the last item in a series unless the sentence structure demands a comma at that point.

> January 15, March 3, and May 20 are the dates of the three letters.
> January 15, March 3, and May 20, 1976, are the dates of the three letters. (The comma following the year is one of the pair that sets off the year. See ¶154.)

166 When *and, or,* or *nor* is used to connect all the items in a series, do not separate the items by commas.

> Invitations are being sent to parents *and* faculty *and* former students.

167 If a series consists of only two items, do not separate the items with a comma. (See also ¶125*f*.)

> You can get in from the airport either *by limousine* or *by taxi.*

NOTE: Use a comma, however, to separate two independent clauses joined by *and, but, or,* or *nor.* (See ¶126*a*.)

▪ *See* ¶¶*184–185 for the use of the semicolon in a series.*

With Adjectives

168 When two consecutive adjectives modify the same noun, separate the adjectives with a comma.

> Most people think of her as a *generous, outgoing* person. (A person who is *generous* and *outgoing.*)

NOTE: Do *not* use a comma between the adjectives if they are connected by *and, or,* or *nor.*

> Most people think of her as a *generous* and *outgoing* person.

169 When two adjectives precede a noun, the first adjective may modify the combined idea of the second adjective plus the noun. In such cases do not separate the adjectives by a comma.

> The estate is surrounded by an *old stone* wall. (A *stone* wall that is *old.*)
> Ms. Klaussen is working on the *annual financial* statement. (A *financial* statement that is *annual.*)

TEST: To decide whether consecutive adjectives should be separated by a comma or not, try using them in a relative clause *after* the noun, with *and* inserted between them. If they read smoothly and sensibly in that position, they should be separated by a comma in their actual position.

> We need an *intelligent, enterprising* person for the job. (One can speak of "a person who is intelligent and enterprising," so a comma is correct in the original wording.)
>
> Throw out your *old winter* coat. (One cannot speak of "a coat that is *old* and *winter*," so no comma should be used in the actual sentence.)

170 When more than two adjectives precede a noun, insert a comma only between those adjectives where *and* could have been used.

> an easy, relaxed, unruffled manner (an easy *and* relaxed *and* unruffled manner)
>
> a competent, efficient legal secretary (a competent *and* efficient legal secretary)
>
> the established American political system (*and* cannot be inserted between these adjectives)

171 Do not use a comma between the final adjective in a series and the following noun.

> I put in a long, hard, *demanding* day on Monday.
>
> (NOT: I put in a long, hard, *demanding,* day on Monday.)

To Indicate Omitted Verbs

172 Use a comma to indicate the omission of a verb in a compound sentence. (This use of the comma usually occurs when clauses are separated by semicolons.)

> The English test was given to all students; the history test, to seniors only; and the math test, to juniors only. (See ¶1048.)

NOTE: If the omitted word is clearly understood from the context, simpler punctuation may be used.

> The English test was given to all students, the history test to seniors only, and the math test to juniors only.

For Clarity

173 Note how the use of the comma prevents misreading.

> As you know, nothing came of the meeting. (NOT: As you know nothing came of the meeting.)
>
> To a liberal like Bill, Buckley seems hard to take.
>
> Soon after, the committee disbanded without accomplishing its goal.

174 Sometimes, for clarity, it is necessary to separate even a subject and a verb.

> All any insurance policy is, is a contract for services.

175 Use a comma to separate repeated words.

> It was a *long, long* time ago.
>
> That was a *very, very* old argument.
>
> *Well, well,* we'll find a way.
>
> *Now, now,* you don't expect me to believe that!

- *Commas with dashes: see ¶¶213, 215b.*
- *Commas with numbers: see ¶461.*
- *Commas with questions within sentences: see ¶¶114–117.*
- *Commas with parentheses: see ¶224a.*
- *Commas inside closing quotation marks: see ¶247.*
- *Commas at the end of a quotation: see ¶¶253–255.*
- *Commas preceding a quotation: see ¶256.*
- *Commas with quotations within a sentence: see ¶¶259–261.*
- *Commas to set off interruptions in quoted matter: see ¶¶262-263.*

The Semicolon

Between Independent Clauses—*And, But, Or,* or *Nor* Omitted

176 When a coordinating conjunction (*and, but, or,* or *nor*) is omitted between two independent clauses, use a semicolon—not a comma—to separate the clauses. (See ¶187.)

> The union was willing to compromise; the management was not.
>
> (**NOT:** The union was willing to compromise, the management was not.)

If the clauses are not closely related, treat them as separate sentences.

> **WEAK:** Thank you for your letter of March 16; we are sorry about the error in the shipment and are rushing the correct items to you.
>
> **BETTER:** Thank you for your letter of March 16. We are sorry about the error in the shipment and are rushing the correct items to you.

Between Independent Clauses—*And, But, Or,* or *Nor* Included

177 A comma is normally used to separate two independent clauses joined by a coordinating conjunction. However, under certain circumstances, a semicolon is appropriate.

a. Use a semicolon in order to achieve a stronger break between clauses than a comma provides.

> **NORMAL BREAK:** Many people are convinced that they could personally solve the problem if given the authority to do so, but no one will come forward with a clear-cut plan that we can evaluate in advance.
>
> **STRONG BREAK:** Many people are convinced that they could personally solve the problem if given the authority to do so; but no one will come forward with a clear-cut plan that we can evaluate in advance.

b. Use a semicolon when one or both clauses have internal commas and a misreading might occur if a comma were also used to separate the clauses.

> **CONFUSING:** I sent you an order for bond letterheads, onionskin paper, carbons, and envelopes, and shipping tags, cardboard cartons, stapler wire, and binding tape were sent to me instead.
>
> **CLEAR:** I sent you an order for bond letterheads, onionskin paper, carbons, and envelopes; and shipping tags, cardboard cartons, stapler wire, and binding tape were sent to me instead.

(Continued on page 34.)

c. If no misreading is likely, a comma is sufficient to separate the clauses, even though commas are also used within the clauses.

> On May 19, 1978, I wrote to Ms. Harriet McGee, your sales manager, but I have not yet had an answer to my letter.
>
> On the whole, his progress has been good, and considering his medical history, I think he will make a complete recovery.

NOTE: If a stronger break is desired between clauses in the two examples above, use a semicolon.

With Transitional Expressions

178 When independent clauses are linked by transitional expressions (see a partial list below), use a semicolon between the clauses. (If the second clause is long or requires special emphasis, treat it as a separate sentence.)

accordingly	however	so (see ¶179)
besides	moreover	that is (see ¶181)
consequently	namely (see ¶181)	then (see ¶139b)
for example (see ¶181)	nevertheless	therefore
furthermore	on the contrary	thus
hence	otherwise	yet (see ¶179)

> The motion was voted down; *moreover*, it was voted down by a large majority.
>
> Our costs have increased; our prices, *however*, have not.
>
> Let's plan to work till one; *then* we can break for lunch.

NOTE: Use a comma after the transitional expression when it occurs at the start of the second clause. (See the first example above.) However, no comma is needed after *hence, then, thus, so,* and *yet* unless a strong pause is wanted at that point. (See the third example above.)

▪ *See ¶¶138–142 for the use of commas with transitional expressions.*

179 An independent clause introduced by *so* (in the sense of "therefore") or *yet* may be preceded by a comma or a semicolon. Use a comma if the two clauses are closely related and there is a smooth flow from the first clause to the second. Use a semicolon if the clauses are long and complicated or if the transition between clauses calls for a long pause or a strong break.

> Sales have been good, *yet* profits are low.
>
> This report explains why production has slowed down; *yet* it does not indicate how to avoid future delays.
>
> These sale-priced toasters are going fast, *so* don't delay if you want one.
>
> We have been getting an excessive number of complaints during the last few months about our service; *so* I would like each of you to review the operations in your department and indicate what corrective measures you think ought to be taken.

180 If both the coordinating conjunction and the transitional expression occur at the start of the second clause, use a comma before the conjunction.

> The site has a number of disadvantages, *and furthermore* the asking price is quite high. (See ¶142b and note.)

REMEMBER: A semicolon is needed to separate independent clauses, not so much because a transitional expression is present but because a coordinating conjunction is absent.

With *For Example, That Is, Namely,* Etc.

181 Before an Independent Clause

a. In general, when two independent clauses are linked by a transitional expression such as *for example* (e.g.), *namely,* or *that is* (i.e.), use a semicolon before the expression and a comma afterward.

> She is highly qualified for the job; *for example,* she has had ten years' experience as a research chemist.

b. If the first independent clause serves to anticipate the second clause and the full emphasis is to fall on the second clause, use a colon before the transitional expression.

> Your proposal covers all but one point: *namely,* who is going to foot the bill?

c. For a stronger but less formal break between clauses, the semicolon or the colon may be replaced by a dash.

> Hampton says he will help—*that is,* he will help if you ask him to.

182 At the End of a Sentence

When *for example, namely,* or *that is* introduces words, phrases, or a series of clauses *at the end of a sentence,* the punctuation preceding the expression may vary as follows:

a. If the first part of the sentence expresses the complete thought and the explanation is added on almost as an afterthought, use a semicolon before the transitional expression.

> Always use figures with abbreviations; *for example,* 6 ft, 9 sq in, 4 p.m. (Here the examples are not anticipated by the earlier part of the sentence.)

b. If the first part of the sentence suggests that an explanation or an illustration will follow, use a colon before the transitional expression to throw emphasis on what *follows.*

> My assistant has three important duties: *namely,* attending all meetings, writing the minutes, and sending out notices. (The word *three* anticipates the enumeration following *namely.*)

NOTE: Use a comma before the transitional expression to throw emphasis on the words that *precede.*

> I checked these figures with three people, *namely, Alix, Andy, and Jim.* (This punctuation emphasizes *three people* rather than the specific names.)

c. If the expression introduces an appositive that explains a word or phrase immediately preceding, a comma should precede the transitional expression.

> Do not use quotation marks to enclose an indirect quotation, *that is, a restatement of a person's exact words.* (Here again, a comma is used because what precedes the transitional expression is more important than what follows.)

(Continued on page 36.)

d. The semicolon, the colon, and the comma in the examples above may be replaced by a dash or by parentheses. The dash provides a stronger but less formal break; the parentheses serve to subordinate the explanatory element.

183   Within a Sentence

When *for example, namely,* or *that is* introduces words, phrases, or clauses *within a sentence,* treat the entire construction as nonessential and set it off with commas, dashes, or parentheses. Dashes will give emphasis to the interrupting construction; parentheses will make the construction appear less important than the rest of the words in the sentence.

> Many of the components, *for example, the motor,* are manufactured by outside suppliers.
>
> Many of the components—*for example, the motor*—are manufactured by . . .
>
> Many of the components (*for example, the motor*) are manufactured by . . .

NOTE: Commas can be used to set off the nonessential element so long as it contains no internal punctuation (other than the comma after the introductory expression). If the nonessential element is internally punctuated with several commas, set it off with either dashes or parentheses.

> Many of the components—*for example, the motor, the batteries, and the cooling unit*—are manufactured by outside suppliers. (Use dashes for emphasis.)
>
> OR: Many of the components (*for example, the motor, the batteries, and the cooling unit*) are manufactured by outside suppliers. (Use parentheses for subordination.)

In a Series

184   Use a semicolon to separate items in a series if any of the items already contain commas.

> Attending the conference in Washington were John McDaniels, executive vice president; Donna Cohen, marketing director; Charles Lindstrom, advertising manager; and Pat Hingle, sales promotion manager.

185   Avoid starting a sentence with a series punctuated with semicolons. Try to recast the sentence so that the series comes at the end.

> AWKWARD: Our sales managers in Portland, Oregon; Flagstaff, Arizona; Lincoln, Nebraska; and Monroe, Louisiana, have been sent invitations.
>
> IMPROVED: Invitations have been sent to our sales managers in Portland, Oregon; Flagstaff, Arizona; Lincoln, Nebraska; and Monroe, Louisiana.

With Dependent Clauses

186   Use semicolons to separate a series of parallel dependent clauses if they are long or contain internal commas. (However, a simple series of dependent clauses requires only commas, just like any other kind of series.)

> They promised that they would review the existing specifications, costs, and sales estimates for the project; that they would analyze Merkle's alternative figures; and that they would prepare a detailed comparison of the two proposals.

If you have tried special clearance sales but have not raised the necessary cash; if you have tried to borrow the money and have not been able to find a lender; if you have offered to sell part of the business but have not been able to find a partner, then your only course of action is to go out of business.

- *Semicolons with dashes: see ¶¶213, 215c.*
- *Semicolons with parentheses: see ¶224a.*
- *Semicolons with quotation marks: see ¶248.*

The Colon

Between Independent Clauses

187 Use a colon between two independent clauses when the second clause explains or illustrates the first clause and there is no coordinating conjunction or transitional expression linking the two clauses.

> The job you have described sounds very attractive: the salary is good and the opportunities for advancement seem excellent.
>
> **BUT:** The job you have described sounds very attractive; for example, the salary is good and the opportunities for advancement seem excellent. (Use a semicolon when a transitional expression links the clauses.)
>
> The job you have described sounds very attractive; it is the kind of job I have been looking for. (Use a semicolon when the second clause does not explain the first clause.)

Before Lists and Enumerations

188 Place a colon before such expressions as *for example, namely,* and *that is* when they introduce words, phrases, or a series of clauses anticipated earlier in the sentence. (See ¶182*b* for examples.)

189 When a clause contains an anticipatory expression (such as *the following, as follows, thus,* and *these*) and directs attention to a series of explanatory words, phrases, or clauses, use a colon between the clause and the series.

> *These* are the job requirements: a college degree, three years' experience in the field, and freedom to travel abroad.
>
> *The following* rules should be observed in writing checks:
> 1. Write them in ink.
> 2. Leave no empty spaces on lines that are to be filled in.
> 3. Make no changes or erasures in an amount of money.

190 Use a colon even if the anticipatory expression is only implied and not stated.

> The house has attractive features: cross ventilation in every room, a two-story living room, and two terraces.

191 Do not use a colon in the following cases:

a. If the sentence in which the anticipatory expression occurs is a long sentence and if the expression occurs near the beginning of that sentence.

(Continued on page 38.)

We have set *the following* restrictions on the return of merchandise, because many customers have abused the privilege. Goods cannot be returned after five days, and price tags must not be removed.

BUT: We have set *the following* restrictions on the return of merchandise: goods cannot be returned . . .

b. If the sentence containing the anticipatory expression is followed by another sentence.

Campers will find that *the following* small items will add much to their enjoyment of the summer. These articles may be purchased from a store near the camp.

Flashlight	Hot-cold food bag
Camera	Fishing gear

c. If an explanatory series follows a preposition or a verb.

The panel consists of Ms. Seidel, Mrs. Kitay, and Mr. Haddad.
(NOT: The panel consists of: Ms. Seidel, Mrs. Kitay, and Mr. Haddad.)

This set of china includes 12 dinner plates, 12 salad plates, and 12 cups and saucers.
(NOT: This set of china includes: 12 dinner plates, 12 salad plates, and 12 cups and saucers.)

NOTE: Retain the colon if the items in the series are listed on separate lines.

This set of china includes:
　　12 dinner plates
　　12 salad plates
　　12 cups and saucers

In Expressions of Time and Proportions

192 When hours and minutes are expressed in figures, separate them with a colon, as in the expression *8:25.* (No space precedes or follows this colon.)

193 A colon is used to represent the word *to* in proportions, as in the ratio *2:1.* (No space precedes or follows this colon.)

After Salutations

194 In business letters, use a colon after the salutation (see also ¶1346). In social letters, use a comma or no punctuation at all (see also ¶1398*b*).

In References to Books or Publications

195 Use a colon to separate:

a. The title and the subtitle of a book.

Tanzi is the author of *The Individual Income Tax and Economic Growth: An International Comparison.*

b. The volume number from the page numbers in a footnote or an entry in a bibliography.

See the *Journal of Public Health,* 5:681–684. (Meaning "Volume 5, pages 681–684.")

■　*See also* ¶1418*b*, e, k, l.

Capitalizing After a Colon

196 Do not capitalize after a colon if the material cannot stand alone as a sentence.

> All cash advances must be countersigned by me, with one exception: when the amount is less than $50. (Dependent clause following a colon.)
>
> Two courses are required: typing and English. (Words following a colon.)

EXCEPTION: Capitalize the first word after the colon if it is a proper noun, a proper adjective, or the pronoun *I*.

> Two courses are required: English and typing.

197 Do not capitalize the first word of an independent clause after a colon if the clause explains, illustrates, or amplifies the thought expressed in the first part of the sentence. (See ¶196, exception.)

> Essential and nonessential elements require altogether different punctuation: the latter should be set off by commas, whereas the former should not.

198 Capitalize the first word of an independent clause after a colon if it requires special emphasis or is presented as a formal rule. (In such cases the independent clause expresses the main thought; the first part of the sentence usually functions only as an introduction.)

> Let me say this: If the company is to recover from its present difficulties, we must immediately devise an entirely new marketing strategy.
>
> Here is the key principle: Nonessential elements must be set off by commas; essential elements should not be set off.

199 Also capitalize the first word after a colon under these circumstances:

a. When the material following the colon consists of two or more sentences.

> There are several drawbacks to this proposal: First, it will tie up a good deal of capital for the next five years. Second, the likelihood of a significant return on the investment has not been shown.

b. When the material following the colon is a quoted sentence.

> Mr. Korman had this to say: "No single person can take full credit for the success of the show." (See ¶256 for the use of a colon before a quoted sentence.)

c. When the material following the colon starts on a new line (for example, the body of a letter following the salutation or the individual items displayed on separate lines in a list).

> Dear Barbara:
>
>   Thank you for your letter of
> May 3. I have talked to Hal . . .

> Capitalize the first word of:
>   a. Every sentence.
>   b. Direct quotations.

d. When the material *preceding* the colon is a short introductory word such as *Note*, *Caution*, or *Wanted*.

> *Note:* All expense reports must be submitted no later than Friday.

- *Colons with dashes: see ¶¶213, 215c.*
- *Colons with parentheses: see ¶224a.*
- *Colons with quotation marks: see ¶¶248, 256.*

PUNCTUATION: OTHER MARKS

THE UNDERSCORE

OTHER MARKS OF PUNCTUATION

TYPEWRITER SPACING WITH PUNCTUATION MARKS (¶299)

Section 2 covers the following punctuation marks: the dash, parentheses, quotation marks, the underscore, the apostrophe, ellipsis marks, the asterisk, the diagonal, and brackets. In addition, it indicates the proper typewriter spacing to be used with all punctuation marks.

The Dash

Although the dash has a few specific functions of its own, it most often serves in place of the comma, the semicolon, the colon, or parentheses. When used as an alternative to these other marks, it creates a much more emphatic separation of words within a sentence. Because of its versatility, careless writers are tempted to use a dash to punctuate almost any break within a sentence. However, the indiscriminate use of dashes is inappropriate; moreover, it serves to destroy the special forcefulness of this mark. Use the dash sparingly—and then only for deliberate effect.

In Place of Commas

201 Use dashes in place of commas to set off a nonessential element that requires special emphasis.

> We intend to see to it that our agents—as well as the transportation companies and the public—receive a fair decision in the matter.
>
> There is a typographical error in one of the paragraphs—the second one.

202 If a nonessential element already contains internal commas, use dashes in place of commas to set the element off. (If dashes provide too emphatic a break, use parentheses instead. See ¶¶183, 219.)

> All large appliances—refrigerators, stoves, washing machines, and dryers—will be on sale throughout the first week of March.
>
> The storm extended the entire length of the Eastern Seaboard—from Eastport, Maine, to Key West, Florida—in hurricane force.

203 To give special emphasis to the second independent clause in a compound sentence, use a dash rather than a comma before the coordinating conjunction.

> Mrs. Gagne's proposal will double our taxes—and I can prove it!

In Place of a Semicolon

204 For a stronger but less formal break, use a dash in place of a semicolon between closely related independent clauses.

> I do the work—he gets the credit!
>
> The job needs to be done—moreover, it needs to be done well.
>
> Wilson is totally unprepared for a promotion—for example, he still does not grasp the basic principles of good management.

In Place of a Colon

205 For a stronger but less formal break, use a dash in place of a colon to introduce explanatory words, phrases, or clauses.

I need only a few items for my meeting with Kaster—namely, a copy of his letter of May 18, a copy of the contract under dispute, and a bottle of aspirin.

My arrangement with Gina is a simple one—she handles sales and promotion, and I take care of production.

In Place of Parentheses

206 Use dashes instead of parentheses when the nonessential element requires strong emphasis. (See ¶¶183, 219.)

Call Mike Habib—he's with Jax Electronics—and get his opinion.

To Indicate an Abrupt Break or an Afterthought

207 Use a dash to show an abrupt break in thought or to set off an afterthought.

Here's gourmet food in a jiffy—economical too!
I believe she said the convention would be held in Portland, Oregon—or was it Portland, Maine?

208 If a *question* or an *exclamation* is broken off abruptly before it has been completed, use a dash followed by a question mark or an exclamation point as appropriate. If the sentence is a *statement,* however, use a dash alone, followed by two spaces.

Do you want to tell him or—? Suppose I wait to hear from you.
If only— Yet there's no point in talking about what might have been.
(NOT: If only—. Yet there's no point in talking about what might have been.)

▪ *See ¶291b for the use of ellipsis marks to indicate a break in thought.*

To Show Hesitation

209 Use a dash to indicate hesitation, faltering speech, or stammering.

The work on the Patterson dam was begun—oh, I should say—well, about May 1—certainly no later than May 15.

To Emphasize Single Words

210 Use dashes to set off single words that require special emphasis.

Money—that is all he thinks about.
She cares about only one thing—success.

With Repetitions and Restatements

211 Use dashes to set off and emphasize words that repeat or restate a previous thought.

Right now—at this very moment—our showrooms are crammed with bargains.
Sometime next week—say, Wednesday—let's plan to meet for lunch.
He himself had the folder—the folder he said I had lost.

Before Summarizing Words

212 Use a dash before such words as *these, they,* and *all* when these words stand as subjects summarizing a preceding list of details.

> A lawn mower, a rake, and a spade—these are the only tools you will need.
>
> Juniors, seniors, and graduate students—all are invited to the Symington lecture on Tuesday.
>
> **BUT:** Juniors, seniors, and graduate students are all invited . . . (No dash is used when the summarizing word is not the subject.)

Punctuation Preceding an Opening Dash

213 An opening dash should not be preceded by a comma, a semicolon, a colon, or a period (except a period following an abbreviation).

> We do a good job—and we do it fast!
> (**NOT:** We do a good job,—and we do it fast!)
> The shipment was sent c.o.d.—as you requested.

Punctuation Preceding a Closing Dash

214 When a *statement* or a *command* is set off by dashes within a sentence, do not use a period before the closing dash (except a period following an abbreviation).

> John Ippolito—he used to head up the sales force at Marker's—now has his own consulting firm.
>
> (**NOT:** John Ippolito—He used to head up the sales force at Marker's.—now has his own consulting firm.)

When a *question* or an *exclamation* is set off by dashes within a sentence, use a question mark or an exclamation point before the closing dash.

> The representative of the Hitchcock Company—do you know her?—has called again for an appointment.
>
> The new sketches—I can't wait to show them to you!—should be ready by Monday.

NOTE: When a complete sentence is set off in dashes, do not capitalize the first word unless it is a proper noun, a proper adjective, the pronoun *I*, or the first word of a quoted sentence.

Punctuation Following a Closing Dash

215 When the sentence construction requires some mark of punctuation following a closing dash, either retain the dash or use the sentence punctuation—but do not use both marks together.

a. When a closing dash falls at the end of a sentence, it should be replaced by the punctuation needed to end the sentence—a period, a question mark, or an exclamation point. (See ¶208 for exceptions.)

> Wheeler's Transport delivers the goods—on time!

b. When a closing dash occurs at a point where the sentence requires a comma, retain the closing dash and omit the comma.

The situation has become critical—indeed dangerous—but no one seems to care. (Here the closing dash is retained, and the comma before the coordinating conjunction is omitted.)

If you feel you are qualified for the job—and you may very well be—you ought to take the employment test. (Here the closing dash is retained, and the comma that separates a dependent clause from an independent clause is omitted.)

Brophy said—and you can check with him yourself—"This office must be vacated by Friday." (Here the closing dash is retained, and the comma before the quotation is omitted.)

c. If a closing dash occurs at a point where the sentence requires a semicolon, a colon, or a closing parenthesis, drop the closing dash and use the required sentence punctuation.

Please try to get your sales projections to us by Wednesday—certainly by Friday at the latest; otherwise, they will be of no use to us in planning the budget.

Here is what Marsha had to say—or at least the gist of it: look for new opportunities for advancement and prepare yourself for them.

You need a volunteer (someone like Louis Morales, for example—he's always cooperative) to play the part of the customer.

Typing Dashes

216 The dash is constructed by striking the hyphen key *twice*, with no space before, between, or after the hyphens.

Improve your English—today!   (**NOT:** Improve your English — today!)

BUT: If he would only try—   (Two spaces follow a dash when a statement breaks off abruptly. See ¶208.)

217 Type a dash at the end of a line (rather than start a new line).

Let's set the date for June 30—   (**NOT:** Let's set the date for June 30
a Wednesday, I believe.   —a Wednesday, I believe.)

Parentheses

Parentheses and dashes serve many of the same functions, but they differ in one significant respect: parentheses can set off only nonessential elements, whereas dashes can set off essential and nonessential elements. In setting off elements, dashes emphasize; parentheses de-emphasize.

With Explanatory Matter

218 Use parentheses to enclose explanatory material that is independent of the main thought of the sentence. The material within parentheses may be a single word, a phrase, or even an entire sentence.

We are disappointed at the very small number of people (five) who have accepted our invitation. (A single word.)

Bids are requested for repaving Sutton Avenue (formerly Lombard Street) in the town of Chester. (A phrase.)

We regret that from now until the end of the year (our fiscal year starts January 1) we can make no further loans. (A sentence.)

(*Continued on page 46.*)

NOTE: Be sure that the parentheses enclose only what is truly parenthetical and not words essential to the construction of the sentence.

> WRONG: I merely said I was averse (not violently opposed *to*) your suggestion.
>
> RIGHT: I merely said I was averse (not violently opposed) *to* your suggestion.

219   Use parentheses to set off a nonessential element when dashes would be too emphatic and commas would be inappropriate or might prove confusing.

> Alma has been named manager of our Portland (Oregon) branch.
>
> BETTER THAN: Alma has been named manager of our Portland, Oregon, branch. (Parentheses are clearer than commas when a city-state expression occurs as an adjective.)
>
> All the classes on this list meet three days a week (Mondays, Wednesdays, and Fridays). (Parentheses are clearer than commas when the nonessential element already contains commas within it.)

With References

220   Use parentheses to set off references and directions.

> Because of unusually heavy expenses to date (see the financial report attached), we are not in a position to make further changes this year.

When a reference falls *at the end of a sentence*, it may be treated as part of the sentence or as a separate sentence.

> The statistics are given in Appendix 4 (see pages 314–316).
>
> OR: The statistics are given in Appendix 4. (See pages 314–316.)

▪ *See also the note following ¶225d.*

With Dates

221   Dates that accompany a person's name or an event are enclosed in parentheses.

> Thomas Jefferson (1743–1826) was the third President of the United States.
>
> At the time of the merger (1948), both parties agreed to establish new headquarters in St. Louis.

With Enumerated Items

222   Use parentheses to enclose numbers or letters that accompany enumerated items within a sentence.

> We need the following information to complete our record of Ms. Pavlick's experience: (1) the number of years she worked for your company, (2) a description of her duties, and (3) the number of promotions she received.
>
> 3. Please include these items on your expense account: (*a*) the cost of your hotel room; (*b*) the cost of meals, including tips; and (*c*) the amount spent on transportation. (Letters are used to enumerate items within a sentence when the sentence itself is part of a *numbered* sequence.)

NOTE: If the enumerated items appear on separate lines, the letters or numbers are usually followed only by periods. (See ¶223.)

223 Subdivisions in outlines are often enclosed in parentheses. When there are many gradations, it is sometimes necessary to use a single closing parenthesis to provide another grade.

```
1. Basic weaves     I. . . . . . . .
   a. Plain            A. . . . . . . .
      (1) Basket          1. . . . . . . .
      (2) Ribbed            a. . . . . . . .
   b. Twill                   (1) . . . . . . .
     etc.                        (a) . . . . . . .
                                    1) . . . . . . .
                                       a) . . . . . . .
```

Parenthetical Items Within Sentences

224 If the item in parentheses falls *within a sentence:*

a. Make sure that any punctuation that comes after the item (such as a comma, a semicolon, a colon, or a dash) falls *outside* the closing parenthesis.

> If you will call me tomorrow (Thursday), I can give you more precise data.
> I wrote to him promptly (as I said I would); however, he has not answered.
> There is only one thing he cares about (and he admits it): himself!
> Your boss's name is mentioned in this week's issue of *Time* (see page 43)—and won't she be delighted!

NOTE: Never insert a comma, a semicolon, a colon, or a dash *before* an opening parenthesis.

b. Do not capitalize the first word of the item in parentheses, even if the item is a complete sentence. **EXCEPTIONS:** Proper nouns, proper adjectives, the pronoun *I*, and the first word of a quoted sentence. (See examples in *c* and *d* below.)

c. Do not use a period before the closing parenthesis except with an abbreviation.

> Mrs. Andrews' letter (please be sure to answer it promptly) makes me question the effectiveness of our order fulfillment procedures.
> Helen Cohen (our public relations representative in Washington, D.C.) could give you that information.
> I want you to meet Ed Pollack (he's our new sales manager) when you come to Omaha.
> **NOT:** I want you to meet Ed Pollack (He's our new sales manager.) when you come to Omaha.

d. Do not use a question mark or an exclamation point before the closing parenthesis unless it applies solely to the parenthetical item *and* the sentence ends with a different mark of punctuation.

> At the coming meeting (will you be able to make it on the 19th?), let's plan to discuss next year's budget. (Question mark used in parentheses because sentence ends with a period.)
> May I still get tickets to the exhibition (and may I bring a friend), or is it now too late? (Question mark omitted in parentheses because sentence ends with a question mark.)
> **NOT:** May I still get tickets to the exhibition (and may I bring a friend?), or is it now too late?

Parenthetical Items at the End of Sentences

225 If the item in parentheses is to be incorporated *at the end of a sentence:*

a. Place the punctuation needed to end the sentence *outside* the closing parenthesis.

> The meeting will be held on March 31 (Friday).
> Have you met John Duff (he's with the Peabody Company)?
> Delivery has been put off again (till next Friday)!

b. Do not capitalize the first word of the item in parentheses, even if the item is a complete sentence. EXCEPTIONS: Proper nouns, proper adjectives, the pronoun *I*, and the first word of a quoted sentence. (See examples in *c* and *d* below.)

c. Do not use a period before the closing parenthesis except with an abbreviation.

> I waited at the airport for hours (until 3 a.m.).
> I waited at the airport for hours (I was there until three).
> NOT: I waited at the airport for hours (I was there until three.).

d. Do not use a question mark or an exclamation point before the closing parenthesis unless it applies solely to the parenthetical element *and* the sentence ends with a different mark of punctuation.

> My new assistant is Bill Romero (didn't you meet him once before?).
> Be sure to send the letter to Portland, Oregon (not Portland, Maine!).
> Then he walked out and slammed the door (can you believe it?)!
> Do you know Ellen Smyth (or is it Smythe)?
> NOT: Do you know Ellen Smyth (or is it Smythe?)?
> I'm through with the job (and I mean it)!
> NOT: I'm through with the job (and I mean it!)!

NOTE: When a complete sentence occurs within parentheses at the end of another sentence, it may be incorporated into the sentence (as in the examples above) so long as it is fairly short and closely related. If the sentence in parentheses is long or requires special emphasis, it should be treated as a separate sentence (see ¶226).

Parenthetical Items as Separate Sentences

226 If the item in parentheses is to be treated as a *separate sentence:*

a. The preceding sentence should close with its own punctuation mark.

b. The item in parentheses should begin with a capital.

c. A period, a question mark, or an exclamation point (whichever is appropriate) should be placed *before* the closing parenthesis.

d. No other punctuation mark should follow the closing parenthesis.

> Many property owners charge that the proposed bond issue will raise the tax rate. (They present no proof of this, however.) Moreover, they claim that new industry will be discouraged.
> She spoke at length on her favorite topic. (How could I stop her?) At the end of an hour, a number of people began to walk out.

- *Parentheses around question marks: see ¶118.*
- *Parentheses around exclamation points: see ¶119, note.*
- *Parentheses around confirming figures: see ¶420.*
- *Parentheses within parentheses: see ¶297.*

Quotation Marks

Quotation marks have three main functions: to indicate the use of someone else's exact words (see ¶¶227–234), to set off words and phrases for special emphasis (see ¶¶235–241), and to display the titles of literary and artistic works (see ¶¶242–244).

For guidance on how to position punctuation marks in relation to the closing quotation mark—that is, *inside* or *outside*—see ¶¶247–251.

For more specific guidance on *when* to use punctuation with quoted matter and which punctuation to use, refer to the following paragraphs:

- *Quotations standing alone: see ¶252.*
- *Quotations at the beginning of a sentence: see ¶¶253–255.*
- *Quotations at the end of a sentence: see ¶¶256–258.*
- *Quotations within a sentence: see ¶¶259–261.*
- *Quotations with interrupting expressions: see ¶¶262–263.*
- *Quotations within quotations: see ¶¶245–246.*
- *Long quotations: see ¶¶264–265.*
- *Quoted letters: see ¶266.*
- *Quoted poetry: see ¶¶267–268.*
- *Quoted dialogues and conversations: see ¶¶269–270.*

With Direct Quotations

227   Use quotation marks to enclose a *direct quotation,* that is, the exact words of a speaker or a writer.

> "I don't like the last paragraph in that letter," said Mr. DeLuca.
> When asked if she planned to attend, Ms. Grunwald simply said "No." (See ¶¶233, 256a.)

228   **a.** Do not use quotation marks for an *indirect quotation,* that is, a restatement or a rearrangement of a person's exact words. (An indirect quotation is often introduced by *that* or *whether* and usually differs from a direct quotation in person, verb tense, or word order.)

> **DIRECT QUOTATION:** Mrs. Knudsen asked her boss, "Am I still being considered for the transfer?"
> **INDIRECT QUOTATION:** Mrs. Knudsen asked her boss whether she was still being considered for the transfer.

NOTE: Sometimes *direct* quotations are introduced by *that.* See ¶256f.

b. In some cases a person's exact words may be treated as either a direct or an indirect quotation, depending on the kind of emphasis desired.

(Continued on page 50.)

Baylis said, "Gutowski should be notified at once." (The use of quotation marks emphasizes that these are Baylis's exact words.)

Baylis said Gutowski should be notified at once. (Without quotation marks, the emphasis falls on the message itself. The fact that Baylis used these exact words is not important.)

229   Do not use quotation marks to set off a *direct question* at the end of a sentence unless it is also a *direct quotation* of someone's exact words.

> DIRECT QUESTION: The question is, How will the tax proposal affect the consumer?
>
> DIRECT QUOTATION: Mr. Rincon then asked, "How will the tax proposal affect the consumer?"
>
> DIRECT QUOTATION: Mr. Rincon then said, "The question is, How will the tax proposal affect the consumer?"

230   When only a word or phrase is quoted from another source, be sure to place the quotation marks around only the words extracted from the original source and not around any rearrangement of those words.

> Bryant said he would decide when he had "all the facts." (Bryant's exact words were, "I will decide when all the facts are in.")
>
> (NOT: Bryant said he would decide "when he had all the facts.")

NOTE: When a quoted word or phrase comes at the end of a sentence, the period goes *inside* the closing quotation mark. See ¶247, particularly examples 2–4.

231   Be particularly sure not to include such words as *a* and *the* at the beginning or *etc.* at the end of the quotation unless these words were actually part of the original material.

> Joe said you turned in a "first-rate" report. (Joe's exact words were, "The report you turned in was first-rate.")
>
> Then end the letter with "I hope to hear from you soon," and so on.

232   When quoting a series of words or phrases in the exact sequence in which they originally appeared, use quotation marks before and after the complete series. However, if the series of quoted words or phrases did not appear in this sequence in the original, use quotation marks around each word or phrase.

> According to Selma, the latest issue of the magazine looked "fresh, crisp, and appealing." (Selma's actual words were, "I think the new issue looks fresh, crisp, and appealing.")
>
> BUT: Selma thinks the magazine looks "fresh" and "crisp."

233   Do not quote the words *yes* and *no* unless you wish to emphasize that these were the exact words spoken.

> Please answer the question yes or no.
>
> Don't say no until you have heard all the terms of the proposal.
>
> Once the firm's board of directors says yes, we can draft the contract.
>
> When asked if he would accept a reassignment, Nick thought for a moment; then, without any trace of emotion, he said "Yes." (The quotation marks imply that Nick said precisely this much and no more. See ¶256a, note, for the use or omission of a comma in constructions like this.)

NOTE: When quoting these words, capitalize them if they represent a complete sentence.

> All she said was "No."
> I would have to answer that question by saying "Yes and no."
> BUT: That question requires something more than a yes-or-no answer.

234 Do not use quotation marks with well-known proverbs and sayings. They are not direct quotations.

> After this experience she surely knows that all that glitters is not gold.

For Special Emphasis

235 In nontechnical material, technical or trade terms should be enclosed in quotation marks when they are first introduced.

> The use of "bleed" illustrations gives the book a handsome graphic effect.

236 Words used humorously or ironically are enclosed in quotation marks.

> They serve "fresh" vegetables all right—fresh out of the can!

237 Slang or poor grammar is enclosed in quotation marks to indicate that such usage is not part of the writer's normal way of speaking.

> Whatever the true facts are, Jeff "ain't sayin'."

NOTE: Quotation marks are not needed for colloquial expressions.

> I thought you were putting me on.

238 Words and phrases introduced by such expressions as *so-called, marked, signed,* and *entitled* are enclosed in quotation marks.

> The carton was marked "Fragile."
> He received a message signed "A Friend."
> The article entitled "Write Your Senator" was in that issue.

NOTE: Titles of complete published works following the expression *entitled* require underscoring rather than quotation marks. (See ¶289 for titles to be underscored; ¶¶242–244 for titles to be quoted.)

239 A word referred to as a word may be enclosed in quotation marks but is now more commonly underscored. (See ¶285.)

240 When a word or an expression is formally defined, the word to be defined is usually underscored (italicized in print) and the definition is usually quoted so that the two elements may be easily distinguished. (See ¶286.)

241 The translation of a foreign expression is enclosed in quotation marks; the foreign word itself is underscored. (See ¶287.)

With Titles of Literary and Artistic Works

242 Use quotation marks around titles that represent only *part* of a complete published work—for example, chapters, lessons, topics, sections, and parts within a book; articles and feature columns in newspapers and magazines; and essays, short poems, lectures, and sermons. (Underscore titles of *complete* published works. See ¶289.)

> When you read Chapter 5, "The Effective Business Letter," give particular attention to the section headed "The Objectives of All Letter Writing."
>
> His most recent article, "Who Speaks for You?" appeared last month. (See ¶¶260–261 for the use of commas with quoted titles.)
>
> Could you recite the poem "The Boy Stood on the Burning Deck" if you were asked to?

NOTE: The titles *Preface, Contents, Appendix,* and *Index* are not quoted, even though they represent parts within a book. They are often capitalized, however, for special emphasis.

> All the supporting data is given in the Appendix. (Often capitalized when referring to another section within the same work.)
>
> BUT: You'll find that the most interesting part of his book is contained in the appendix. (Capitalization is not required when reference is made to a section within another work.)

243 Use quotation marks around the titles of *complete but unpublished* works, such as manuscripts, dissertations, and reports.

> I would like to get a copy of Sandor's special study, "Criteria for Evaluating Staff Efficiency."

244 Use quotation marks around titles of songs and other short musical compositions and around titles of television and radio series and programs.

> Everyone sang "Happy Birthday" to Mr. Schildkraut.
>
> She will appear on "Face the Nation" next Sunday.

Quotations Within Quotations

245 A quotation within another quotation is enclosed in single quotation marks. On a typewriter, use the apostrophe key for a single quotation mark.

> "Tanned skin was a fashionable 'must' about thirty years ago."

246 If a quotation appears within the single-quoted matter, revert to double quotation marks for the inner portion.

> Mrs. DeVries then remarked, "I thought it a bit strange when Mr. Fowler said, 'Put these checks in an envelope marked "Personal Funds," and set them aside for me.'" (When single and double quotation marks occur together, do not insert any extra space between them in typewritten material.)

NOTE: For the positioning of punctuation in relation to a single quotation mark, see:

- ¶247, note, *for placement of periods and commas.*
- ¶248, note, *for placement of semicolons and colons.*
- ¶249, note, *for placement of question marks and exclamation points.*
- ¶250b *for placement of dashes.*

The following rules (¶¶247–251) indicate how to position punctuation marks in relation to the closing quotation mark—inside or outside.

With Periods and Commas

247 Periods and commas always go *inside* the closing quotation mark. This is the preferred American style. (Some writers in this country follow the British style: Place the period *outside* when it punctuates the whole sentence, *inside* when it punctuates only the quoted matter. Place the comma *outside,* since it always punctuates the sentence, not the quoted matter.)

> As I was leaving his office, Mr. Rossi said, "Mr. Ward, we will need five copies of that agreement."
> We agreed that the draft would be payable "six months after date."
> The bill had been stamped "Paid."
> Retain all copies marked "A."
> "I will call you tomorrow," he said.
> "Please try to arrive by 9:30 a.m.," she announced.
> His latest article, "Systems Management and Education," appeared in May.
> "Witty," "clever," "vastly amusing," and "hilarious" are only a few of the adjectives that are being applied to her new book.
> The package was clearly labeled "Fragile," but apparently labels mean nothing to your delivery crew.

NOTE: Periods and commas also go *inside* the single closing quotation mark.

> Mr. Poston said, "Please let me see all the orders marked 'Rush.'"
> "All he would say was 'I don't remember,'" answered the witness.

With Semicolons and Colons

248 Semicolons and colons always go *outside* the closing quotation mark.

> Last Tuesday you said, "I will mail a check today"; however, it has not yet arrived.
> When the announcement of the changeover was made, my reaction was "Why?"; John's only reaction was "When?"
> Please get these supplies from the shelf marked "Editorial": 20 blue file folders, 12 No. 2 pencils, and 3 boxes of correction tape.

NOTE: Semicolons and colons also go *outside* the single quotation mark.

> Ms. Fennel said, "Please get these supplies from the shelf marked 'Editorial': 20 blue file folders, 12 No. 2 pencils, and 3 boxes of correction tape."

With Question Marks and Exclamation Points

249 a. A *question mark* or an *exclamation point* goes *inside* the closing quotation mark when it applies only to the quoted material.

> He asked, "Did you enjoy that book?" (Quoted question at the end of a statement.)
> My boss's favorite remark is, "This is a rush job!" (Quoted exclamation at the end of a statement.)

(Continued on page 54.)

b. A question mark or an exclamation point goes *outside* the closing quotation mark when it applies to the entire sentence.

> Why did Sally say, "Don't expect to see me tomorrow"? (Quoted statement at the end of a question.)
> Don't keep saying, "Take it easy"! (Quoted statement at the end of an exclamation.)

c. If the quoted material and the entire sentence each require the same mark of punctuation, use only one mark—the one that comes first. (See also ¶¶257–258.)

> Have you seen the advertisement that starts, "Why pay more?" (Quoted question at the end of a question.)
> Let's not panic and yell "Fire!" (Quoted exclamation at the end of an exclamation.)

NOTE: These same principles govern the placement of a question mark or an exclamation point in relation to a single quotation mark.

> What prompted her to say, "Be careful in handling documents marked 'Confidential'"? (Quoted phrase within a quoted statement within a question.)
> Dr. Marks asked, "Was the check marked 'Insufficient Funds'?" (Quoted phrase within a quoted question within a statement.)
> Miss Parsons then said, "How did you answer him when he asked you, 'How do you know?'" (Quoted question within a quoted question within a statement.)

With Dashes

250 **a.** A *dash* goes *inside* the closing quotation mark to indicate that the speaker's or writer's words have broken off abruptly.

> Eileen said, "When I see Mary—" We could all guess what she would say to Mary.

b. A dash goes *outside* the closing quotation mark when the sentence breaks off abruptly *after* the quotation.

> If one more person speaks to me about "innovation"—
> BUT: Mr. Ballard said, "If one more person speaks to me about 'innovation'—"

c. A closing dash goes *outside* the closing quotation mark when the quotation itself is part of a nonessential element being set off by a pair of dashes.

> Get the latest draft—it's the one with the notation "Let's go with this"—and take it to Miss Pomeroy for her approval.

With Parentheses

251 **a.** The closing *parenthesis* goes *inside* the closing quotation mark when the parenthetical element is part of the quotation.

> The meeting was to be held "no later than Wednesday (May 15)" because of the need for a decision by the end of that week.

b. The closing parenthesis goes *outside* the closing quotation mark when the quotation is part of the parenthetical element.

Joe Elliott (the one everyone calls "Harper's fair-haired boy") will probably get the job.

The following rules (¶¶252–270) indicate what punctuation to use with various kinds of quoted matter.

Punctuating Quotations That Stand Alone

252 When a quoted sentence stands alone, put the appropriate mark of terminal punctuation—a period, a question mark, or an exclamation point—*inside* the closing quotation mark.

> "I can recommend Ruth Vilas without any reservation."
> "May I see you for about a half hour tomorrow?"
> "This transcript is worse than the one before!"

Punctuating Quotations at the Beginning of a Sentence

253 When a quoted *statement* occurs at the beginning of a sentence, omit the period before the closing quotation mark and use a comma instead.

> "I can recommend Ruth Vilas without any reservation," he said.
> (**NOT:** . . . reservation.," he said.)

EXCEPTION: Retain the period if it accompanies an abbreviation.

> "By next May I expect to have my Ph.D.," she said.

254 When a quoted *question* or *exclamation* occurs at the beginning of a sentence, retain the question mark or the exclamation point before the closing quotation mark and do *not* insert a comma.

> "May I see you for about a half hour tomorrow?" he asked.
> (**NOT:** . . . tomorrow?," he asked.)

> "This transcript is worse than the one before!" she said.
> (**NOT:** . . . before!," she said.)

255 When a quoted *word* or *phrase* occurs at the beginning of a sentence, no punctuation should accompany the closing quotation mark unless required by the overall construction of the sentence.

> "A smash hit" was the phrase used by more than one critic.
> "How to Get a Job," the last chapter in the manuscript, does not read as well as the rest of the material you have submitted. (The comma that follows the chapter title is the first of a pair needed to set off a nonessential expression.)

Punctuating Quotations at the End of a Sentence

256 **a.** When a quoted *statement, question,* or *exclamation* comes at the end of a sentence and is introduced by an expression such as *he said* or *she said,* a comma usually precedes the opening quotation mark.

> Mr. Kelley said, "We'll close early on Friday."
> In her letter Diana said, "I plan to arrive on Thursday at 6 p.m."

(*Continued on page 56.*)

NOTE: If the quotation is quite short or is woven into the flow of the sentence, omit the comma.

All she said was "No." **OR:** All she said was, "No." (The comma creates a slight pause and throws greater emphasis on the quotation.)

Why does he keep saying "It won't work"?

b. Use a colon in place of a comma if the introductory expression is an independent clause.

Gordon did tell me this: "I'm willing to sign the contract with Harry."

This is what she said in her letter: "I plan to arrive on Thursday at 6 p.m."

c. Use a colon in place of a comma if the quotation contains more than one sentence.

Ms. Frost said: "In this case there is not much point in trying to fix the blame for what happened. The important thing is to establish procedures and safeguards to ensure that there are no recurrences."

d. Use a colon in place of a comma if the quotation is set off on separate lines as an extract. (See also ¶265.)

Sheila's letter said in part:

I have always valued your assistance on our various projects. You have always acted as if you were actually part of our staff, with our best interests in mind . . . .

e. Do not use either a comma or a colon before an indirect quotation.

Sheila said that she had always valued Bob's assistance on various projects.

f. Do not use either a comma or a colon when a direct quotation is introduced by *that* or is otherwise woven into the flow of the sentence.

In a previous letter to you, I noted that "you have always acted as if you were actually part of our staff, with our best interests in mind."

NOTE: The first word of the quotation is not capitalized in this case, even though it was capitalized in the original. Compare *you* here with *You* in the example in *d* above. (See ¶272 for the rule on capitalization.)

257 When a quoted *sentence* (a statement, a question, or an exclamation) falls at the end of a larger sentence, do not use double punctuation—that is, one mark to end the quotation and another to end the sentence. Choose the stronger mark. (**REMEMBER:** *A question mark is stronger than a period; an exclamation point is stronger than a period or a question mark.*) If the same mark of punctuation is required for both the quotation and the sentence as a whole, use the first mark that occurs—the one within quotation marks.

Quoted Sentences at the End of a Statement
Fred said, "Let's make the best of the situation." (Not .".)
Miss Harris asked, "Shall I put through that call now?" (Not ?".)
Mr. Vogt exclaimed, "These rumors must stop!" (Not !".)

Quoted Sentences at the End of a Question
Did you say, "I'll help out"? (Not ."?)
Why did Mary ask, "Will Joe be there?" (Not ?"?)
Who yelled "Watch out!" (Not !"?)

Quoted Sentences at the End of an Exclamation

How could you forget to follow up when you were specifically told, "Give this order special attention"! (Not ."!)

Stop saying "How should I know"! (Not ?"!)

How I'd like to walk into his office and say, "I quit!" (Not !"!)

NOTE: When a quoted sentence ends with an abbreviation, retain the abbreviation period, even though a question mark or an exclamation point follows as the terminal mark of punctuation.

The interviewer asked, "How long did you work for Pierson Inc.?"

Didn't Sue say, "I am now working for an LL.B."?

However, if a period is required as the terminal mark of punctuation, use only one period to mark the end of the abbreviation and the end of the sentence.

Edna said, "The conference will begin at 9:30 a.m." (Not .".)

- See ¶247 for placement of periods; ¶249 for placement of question marks and exclamation points.

258 When a quoted *word* or *phrase* occurs at the end of a sentence, punctuate according to the appropriate pattern shown below. (**NOTE:** If the quoted word or phrase represents a complete sentence, follow the patterns shown in ¶257.)

Quoted Words and Phrases at the End of a Statement

He says he is willing to meet "at your convenience." (Not ".)

I thought her letter said she would arrive "at 10 p.m." (Not .".)

I've been meaning to read "Who Pays the Bill?" (Not ?".)

Critics have praised his latest article, "Freedom Now!" (Not !".)

Quoted Words and Phrases at the End of a Question

Why is he so concerned about my "convenience"?

Didn't she clearly state she would arrive "at 10 p.m."?

Have you had a chance to read "Who Pays the Bill?" (Not ?"?)

What did you think of the article "Freedom Now!"?

Quoted Words and Phrases at the End of an Exclamation

He couldn't care less about my "convenience"!

You're quite mistaken—she clearly said "at 10 a.m."!

Don't waste your time reading "Who Pays the Bill?"!

What a reaction he got with his article "Freedom Now!" (Not !"!)

Punctuating Quotations Within a Sentence

259 Do not use a comma before or after a quotation when it is woven into the flow of the sentence.

Don't say "I can't do it" without trying.

No considerate person would say "Why should I care?" under those circumstances.

The audience shouted "Bravo!" and "Encore!" at the end of the concerto.

(Continued on page 58.)

NOTE: In such cases do not use a period at the end of a quoted statement, but retain the question mark or the exclamation point at the end of a quoted question or exclamation (as illustrated on the preceding page).

260 Do not set off a quotation that occurs within a sentence as an *essential* expression. (See ¶149.)

> The famous words "Don't give up the ship" have been attributed to several people.
> The chapter entitled "Factors of Production" should help you answer that question.

261 When a quotation occurs within a sentence as a *nonessential* expression, use a comma before the opening quotation mark and before the closing quotation mark.

> His parting words, "I hardly know how to thank you," were sufficient.
> The next chapter, "The Role of Government," further clarifies the answer.

However, if the quoted matter requires a question mark or an exclamation point before the closing quotation mark, omit the comma at that point.

> The final chapter, "Where Do We Go From Here?" shows how much remains to be accomplished.
> Your last question, "How can we improve communications between departments?" can best be answered by you.

NOTE: As an alternative, use a pair of dashes or parentheses to set off the quoted matter.

> Your last question—"How can we improve communications between departments?"—can best be answered by you.

Punctuating Quoted Sentences With Interrupting Expressions

262 When a quoted sentence is *interrupted* by an expression such as *he said* or *she said,* use a comma and a closing quotation mark before the interrupting expression and another comma after it. Then resume the quotation with an opening quotation mark and put the first word in small letters.

> "For the fifth successive week," the report began, "we have chalked up increased sales in our New England territory."

263 If the interrupting expression ends the sentence and the quotation continues in a new sentence, put a period after the interrupting expression and start the new sentence with an opening quotation mark and a capital letter.

> "We'll be late for the ceremonies," she said. "However, late or not, we have to attend."

Punctuating Long Quotations

264 If a quotation consists of more than one sentence without any interrupting elements, use quotation marks only at the beginning and at the end of the quotation. Do not put quotation marks around each sentence within the quotation.

> Here is what he wrote in his letter: "I hereby tender my resignation. I have reached what is considered a good age to retire. It is time for someone younger to take over."

265 A long quotation that will make four or more typewritten lines may be handled in one of the following ways:

a. Display the quoted matter by typing it single-spaced on a shorter line length than is used for the remainder of the material. (Indent all lines five spaces from each side margin.) Do not enclose the quoted matter in quotation marks; the indentation replaces the quotes. This style is preferred. (See page 235.)

NOTE: Ordinarily, start typing the quoted matter flush left on the shorter line length; however, if a paragraph indention was called for in the original, indent the first line five spaces. Indent the first line of any additional paragraphs five spaces also.

b. Type the quoted matter using the same line length and spacing as for the remainder of the material.

(1) If the quoted matter consists of one paragraph only, place quotation marks at the beginning and end of the paragraph. Use the normal paragraph indention of five spaces.

(2) If the quoted matter consists of two or more paragraphs, place a quotation mark at the start of each paragraph but at the end of only one paragraph—the last one.

(3) Change double quotation marks within the quoted matter to single quotation marks, and vice versa. (See ¶¶245–246.)

> "When writing a letter that grants a request, you can follow this pattern:
> "First, express appreciation for the writer's interest in the company's product or service.
> "Next, give the exact information requested and, if possible, additional information that may be of interest.
> "Finally, express willingness to 'be of further help.'"

Quoting Letters

266 Letters and other business documents that are to be copied word for word may be handled in one of the following ways:

a. Type the material on a separate sheet of paper headed *COPY*. In this case no quotation marks are used.

b. Make a photocopy of the material. In this case neither the heading *COPY* nor quotation marks are used.

c. The material, if short, may be treated like a long quotation (see ¶265). If it is typed on a shorter line length, omit the quotation marks. If it is typed on the same line length as other material on the page, then type the opening quotation mark before the first word (in a letter, the date line); type the closing quotation mark after the last word (in a letter, the last word in the signature block).

Quoting Poetry

267   When quoting a complete poem (or an extended portion of one) in a letter or a report, type it line for line, single-spaced (except for stanza breaks). If the line length is shorter than that of the normal text above and below the poem, no quotation marks are needed; the poem will stand out sufficiently as an extract. If, however, quotation marks are needed to indicate the special nature of the material, place a quotation mark at the beginning of each stanza and at the end of only the last stanza. (See also ¶284*b*.)

268   A short extract from a poem is sometimes woven right into a sentence or a paragraph. In such cases use quotation marks at the beginning and end of the extract and a diagonal line to indicate where each line would break in the original arrangement of the poem.

> As Alexander Pope put it, "A little learning is a dang'rous thing; / Drink deep, or taste not the Pierian spring . . . ." (Note that one space precedes and follows the diagonal.)

Quoting Dialogues and Conversations

269   When quoting dialogues and conversations, start the remarks of each speaker as a new paragraph, no matter how brief.

> "Are those the only styles you can show me?" the customer inquired.
> "I'm afraid so," replied the sales manager, "but I can order anything shown in this catalog for you."
> "How long would it take to get the items?"
> "Two weeks."

270   In plays and court testimony, where the name of the speaker is indicated, quotation marks are not needed.

> George: What you say is impossible!
> Henry: I tell you it's true!
> George: I must have more proof than your word before I'll believe it.

———————————

The following rules (¶¶271–284) cover a number of stylistic matters, such as how to capitalize in quoted matter (¶¶272–273), how to handle omissions in quoted matter (¶¶274–280), and how to handle insertions in quoted matter (¶¶281–283).

Style in Quoted Matter

271   In copying quoted matter, follow the style of the extract exactly in punctuation, spelling, hyphenation, and number style. (See ¶282 for the use of [*sic*] to indicate errors in the original.)

Capitalization in Quoted Matter

272 Ordinarily, capitalize the first word of every complete sentence in quotation marks.

> I heard Maria say, "Anyone could do that job."
> My lawyer gave me this advice: "Try to settle this claim out of court."

NOTE: If the quoted sentence is preceded by *that* or is otherwise incorporated into the flow of a larger sentence, do not capitalize the first word (unless it is a proper noun, a proper adjective, or the pronoun *I*).

> Maria is reported to have said that "anyone could do that job."
> My lawyer advised me "to settle this claim out of court."

273 When quoting a word or phrase, do not capitalize the first word unless it meets *one* of these conditions:

a. It is a proper noun, a proper adjective, or the pronoun *I*.

> Mr. Sewara paid tribute to "American know-how."

b. It was capitalized in its original use.

> He wrote "Paid" across the face of the bill.

c. The quoted word or phrase occurs at the beginning of a sentence.

> "Electrifying" was the word one critic applied to Caliano's new play. (Even if the expression was not capitalized in the original material, it must be capitalized here to mark the start of the sentence.)

d. It represents a complete sentence.

> Pete flatly said "No"; Phil said "Maybe."
> **BUT:** Ella said she would not pay the bill "until certain adjustments are made." (Ella's exact words were, "I won't pay until certain adjustments are made.")

- See ¶¶277–278 on capitalizing the first word of a quoted sentence fragment.

Omissions in Quoted Matter

274 If one or more words are omitted *within a quoted sentence,* use ellipsis marks (three spaced periods, with one typewriter space before and after each period) to indicate the omission.

> "During the past twenty years . . . we have been witnessing a change in buying habits, particularly with respect to food."

NOTE: Omit any marks of internal punctuation (a comma, a semicolon, a colon, or a dash) on either side of the ellipsis marks unless they are required for the sake of clarity.

> **ORIGINAL VERSION:** "The objectives of the proposed bill are admirable, I will cheerfully concede; the tactics being used to gain support for the bill are not."
> **CONDENSED VERSION:** "The objectives of the proposed bill are admirable . . . ; the tactics being used to gain support for the bill are not." (The comma preceding the omitted phrase is not needed; however, the semicolon following the omitted phrase must be retained for clarity.)

275   If one or more words are omitted *at the end of a quoted sentence,* use three spaced periods followed by the necessary terminal punctuation for the sentence as a whole.

> "Can anyone explain why . . . ?" (The original question read, "Can anyone explain why this was so?")

> "During the past twenty years, starting in the late 1950s, we have been witnessing a change in buying habits . . . . Consumers have become more concerned with what's in the package rather than with the package itself." (The first three periods represent the omitted words "particularly with respect to food"; the fourth period marks the end of the sentence. Two typewriter spaces follow before the next sentence.)

NOTE: If the quotation is intended to trail off, use only three spaced periods at the end of the sentence. (See also ¶291*b*.)

> His reaction was, "If I had only known . . ."

276   If one or more sentences are omitted *between other sentences* within a long quotation, use three spaced periods *after* the terminal punctuation of the preceding sentence.

> "During the past twenty years, starting in the late 1950s, we have been witnessing a change in buying habits, particularly with respect to food. . . . How far this pattern of change will extend cannot be estimated."

NOTE: There is no space between *food* and the first period because that period marks the end of a sentence. The remaining three periods signify the omission of one or more complete sentences. Two spaces follow before the next sentence.

277   If only a fragment of a sentence is quoted within another sentence, it is not necessary to signify the omission of words before or after the fragment.

> According to Robertson's report, there has been "a change in buying habits" during the past twenty years.

Moreover, if the fragment as given can be read as a complete sentence, capitalize the first word in the quoted fragment, even though this word was not capitalized in the original. (Compare *We* in the following example with *we* in the example in ¶276.)

> According to Robertson's report, "We have been witnessing a change in buying habits, particularly with respect to food."

278   If a displayed quotation starts in the middle of a sentence, use three spaced periods at the beginning of the quotation.

> According to Robertson's report, there has been
>> . . . a change in buying habits, particularly with respect to food. . . . How far this pattern of change will extend cannot be estimated.

If the fragment, however, can be read as a complete sentence, capitalize the first word of the fragment and omit the ellipsis marks. (Compare *Starting* in the following example with *starting* in the example in ¶276.)

According to Robertson's report:
> Starting in the late 1950s, we have been witnessing a change in buying habits, particularly with respect to food.

279 When a long quotation starts with a complete sentence and ends with a complete sentence, do not use three spaced periods at the beginning or the end of the quotation unless there is a need to emphasize that the quotation has been extracted from a larger body of material.

280 If one or more paragraphs are omitted within a long quotation, indicate the omission by adding three spaced periods *after* the terminal punctuation that concludes the preceding paragraph.

Insertions in Quoted Matter

281 For clarity it is sometimes necessary to insert explanatory words or phrases within quoted matter. Enclose such insertions in brackets. (See also ¶¶296–298.)

> Miss Rawlings added, "At the time of the first lawsuit [1976], there was clear-cut evidence of an intent to defraud."

282 When the original wording contains a misspelling, a grammatical error, or a confusing expression of thought, insert the term *sic* (meaning "so" or "this is the way it was") in brackets to indicate that the error existed in the original material.

> As he wrote in his letter, "I would sooner go to jail then [*sic*] have to pay your bill." (The word *sic* is not underscored in typed material.)

283 For emphasis, it is sometimes necessary to underscore words that were not so treated in the original. In such cases, an expression like *emphasis added* should be typed in brackets at the end of the quotation.

> Upon cross-examination, she replied, "I never met Mr. Norman in my life, to the best of my recollection. [Emphasis added.]"

- See ¶¶262–263 *for simple interruptions such as* he said *or* she said.

Typing Quotation Marks

284 **a.** In a typed list, any opening quotation mark should align with the first letter of the other items.

> I need the following stationery items:
> > Paper clips
> > Rubber bands
> > "Fragile" labels
> > White cord

b. In poems, the opening quotation mark at the beginning of each stanza should clear the left margin so that the first letter of each line will be in alignment. (See also ¶267.)

> "I think that I shall never see
> A billboard lovely as a tree.
> Perhaps, unless the billboards fall,
> I'll never see a tree at all."

The Underscore

Underscoring in typewritten material is the counterpart of using *italics* in printed material.

For Special Emphasis

285 A word referred to as a word is usually underscored, but it may be enclosed in quotation marks instead. A word referred to as a word is often introduced by the expression *the term* or *the word*.

> The words <u>carton</u> and <u>cartoon</u> have quite different meanings. (**ALSO:** The words "carton" and "cartoon" have quite different meanings.)
>
> If you used fewer compound sentences, you wouldn't have so many <u>and</u>s in your writing. (Only the root word is underscored, not the *s*.)
>
> **BUT:** She refused to sign the contract because she said it had too many ands, ifs, and buts. (No underscores are required for the phrase *ands, ifs, and buts* because the writer is not referring literally to these words as words. The phrase means "too many conditions and qualifications.")

286 In a formal definition the word to be defined is usually underscored and the definition is usually quoted. In this way the two elements may be easily distinguished.

> The term <u>psychosomatic</u> has an interesting derivation: the prefix <u>psycho</u> means "of the mind"; the root word <u>soma</u> refers to the body.

NOTE: An informal definition does not require any special punctuation.

> A chandler is a person who makes candles.

287 Underscore foreign expressions that are not considered part of the English language. (Use quotation marks to set off translations of foreign expressions.)

> It's true, <u>n'est-ce pas</u>? (Meaning "isn't that so?")

NOTE: Once an expression of foreign origin has become established as part of the English language, underscoring is no longer necessary. (Most dictionaries offer guidance on this point.) Here are some frequently used expressions that no longer require underscoring or any other special display:

a la carte	bona fide	laissez faire	pro tem
a la mode	carte blanche	non sequitur	quid pro quo
a priori	et al.	op. cit.	rendezvous
ad hoc	etc.	per annum	repertoire
ad infinitum	ex officio	per se	résumé
alma mater	habeas corpus	prima facie	status quo
alter ego	ibid.	pro rata	vice versa

288 The *individual* names of ships, trains, airplanes, and spacecraft may be underscored for special display or written simply with initial caps.

> The S.S. <u>Ballou</u> will dock at Pier 34.   **OR:** The S.S. Ballou . . .
>
> **BUT:** I flew to Miami on an Electra and came back on a DC-10. (No special display is needed for the names *Electra* or *DC-10* because they identify classes of aircraft but are not the individual names of planes.)

With Titles of Literary and Artistic Works

289 Underscore titles of *complete* works that are published as separate items—for example, books, pamphlets, long poems, magazines, and newspapers. Also underscore titles of movies, plays, musicals, operas, long musical compositions, paintings, and pieces of sculpture.

> Every office worker will find <u>Etiquette in Business</u> helpful.
> We find it beneficial to advertise occasionally in <u>The New York Times</u>.
> Next Saturday they are going to hear the opera <u>La Traviata</u>.

a. Titles of complete works may be typed in all capitals as an alternative to underscoring.

> Every office worker will find ETIQUETTE IN BUSINESS helpful.

NOTE: The use of all capitals is acceptable (1) in business correspondence where titles occur frequently (as in the correspondence of a publishing house) and (2) in advertising and sales promotion copy where the use of all capitals is intended to have an eye-catching effect. In other circumstances, use underscoring.

b. In typewritten material that is *to be set in type*, titles of complete works must be underscored. The underscoring indicates to the printer that the title should be set in italics.

> Every secretary will find *Etiquette in Business* helpful.

c. In titles of magazines, do not underscore or capitalize the word *magazine* unless it is part of the actual title.

> <u>Time</u> magazine   **BUT:** <u>The New York Times Magazine</u>

d. In some cases the name of the publishing company is the same as the name of the publication. Underscore the name when it refers to *the publication* but not when it refers to *the company*.

> I saw her column in <u>Newsweek</u>.
> **BUT:** I wrote to Newsweek about a job.

- See ¶¶242–244 for the use of quotation marks with titles of literary and artistic works.

Typing Underscores

290 Underscore as a unit whatever should be stressed as a unit—individual words, titles, phrases, or even whole sentences.

a. When underscoring a unit consisting of two or more words, be sure to underscore the space between words.

> I plan to read <u>War and Peace</u> next summer.
> **BUT:** Do you understand the meaning of such terms as <u>quasi</u>, <u>ergo</u>, and <u>ipso facto</u>? (Only the individual units are underscored, not the series as a whole.)

b. Do not underscore a mark of *sentence punctuation* that comes directly after the underscored matter. (However, underscore all punctuation marks that are an integral part of the underscored matter.)

(*Continued on page 66.*)

This week the Summertime Playhouse is presenting <u>Oklahoma</u>!, next week <u>Where's Charley</u>?, and the following week <u>My Fair Lady</u>.

c. Do not underscore a possessive or plural ending that is added on to an underscored word.

the <u>Times</u>'s editorial   too many <u>ands</u>

Other Marks of Punctuation

The Apostrophe (')

The use of the apostrophe is covered in the following paragraphs:

- *As a single quotation mark, see ¶¶245–246.*
- *To indicate the omission of figures in dates, see ¶412.*
- *As a symbol for feet, see ¶432.*
- *To form contractions, see ¶505.*
- *To form plurals of figures, letters, etc., see ¶¶623–626.*
- *To form possessives, see ¶¶627–650.*

Ellipsis Marks (. . .)

291   **a.** Ellipsis marks (three spaced periods, with one typewriter space before and after each period) are often used, especially in advertising, to display individual items or to connect a series of loosely related phrases.

The Inn at the End of the Road . . . where you may enjoy the epicure's choicest offerings . . . by reservation only . . . closed Tuesdays.

Where can you match these services—
. . . Free ticket delivery
. . . Flight insurance
. . . On-time departures

b. Ellipsis marks are also used to indicate that a sentence trails off before the end. The three spaced periods create an effect of uncertainty or suggest an abrupt suspension of thought. (No terminal punctuation is used with ellipsis marks in this kind of construction.)

He could easily have saved the situation by . . . But why talk about it?

- *See ¶¶274–280 for the use of ellipsis marks to indicate omissions in quoted matter.*

The Asterisk (*)

292   The asterisk is used to refer the reader to a footnote placed at the bottom of a page.

"Because they won't let you wear it unless it fits."*

---

*Reg. U.S. Pat. Off.

a. When the asterisk and some other mark of punctuation occur together within a sentence, the asterisk *follows* the punctuation mark, with no intervening space. (See also ¶1414c.)

b. In the footnote itself, leave no space after the asterisk.

293 Asterisks are used to replace words that are considered unprintable.

> We were shocked to hear Mr. Scott refer to Mr. Frost as a ***.

NOTE: If your typewriter does not have an asterisk key, a fair substitute can be made by typing a capital *A* over a small *v*.

The Diagonal (/)

294 The diagonal occurs (without space before or after) in certain abbreviations and expressions of time.

> B/L   bill of lading   km/h   kilometers per hour   c/o   care of
>
> Check the figures for fiscal year 1978/79.

295 The diagonal is also used in writing fractions (for example, 4/5) and in some code and serial numbers (for example, 2S/394756).

> ▪ *See ¶268 for the use of the diagonal when quoting poetry; also see the entry for and/or in ¶1101.*

Brackets ([ ])

296 A correction or an insertion in a quoted extract should be enclosed in brackets. (See also ¶¶281–283.)

> "During the height of the storm, winds exceeded 55 miles an hour [the local weather station recorded 60 miles an hour], with gusts up to 65 miles an hour."
>
> "We cannot allow this situation to continue. [Extended applause.] The time for action is now."

297 When a parenthetical element falls within another parenthetical element, enclose the smaller element in brackets and the larger element in parentheses.

> Scalzo said on television yesterday that prices would begin to fall sharply. (However, in an article published in the *Times* [May 12, 19—], he was quoted as saying that prices would remain at their current levels for the foreseeable future.)

298 If brackets do not appear on the typewriter keyboard, you may either construct them (as shown in the illustration below) or leave a space at the point where each mark should appear and insert the marks in pen after the paper has been removed from the typewriter.

> "We returned to Salem /Massachusetts/ the following year."

Typewriter Spacing With Punctuation Marks

299 Period

Two spaces *after* the end of a sentence.
One space *after* an abbreviation within a sentence. (See also ¶511.)
No space *after* a decimal point.
No space *after* when another mark of punctuation immediately follows the period (for example, a closing quotation mark, a closing parenthesis, or a comma following an "abbreviation" period).
Two spaces *after* a number or letter that indicates an enumeration. (See ¶106, note, for an exception.)

Question Mark or Exclamation Point

Two spaces *after* the end of a sentence.
No space *after* when another mark of punctuation immediately follows (for example, a closing quotation mark, a closing parenthesis, or a closing dash).

Comma

No space *before*—ever.
One space *after*, unless a closing quotation mark immediately follows the comma.
No space *after* commas within a number.

Semicolon

No space *before;* one space *after*.

Colon

No space *before*.
Two spaces *after* within a sentence.
No space *before* or *after* in expressions of time (*8:20 p.m.*) or proportions (*2:1*).

Dash

No space *before, between,* or *after* two hyphens used to represent a dash.
Two spaces *after* a dash at the end of a statement that breaks off abruptly. (See ¶208.)

Opening Parenthesis or Bracket

One space *before* when parenthetic matter is within a sentence.
Two spaces *before* when parenthetic matter follows a sentence. In this case the parenthetic matter starts with a capital and closes with its own sentence punctuation. (See ¶¶226, 296.)
No space *after*.

Closing Parenthesis or Bracket

No space *before*.
One space *after* when parenthetic matter is within a sentence.
Two spaces *after* when parenthetic matter is itself a complete sentence and another sentence follows. (See ¶¶226, 296.)
No space *after* if another mark of punctuation immediately follows.

Opening Quotation Mark

Two spaces *before* when quoted matter starts a new sentence or follows a colon.
No space *before* when a dash or an opening parenthesis precedes.
One space *before* in all other cases.
No space *after*.

Closing Quotation Mark

No space *before*.
Two spaces *after* when quoted matter ends the sentence.
No space *after* when another mark of punctuation immediately follows (for example, a semicolon or a colon).
One space *after* in all other cases.

Single Quotation Mark

No space between single and double quotation marks. (See ¶246.)

Apostrophe (')

No space *before*, either within a word or at the end of a word.
One space *after* only if it is at the end of a word within a sentence.

Ellipsis Marks (. . .)

One space *before* and *after* each of the three periods within a sentence. (See ¶¶274–275.)
No space *before* when an *opening* quotation mark precedes the ellipsis marks.
No space *after* when a *closing* quotation mark follows the ellipsis marks. (See last example in ¶275.)
Two spaces *after* ellipsis marks that follow a period, question mark, or exclamation point at the end of a sentence. (See example in ¶276.)

Asterisk (*)

No space *before* an asterisk following a word or punctuation mark within a sentence or at the end of a sentence.
Two spaces *after* an asterisk at the end of a sentence.
One space *after* an asterisk following a word or punctuation mark within a sentence.
No space *after* an asterisk in a footnote. (See ¶292.)

Diagonal (/)

No space *before* or *after* a diagonal line. (See ¶268 for an exception in poetry.)

CAPITALIZATION

The function of capitalization is to give distinction, importance, and emphasis to words. Thus the first word of a sentence is capitalized to indicate distinctively and emphatically that a new sentence has begun. Moreover, proper nouns like *George, Chicago, Dun & Bradstreet, the Parthenon, January,* and *Friday* are capitalized to signify the special importance of these words as the official names of particular persons, places, and things. A number of words, however, may function either as proper nouns or as common nouns—for example, terms like *the board of directors* or *the company.* For words like these, capitalization practices vary widely, but the variation merely reflects the relative importance each writer assigns to the word in question.

Despite disagreements among authorities on specific rules, there is a growing consensus against overusing capitalization in business writing. When too many words stand out, none stand out. The current trend, then, is to use capitalization more sparingly—to give importance, distinction, or emphasis only when and where it is warranted.

The following rules of capitalization are written with the ordinary business office in mind. If you work in a specialized situation, such as a government office or an advertising agency, you might be asked to capitalize some of those terms that would not be capitalized ordinarily. Whenever your office has a particular preference, follow that style.

Basic Rules

First Words

301 Capitalize the first word of:

a. Every sentence. (See ¶302 for exceptions.)

Up-to-date sales reports will be released tomorrow.
Will the computations be ready by then?
The news is unbelievable!

b. An expression used as a sentence. (See also ¶¶102, 111, 119–120.)

So much for that. Really? No!

c. A quoted sentence. (See also ¶¶272–273.)

Mr. Jarvis said, "The estimates will be submitted on Monday."

d. An independent question within a sentence. (See also ¶¶115–117.)

The question is, Will this policy reduce staff turnover?

e. Each item displayed in a list or an outline. (See also ¶107.)

f. Each line in a poem. (Always follow the style of the poem itself, however.)

When to the sessions of sweet silent thought
I summon up remembrance of things past,
I sigh the lack of many a thing I sought,
And with old woes new wail my dear time's waste.
—William Shakespeare

(*Continued on page 72.*)

g. The first word in the salutation and the complimentary closing of a letter.

> *Dear* Mrs. Barbetta: *Sincerely* yours,
> My dear Mrs. Barbetta: Yours very truly,

302 Do not capitalize the first word of a sentence when it is set off by *dashes* or *parentheses* within another sentence. (See ¶¶214, 224–225 for examples.) Moreover, do not capitalize the first word of a sentence following a colon except under certain circumstances. (See ¶¶196–199.)

Proper Nouns

303 Capitalize every *proper noun,* that is, the official name of a particular person, place, or thing. Also capitalize the pronoun *I.*

> James E. Carter   Friday, June 2
> Eau Claire, Wisconsin   the New Deal
> Ford Motor Company   the Atomic Energy Act
> the United Fund   the Chinese
> the National Security Council   Venus and Mercury
> Temple University   History 308
> the Department of Labor (see ¶320, note)   Frigidaire
> the Washington Monument   *War and Peace* (see ¶360)

304 Capitalize adjectives derived from proper nouns.

> Elizabeth (n.), Elizabethan (adj.)   America (n.), American (adj.)
>
> EXCEPTIONS: Congress, congressional; the Constitution (U.S.), constitutional. (See also ¶306.)

305 Capitalize imaginative names and nicknames that designate particular persons, places, or things. (See ¶¶333–335 for imaginative place names; ¶344 for imaginative names of historical periods.)

> the First Lady   the Establishment
> Down Under (for Australia)   the Big Ten
> the Granite State (for New Hampshire)   Tommy
> the Stars and Stripes   Crazy Louie
> the White House   the Oval Office

306 Some words that were originally proper nouns or adjectives are now considered common nouns and should not be capitalized.

> plaster of paris   venetian blind   ampere   roman numeral
> manila envelope   morocco leather   watt   (BUT: Roman history)
>
> NOTE: Check an up-to-date dictionary to determine capitalization for words of this type.

Common Nouns

307 A *common noun* names a class of things (for example, *books*), or it may refer indefinitely to one or more things within that class (*a book, several* *books*). Nouns used in this way are considered general terms of classification and are often modified by indefinite words such as *a, any, every,* or *some.* Do not capitalize nouns used as general terms of classification.

a company   every board of directors
any corporation   some senators

308 A common noun may also be used to name a *particular* person, place, or thing. Nouns used in this way are often modified by *the, this, these, that,* or *those,* or by possessive words such as *my, your, his, our,* or *theirs.* Do not capitalize a general term of classification, even though it refers to a particular person, place, or thing.

COMMON NOUN: our doctor   the hotel   the river
PROPER NOUN: Dr. Halliday   Hotel Plaza   the Hudson River

309 Capitalize a common noun when it is part of a proper name but not when it is used alone in place of the full name. (See ¶310 for exceptions.)

Professor Hildebrandt   BUT: the professor
the Chase Corporation   the corporation
the Easton Municipal Court   the court
Elston Avenue   the avenue
the Clayton Antitrust Act   the act

NOTE: Also capitalize the plural form of a common noun in expressions such as *the Republican and the Democratic Parties, Main and Tenth Streets, the Hudson and Ohio Rivers,* and *the Atlantic and Pacific Oceans.*

310 Some *short forms* (common-noun elements replacing the complete proper name) are capitalized when they are intended to carry the full significance of the complete proper name. It is in this area, however, that the danger of overcapitalizing most often occurs. Therefore, do not capitalize a short form unless it clearly warrants the importance, distinction, or emphasis that capitalization conveys. The following kinds of short forms are commonly capitalized:

PERSONAL TITLES: Capitalize titles replacing names of high-ranking national, state, and international officials (but not ordinarily local officials or company officers). (See ¶313.)

ORGANIZATIONAL NAMES: Do not capitalize short forms of company names except in formal or legal writing. (See ¶321.)

GOVERNMENTAL NAMES: Capitalize short forms of names of national and international bodies (but not ordinarily state or local bodies). (See ¶¶326–327, 334–335.)

PLACE NAMES: Capitalize only well-established short forms. (See ¶¶332, 335.)

NOTE: Do not use a short form to replace a full name unless the full name has been mentioned earlier or will be clearly understood from the context.

Special Rules

Personal Names

311 Treat a person's name—in terms of capitalization, spelling, and spacing—exactly as the person does.

Ellen Rodriguez	A. Wilson Krieger
Henry Lang Underhill	C. M. Pastore
Esther T. Gregorowicz	JFK (see ¶516)

a. Respect individual preferences in the spelling of personal names.

Ann Marie, Anne Marie, Anna Marie, Annemarie, Annamarie, Anne-Marie, AnneMarie

Macmillan, MacMillan, Mac Millan, Macmillen, MacMillen, MacMillin McMillan, Mc Millan, McMillen, McMillin

b. In names containing the prefix *O'*, always capitalize the *O* and the letter following the apostrophe; for example, *O'Brian* or *O'Brien*.

c. Watch for differences in capitalization and spacing in names containing prefixes like *d', da, de, del, della, di, du, l', la, le, van,* and *von.*

D'Amelio, d'Amelio, Damelio	deLaCruz, DeLacruz, Dela Cruz, DelaCruz
LaCoste, Lacoste, La Coste	VanDeVelde, Van DeVelde, vandeVelde, van deVelde

d. When a surname with an uncapitalized prefix stands alone (that is, without a first name, a title, or initials preceding it), capitalize the prefix to prevent a misreading.

Anthony de Luca	Mr. de Luca	A. R. de Luca

BUT: I hear that *De Luca* is leaving the company.

e. When names that contain prefixes are to be typed in all-capital letters, follow these principles: If there is no space after the prefix, capitalize only the initial letter of the prefix. If space follows the prefix, capitalize the entire prefix.

Normal Form	**All-Capital Form**
MacDonald	MacDONALD
BUT: Mac Donald	MAC DONALD

- See ¶¶615–616 for plurals of personal names; ¶¶630–633 for possessives of personal names.

Titles With Personal Names

312 Capitalize all official titles of honor and respect when they *precede* personal names.

PERSONAL TITLES:
Mrs. Della Rogers (see ¶517)   Mr. Clampitt

EXECUTIVE TITLES:
President Sarah Orwell   Vice President Degnan

PROFESSIONAL TITLES:
Professor Floyd Bergquist   Dr. Chang (see ¶517)

CIVIC TITLES:
Governor Ella T. Grasso
Mayor-elect Hector Diaz (see ¶317)

Ambassador Berenson
ex-Senator Ball (see ¶317)

MILITARY TITLES:
General Martin O. Johnson

Commander Wilkinson

RELIGIOUS TITLES:
the Reverend John S. Czarnecki

Rabbi Silverman

a. Do not capitalize such titles when the personal name that follows is in apposition and is set off by commas.

The *president*, Sarah Orwell, will address the faculty tomorrow afternoon.
BUT: *President* Sarah Orwell will address the faculty tomorrow afternoon.

b. Do not capitalize occupational titles (such as *author, surgeon, publisher,* and *lawyer*) preceding a name.

Among those attending the opening was *the banker* John Hamstra (NOT: Banker John Hamstra).

NOTE: Occupational titles can be distinguished from official titles in that only official titles can be used with a last name alone. Since one would not address a person as "Author Mailer" or "Publisher Johnson," these are not official titles and should not be capitalized.

313 In general, do not capitalize titles of honor and respect when they *follow* a personal name or are used *in place of* a personal name.

Dr. Sarah Orwell, *president* of Cromwell University, will speak tomorrow night at eight. The *president's* topic is . . .

However, exceptions are made for important officials and dignitaries, as indicated in the following paragraphs.

a. Retain the capitalization in titles of high-ranking national, state, and international officials when they *follow* or *replace* a specific personal name. Below are examples of titles that remain capitalized.

NATIONAL OFFICIALS: the *President*, the *Vice President*, Cabinet members (such as the *Secretary of State* and the *Attorney General*), the heads of government agencies and bureaus (such as the *Director* or the *Commissioner*), the *Chief Justice*, the *Ambassador*, the *Senator*, the *Representative*.

STATE OFFICIALS: the *Governor*, the *Lieutenant Governor*. (BUT: the *attorney general*, the *senator*.)

FOREIGN DIGNITARIES: the *Queen of England*, the *King*, the *Prime Minister*, the *Premier*.

INTERNATIONAL FIGURES: the *Pope*, the *Secretary General of the United Nations*.

b. Titles of local governmental officials and those of lesser federal and state officials are not usually capitalized when they follow or replace a personal name. However, these titles are sometimes capitalized in writing intended for a limited readership (for example, in a local newspaper, in internal communications within an organization, or in correspondence coming from or directed to the official's office), where the person in question would be considered to have high rank by the intended reader.

(Continued on page 76.)

The *Mayor* announced today that the strike had been settled. (Item in a local newspaper.)

BUT: John Nowicki, *mayor* of Waterville, Pennsylvania, was interviewed in New York today before leaving for Europe. The *mayor* indicated . . . (From a national news service release.)

I would like to request an appointment with the *Attorney General*. (In a letter sent to the state attorney general's office.)

BUT: I have written for an appointment with the *attorney general* and expect to hear from his office soon.

c. Titles of *company officials* (for example, the *president*, the *general manager*) should not be capitalized when they follow or replace a personal name. Exceptions are made in formal minutes of meetings and in rules and bylaws.

The *president* will visit thirteen countries in a tour of company installations abroad. (Normal style.)

The *Secretary's* minutes were read and approved. (In formal minutes.)

NOTE: Some companies choose to capitalize these titles in all their communications because of the great respect the officials command within the company. However, this practice confers excessive importance on people who are neither public officials nor eminent dignitaries, and it should be avoided.

d. In general, do not capitalize job titles when they stand alone. (**NOTE:** In procedures manuals and company memos and announcements, job titles are sometimes capitalized for special distinction and emphasis.)

Marion Conroy has been promoted to the position of *senior accountant* (**OR** *Senior Accountant*).

e. Titles *following* a personal name or *standing alone* are sometimes capitalized in formal citations and acknowledgments.

314 Do not capitalize titles used as general terms of classification. (See ¶307.)

a United States senator   every king
a state governor   any ambassador

EXCEPTION: Because of the special regard for the office of the President of the United States, this title is capitalized even when used as a general term of classification (for example, a *President*, every *President*).

315 Capitalize any title (even if not of high rank) when it is used in *direct address* (that is, quoted or unquoted speech made directly to another person).

DIRECT ADDRESS: Tell me, *Professor*, what you think of Allen's work.

INDIRECT ADDRESS: I asked the *professor* to tell me what he thought of Allen's work.

NOTE: In direct address, do not capitalize a term like *madam* or *sir* if it stands alone without a proper name following.

Please tell me, *sir*, how we can help you.

316 In the *inside address* of a letter, in the *writer's identification block*, and on an *envelope*, capitalize all titles whether they precede or follow the name. (See ¶¶1322–1325, 1362–1368, and the illustrations on page 263.)

317 Do not capitalize *former, late, ex-,* or *-elect* when used with titles. (See ¶362 for the style in headings.)

> the late President Roosevelt   ex-President Ford   Governor-elect Ott

Family Titles

318 Capitalize words such as *mother, father, aunt,* and *uncle* when they stand alone or are followed by a personal name.

> I spoke to *Mother* and *Dad* on the phone last night.
> Let's invite *Uncle Bob* and *Aunt Eleanor.*
> I know that *Grandmother Morrison* will help us if we ask her.

319 Do not capitalize family titles when they are preceded by possessives (such as *my, your, his, our,* and *their*) and simply describe a family relationship.

> I spoke to both my *mother* and my *uncle* on the phone last night.
> We have often heard Edith speak of her *sister* Kate.

NOTE: If the words *uncle, aunt,* or *cousin* form a unit when used together with a first name, capitalize these titles, even when they are preceded by a possessive.

> Frank wants us to meet his *Uncle John.* (Here *Uncle John* is a unit.)
> **BUT:** Frank wants us to meet his *uncle,* John Cunningham. (Here *uncle* simply describes a family relationship.)
> I hope you can meet my *Cousin May.* (The writer thinks of her as *Cousin May.*)
> **BUT:** I hope you can meet my *cousin* May. (Here the writer thinks of her as *May;* the word *cousin* merely indicates relationship.)

Names of Organizations

320 Capitalize the names of companies, associations, societies, independent committees and boards, schools, political parties, conventions, fraternities, clubs, and religious bodies. (Follow the style established by the organization itself, as shown in the letterhead or some other written communication from the organization.)

> the Andersen Hardware Company
> the Young Women's Christian Association
> the Committee for Economic Development
> the Board of Realtors of Morris County Inc.
> the League of Women Voters
> the Farmington Chamber of Commerce
> the University of Montana
> the Democratic and Liberal Parties
> the Republican National Convention
> the Glen Ridge Country Club
> the American Red Cross
> St. Luke's Episcopal Church

NOTE: Prepositions (like *for* and *of*) and conjunctions (like *and*) are not capitalized unless they have four or more letters. (See also ¶360.) The articles *a* and *an* are not capitalized; the article *the* is capitalized only under special circumstances (see ¶324).

See also ¶¶520–522 for the capitalization of abbreviations and acronyms used as organizational names.

321   When the common-noun element is used in place of the full name (for example, *the company* in place of *the Andersen Hardware Company*), do not capitalize the short form unless special emphasis or distinction is required (as in legal documents, minutes of meetings, bylaws, and other formal communications, where the short form is intended to invoke the full authority of the organization). In most cases, however, capitalization is unnecessary because the short form is used only as a general term of classification (see ¶¶307–308).

The *company,* in my opinion, has always made a conscientious effort to involve itself in community affairs. (As used here, *company* is a general term of classification.)

BUT: On behalf of the *Company,* I am authorized to accept your bid. (Here the full authority of the company is implied; hence the capital *C*.)

Mr. Weinstock has just returned from a visit to Haverford College. He reports that the *college* is planning a new fund-raising campaign.

BUT: The *College* hopes to raise an additional $10,000,000 this year to finance the construction of the new instructional resource center. (Announcement in the alumni bulletin.)

NOTE: Do not capitalize the short form if it is modified by a word other than *the.* In constructions such as *our company, this company,* and *every company,* the noun is clearly a general term of classification. (See also ¶308.)

322   Common organizational terms such as *advertising department, manufacturing division, finance committee,* and *board of directors* are ordinarily capitalized when they are the actual names of units within the writer's own organization. These terms are not capitalized when they refer to some other organization unless the writer has reason to give these terms special importance or distinction.

The *Board of Directors* will meet next Thursday at 2:30. (From a company memorandum.)

BUT: Julia Perez has been elected to the *board of directors* of the Kensington Trade Corporation. (From a news release intended for a general audience.)

The *Finance Committee* will meet all week to review next year's budget. (Style used by insiders.)

BUT: Gilligan says his company can give us no encouragement until its *finance committee* has reviewed our proposal. (Style normally used by outsiders.)

NOTE: These terms should not be capitalized when modified by a word other than *the;* for example, *this credit department, their credit department.* (See also ¶321, note.) When *our* or *your* is used as a modifier, the preferred form is *our credit department* or *your credit department.* However, the form *our Credit Department* or *your Credit Department* may be used for special emphasis.

I would like to learn more about the position you have open in your *Advertising Department.* (Outsiders may capitalize the name of the department to indicate the special importance they assign to it.)

323 Capitalize such nouns as *marketing, advertising,* or *promotion* when they are used alone to designate a department within an organization.

> Ann Heller of *Customer Relations* is the person to see.
> I want to get a reaction from our people in *Marketing* first.
> **BUT:** I want to talk to our *marketing* people first. (Here *marketing* is simply a descriptive adjective.)

324 Capitalize the word *the* preceding the name of an organization only when it is part of the legal name of the organization.

> The Associated Press   The New York Times (see ¶289d)

a. Even when part of the organizational name, *the* is often uncapitalized except in legal or formal contexts where it is important to give the full legal name.

b. Do not capitalize *the* when the name is used as a modifier or is abbreviated.

> the Associated Press report   the AP   works for the Times

Names of Government Bodies

325 Capitalize the names of countries and international organizations as well as national, state, county, and city bodies and their subdivisions.

> the Republic of Panama   the Ohio Legislature
> the Ninety-fourth Congress   the Court of Appeals of the State of
>   (see ¶362)   Wisconsin (see ¶320, note)
> the United Nations   the New York State Board of Education
> the Carter Administration   the Fairfax County Shade Tree Commission
> the Cabinet   the Boston City Council

- *See ¶¶334–335 for city and state names.*

326 Capitalize short forms of names of national and international bodies and their major divisions.

> the House (referring to the House of Representatives)
>
> the Department (referring to the Department of Defense, the State Department, the Department of Labor, etc.)
>
> the Bureau (referring to the Bureau of the Budget, the Federal Bureau of Investigation, etc.)
>
> the Court (referring to the United States Supreme Court, the International Court of Justice, etc.)

As a rule, do not capitalize short forms of names of state or local governmental groups, except when special circumstances warrant emphasis or distinction. (See ¶327.)

327 Common terms such as *police department, board of education,* and *county court* need not be capitalized (even when referring to a specific body) since they are terms of general classification. However, such terms should be capitalized when the writer intends to refer to the organization in all of its official dignity.

(Continued on page 80.)

The *Police Department* has announced the promotion of Robert Boyarsky to the rank of sergeant. (The short form is capitalized here because it is intended to have the full force of the complete name, the *Cranfield Police Department*.)

BUT: The Cranfield *police department* sponsors a youth athletic program that we could well copy. (No capitalization is used here because the writer is referring to the department in general terms and not by its official name.)

NOTE: Do not capitalize the short form if it is not actually derived from the complete name. For example, do not capitalize the short form *police department* if the full name is *Department of Public Safety*.

328 Capitalize *federal* only when it is part of the official name of a federal agency, a federal act, or some other proper noun.

> the *Federal* Reserve Board   the *Federal* Insurance Contributions Act
> **BUT:** . . . subject to *federal*, state, and local laws.

329 The terms *federal government* and *government* (referring specifically to the United States government) are now commonly written in small letters because they are considered terms of general classification. In government documents and correspondence, and in other communications where these terms are intended to have the force of an official name, they are capitalized.

330 Capitalize the words *union* and *commonwealth* only when they refer to a specific government.

> Wilkins has lectured on the topic in almost every state in the *Union*.

Names of Places

331 Capitalize the names of places, such as streets, buildings, parks, monuments, rivers, oceans, and mountains. Do not capitalize short forms used in place of the full name.

Fulton Street	**BUT:** the street	the Rocky	**BUT:** the mountains
the Empire State	the building	Mountains	
Building		the Statue of	the statue
Central Park	the park	Liberty	
the Ohio River	the river	Death Valley	the valley
Lake Superior	the lake	O'Hare Airport	the airport
Hotel Pierre	the hotel	Union Station	the station

- *For plural expressions like* the Atlantic and Pacific Oceans, *see ¶309, note. For the treatment of prepositions and conjunctions in proper names, see ¶320, note.*

332 A few short forms are capitalized because of clear association with one place.

> the Coast (the West Coast)   the Hill (Capitol Hill)
> the Continent (Europe)   the Canal (the Panama Canal)

333 Capitalize imaginative names that designate specific places.

> the Bay Area (San Francisco)   the Eternal City (Rome)
> the Loop (in Chicago)   the Twin Cities (Minneapolis and St. Paul)
> the Great White Way   the Garden State (New Jersey)
> (in New York)   the City of Brotherly Love (Philadelphia)

334 Capitalize the word *city* only when it is part of the corporate name of the city or part of an imaginative name.

> Kansas City   the Windy City (Chicago)   **BUT:** the city of San Francisco

335 Capitalize *state* only when it follows the name of a state or is part of an imaginative name.

> New York *State* is also called the Empire *State.*
> The *state* of Alaska is the largest in the Union.
> After a two-year assignment overseas, we returned to the *States.* (Meaning the United States.)

> **NOTE:** Do not capitalize *state* even when used in place of the actual state name.

> He is an employee of the *state.* (People working for the state government, however, might write *State.*)

336 Capitalize *the* only when it is a part of the official name of a place.

> The Dalles   The Hague   **BUT:** the Bronx   the Netherlands

337 Capitalize the words *upper* and *lower* only when they are part of an actual place name or a well-established imaginative name.

> Upper Peninsula   Lower California
> Upper West Side   Lower East Side

Points of the Compass

338 Capitalize *north, south, east, west,* and derivative words when they designate definite regions or are an integral part of a proper name.

> in the North   the Far North   North Dakota
> back East   the Near East   the Eastern Seaboard
> down South   the Deep South   the South Side
> out West   the Middle West   the West Coast

Do not capitalize these words when they merely indicate direction or general location.

> Many textile plants have moved from the *Northeast* and relocated in the *South.* (Region.)
> They maintain a villa in the *south* of France. (General location.)
> Go *west* on Route 517 and then *south* on 195. (Direction.)
> John is coming back *East* after three years on the West Coast. (Region.)
> **BUT:** The *west coast* of the United States borders on the Pacific. (Referring only to the shoreline, not the region.)
> Most of our customers live on the *East Side.* (Definite locality.)
> **BUT:** Most of our customers live on the *east side* of town. (General location.)

339 Capitalize such words as *Northerner, Southerner,* and *Midwesterner.*

340 Capitalize such words as *northern, southern, eastern,* and *western* when these words pertain to the people in a region and to their political, social, or cultural activities. Do not capitalize these words, however, when they merely indicate general location or refer to the geography or climate of the region.

Eastern bankers	**BUT:** the eastern half of Pennsylvania
Southern hospitality	southern temperatures
Western civilization	westerly winds
the Northern vote	a northern winter

The *Northern* states did not vote as they were expected to. (Political activities.)
BUT: The drought is expected to continue in the *northern* states. (Climate.)

My sales territory takes in most of the *southeastern* states. (General location.)

NOTE: When terms like *western region* and *southern district* are used to name organizational units within a company, capitalize them.

The *Western Region* (referring to a part of the national sales staff) reports that sales are 12 percent over budget for the first six months this year.

341 When words like *northern, southern, eastern,* and *western* precede a place name, they are not capitalized because they merely indicate general location within a region. In a few cases, where these words are actually part of the place name, they must be capitalized. (Check an atlas or the geographical listings in a dictionary when in doubt.)

Preceding a Place Name	**Part of a Place Name**
northern New Jersey	**BUT:** Northern Ireland
western Massachusetts	Western Australia

Days of the Week, Months, Holidays, Seasons, Events, Periods

342 Capitalize names of days, months, holidays, and religious days.

Wednesday	Good Friday
February	Passover
New Year's Eve	the Fourth of July
Veterans Day (no apostrophe)	Mother's Day

343 Capitalize the names of the seasons only when they are personified.

Come, gentle *Spring,* with your blessed showers.
BUT: Our order for *spring* merchandise was mailed today.

344 Capitalize the names of historical events and imaginative names given to historical periods.

the American Revolution	the Middle Ages
World War II	Prohibition
Fire Prevention Week	the Great Depression

NOTE: Terms like *space age, atomic age,* and *nuclear age* are usually not capitalized.

345 Do not capitalize the names of decades and centuries.

during the thirties	in the twentieth century
in the nineteen-seventies	during the eighteen hundreds

NOTE: Decades are capitalized, however, in special expressions.

the Gay Nineties   the Roaring Twenties

Acts, Laws, Bills, Treaties

346   Capitalize formal titles of acts, laws, bills, and treaties, but do not capitalize common-noun elements that stand alone in place of the full name.

the Social Security Act	the act
Public Law 85-1	the law
the Treaty of Versailles	the treaty
the Constitution of the United States	**BUT:** the Constitution

Programs, Movements, Concepts

347   Do not capitalize the names of programs, movements, or concepts when used as general terms.

social security benefits (**BUT:** the Social Security Administration)
medicare payments (**BUT:** the Medicare Act)
socialism (**BUT:** the Socialist Labor Party)
the civil rights movement
women's lib

NOTE: Imaginative names like the *New Deal* are capitalized.

Races, Peoples, Languages, Religions

348   Capitalize the names of races, peoples, tribes, religions, and languages.

Chinese	Afro-American	Chicanos	**BUT:** the blacks
Judaism	Sanskrit	Negroes	the whites

Supreme Being

349   Capitalize all references to a supreme being.

God	the Supreme Being	the Almighty
the Lord	the Messiah	the Holy Spirit

350   Capitalize personal pronouns referring to a supreme being when they stand alone, without an antecedent nearby.

Offer thanks unto *Him.*   **BUT:** Ask the Lord for *his* blessing.

Heavenly Bodies

351   Capitalize the names of planets (*Jupiter, Mars*), stars (*Polaris, the North Star*), and constellations (*the Big Dipper, the Milky Way*). However, do not capitalize the words *sun, moon,* or *earth* unless they are used in connection with the capitalized names of other planets or stars.

The *sun* was hidden behind the cloud.
The *earth* revolves on its axis.
Compare the orbits of *Mars, Venus,* and *Earth.*

Course Titles, Subjects, Academic Degrees

352 Capitalize the names of specific course titles. However, do not capitalize names of subjects or areas of study except for any proper nouns or adjectives in such names.

> *American History 201* meets on Tuesdays and Thursdays. (Course title.)
> Harriet has decided to major in *American history*. (Area of study.)

353 Do not capitalize academic degrees used as general terms of classification (for example, *a bachelor of arts degree, working on her master's*). However, capitalize a degree used after a person's name (*Claire Hurwitz, Doctor of Philosophy*).

354 Do not capitalize the words *freshman, sophomore, junior,* or *senior* in references to academic years.

> She plans to spend her *junior* year abroad.
> All *seniors* must return library books by May 15.

Commercial Products

355 Capitalize trademarks, brand names, proprietary names, names of commercial products, and market grades. The common noun following the name of a product should not ordinarily be capitalized; however, manufacturers and advertisers often capitalize such words in the names of their own products for special emphasis.

> Ivory soap   Hotpoint dishwasher   Choice lamb (market grade)

356 Capitalize all trademarks except those that have become clearly established as common nouns. To be safe, check an up-to-date dictionary or consult the United States Trademark Association (6 East 45 Street, New York, New York 10017).

Coca-Cola, Coke	Teflon	Dacron	Dictaphone
Pyrex	TelePrompTer	Teletype	Frigidaire
Photostat	Xerox	Scotch tape	Kleenex
Band-Aid	Jeep	Levi's	Realtor

BUT: nylon, cellophane, mimeograph, dry ice, aspirin

Advertising Material

357 Words ordinarily written in small letters may be capitalized in advertising copy for special emphasis. (This style is inappropriate in all other kinds of written communication.)

> Save money now during our *Year-End Clearance Sale.*
> It's the event *Luxury Lovers* have been waiting for . . . from Whitehall's!

Legal Correspondence

358 In legal documents many words that ordinarily would be written in small letters are written with initial capitals or all capitals—for example, references to parties, the name of the document, special provisions, and sometimes spelled-out amounts of money (see ¶420).

Whereupon I, the said Notary, at the request of the aforesaid, did PROTEST, and by these presents do publicly and solemnly PROTEST, as well against Maker and Indorser of said note . . .

THIS AGREEMENT, made this 31st day of January, 1977 . . .

. . . hereinafter called the SELLER . . .

WHEREAS the Seller has this day agreed . . .

WITNESS the signatures . . .

Nouns With Numbers or Letters

359 Capitalize a noun followed by a number or a letter that indicates sequence. EXCEPTIONS: Do not capitalize the nouns *line, note, page, paragraph, size,* and *verse.*

Act I	Class 4	Lesson 20	Policy 394857
Appendix A	Column 1	line 4	Room 501
Article 2	Diagram 4	Model B671-4	Section 1
Book III	Exercise 8	note 1	size 10
Bulletin T-119	Exhibit A	page 158	Table 7
Car 8171	Figure 9	paragraph 2a	Track 2
Chapter V	Flight 626	Part Three	Unit 2
Chart 3	Illustration 19	Plate XV	verse 3
Check 181	Invoice 270487	Platform 3	Volume II

NOTE: It is often unnecessary to use *No.* before the number. (See ¶455.)

Purchase Order 4713 (RATHER THAN: Purchase Order *No.* 4713)

Titles of Literary and Artistic Works; Headings

360 In titles of literary and artistic works and in displayed headings, capitalize all words with *four or more* letters. Also capitalize words with fewer than four letters except:

ARTICLES: *the, a, an*

SHORT CONJUNCTIONS: *and, as, but, if, or, nor*

SHORT PREPOSITIONS: *at, by, for, in, of, off, on, out, to, up*

How to Succeed in Business Without Really Trying
"Redevelopment Proposal Is Not Expected to Be Approved"

NOTE: Even articles, short conjunctions, and short prepositions should be capitalized under the following circumstances:

a. Capitalize the first and last word of a title.

"A Home to Be Proud Of"

CAUTION: Do not capitalize *the* at the beginning of a title unless it is actually part of the title.

For further details check the *Encyclopaedia Britannica.*
This clipping is from *The New York Times.*

b. Capitalize the first word following a dash or colon in a title.

Abraham Lincoln—The Early Years
The Treaty of Versailles: A Reexamination

(Continued on page 86.)

c. Capitalize short words like *in, out, off,* and *up* in titles when they serve as adverbs rather than as prepositions. (These words may occur in verb phrases or in hyphenated compounds derived from verb phrases.)

> "IBM Chalks *Up* Record Earnings for the Year"
> "LeClaire Is Runner-*Up* in Election" (see also ¶362)
> **but:** "Sailing *up* the Mississippi"

d. Capitalize short prepositions like *in* and *up* when used together with prepositions having four or more letters.

> "Sailing *Up* and *Down* the Mississippi"
> "Happenings *In* and *Around* Town"

- See ¶242, note, for the capitalization of Preface, Contents, Appendix, and Index.
- See ¶289a for the use of all capitals with titles.

361 Do not capitalize a book title when it is incorporated into a sentence as a descriptive phrase.

> In his book on *economics* Samuelson points out that . . .
> **but:** In his book *Economics* Samuelson points out that . . .

Hyphenated Words

362 *Within a sentence,* capitalize only those elements of a hyphenated word that are proper nouns or proper adjectives. *At the beginning of a sentence,* capitalize the first element in the hyphenated word but not other elements unless they are proper nouns or adjectives. *In a heading or title,* capitalize all the elements except articles, short prepositions, and short conjunctions (see ¶360).

Within Sentences	Beginning Sentences	In Headings
up-to-date	Up-to-date	Up-to-Date
Spanish-American	Spanish-American	Spanish-American
English-speaking	English-speaking	English-Speaking
mid-September	Mid-September	Mid-September
ex-President Ford	Ex-President Ford	Ex-President Ford
Senator-elect Murray	Senator-elect Murray	Senator-Elect Murray
self-confidence	Self-confidence	Self-Confidence
de-emphasize	De-emphasize	De-Emphasize
follow-up	Follow-up	Follow-Up (see ¶360c)
Ninety-fifth Congress	Ninety-fifth Congress	Ninety-Fifth Congress
one-sixth	One-sixth	One-Sixth
post-World War II	Post-World War II	Post-World War II

- *Capitalization of questions within sentences: see ¶¶115, 117.*
- *Capitalization after a colon: see ¶¶196–199.*
- *Capitalization after an opening dash: see ¶214, note.*
- *Capitalization after an opening parenthesis: see ¶¶224–226.*
- *Capitalization after an opening quotation mark: see ¶¶272–273.*
- *Capitalization of abbreviations: see ¶514.*

NUMBERS

BASIC RULES

SPECIAL RULES

There is a significant difference between using figures and using words to express numbers. Figures are big (like capital letters) and compact and informal (like abbreviations); when used in a sentence, they stand out clearly from the surrounding words. By contrast, numbers expressed in words are unemphatic and formal; they do not stand out in a sentence. It is this functional difference between figures and words that underlies all aspects of number style.

Basic Rules

The rules for expressing numbers would be quite simple if writers would all agree to express numbers entirely in figures or entirely in words. But in actual practice the exclusive use of figures is considered appropriate only in tables and statistical matter, whereas the exclusive use of words to express numbers is found only in ultraformal documents (such as proclamations and social invitations). In writing that is neither ultraformal nor ultratechnical, most style manuals call for the use of both figures and words in varying proportions. Although authorities do not agree on details, there are two sets of basic rules in wide use: the *figure style* (which uses figures for most numbers above 10) and the *word style* (which uses figures for most numbers above 100). Unless you deal with a very limited type of business correspondence, you should be familiar with both styles and be prepared to use each appropriately as the situation demands.

Figure Style

The figure style is most commonly used in ordinary business correspondence (dealing with sales, production, advertising, and other routine commercial matters). It is also used in journalistic and technical material. In writing of this kind most numbers represent significant quantities or measurements that should stand out for emphasis or quick comprehension.

401   Spell out numbers from 1 through 10; use figures for numbers above 10. This rule applies to both exact and approximate numbers.

> We need *ten* samples, but they can give us only *four* or *five*.
> Please send us *35* copies of your latest bulletin.
> About *60* to *70* contracts are missing from the files.
> I have received some *30-odd* letters about Tuesday's column.
> Our group has already sold over *1,200* (or *1200*) tickets. (See ¶461 on commas in four-digit figures.)
> This stadium can seat more than *80,000* people.

a. Use all figures—even for the numbers 1 through 10 (as in this sentence)—when they have technical significance or need to be emphasized for quick comprehension.

NOTE: This style is used in tables, statistical matter, and in expressions of dates (*May 3*), money (*$6*), clock time (*4 p.m.*), proportions, ratios, percentages (*8 percent*), and scores (*3 to 1*). This style is also used with abbreviations and symbols (*12 cm, 8°F*), with numbers referred to as numbers (*any number from 1 to 10*), and with technical or emphatic references to age (*a clinical study of 5-year-olds*), periods of time (*a 6-month loan*), and measurements (*parcels over 3 pounds*).

b. In isolated cases spell out a number above 10 in order to de-emphasize the number or make it seem indefinite. (See ¶¶465–467 for rules on how to express numbers in words.)

> He could give you *a thousand and one* reasons for his decision.
> I have *a hundred* things to do today. (In this context *100 things* would seem too precise, too exact.)

NOTE: Also use words for numbers at the beginning of a sentence, for most ordinals (*our twenty-fifth anniversary*), for fractions (*one-third of our sales*), and for nontechnical or nonemphatic references to age (*my son just turned twelve*), periods of time (*twenty years ago*), and measurements (*I'd like to lose another three pounds*).

402 Use the same style to express *related* numbers above and below 10. (If any of the numbers are above 10, put them all in figures.)

> Smoke damaged *five* dresses and *eight* suits.
> **BUT:** Smoke damaged *5* dresses, *8* suits, and *11* coats.
>
> I have requisitioned *16* reams of bond paper, *120* scratch pads, and *8* boxes of envelopes for the *four* secretaries. (Figures are used for related items of stationery; the number of secretaries is not related.)

403 For fast comprehension, numbers in the *millions* or higher may be expressed as follows:

> 21 million (in place of 21,000,000)   14½ million (in place of 14,500,000)
> 3 billion (in place of 3,000,000,000)   2.4 billion (in place of 2,400,000,000)

a. This style may be used only when the amount consists of a whole number with nothing more than a simple fraction or decimal following. A number such as *4,832,067* must be written all in figures.

b. Treat related numbers alike.

> Last year we sold *21,557,000* items; this year, nearly *23,000,000*. (**NOT:** 23 million.)

- *See ¶416 for examples involving money.*

Word Style

The word style of numbers is used in high-level executive correspondence and in nontechnical material, where the writing is of a more formal or literary nature and the use of figures would give numbers an undesired emphasis and obtrusiveness. Here are the basic rules for the word style.

404 Spell out all numbers, whether exact or approximate, that can be expressed in one or two words. (A hyphenated compound number like *twenty-one* or *ninety-nine* counts as one word.) In effect, spell out all numbers from 1 through 100 and all round numbers above 100 that require no more than two words (such as *sixty-two thousand* or *forty-five million*).

(Continued on page 90.)

Mr. Ryan received *twenty-three* letters praising his talk at the Rotary Club.

Last year more than *twelve million* people attended the art exhibition our company sponsored.

Some *sixty-odd* people have called to volunteer their services.

Over *two hundred* people attended the reception for Helen and Frank Russo. **BUT:** Over *250* people attended the reception. (Use figures when more than two words are required.)

NOTE: In writing of an ultraformal nature—proclamations, social invitations, and many legal documents—even a number that requires more than two words is spelled out. However, as a matter of practicality the word style ordinarily uses figures when more than two words are required.

- See ¶¶465–467 for rules on how to express numbers in words.

405   Express related numbers the same way, even though some are above 100 and some below. If any are in figures, put all in figures.

We sent out *three hundred* invitations and have already received over *one hundred* acceptances.

BUT: We sent out *300* invitations and have already received *125* acceptances. (**NOT:** three hundred . . . 125 . . .)

406   Numbers in the millions or higher *that require more than two words when spelled out* may be expressed as follows:

231 million (in place of 231,000,000)
9¾ billion (in place of 9,750,000,000)
671.4 million (in place of 671,400,000)

Even a two-word number such as *sixty-two million* should be expressed as *62 million* when it is related to a number such as *231 million* (which cannot be spelled in two words). Moreover, it should be expressed as *62,000,000* when it is related to a number such as *231,163,520*.

Special Rules

The preceding rules on figure style (¶¶401–403) and word style (¶¶404–406) are basic guidelines that govern in the absence of more specific principles. The following rules cover those situations which require special handling (for example, expressions of dates and money). In a number of cases where either figures or words are acceptable, your choice will depend on whether you are striving for emphasis or formality.

Dates

These rules apply to dates in sentences. See ¶1314 for date lines in correspondence.

407   When the day *precedes* the month or *stands alone*, express it either in ordinal figures (*1st, 2d, 3d, 4th*, etc.) or in ordinal words (the *first*, the *twelfth*, the *twenty-eighth*).

Our meeting starts on the *21st* of July and runs through the *23d*. (For emphasis.)
I arrive on the *ninth* of March and leave on the *thirty-first*. (For formality.)

408 When the day *follows* the month, always express it in cardinal figures (*1, 2, 3,* etc.).

on March 6 (**NOT:** March 6*th* or March *sixth*)

409 **a.** Express complete dates in month-day-year sequence.

March 6, 1979

NOTE: In United States military correspondence and in letters from foreign countries, the complete date is expressed in day-month-year sequence.

6 March 1979

b. The form *3/6/79* (representing a *month*-day-year sequence) is acceptable on business forms and in informal letters and memos. Avoid this form, however, if there is any chance your reader could misinterpret it as a *day*-month-year sequence.

c. Avoid the following forms: *March 6th, 1979; Mar. 6, 1979; the 6th of March, 1979; the sixth of March, 1979.*

410 Note the current use of commas and other punctuation with expressions of dates.

On *March 12, 1975,* construction began on our present headquarters. (Two commas set off the year following the month and day.)

The corporation was founded on *May 1, 1930;* it filed for bankruptcy on *July 12, 1977* (the same day merger plans failed). (Omit the second comma when other punctuation is required at that point.)

The records for *June 1973* (**OR** *June, 1973,*) have been charged out to Ms. Gerson. (The current trend is to omit commas around the year when it follows the month alone.)

The *March 1975* issue of *Harper's* carried the article. (No commas are used when the month and year serve as an adjective.)

BUT: The *March 15, 1975,* issue of *Time* . . . (Use two commas to set off the year when a complete date serves as an adjective. See ¶154.)

In *1975* Mr. Richardson and Mrs. Fein were elected to the board. (No comma follows the year in a short introductory phrase.)

On *January 15* we met to review your proposal. (No comma follows the month and day in a short introductory phrase.)

BUT: On *January 15, 22* new employees will be added to the staff. (Insert a comma when another figure immediately follows. See ¶456.)

- *See ¶152 for the use or omission of a comma when a date is followed by a related phrase or clause.*

411 In formal legal documents, formal invitations, and proclamations, spell out the day and the year. A number of styles may be used:

May twenty-first	nineteen hundred and seventy-nine
the twenty-first of May	one thousand nine hundred and seventy-nine
this twenty-first day of May	in the year of Our Lord one thousand nine hundred and seventy-nine

412 Class graduation years and well-known years in history may appear in abbreviated form.

the class of '74   the blizzard of '88

■ *See ¶¶438–439 for the expression of centuries and decades; ¶¶458–460 for dates in a sequence.*

Money

413 Use figures to express exact or approximate amounts of money.

$5	about $200	over $1,000,000	a $20 bill
$9.75	nearly $1,000	a $20,000-a-year job	$2,000 worth

NOTE: An isolated, nonemphatic reference to money may be spelled out.

five hundred dollars	a twenty-dollar bill
nearly a thousand dollars	two thousand dollars' worth (note the
a half-dollar	apostrophe with *dollars'*)

414 Spell out indefinite amounts of money.

a few million dollars   many thousands of dollars

415 Do not add a decimal point or ciphers to a *whole* dollar amount when it occurs in a sentence.

I am enclosing a check for *$125* as payment in full.
This model costs $12.50; that one costs *$10*.

In a column, however, if any amount contains cents, add a decimal point and two ciphers to all *whole* dollar amounts to maintain a uniform appearance.

$150.50
25.00
8.05
$183.55

416 Money in round amounts of a million or more may be expressed partially in words. (The style given in the first column is preferred.)

$12 million	OR	12 million dollars			
$10½ million	OR	10½ million dollars			
$10.5 million	OR	10.5 million dollars			
$6¼ billion	OR	6¼ billion dollars	OR	$6,250 million	
$6.25 billion	OR	6.25 billion dollars	OR	6,250 million dollars	

a. This style may be used only when the amount consists of a whole number with nothing more than a simple fraction or decimal following. Write an amount like *$10,235,000* entirely in figures.

b. Express related amounts the same way.

from $500,000 to $1,000,000 (NOT: from $500,000 to $1 million)

c. Repeat the word *million* (*billion*, etc.) with each figure to avoid misunderstanding.

$5 million to $10 million (NOT: $5 to $10 million)

417 Fractional expressions of large amounts of money should be either completely spelled out or converted to an all-figure style.

one-quarter of a million dollars **or** $250,000
(**but not:** ¼ of a million dollars **or** $¼ million)
a half-billion dollars **or** $500,000,000
(**but not:** ½ billion dollars **or** $½ billion)

418 For amounts under a dollar, use figures and the word *cents*.

I am sure that customers will not pay more than *50 cents* for this item.

This machine can be fixed with *80 cents'* worth of parts. (Note the apostrophe with *cents'*.)

note: An isolated, nonemphatic reference to cents may be spelled out.

I wouldn't give *two cents* for that car.

a. Do not use the style $.75 in sentences except when related amounts require a dollar sign.

It will cost you $2.42 a copy to do the company manual: $.43 for the paper, $.77 for the printing, and $1.22 for the special binder.

b. The symbol ¢ may be used in technical and statistical matter containing many price quotations.

Yesterday's wholesale prices for food commodities were as follows: coffee, 73¢; cocoa, 83¢; sugar, 11¢; butter, 87¢.

419 When using the dollar sign or the cent sign with a price range or a series of amounts, use the sign with each amount.

$5,000 to $10,000 $10 million to $20 million
10¢ to 20¢   (**not:** $10 to $20 million)

These three properties are valued at $32,900, $54,500, and $87,000, respectively.

If the term *dollars* or *cents* is to be spelled out, use it only with the final amount.

10 to 20 cents   10 million to 20 million dollars (see ¶416c)

420 In legal documents, amounts of money are often expressed first in words and then, within parentheses, in figures. (See also ¶¶465–467.)

One Hundred Dollars ($100)   **or**   One Hundred (100) Dollars
but not: One Hundred ($100) Dollars
Three Thousand One Hundred and 50/100 Dollars ($3,100.50)

a. When spelling out amounts of money, omit the *and* between hundreds and tens of dollars if *and* is used before the fraction representing "cents."

Six Hundred Thirty-two and 75/100 Dollars

note: In whole dollar amounts, the use of *and* between hundreds and tens of dollars is optional.

Six Hundred Thirty-two Dollars   **or**   Six Hundred and Thirty-two Dollars

b. The capitalization of spelled-out amounts may vary. Sometimes the first letter of each main word is capitalized (as in the examples above); sometimes only the first letter of the first word is capitalized (as on checks); sometimes the entire amount is given all in capitals.

¶¶421–428 cover situations in which numbers are usually spelled out: at the beginning of sentences and in expressions using indefinite numbers, ordinal numbers, and fractions.

At the Beginning of a Sentence

421 Spell out a number that begins a sentence, as well as any related numbers.

> *Forty-six* glasses were broken in the last shipment you sent us.
> *Five hundred* people attended the reception for Mr. and Mrs. Santangelo.
> *Twenty* to *thirty* percent of the castings proved to be defective.
> (**NOT:** *Twenty* to *30* percent of the castings proved to be defective.)

422 If the number requires more than two words when spelled out or if figures are preferable for emphasis or quick reference, reword the sentence.

> The company sent out *298* copies of its consumer guidelines last month.
> (**NOT:** *Two hundred and ninety-eight* of its consumer guidelines were sent out by the company last month.)
> We had a good year in *1977.*
> (**NOT:** *Nineteen hundred seventy-seven* **OR** *1977* was a good year for us.)
> Our mining operations provide *60* to *70* percent of our revenues.
> (**INSTEAD OF:** *Sixty* to *seventy* percent of our revenues come from our mining operations.)

Indefinite Numbers and Amounts

423 Spell out indefinite numbers and amounts.

> a few hundred votes   hundreds of customers
> several thousand orders   thousands of questionnaires
> a multimillion-dollar program   many millions of dollars
> a woman in her fifties   a stack of twenties

- *For the treatment of approximate numbers, see ¶401 (figure style) and ¶404 (word style).*

Ordinal Numbers

424 In general, spell out all ordinal numbers (*first, second, third,* etc.) that can be expressed in one or two words. (A hyphenated number like *twenty-first* counts as one word.)

> in the twentieth century   the Twenty-third Assembly District
> on your thirty-fifth birthday   the ten millionth visitor to the United
> the Ninety-fourth Congress (in text)   Nations
> the Ninety-Fourth Congress (in head-   the store's one hundredth anniversary
> ings and titles)   **BUT:** the store's 125th anniversary

- *See ¶465 for the rule on how to express ordinal numbers in words; ¶427d for the distinction between ordinals and fractions.*

425 Use figures for ordinals in certain expressions of dates (see ¶¶407–409), in numbered street names above 10 (see ¶1333b), and for special emphasis.

In Advertising Copy

Come to our *25th* Anniversary Sale! (Figures for emphasis.)

Come to our *Twenty-fifth* Anniversary Sale! (Words for formality.)

In Ordinary Correspondence

Watkins & Glenn is having a *twenty-fifth* anniversary sale.

NOTE: Ordinal figures are expressed as follows: *1st, 2d* or *2nd, 3d* or *3rd, 4th, 5th, 6th,* etc. Do not use an "abbreviation" period following an ordinal figure.

- See ¶504 for the use of 2d in preference to 2nd.

426 Use figures or roman numerals for ordinals that follow a name.

James A. Wilson 3d   **OR**   James A. Wilson III

Fractions

427 Fractions Standing Alone

a. Ordinarily spell out a fraction that stands alone (i.e., without a whole number preceding). Use figures, however, if the spelled-out form is long and awkward or if the fraction is used in a technical measurement or a computation.

one-half the vote (see ¶427c)	three-fourths of the voters
a two-thirds majority	half an hour later (**OR:** a half hour later)

3/4-yard lengths (**BETTER THAN:** three-quarter-yard lengths)

5/32 inch (**BETTER THAN:** five thirty-seconds of an inch)

multiply by 2/5

b. When a fraction is spelled out, the numerator and the denominator should be connected by a hyphen unless either element already contains a hyphen.

seven-twelfths	five thirty-seconds
nine-sixteenths	twenty-five thirty-seconds

c. Do not hyphenate *one half* in constructions like the following:

One half of the shipment was damaged beyond use; the *other half* was partially salvageable.

d. Distinguish between large spelled-out fractions (which are hyphenated) and large spelled-out ordinals (which are not).

The difference is less than *one-hundredth* of 1 percent. (Hyphenated fraction referring to 1/100.)

BUT: This year the company will be celebrating the *one hundredth* anniversary of its founding. (Unhyphenated ordinal referring to 100th.)

e. Fractions expressed in figures should not be followed by endings like *sts, ds, nds,* or *ths* or by an *of* phrase.

3/200 (**NOT:** 3/200ths)   9/64 inch (**NOT:** 9/64ths of an inch)

If a sentence requires the use of an *of* phrase following the fraction, spell the fraction out.

three-quarters of an hour (**NOT:** 3/4 of an hour)

428 Fractions in Mixed Numbers

a. A mixed number (a whole number plus a fraction) is written in figures except at the beginning of a sentence.

> This year's sales are 3¼ times as great as they were five years ago.
> *Five and one-quarter* (**or** *Five and a quarter*) inches of snow fell last night. (Note the use of *and* between the whole number and the fraction.)

b. When constructing fractions that do not appear on the typewriter, use the diagonal (/). Separate a whole number from a fraction by a space (not by a hyphen).

> The rate of interest was *3 7/8* percent. (**not:** 3-7/8 percent.)

c. In the same sentence, do not mix constructed fractions (7/8, 5/16) with those that appear on the typewriter (½, ¼).

> The interest rate rose from *7 1/2* to *7 5/8* percent. (**not:** 7½ to *7 5/8* percent.)

¶¶429–442 deal with measurements and with expressions of age and time (elements that often function as measurements). When these elements have technical or statistical significance, they are expressed in figures; otherwise, they are expressed in words.

Measurements

429 Most measurements have a technical significance and should be expressed in figures (even from 1 through 10) for emphasis or quick comprehension. However, spell out an isolated measurement that lacks technical significance.

> A higher rate is charged on parcels over *2 kilograms.*
> **but:** I'm afraid I've gained another *two kilograms* this week.
> Add *1 quart* of sugar for each *4 quarts* of strawberries.
> **but:** Last weekend we picked *four quarts* of strawberries from our own patch.
> There is no charge for delivery within a *30-mile* radius of Chicago.
> **but:** It's only an *eighty-mile* drive up to our summer place.

note: Dimensions, sizes, and temperature readings are always expressed in figures.

> The dimensions of my new office are *4 by 5 meters.* (See also ¶432.)
> Your order for one pair of tennis shoes, *size 6,* has been delayed.
> The thermometer now stands at *28,* a rise of three degrees in the last hour.

430 When a measurement consists of several words, do not use commas to separate the words. The measurement is considered a single unit.

> The parcel weighed *6 pounds 14 ounces.*   I am *6 feet 2 inches* tall.
> The punch bowl holds *4 quarts 1 pint.*   He has *20/20* vision.

431 The unit of measure may be abbreviated or expressed as a symbol in technical matter or in tables. (See ¶¶535–538 for the style of abbreviations for units of measure; ¶454 for the repetition of abbreviations and symbols in a range of numbers.)

432 Dimensions may be expressed as follows:

GENERAL USAGE:	a room 15 by 30 feet	a 15- by 30-foot room
TECHNICAL USAGE:	{ a room 15 x 30 ft	a 15- x 30-ft room
	{ a room 15' x 30'	a 15' x 30' room
GENERAL USAGE:	a room 5 by 10 meters	a 5- by 10-meter room
TECHNICAL USAGE:	a room 5 x 10 m	a 5- x 10-m room
GENERAL USAGE:	15 feet 6 inches by 30 feet 9 inches	
TECHNICAL USAGE:	15 ft 6 in x 30 ft 9 in OR 15' 6" x 30' 9"	

Ages and Anniversaries

433 Express ages in figures (even from 1 through 10) when they are used as significant statistics or as technical measurements.

> Ralph Martinez, *43,* has been promoted to professor of law.
> At the age of *50,* a policyholder may collect disability benefits. (Avoid the abrupt construction *at age 50.*)
> We are making a citywide study of the reading skills of all *9-year-olds.*
> You cannot disregard the job application of a person aged *58.* (NOT: age 58.)

NOTE: When age is expressed in years, months, and days, do not use commas to separate the elements; they make up a single unit.

> On January 1 she will be *19 years 4 months and 17 days old.* (The *and* linking months and days is often omitted.)

434 Spell out ages in nontechnical references and in formal writing.

> My daughter will be *five years old* tomorrow.
> The woman is in her early *thirties;* her husband is in his *mid-fifties.*

435 Spell out ordinals in references to birthdays and anniversaries except where special emphasis or more than two words are required. (See also ¶¶424–425.)

> on her twenty-first birthday
> their fortieth anniversary
> the company's 125th anniversary

Periods of Time

436 Use figures (even from 1 through 10) to express periods of time when they are used as technical measurements or significant statistics (as in discounts, interest rates, and credit terms).

> a 5-minute warmup   a note due in 6 months
> payable in 30 days   a 30-year mortgage

437 Spell out nontechnical references to periods of time unless the number requires more than two words.

> a twenty-minute wait   in the last thirty years
> eight hours later   forty-odd years ago
> twelve days from now   three hundred years ago
> in twenty-four months   BUT: 350 years ago

438 Centuries may be expressed as follows:

the 1900s **or** the nineteen hundreds
the twentieth century
nineteenth-century business customs

439 Decades may be expressed as follows:

the 1970s **or** the nineteen-seventies **or** the seventies **or** the '70s
the mid-1960s **or** the mid-sixties **or** the mid-'60s
during the years 1960–1970 **or** from 1960 to 1970 (see ¶459) **or** between 1960
and 1970

note: Decades are not capitalized except in special expressions such as
the Gay Nineties, the Roaring Twenties.

Clock Time

440 **With *A.M., P.M., Noon,* and *Midnight***

a. Always use figures with *a.m.* or *p.m.*

The boat sails at *11:30 a.m.*   The train leaves at *2 p.m.*
By *8 p.m.*, CST, the first election returns should be in.
or: By *8 p.m.* (CST) the first election returns should be in.

b. the abbreviations *a.m.* and *p.m.* are typed in small letters without
spaces. (In printed matter they usually appear in small capitals: A.M., P.M.)

c. For time "on the hour," ciphers are not needed to denote minutes.

Our store is open from 9:30 a.m. to *6 p.m.* (**not:** 6:00 p.m.)
We always close from *12 noon* to 1:30 p.m.
You can buy your tickets between *9* and *10 a.m.*

In tables, however, when some entries are given in
hours and minutes, add a colon and two ciphers to
exact hours to maintain a uniform appearance. (See
also ¶442 for the use of ciphers.)

ARR	DEP
8:45	9:10
9:00	9:25
9:50	10:00

d. Do not use *a.m.* or *p.m.* unless figures are used.

this morning (**not:** this a.m.)   tomorrow afternoon (**not:** tomorrow p.m.)

e. Do not use *a.m.* or *p.m.* with *o'clock.*

6 o'clock **or** 6 p.m.   ten o'clock **or** 10 a.m.
(**not:** 6 p.m. o'clock)   (**not:** 10 a.m. o'clock)

note: The expression *o'clock* is more formal than *a.m.* or *p.m.*

f. Do not use *a.m.* or *p.m.* with the expressions *in the morning, in the
afternoon, in the evening,* or *at night.* The abbreviations themselves
already convey one of these meanings.

at 9 p.m. **or** at nine in the evening (**not:** at 9 p.m. in the evening)

g. Use a colon (without space before or after) to separate hours from
minutes (as in *3:22*).

h. The times *noon* and *midnight* may be expressed in words alone. However, use the forms *12 noon* and *12 midnight* when these times are given with other times expressed in figures.

> The second shift ends at *midnight*.
> **BUT:** The second shift runs from *4 p.m.* to *12 midnight*.

441   With *O'Clock*

a. With *o'clock* use figures for emphasis or words for formality.

> 3 o'clock (for emphasis)   three o'clock (for formality)

b. To express hours and minutes with *o'clock*, use this style: *half past four o'clock* or *half after four o'clock* (but not *four-thirty o'clock*).

c. Expressions of time containing *o'clock* may be reinforced by such phrases as *in the morning, in the afternoon,* and the like.

> 10 o'clock at night   seven o'clock in the morning

For quick comprehension, the forms *10 p.m.* and *7 a.m.* are preferable.

442   Without *A.M., P.M.,* or *O'Clock*

When expressing time without *a.m., p.m.,* or *o'clock,* either spell the time out or—for quick comprehension—convert the expression to an all-figure style.

> arrive at eight   **OR**   arrive at 8:00
> five after six   **OR**   6:05
> a quarter past ten   **OR**   10:15
> twenty of four   **OR**   3:40
> a quarter to five   **OR**   4:45
> half past nine   **OR**   nine-thirty   **OR**   9:30
> nine forty-two   **OR**   9:42

NOTE: A hyphen is used between hours and minutes (*seven-thirty*) but not if the minutes must be hyphenated (seven *thirty-five*).

The following paragraphs, ¶¶443–455, deal with situations in which numbers are always expressed in figures.

Decimals

443 Always write decimals in figures. Never insert commas in the decimal part of a number.

> 665.3184368 (no comma in decimal part of the number)
> 8,919.23785 (comma used in whole part of the number)

▪ *See ¶461b for the metric style of writing decimals.*

444 When a decimal stands alone (without a whole number preceding the decimal point), insert a cipher before the decimal point. (Reason: The cipher keeps the reader from overlooking the decimal point.)

> 0.55 inch   0.08 gram   **EXCEPTIONS:** a Colt .45; a .36 caliber revolver

445 Ordinarily, drop the cipher at the end of a decimal (for example, write 2.787 rather than 2.7870). However, retain the cipher (a) if you wish to emphasize that the decimal is an exact number or (b) if the decimal has been rounded off from a longer figure. In a column of numbers add ciphers to the end of a decimal in order to make the number as long as other numbers in the column.

446 Do not begin a sentence with a decimal figure.

> The temperature reading at 8 a.m. was 63.7.
> (NOT: 63.7 was the temperature reading at 8 a.m.)

Percentages

447 Express percentages in figures, and spell out the word *percent*. (See ¶¶421–422 for percentages at the beginning of a sentence.)

> They are willing to give us a discount of *15 percent*.
> We have had an *8 percent* increase in sales this year. (NOT: 8-percent.)
> Our terms are *2 percent* 10 days, net 30 days. (These credit terms may be abbreviated as *2/10, n/30* on invoices and other business forms.)

NOTE: The % symbol may be used in tables, on business forms, and in statistical or technical matter.

448 **a.** Fractional percentages *under 1 percent* may be expressed as follows:

> one-half of 1 percent   OR   0.5 percent

NOTE: The cipher before the decimal point in *0.5 percent* prevents misreading the amount as *5 percent*.

b. Fractional percentages *over 1 percent* should be expressed in figures.

> 7½ percent   OR   7.5 percent   9¼ percent   OR   9.25 percent

449 In a range or series of percentages, the word *percent* follows the last figure only. The symbol %, if used, must follow each figure (see ¶447, note).

> Price reductions range from *20 to 50 percent*. (BUT: from 20% to 50%.)
> We give discounts of *10, 20, and 30 percent*. (BUT: 10%, 20%, and 30%:)

▪ See ¶1506 for the use of % in a column of figures.

Ratios and Proportions

450 Always write ratios and proportions in figures.

> a proportion of 5 to 1   OR   a 5-to-1 ratio   OR   a 5:1 ratio
> the odds are 100 to 1   OR   a 100-to-1 shot
> 7 parts benzene to 3 parts water
> a 50-50 chance to recover

Scores and Voting Results

451 Use figures (even for 1 through 10) to express scores and voting results.

> a score of 85 on the test   New York 8, Chicago 6   a vote of 17 to 6

Numbers Referred to as Numbers

452   Always use figures to express numbers referred to as numbers.

> pick a number from 1 to 10   divide by 3
> the number 7 is considered lucky   multiply by ¼

Figures With Abbreviations and Symbols

453   Always use figures with abbreviations and symbols.

> $25   90¢   50%   9 a.m.   6:30 p.m.   No. 985   6 in **or** 6″   50 km (see ¶537)

454   If a symbol is used in a range of numbers, it should be repeated with each number. A full word or an abbreviation used in place of the symbol is given only with the last number.

> 20°–30°C   **but:** 20 to 30 degrees Celsius (see ¶537, note)
> 5½″ x 8″   5½ by 8 inches   **or**   5½ x 8 in
> 9′ x 12′   9 by 12 feet   **or**   9 x 12 ft
> 30%–40%   30 to 40 percent
> 50¢–60¢   50 to 60 cents
> $70–$80   seventy to eighty dollars

note: A symbol should also be repeated when used with a series of numbers.

> discounts of 5%, 10%, and 15%   **but:** discounts of 5, 10, and 15 percent

No. or # With Figures

455   If the term *number* precedes a figure, express it as an abbreviation (singular: *No.;* plural: *Nos.*). At the beginning of a sentence, however, spell out *Number* to prevent misreading.

> Our check covers the following invoices: *Nos.* 8592, 8653, and 8654.
> *Number* 82175 has been assigned to your new policy.

a. If an identifying noun precedes the figure (such as *Invoice, Check, Room, Box,* or the like), the abbreviation *No.* is usually unnecessary.

> Our check covers *Invoices* 8592, 8653, and 8654.
> **exceptions:** License No. HLM 744; Social Security No. 169–35–8142; Patent No. 953,461

b. The symbol # may be used on business forms (such as invoices) and in technical matter.

▪ See ¶359 for the capitalization of nouns preceding figures.

¶¶456–468 deal with two technical aspects of style: treating numbers that are adjacent or in a sequence and expressing numbers in figures, words, or roman numerals.

Adjacent Numbers

456 When two numbers come together in a sentence and both are in figures or both are in words, separate them with a comma.

>In 1975, 440 employees received bonuses.
>Out of *ten, two* were defective.
>On page *31,* 90 cents is incorrectly given as the price.
>On Account *4613,* $18.60 is the amount still due.

NOTE: No comma is necessary when one number is in figures and the other is in words.

>On *March 3 eight* cases of measles were reported.

457 When two numbers come together and one is part of a compound modifier (see ¶817), express one of the numbers in figures and the other in words. As a rule, spell the first number unless the second number would make a significantly shorter word.

| two 8-room houses | **BUT:** 500 four-page leaflets |
| sixty $5 bills | 150 five-dollar bills |

Numbers in a Sequence

458 Use commas to separate numbers that do not represent a continuous sequence.

| on pages 18, 20, and 28 | data for the years 1972, 1976, and 1978 |

459 A hyphen may be used in place of the word *to* to link two figures that represent a continuous sequence. (Do not leave any space before or after the hyphen.)

| on pages 18–28 | in Articles I–III |
| during the week of May 15–21 | during the years 1975–1980 |

Do not use the hyphen if the sequence is introduced by the word *from* or *between*.

| from 1975 to 1980 | between 1977 and 1982 |
| (**NOT:** from 1975–1980) | (**NOT:** between 1977–1982) |

460 In a continuous sequence of figures connected by hyphens, the second figure may be expressed in abbreviated form. This style is used for sequences of page numbers or years only when they occur quite frequently. (In isolated cases, do not abbreviate.)

| 1970–75 (**OR** 1970–1975) | pages 110–12 (**OR** pages 110–112) |
| 1901–2 (**OR** 1901–1902) | pages 101–2 (**OR** pages 101–102) |

a. Do not abbreviate the second number when the first number ends in two zeros.

| 1900–1975 | pages 100–101 |

b. Do not abbreviate the second number when it starts with different digits.

| 1890–1902 | pages 998–1004 |

c. Do not abbreviate the second number when it is under 100.

46–48 A.D.   pages 46–48

Expressing Numbers in Figures

461 **a.** When numbers run to four or more figures, use commas to separate thousands, hundreds of thousands, millions, etc., in whole numbers.

2,375   147,300 $11,275,478   4,300,000,000   BUT: 70,650.37248

NOTE: A growing trend is to omit the comma in four-digit numbers unless these numbers occur together with larger numbers that require commas.

3,500 OR 3500 $2,000 OR $2000

b. In metric quantities use a space (not a comma) to separate digits into groups of three. Separate whole numbers and decimal fractions, counting from the decimal point.

12 945 181 (RATHER THAN 12,945,181)   0.594 31 (RATHER THAN 0.59431)

NOTE: When a four-digit number is used as a metric quantity, do not leave a space unless the number is used in a column with larger numbers.

5181 OR 5 181   0.3725 OR 0.372 5

462 Do not use commas in year numbers, page numbers, house or building numbers, room numbers, ZIP Code numbers, telephone numbers, heat units, and decimal parts of numbers.

1973	8760 Sunset Drive	New York, New York 10021	1500°C
page 1246	Room 1804	(212) 997–2174	13,664.9999

463 Serial numbers (for example, invoice, style, model, or lot numbers) are usually written without commas. However, some serial numbers are written with hyphens, spaces, or other devices. In all cases follow the style of the source.

Invoice 38162   BUT: Social Security No. 152–22–8285
Model G-43348   License No. SO14 785 053
Lot 75/23512   Patent No. 222,341

▪ *See ¶359 for the capitalization of nouns before numbers; see ¶455 for the use of No.*

464 To form the plurals of figures, add *s*.

in the 1970s   temperatures in the 80s

Expressing Numbers in Words

465 When expressing numbers in words, hyphenate all compound numbers between *21* and *99* (or *21st* and *99th*), whether they stand alone or are part of a number over 100.

twenty-one   twenty-one hundred
twenty-first   twenty-one hundredth

(Continued on page 104.)

seven hundred and twenty-five (*and* may be omitted)
five thousand seven hundred and twenty-five (no commas)

Do not hyphenate other words in a spelled-out number over 100.

one hundred	nineteen hundred
two thousand	three hundred thousand
four million	six hundred million
twenty-three billion	fifty-eight trillion

- See ¶362 *for capitalization of hyphenated numbers.*

466 When spelling out round numbers, use the form *twelve hundred* rather than *one thousand two hundred*. (The longer form is rarely used except in formal expressions of dates; see ¶411 for examples.)

467 To form the plurals of spelled-out numbers, add *s* or *es*. (For numbers ending in *y*, change the *y* to *i* before *es*.)

ones	twos	threes	sixes	twenty-fives
thirds	sixths	eighths	twenties	thirty-seconds

- *For spelled-out dates, see* ¶411; *for spelled-out amounts of money, see* ¶420; *for spelled-out fractions, see* ¶427.

Expressing Numbers in Roman Numerals

468 Roman numerals are used chiefly for the important divisions of literary and legislative material, for main topics in outlines, and in dates on public buildings. (For methods of forming roman numerals, consult the table below.)

Chapter X	Part II
Volume I	MCMLXXVII (1977)

NOTE: Pages in the front section of a book (such as the preface and table of contents) are usually numbered in small roman numerals; *iii, iv, v,* etc. Other pages are numbered in arabic numerals: *1, 2, 3,* etc.

1	I	13	XIII	60	LX	900	CM
2	II	14	XIV	70	LXX	1000	M
3	III	15	XV	80	LXXX	1100	MC
4	IV	19	XIX	90	XC	1200	MCC
5	V	20	XX	100	C	1300	MCCC
6	VI	21	XXI	200	CC	1400	MCD
7	VII	24	XXIV	300	CCC	1500	MD
8	VIII	25	XXV	400	CD	1600	MDC
9	IX	29	XXIX	500	D	1700	MDCC
10	X	30	XXX	600	DC	1800	MDCCC
11	XI	40	XL	700	DCC	1900	MCM
12	XII	50	L	800	DCCC	2000	MM

- *Division at the end of a line: see* ¶915.
- *House, street, and ZIP Code numbers: see* ¶¶1332–1333, *1339, 1341b.*

ABBREVIATIONS

BASIC RULES

SPECIAL RULES

Basic Rules

When to Use Abbreviations

501 An abbreviation is a shortened form of a word or phrase used primarily to save space. Abbreviations occur most frequently in technical writing, statistical matter, tables, and footnotes.

502 In business writing, abbreviations are appropriate in "expedient" documents (such as business forms, catalogs, and routine memos and letters between business offices), where the emphasis is on communicating data in the briefest form. In other kinds of business writing, where a more formal style is appropriate, use abbreviations sparingly. When in doubt, spell it out.

a. Some abbreviations are always acceptable, even in the most formal contexts: those that precede or follow personal names (such as *Mr., Ms., Mrs., Jr., Sr., Esq., Ph.D., S.J.*); those that are part of an organization's legal name (such as *Co., Inc., Ltd.*); those used in expressions of time (such as *a.m., p.m., CST, EDT*); and a few miscellaneous expressions (such as *A.D., B.C., R.S.V.P.*).

b. Organizations with long names are now commonly identified by their initials in all but the most formal writing (for example, *IBM, AT&T, AFL-CIO, UNESCO, FBI, CBS*).

c. Days of the week, names of the months, geographical names, and units of measure should be abbreviated only on business forms, in "expedient" correspondence, and in tables and lists where space is tight.

503 Be consistent within the same material: do not abbreviate a term in some sentences and spell it out in other sentences.

NOTE: When using an abbreviation that may not be familiar to the reader, spell out the full term along with the abbreviation when it is first used.

504 Consult a dictionary or an authoritative reference work for the acceptable forms of abbreviations. When a term may be abbreviated in several ways, choose the form that is shortest without sacrifice of clarity.

continued:	Use *cont.* rather than *contd.*
2 pounds:	Use *2 lb* rather than *2 lbs* (see ¶621).
Enclosures 2:	Use *Enc. 2* rather than *Encs. 2* or *Encl. 2.*
second, third:	Use *2d, 3d* rather than *2nd, 3rd* (see also ¶425, note).

NOTE: Having selected one form of an abbreviation (say, *a.m.*), do not use a different style (*A.M.*) elsewhere in the same material.

505 Given a choice between an abbreviation or a contraction, choose the abbreviation. It not only looks better but is easier to type.

cont. (**RATHER THAN:** cont'd)	govt. (**RATHER THAN:** gov't)
dept. (**RATHER THAN:** dep't)	mfg. (**RATHER THAN:** m'f'g)

NOTE: When a word or phrase is shortened by contraction, an apostrophe is inserted at the exact point where letters are omitted and no period follows the contraction except at the end of a sentence. (**EXAMPLES:** *nat'l* for *national; doesn't* for *does not*.) As a rule, contractions are used only in informal writing or in tabular matter where space is limited. However, contractions of verb phrases (such as *can't* and *shouldn't*) are commonly used in business letters where the writer is striving for an easy, colloquial tone. In formal writing, contractions are not used (except for *o'clock*, which is a more formal way to express time than *a.m.* or *p.m.*).

Punctuation and Spacing With Abbreviations

506 The abbreviation of a single word requires a period at the end.

Mr.	Jr.	Dr.	cont.	Nos.
Mon.	Inc.	Co.	mfg.	pp.

NOTE: Units of measurement are now commonly written without periods. (See ¶¶535*a*, 538*a*.)

507 Small-letter abbreviations made up of single initials require a period after each initial but no space after each internal period.

a.m.   e.g.   f.o.b.   a.k.a.   **BUT:** rpm, ips (see ¶535*a*)

508 All-capital abbreviations made up of single initials normally require no periods and no internal space.

RCA	ASME	FTC	NBC	IQ
UAW	BPOE	HEW	WEEI	FM

EXCEPTIONS: Retain the periods in abbreviations of geographical names (such as *U.S.A., U.S.S.R.*), academic degrees (such as *B.A., M.S.*), and a few miscellaneous expressions (such as *A.D., B.C., P.O., R.S.V.P.,* and *V.P.*).

509 If an abbreviation stands for two or more words and consists of more than single initials, insert a period and a space after each element in the abbreviation.

N. Dak.   Maj. Gen.   Lt. Gov.   op. cit.   nol. pros.

EXCEPTIONS: Academic abbreviations such as *Ph.D., Ed.D., LL.B.,* and *Litt.D.,* are written with periods but no spaces. Units of measurement such as *sq ft* and *cu cm* are written with spaces but no periods.

510 A number of shortened forms of words are not abbreviations and should not be followed by periods.

memo	ad	photo	info	before the 3d
stereo	auto	co-op	math	on the 14th

511 *One space* should follow an abbreviation within a sentence unless another mark of punctuation follows immediately.

Dr. Wilkins works in Washington, D.C., but his home is in Bethesda.

Please call tomorrow afternoon (before 5:30 p.m.).

Get PRV's approval before you send the letter. (See ¶¶638–639 for possessive forms of abbreviations.)

512 *Two spaces* should follow an abbreviation at the end of a statement.

> The vase dates back to 400 B.C.   (The period that marks the end of the abbreviation also marks the end of the sentence.)

513 *No space* should follow an abbreviation at the end of a question or an exclamation.

> Can you see me tomorrow at 10:30 a.m.?

Capitalization and Hyphenation

514 Abbreviations usually follow the capitalization and hyphenation of the full words for which they stand.

Mon.	Monday	a.m.	ante meridiem
ft-lb	foot-pound	D.C.	District of Columbia

EXCEPTIONS: PTA   Parent-Teacher's Association   A.D.   anno Domini

NOTE: For abbreviations with two forms (*COD* or *c.o.d.*), see ¶542.

The following rules (¶¶515–547) offer guidance on specific types of abbreviations.

Special Rules

Personal Names and Initials

515 Use periods with abbreviations of first or middle names but not with nicknames.

Thos.	Jas.	Jos.	Wm.	Robt.	Saml.	Benj.	Edw.
Tom	Jim	Joe	Bill	Bob	Sam	Ben	Ed

Note: Do not abbreviate first or middle names except (1) in a list where space is tight or (2) in a context where it is necessary to give a person's name exactly as he or she signs it. (See also ¶1322, note.)

516 **a.** Initials in a person's name should each be followed by a period and one space.

> John T. Noonan   Mr. L. Bradford Anders
> J. T. Noonan & Co.   L. B. Anders Inc. (see also ¶159)

b. When personal initials stand alone, type them preferably without periods or space. If periods are used, omit the internal space.

> JTN   **OR**   J.T.N.

c. For names with prefixes, initials are formed as follows:

> JDM (for John D. MacDonald)   FGO (for Frances G. O'Brien)

d. Do not use a period when the initial is only a letter used in place of a real name. (See also ¶109a.)

I have selected three case studies involving a Ms. A, a Mr. B, and a Miss C. (Letters used in place of real names.)

BUT: Call Mrs. G. when you get a chance. (Here G. is an initial representing an actual name like *Galanos*.)

Abbreviations With Personal Names

517 **a.** Always abbreviate the following titles when they are used with personal names: *Dr., Mr., Messrs.* (plural of *Mr.* and pronounced *messers*), *Mrs., Mme.* (short for *Madame*), *Ms.* (pronounced *mizz*), and *Mses.* or *Mss.* (plural form of *Ms.*). The plural of *Mme.* may either be spelled out (*Mesdames*, pronounced *may-dáhm*) or abbreviated (*Mmes.*). The titles *Miss* and *Misses* are not abbreviations and should not be followed with periods.

> *Ms.* Thelma Sandford has been promoted to senior programmer.

> *Dr.* Galloway will be staying with *Mr. and Mrs.* Sachs. (See ¶519*b* for the use of *Dr.* with degrees.)

NOTE: The abbreviation *Ms.* is used (1) when a woman has indicated that she prefers this title, (2) when a woman's marital status is unknown, or (3) when a woman's marital status is considered not relevant to the situation. (See also ¶¶618, 1322*b*, 1366*a*.)

b. In general, spell out all other titles used with personal names.

> Professor Joan Pulaski   Governor Byrne
> President William McGill   Senator Fong

c. Long military, religious, and honorable titles are spelled out in formal correspondence but may be abbreviated in informal correspondence.

> **Formal**   **Informal**
> Major General George O. Young   Maj. Gen. George O. Young
> Lieutenant Commander Sylvia Heller   Lt. Comdr. Sylvia Heller

NOTE: Spell out *Rev.* and *Hon.* when preceded by *the.*

> **Formal**   **Informal**
> *the Reverend* Henry B. Niles   Rev. Henry B. Niles
> *the Honorable* Bella Abzug   Hon. Bella Abzug

- *See ¶¶1322–1323 for the treatment of titles in addresses; ¶¶1347–1350 for the treatment of titles in salutations.*

518 Always abbreviate *Jr., Sr.,* and *Esq.* when they follow personal names. The terms *2d* or *II* and *3d* or *III* are not abbreviations and should not be used with periods.

a. The forms *Jr.* and *Sr.* should be used only with a full name, not with a surname alone. A title like *Mr.* or *Dr.* may precede the name.

> Mr. Warren B. Kelly Jr.   **NOT:** Mr. Kelly Jr.

- *See ¶156 for the use or omission of commas with Jr. and Sr.*

b. The form *Esq.* should also be used only with a full name, but no title should precede the name.

> George W. LaBarr, *Esq.*   **NOT:** *Mr.* George W. LaBarr, Esq.

Academic Degrees and Religious Orders

519 Abbreviations of academic degrees and religious orders require a period after each *element* in the abbreviation but no internal space.

B.A.	Ph.D.	LL.B.	B.Ch.E.	M.D.	S.J.
M.S.	Ed.D.	Litt.D.	B.Arch.	D.D.S.	O.S.B.

a. Write *CPA* without periods when it is used alone but with periods when it is used together with other academic degrees.

Joseph Fortunato, CPA   **BUT:** Joseph Fortunato, B.S., M.B.A., *C.P.A.*

b. When academic degrees follow a person's name, do not use such titles as *Dr., Mr., Ms., Miss,* or *Mrs.* before the name.

Dr. Helen Garcia   **OR**   Helen Garcia, M.D. (**BUT NOT:** Dr. Helen Garcia, *M.D.*)

However, other titles may precede the name as long as they do not convey the same meaning as the degree that follows.

Professor George Perrier, Ph.D.   the Reverend John Day, *D.D.*
President Grace Dillard, L.H.D.   **OR:** the Reverend *Dr.* John Day
Dean Marion Konopka, J.S.D.   (**BUT NOT:** the Reverend *Dr.* John Day, *D.D.*)

▪ *See also* ¶¶1324c, 1324d, 1364a.

c. Academic degrees standing alone may be abbreviated except in very formal writing.

I am now completing my *Ph.D.* thesis.
She received her *M.A.* degree last year.
OR . . . her *master of arts* degree last year. (See also ¶353.)

Names of Organizations

520 Names of well-known business organizations, labor unions, societies, and associations (trade, professional, charitable, and fraternal) are often abbreviated (except in the most formal writing). When these abbreviations consist of all-capital initials, they are typed without periods or spaces.

IBM	International Business Machines
AT&T	American Telephone & Telegraph
AFL-CIO	American Federation of Labor and Congress of Industrial Organizations
ILGWU	International Ladies' Garment Workers' Union
NAACP	National Association for the Advancement of Colored People
AMS	Administrative Management Society
ASCAP	American Society of Composers, Authors, and Publishers
NAM	National Association of Manufacturers
CED	Committee for Economic Development
YMCA	Young Men's Christian Association
IOOF	Independent Order of Odd Fellows

521 The following terms are often abbreviated in the names of business organizations. However, follow the individual company's preference for abbreviating or spelling out.

Mfg.	Manufacturing	Co.	Company	Inc.	Incorporated
Mfrs.	Manufacturers	Corp.	Corporation	Ltd.	Limited

Bro.	Brother	Cie	Company (from the French *Compagnie*)
Bros.	Brothers	N.V.	Limited (from the Dutch *Naamloze Vennootschap*)

Acronyms

522 An acronym—for example, COBOL—is a shortened form derived from the initial letters of the words that make up the complete form. Thus *COBOL* is derived from <u>CO</u>mmon <u>B</u>usiness-<u>O</u>riented <u>L</u>anguage. Like all-capital abbreviations such as *IBM* and *NAM*, acronyms are usually written in all capitals and without periods; however, unlike those abbreviations, which are pronounced letter by letter, acronyms are pronounced like words. Because they have been deliberately coined to replace the longer expressions they represent, acronyms are appropriate for use on all occasions.

NOW	National Organization for Women
UNESCO	United Nations Educational, Scientific, and Cultural Organization
PERT	program evaluation and review technique
ZIP (Code)	Zone Improvement Plan
PUSH	People United to Save Humanity
SALT	strategic arms limitation talks

NOTE: Some coined names use more than the first letters of the words they represent. Such names are usually written with only the first letter capitalized.

Nabisco	Aramco	Amtrak

Names of Broadcasting Stations and Systems

523 The names of radio and television broadcasting stations and the abbreviated names of broadcasting systems are written in capitals without periods and without spaces.

Station KFRC	Station WPIX-Channel 11
Station WQXR-FM	Station WCBS-TV
ABC reporters	NBC officials

Names of Government and International Agencies

524 The names of well-known government and international agencies are often abbreviated. They are written without periods or spaces.

FCC	Federal Communications Commission	SEC	Securities and Exchange Commission
UN	United Nations	ITO	International Trade Organization

525 The name *United States* is usually abbreviated when it is part of the name of a government agency. When used as an adjective, the name is often abbreviated, though not in formal usage. When used as a noun, the name is always spelled out.

(*Continued on page 112.*)

U.S. Office of Education   OR   USOE
U.S. Department of Agriculture   USDA
U.S. Air Force   USAF
the United States government   the U.S. government
United States foreign policy   U.S. foreign policy

throughout the United States (NOT: throughout the U.S.)

Geographical Names

526 Do not abbreviate geographical names except in tables, business forms, and "expedient" correspondence (see ¶502). EXCEPTION: *U.S.S.R.* is often used in place of the full name, *Union of Soviet Socialist Republics.*

527 When abbreviating state names in addresses, use the two-letter abbreviations (without periods) shown in ¶1341. In all other situations, use the following abbreviations (with periods and spacing as shown).

Alabama	Ala.	Missouri	Mo.
Alaska	—	Montana	Mont.
Arizona	Ariz.	Nebraska	Nebr.
Arkansas	Ark.	Nevada	Nev.
California	Calif.	New Hampshire	N.H.
Canal Zone	C.Z.	New Jersey	N.J.
Colorado	Colo.	New Mexico	N. Mex.
Connecticut	Conn.	New York	N.Y.
Delaware	Del.	North Carolina	N.C.
District of		North Dakota	N. Dak.
Columbia	D.C.	Ohio	—
Florida	Fla.	Oklahoma	Okla.
Georgia	Ga.	Oregon	Oreg.
Guam	—	Pennsylvania	Pa.
Hawaii	—	Puerto Rico	P.R.
Idaho	—	Rhode Island	R.I.
Illinois	Ill.	South Carolina	S.C.
Indiana	Ind.	South Dakota	S. Dak.
Iowa	—	Tennessee	Tenn.
Kansas	Kans.	Texas	Tex.
Kentucky	Ky.	Utah	—
Louisiana	La.	Vermont	Vt.
Maine	—	Virgin Islands	V.I.
Maryland	Md.	Virginia	Va.
Massachusetts	Mass.	Washington	Wash.
Michigan	Mich.	West Virginia	W. Va.
Minnesota	Minn.	Wisconsin	Wis.
Mississippi	Miss.	Wyoming	Wyo.

NOTE: Alaska, Guam, Hawaii, Idaho, Iowa, Maine, Ohio, and Utah are not abbreviated.

▪ *See ¶¶1334–1337, 1340–1341, 1343–1344 for the abbreviation or the spelling out of names of streets, cities, states, and countries.*

528 Geographical abbreviations made up of single initials require a period after each initial but *no* space after each internal period.

U.S.A.   U.S.S.R.   U.A.R.   S.A.   B.W.I.

If the geographical abbreviation contains more than single initials, space once after each internal period.

N. Mex.   N. Dak.   W. Va.   W. Aust.

Compass Points

529 Spell out compass points included in street names; for example, *East 123*

The company has large landholdings in the *Southwest*.
We purchased a lot at the *southwest* corner of Green and Union Streets.

- See ¶¶338–341 *for the capitalization of compass points.*

530 Spell out compass points included in street names; for example, *East 123 Street.* (See also ¶1334.) However, abbreviate compass points (with periods but no internal space) when they are used *following* a street name to indicate the section of the city.

1895 North 179 Street, N.W.

531 In technical material (real estate, legal, nautical), abbreviate compass points but omit the periods.

S   south   SW   southwest   SSW   south-southwest

Days and Months

532 Do not abbreviate names of days of the week and months of the year except in tables or lists where space is limited. In such cases the following abbreviations may be used:

Sun.	Thurs., Thu.	Jan.	May	Sept., Sep.
Mon.	Fri.	Feb.	June, Jun.	Oct.
Tues., Tue.	Sat.	Mar.	July, Jul.	Nov.
Wed.		Apr.	Aug.	Dec.

NOTE: When space is extremely tight, the following one- and two-letter abbreviations may be used.

Su M Tu W Th F Sa   Ja F Mr Ap My Je
                                Jl Au S O N D

Time and Time Zones

533 Use the abbreviations *a.m.* and *p.m.* in expressions of time (see ¶440). Small letters are preferred for these abbreviations. For more formal expressions of time, use *o'clock* (see ¶441).

534 The standard time zones are abbreviated as follows: EST, CST, MST, and PST. When daylight saving prevails, the following forms are used:

DST (daylight saving time)   **OR**   EDT (Eastern daylight time)
                                      CDT (Central daylight time)
                                      MDT (Mountain daylight time)
                                      PDT (Pacific daylight time)

- See ¶440a *for examples.*

Customary Measurements

535   Abbreviate units of measure when they occur frequently, as in technical and scientific work, on invoices and other business forms, and in tables.

a. Units of measure are now commonly abbreviated without periods.

yd (yard, yards)	rpm (revolutions per minute)
oz (ounce, ounces)	ips (inches per second)
gal (gallon, gallons)	mpg (miles per gallon)
lb (pound, pounds)	mph (miles per hour)

NOTE: Even the abbreviation *in* (for inch or inches) may be written without a period so long as it is not likely to be confused with the preposition *in*.

8 in   **OR**   8 in.   **BUT:** 8 sq in   8 ft 2 in

b. In a range of numbers, an abbreviation is given only with the last number; a symbol is repeated with each number. (See also ¶454.)

a room 10 ft 6 in x 19 ft 10 in   35° to 45°F
OR: a room 10′ 6″ x 19′ 10″ (see ¶432)   **OR:** 35°–45°F

536   In nontechnical writing, spell out units of measure.

a 20-gallon container	a 20-degree drop in temperature
a 150-acre estate	8½ by 11 inches
14 yards of cotton	an 8½- by 11-inch book (see ¶817)

Metric Measurements

The following rules of style are based on the *Metric Editorial Guide,* published in January 1978 by the American National Metric Council (Washington, D.C.). For a full listing of metric terms and for the proper pronunciation of these terms, consult a dictionary.

537   The most common metric measurements are derived from three basic units and several prefixes indicating multiples or fractions of a unit, as shown below. The abbreviations for these terms are given in parentheses.

Basic Units

meter	(m)	One meter is 10 percent longer than a yard (39.37 inches).
gram	(g)	A thousand grams (a *kilogram*) is 10 percent heavier than 2 pounds (2.2 pounds).
liter	(L)	A liter is about 5 percent bigger than a quart (1.057 quarts).

Prefixes Indicating Fractions*

deci	(d)	1/10	A *decimeter* (dm) equals 1/10 meter.
centi	(c)	1/100	A *centigram* (cg) equals 1/100 gram.
milli	(m)	1/1000	A *milliliter* (mL) equals 1/1000 liter.

Prefixes Indicating Multiples*

deka	(da)	10	A *dekameter* (dam) equals 10 meters (about 11 yards).
hecto	(h)	100	A *hectogram* (hg) equals 100 grams (about 3½ ounces).
kilo	(k)	1000	A *kilometer* (km) equals 1000 meters (about 5/8 mile).

*Accent the first syllable of every prefix. For example, *kilometer* is pronounced *kill*-oh-meter (**NOT** kil-*lom*-eter).

NOTE: Temperatures are expressed in terms of degrees on the Celsius scale (abbreviated *C*).

Water freezes at 0°C (32°F) and boils at 100°C (212°F).
With a temperature of 37°C (98.6°F), you can't be very sick.

The temperature here on the island stays between 20° and 30°C (68° and 86°F). (See also ¶535*a*, note.)

▪ *See ¶461b for the use of spaces in figures expressing metric quantities.*

538 Metric units of measurement, like the customary units of measurement described in ¶535, are abbreviated in technical and scientific work, on business forms, and in tables. In nontechnical writing, metric units are ordinarily spelled out, but some expressions are abbreviated (for example, *35-mm film*).

a. Abbreviations of metric units of measurement are written without periods except at the end of a sentence.

100-mm cigarettes (10 centimeters or about 4 inches)
a 30-cm width (about 12 inches or 1 foot)
a 1000-km trip (620 miles)
weighs 100 kg (about 220 pounds)
50 to 75 kg (about 110 to 165 pounds)
feels like 10°C weather (50°F weather)

NOTE: In abbreviations of expressions like *kilometers per hour,* a diagonal is used to express *per*.

an 80 km/h speed limit (50 miles per hour)

b. Metric abbreviations are the same for the singular and the plural.

1 kg (1 kilogram)   5 kg (5 kilograms)

c. When expressing temperatures, leave no space between the number and the degree symbol or between the degree symbol and the abbreviation for Celsius.

14°C   (NOT: 14° C)

d. In printed material, metric measurements for area and volume are usually expressed with raised numbers.

m^2 square meter cm^3 cubic centimeter

In typewritten material, these measurements may be expressed as shown above or in another form (to avoid typing raised numbers).

sq m   square meter   cu cm   cubic centimeter

NOTE: The forms *sq m* and *cu cm* are also recommended in typewritten material which uses raised numbers for footnote references.

Chemical and Mathematical Expressions

539 Do not use a period after the symbols that represent chemical elements and formulas.

K (potassium) H_2O (water)   NaCl (sodium chloride—table salt)

540 Do not use a period after such mathematical abbreviations as *log* (for *logarithm*) and *tan* (for *tangent*).

Business Expressions

541 A number of terms are commonly abbreviated on business forms, in tables, and in routine business correspondence.

@	at	ft.	foot, feet
acct.	account	ft-tn	foot-ton(s)
addl.	additional	fwd.	forward
a.k.a.	also known as	FYI	for your information
amt.	amount	g	gram(s)
ASAP	as soon as possible	gal	gallon(s)
astd.	assorted	gr.	gross
Attn.	Attention	gr. wt.	gross weight
avg.	average	hdlg.	handling
bal.	balance	hdqrs.	headquarters
bbl	barrel(s)	hr.	hour(s)
bl	bale(s)	in OR in.	inch(es) (see ¶535a, note)
B/L	bill of lading	Inc.	Incorporated
bldg.	building	ins.	insurance
B/S	bill of sale	inv.	invoice
bu	bushel(s)	ips	inches per second
C	100; Celsius (temperature)	kg	kilogram(s)
cg.	centigram(s)	km	kilometer(s)
chg.	charge	km/h	kilometers per hour
c.i.f. OR	cost, insurance, and	L	liter(s) (see ¶538c)
CIF	freight (see ¶542)	l., ll.	line, lines
cm	centimeter(s)	lb	pound(s)
Co.	Company	l.c.l. OR	less-than-carload lot
c/o	care of	LCL	(see ¶542)
c.o.d. OR	cash (or collect) on	Ltd.	Limited
COD	delivery (see ¶542)	m	meter(s)
cont.	continued	M	1,000
Corp.	Corporation	max.	maximum
cr.	credit	mdse.	merchandise
ctg.	cartage	mfg.	manufacturing
ctn.	carton	mg	milligram(s)
cwt.	hundredweight	mgr.	manager
dept.	department	min	minute(s)
dis.	discount	min.	minimum
distr.	distributor, distribution,	misc.	miscellaneous
	distributed	mL	milliliter(s)
div.	division	mm	milligram(s)
doz	dozen	mo	month(s)
dr.	debit	MO	mail order, money order
dstn.	destination	mph	miles per hour
dtd.	dated	n/30	net in 30 days
ea.	each	NA	not applicable, not available
e.o.m. OR	end of month (see ¶542)	No.	number (see ¶455)
EOM		nt. wt.	net weight
Esq.	Esquire	opt.	optional
ETA	estimated time of arrival	OS	out of stock
F	Fahrenheit (temperature)	oz	ounce(s)
f.a.s. OR	free alongside ship	p., pp.	page, pages
FAS	(see ¶542)	pd.	paid
f.o.b. OR	free on board (see ¶542)	pkg.	package(s)
FOB		PO	purchase order

P.O.	post office	reg.	registered
p.o.e. **OR** POE	port of entry (see ¶542)	req.	requisition
		rm	ream(s)
PP	parcel post	rpm	revolutions per minute
ppd.	postpaid, prepaid (postage paid in advance)	/S/	signed (before a copied signature)
pr.	pair(s)	shtg.	shortage
PS, PS.	postscript	SO	shipping order
pstg.	postage	std.	standard
pt	pint(s)	stge.	storage
pt.	part, point(s), port	stmt.	statement
		V.P.	vice president
qr	quire(s)	wt.	weight
qt	quart(s)	yd	yard(s)
qtr.	quarter(ly)	yr	year(s)
qty.	quantity	#	number (before a figure); pounds (after a figure)
recd.	received		

542 A few common business abbreviations listed in ¶541 above are often typed in small letters (with periods) when they occur within sentences but are typed in all-capital letters (without periods) when they appear on invoices or other business forms.

c.i.f.	**OR**	CIF	e.o.m.	**OR**	EOM	l.c.l.	**OR**	LCL
c.o.d.	**OR**	COD	f.o.b.	**OR**	FOB	p.o.e.	**OR**	POE

Foreign Expressions

543 Many foreign expressions contain short words, some of which are abbreviations and some of which are not. Use periods only with abbreviations.

ad hoc	(meaning "for a particular purpose")
ad val.	(*ad valorem,* meaning "according to the value")
c. **OR** ca.	(*circa,* meaning "approximately")
cf.	(*confer,* meaning "compare")
e.g.	(*exempli gratia,* meaning "for example")
et al.	(*et alii,* meaning "and other people")
etc.	(*et cetera,* meaning "and other things," "and so forth")
ibid.	(*ibidem,* meaning "in the same place")
idem	(meaning "the same")
i.e.	(*id est,* meaning "that is")
infra	(meaning "below")
loc. cit.	(*loco citato,* meaning "in the place cited")
N.B.	(*nota bene,* meaning "note well")
nol. pros.	(*nolle prosequi,* meaning "to be unwilling to prosecute")
non seq.	(*non sequitur,* meaning "it does not follow")
op. cit.	(*opere citato,* meaning "in the work cited")
pro tem.	(*pro tempore,* meaning "for the time being")
prox.	(*proximo,* meaning "in the next month")
Q.E.D.	(*quod erat demonstrandum,* meaning "which was to be demonstrated")
q.v.	(*quod vide,* meaning "which see")
re **OR** in re	(meaning "in the matter of," "concerning")
R.S.V.P.	(*Répondez s'il vous plaît,* meaning "please reply")
supra	(meaning "above")
ult.	(*ultimo,* meaning "in the last month")
viz.	(*videlicet,* meaning "namely")

Miscellaneous Expressions

544 The following list of expressions presents common abbreviations acceptable in general (but not formal) usage.

AV	audiovisual	a list of AV materials
ESP	extrasensory perception	their sales manager must have ESP
FIFO	first in, first out	the FIFO system of cost accounting
GNP	gross national product	the GNP for the fourth quarter
ID	identification data	show your ID card
IQ	intelligence quotient	take an IQ test
LIFO	last in, first out	use the LIFO method for costs
PA	public address	a problem with our PA system
PERT	program evaluation and review technique	draw up a PERT chart
P.O.	post office	send it to P.O. Box 315
PR	public relations	need to work on your PR campaign
R&D	research and development	need a bigger R&D budget
SRO	standing room only	an SRO audience at our presentation
TLC	tender, loving care	give this customer some TLC
TV	television	watch for it on TV
UFO	unidentified flying object	took off like a UFO
VIP	very important person	treat these dealers like VIPs

545 Do not use periods with capitalized letters that are not abbreviations.

IOU	Brand X	SOS
T-shirt	I beam	X ray

546 The abbreviation *OK* is written without periods. In sentences, the forms *okay, okayed,* and *okaying* look better than *OK, OK'd,* and *OK'ing,* but the latter forms can be used.

547 The dictionary recognizes *x* as a verb; however, *cross out, crossed out,* and *crossing out* look better than *x out, x-ed out,* and *x-ing out.*

- *Plurals of abbreviations: see ¶¶620–624.*
- *Possessives of abbreviations: see ¶¶638–649.*

6 PLURALS AND POSSESSIVES

FORMING PLURALS

FORMING POSSESSIVES

Forming Plurals

When you are uncertain about the plural form of a word, consult the dictionary. If no plural is shown, form the plural according to the rules in ¶¶601–605.

Basic Rule

601 Plurals are regularly formed by adding s to the singular form.

park	parks	employee	employees
price	prices	taxi	taxis
area	areas	menu	menus

Nouns Ending in *S, X, CH, SH,* or *Z*

602 When the singular form ends in s, x, ch, sh, or z, the plural is formed by adding *es* to the singular.

lens	lenses	church	churches
business	businesses	crash	crashes
annex	annexes	quartz	quartzes

603 Singular nouns ending in silent s do not change their forms in the plural.

| one corps | two corps | one chassis | two chassis |

Nouns Ending in *Y*

604 When a singular noun ends in y preceded by a *consonant*, the plural is formed by changing the y to i and adding *es* to the singular.

| company | companies | category | categories |
| vacancy | vacancies | authority | authorities |

605 When a singular noun ends in y preceded by a *vowel*, the plural is formed by adding s to the singular.

| attorney | attorneys | EXCEPTION: soliloquy | soliloquies |

Nouns Ending in *O*

606 Singular nouns ending in o preceded by a *vowel* form their plurals by adding s to the singular.

| studio | studios | duo | duos |
| cameo | cameos | tattoo | tattoos |

607 Singular nouns ending in o preceded by a *consonant* form their plurals differently.

a. Some nouns in this category simply add s.

| piano | pianos | memo | memos |

b. Some add es.

| potato | potatoes | hero | heroes |

c. Some have two plural forms. (The preferred form is given first.)

cargo	cargoes, cargos	zero	zeros, zeroes

- See ¶614 for foreign nouns ending in o.

Nouns Ending in *F*, *FE*, or *FF*

608 **a.** Most singular nouns that end in *f*, *fe*, or *ff* form their plurals by adding *s* to the singular form.

brief	briefs	safe	safes
proof	proofs	tariff	tariffs

b. Some commonly used nouns in this category form their plurals by changing the *f* or *fe* to *ve* and adding *s*.

half	halves	shelf	shelves
wife	wives	knife	knives
leaf	leaves	life	lives

c. A few of these nouns have two plural forms. (The preferred form is given first.)

scarf	scarves, scarfs	dwarf	dwarfs, dwarves

Nouns With Irregular Plurals

609 The plurals of some nouns are formed by a change of letters within.

woman	women	foot	feet
mouse	mice	goose	geese

610 A few plurals end in *en*.

ox	oxen	child	children
brother	brethren (*an alternative plural to* brothers)		

Compound Nouns

611 When a compound noun is a *solid* word, pluralize the final element in the compound as if it stood alone.

courthouse	courthouses	step*child*	step*children*
hat*box*	hat*boxes*	fore*foot*	fore*feet*
straw*berry*	straw*berries*	tooth*brush*	tooth*brushes*
book*shelf*	book*shelves*	mouse*trap*	mouse*traps*

EXCEPTION: passerby   passersby

612 The plurals of *hyphenated* or *spaced* compounds are formed by pluralizing the chief element of the compound.

brother-in-law	brothers-in-law	*bill* of lading	*bills* of lading
senator-elect	senators-elect	*editor* in chief	*editors* in chief
looker-on	lookers-on	*runner*-up	*runners*-up

account receivable	*accounts* receivable
deputy *chief* of staff	deputy *chiefs* of staff
brigadier *general*	brigadier *generals*

(Continued on page 122.)

a. When a hyphenated compound does not contain a noun as one of its elements, simply pluralize the final element.

go-*between*	go-*betweens*	tie-*in*	tie-*ins*
write-*up*	write-*ups*	hand-me-*down*	hand-me-*downs*
also-*ran*	also-*rans*	get-*together*	get-*togethers*

b. Some of these compounds have two recognized plural forms. (The first plural form shown below is preferred because it adds the plural sign to the chief element of the compound.)

court-martial	*courts*-martial, court-*martials*
notary public	*notaries* public, notary *publics*
attorney general	*attorneys* general, attorney *generals*

613 The plurals of compounds ending in *ful* are formed by adding *s*.

armful	armfuls	handful	handfuls
cupful	cupfuls	teaspoonful	teaspoonfuls

Compare the difference in meaning in these phrases:

six *cupfuls* of sugar (a quantity of sugar that would fill one cup six times)
six *cups full* of sugar (six separate cups, each filled with sugar)

Foreign Nouns

614 Many nouns of foreign origin retain their foreign plurals, others have been given English plurals, and still others have two plurals—an English and a foreign one. When two plural forms exist, one may be preferred to the other or there may be differences in meaning that govern the use of each. Consult your dictionary to be sure of the plural forms and the meanings attached to them.

- See ¶1018 for agreement of foreign-plural subjects with verbs.

WORDS ENDING IN *US*

Singular	**English Plural**	**Foreign Plural**
alumnus		alumni
campus	campuses	
census	censuses	
nucleus	nucleuses	nuclei*
prospectus	prospectuses	
radius	radiuses	radii*
status	statuses	
stimulus		stimuli
stylus	styluses	styli*
syllabus	syllabuses	syllabi*

WORDS ENDING IN *A*

Singular	**English Plural**	**Foreign Plural**
agenda	agendas	
alumna		alumnae
antenna	antennas (of radios)	antennae (of insects)
formula	formulas*	formulae
minutia		minutiae

*Preferred form.

WORDS ENDING IN *UM*

Singular	English Plural	Foreign Plural
addendum		addenda
bacterium		bacteria
curriculum	curriculums	curricula*
datum	datums	data* (see ¶1018)
erratum		errata
medium	mediums	media (for advertising and communication)
memorandum	memorandums*	memoranda

WORDS ENDING IN *IX* OR *EX*

Singular	English Plural	Foreign Plural
appendix	appendixes*	appendices
index	indexes (of books)	indices (math symbols)
matrix	matrixes	matrices*

WORDS ENDING IN *IS*

Singular	English Plural	Foreign Plural
analysis		analyses
axis		axes
basis		bases
crisis		crises
diagnosis		diagnoses
hypothesis		hypotheses
parenthesis		parentheses
synopsis		synopses
synthesis		syntheses
thesis		theses

WORDS ENDING IN *O*

Singular	English Plural	Foreign Plural
graffito		graffiti
libretto	librettos*	libretti
virtuoso	virtuosos*	virtuosi

WORDS ENDING IN *ON*

Singular	English Plural	Foreign Plural
criterion	criterions	criteria*
phenomenon	phenomenons	phenomena*

WORDS ENDING IN *EAU*

Singular	English Plural	Foreign Plural
bureau	bureaus*	bureaux
plateau	plateaus*	plateaux
trousseau	trousseaus	trousseaux*

NOTE: The x ending for these foreign plurals is pronounced like z.

*Preferred form.

Proper Names

615 **a.** Most *surnames* are pluralized by the addition of s.

Mr. and Mrs. Brinton	the Brintons
Mr. and Mrs. Romano	the Romanos

(Continued on page 124.)

b. When a surname ends in s, x, *ch*, *sh*, or z, add *es* to form the plural.

Mr. and Mrs. Banks	the Bankses
Mr. and Mrs. Van Ness	the Van Nesses
Mr. and Mrs. Maddox	the Maddoxes
Mr. and Mrs. March	the Marches
Mr. and Mrs. Welsh	the Welshes
Mr. and Mrs. Katz	the Katzes
Mr. and Mrs. Jones	the Joneses
Mr. and Mrs. James	the Jameses
Mr. and Mrs. Barnes	the Barneses

NOTE: If the addition of *es* would make the plural surname awkward to pronounce, omit the *es*.

the Hodges (NOT: Hodgeses)   the Hastings (NOT: Hastingses)

c. Never change the original spelling of a surname when forming the plural. Simply add s or *es*, according to *a* and *b* above.

Mr. and Mrs. McCarthy	the McCarthys (NOT: McCarthies)
Mr. and Mrs. Wolf	the Wolfs (NOT: Wolves)
Mr. and Mrs. Martino	the Martinos (NOT: Martinoes)
Mr. and Mrs. Goodman	the Goodmans (NOT: Goodmen)

d. When a surname is followed by *Jr.*, *Sr.*, or a number like *2d* or *II*, the plural can be formed two ways:

ORDINARY USAGE: the Roy Van Allen *Jrs.*   the Ellsworth Hadley *3ds*
FORMAL USAGE: the Roy Van *Allens* Jr.   the Ellsworth *Hadleys* 3d

616 To form the plurals of *first names*, add s or *es* but do not change the original spellings.

Marie	Maries	Mary	Marys
Thomas	Thomases	Max	Maxes
Charles	Charleses	Otto	Ottos

617 To form the plural of other proper names, add s or *es* but do not change the original spelling.

the Russians	the Dakotas
Marches	the two Kansas Citys (NOT: Cities)

EXCEPTIONS:
the Alleghenies (for Allegheny Mountains)
the Rockies (for Rocky Mountains)

Personal Titles

618 The plural of *Mr.* is *Messrs.*; the plural of *Ms.* is *Mses.* or *Mss.*; the plural of *Mrs.* or *Mme.* is *Mmes.*; the plural of *Miss* is *Misses* (no period follows).

Messrs. Strehle and Vlasek have been appointed to the Finance Committee.
Mmes. DeGrasse and Hansen will handle all the arrangements for the luncheon.
Misses Eleanor Rustin and Frances Mendoza will arrange for transportation.

NOTE: If the use of plural titles seems too formal or stilted for the situation, simply retain the singular form and repeat it with each name.

Ms. Jane Covello and Ms. Angela Byrd will handle publicity.

619 When personal titles apply to two or more people with the same surname, the plural may be formed in two ways: (*a*) pluralize only the title (formal usage); (*b*) pluralize only the surname (ordinary usage).

Formal Usage	**Ordinary Usage**
the Messrs. Thomas	the Mr. Thomases
the Mmes. (**or** Mesdames) Bergeret	the Mrs. Bergerets
the Misses Corby	the Miss Corbys
the Mses. (**or** Mss.) Hathaway	the Ms. Hathaways

Abbreviations, Letters, Numbers, and Words

620 The plurals of most abbreviations are formed by adding *s* to the singular.

dept.	depts.	No.	Nos.
vol.	vols.	Dr.	Drs.
engr.	engrs.	Bro.	Bros.

621 **a.** The abbreviations of many customary units of weight and measure, however, are the same in both the singular and plural.

oz (ounce **or** ounces)	ft (foot **or** feet)
deg (degree **or** degrees)	in (inch **or** inches)
bbl (barrel **or** barrels)	mi (mile **or** miles)

NOTE: For a number of these abbreviations, two plural forms have been widely used: for example, *lb* or *lbs* (meaning "pounds"), *yd* or *yds* (meaning "yards"), *qt* or *qts* (meaning "quarts"). However, the trend is toward using *lb, yd,* and *qt* to signify the plural.

b. The abbreviations of metric units of weight and measure are the same in both the singular and plural. (See also ¶¶537–538.)

km (kilometer **or** kilometers)	cg (centigram **or** centigrams)
mL (milliliter **or** milliliters)	dam (dekameter **or** dekameters)

622 The plurals of a few single-letter abbreviations (such as *p.* for *page* and *f.* for *the following page*) consist of the same letter doubled.

p. 39 (page 39)
pp. 39–43 (pages 39 through 43)
pp. 12 f. (page 12 and the following page)
pp. 12 ff. (page 12 and the following pages)

623 Capital letters and abbreviations ending with capital letters are pluralized by adding *s* alone.

four Cs	IQs	PTAs	M.D.s	three Rs	YWCAs	Ph.D.s

NOTE: Some authorities still sanction the use of an apostrophe before the *s* (for example, *four C's, PTA's*). However, the apostrophe is functionally unnecessary except where confusion might otherwise result.

three A's   too many I's   two U's on his report card

624 For the sake of clarity, uncapitalized letters and uncapitalized abbreviations with internal periods are pluralized by adding an apostrophe plus *s*.

dotting the *i*'s   counting the c.o.d.'s   *p*'s and *q*'s

625 Numbers expressed in figures are pluralized by the addition of s alone. (See, however, ¶623, note.)

> in the 1980s   temperature in the 40s   sort these 1040s and W-2s

Numbers expressed in words are pluralized by the addition of s or es.

> ones   twos   sixes   twenties   twenty-fives

626 **a.** When words taken from other parts of speech are used as nouns, they are usually pluralized by the addition of s or es.

> ands, ifs, and buts   pros and cons
> dos and don'ts   whys and wherefores
> yeses and noes   yeas and nays
> the haves and the have-nots the ins and outs

b. If the pluralized form is unfamiliar or is likely to be misread, use an apostrophe plus s to form the plural.

> which's and that's   or's and nor's

If the singular form already contains an apostrophe, simply add s to form the plural.

> ain'ts   doesn'ts   don'ts

- See ¶285 for the underscoring of words referred to as words.

Forming Possessives

Possession Versus Description

627 An s-ending noun is usually in the possessive form if it is followed immediately by another noun.

> the employee's record (meaning the record of the employee)
> Saunders' merchandise (meaning the merchandise of the Saunders store)
> Thackeray's novels (meaning novels written by Thackeray)

To be sure that the possessive form should be used, try substituting an *of* phrase or a *by* phrase as in the examples above. If the substitution works, the possessive form is correct.

628 Do not mistake a descriptive form ending in s for a possessive form.

> sales effort (*sales* describes the kind of effort)
>
> savings account (*savings* describes the kind of account)

- See ¶640 for descriptive and possessive forms in organizational names.

629 In a number of cases, only a slight difference in wording distinguishes a descriptive phrase from a possessive phrase.

Descriptive	Possessive
a two-week vacation	a two weeks' vacation
the New Jersey sales tax	New Jersey's sales tax
the Hess estate	Hess's estate
the Wilson house	the Wilsons' house
	OR Mr. and Mrs. Wilson's house

Singular Nouns

630 To form the possessive of a singular noun *not* ending in an s sound, add an apostrophe plus s to the noun.

a person's self-respect	Mr. and Mrs. Fenton's claim
a master's degree	Sylvia's promotion
the corps's morale	Arkansas's tourist industry

631 To form the possessive of a singular noun that ends in an s sound, be guided by the way the word is pronounced.

a. If a new syllable is formed in the pronunciation of the possessive, add an apostrophe plus s.

my boss's calendar	Mr. and Mrs. Harris's apartment
the witness's testimony	Ms. Hertz's book
an actress's entrance	Miss Marx's memo

b. If the addition of an extra syllable would make an s-ending word hard to pronounce, add the apostrophe only.

Miss Hastings' order	for goodness' sake
Mr. Phillips' pen	Jesus' teachings
Simmons' factory	Moses' journey

CAUTION: In forming the possessive of any noun ending in s, always place the apostrophe at the end of the original word, never within it.

Mr. Hodges' message (**NOT:** Mr. Hodge's message)

Plural Nouns

632 For a *regular* plural noun (one that ends in s), add only an apostrophe to form the plural possessive. (See ¶¶639–640 for the use of the apostrophe in organizational names.)

students' marks	attorneys' offices
the witnesses' testimonies	the companies' joint assets
the United States' concern	the Joneses' contributions

NOTE: Since the singular and plural possessives for the same word usually sound exactly alike, pay particularly close attention to the meaning in order to determine whether the noun in question is singular or plural.

A student's marks should be considered along with other factors.
BUT: Students' marks must be submitted by Friday.

We have been invited to Mr. and Mrs. Jones's home.
BUT: We have been invited to the Joneses' home.

633 For an *irregular* plural noun (one that does not end in s), add an apostrophe plus s to form the plural possessive.

men's suits	children's shoes

IMPORTANT NOTE: To avoid mistakes in forming the possessive of plural nouns, form the plural first; then apply the rule in ¶632 or ¶633, whichever fits.

(*Continued on page 128.*)

Singular	Plural	Plural Possessive
boy	boys (regular)	boys'
boss	bosses (regular)	bosses'
Mr. and Mrs. Fox	the Foxes (regular)	the Foxes'
child	children (irregular)	children's
alumnus	alumni (irregular)	alumni's
son-in-law	sons-in-law (irregular)	sons-in-law's

Compound Nouns

634 To form the *singular* possessive of a compound noun (whether solid, spaced, or hyphenated), add an apostrophe plus s to the last element of the compound.

my mother-in-law's will   my stockbroker's advice
the secretary-treasurer's report   the attorney general's power

635 To form the *plural* possessive of a compound noun, first form the plural.

a. If the plural form ends in s, add only an apostrophe.

Singular	Plural	Plural Possessive
stockholder	stockholders	stockholders'
vice president	vice presidents	vice presidents'
clerk-typist	clerk-typists	clerk-typists'

b. If the plural form does not end in s, add an apostrophe plus s.

Singular	Plural	Plural Possessive
salesclerk	salesclerks	salesclerks'
editor in chief	editors in chief	editors in chief's
brother-in-law	brothers-in-law	brothers-in-law's

NOTE: To avoid the awkwardness of a plural possessive such as *editors in chief's* or *brothers-in-law's*, rephrase the sentence.

    AWKWARD: Mr. Ahmed's statement agrees with both *attorneys general's* views.
    BETTER: Mr. Ahmed's statement agrees with the views of both *attorneys general.*

Pronouns

636 The possessive forms of *personal pronouns* and of the relative pronoun *who* do not require the apostrophe. These pronouns have their own special possessive forms.

I: my, mine	she: her, hers	they: their, theirs
you: your, yours	it: its	who: whose
he: his	we: our, ours	

My copy of the letter arrived last week, so she should have received *hers* by now. (**NOT:** her's.)

Each unit comes carefully packed in *its* own carton. (**NOT:** it's.)

CAUTION: Do not confuse personal possessive pronouns with similarly spelled contractions. (See ¶1056d for examples.)

637 Some *indefinite pronouns* have regular possessive forms.

one's choice	the other's claim	anybody's guess
anyone else's job	the others' claim	no one's responsibility
one another's time	each other's claim	someone's chance

For those indefinite pronouns that do not have possessive forms, use an *of* phrase.

> Although children in this group seem very much alike, the needs *of each* are different. (**NOT:** each's needs.)

Abbreviations

638 To form the singular possessive of an abbreviation, add an apostrophe plus *s*. To form the plural possessive, add an *s* plus an apostrophe to the singular form. (See also ¶639.)

Mr. C.'s opinion	the M.D.s' diagnoses	the CPA's audit
the FCC's ruling	the Ph.D.s' theses	the CPAs' meeting

Personal and Organizational Names

639 To form the possessive of a personal or organizational name that ends with an abbreviation, a number, or a prepositional phrase, add an apostrophe plus *s* at the end of the complete name.

the A. & V. Co.'s ad	Henry Ford II's announcement
George Thompson Inc.'s stationery	Mr. John Smith Jr.'s new house
the Knights of Columbus's drive	**BUT:** the George Herrick Jrs.' estate

■ See ¶¶156 and 159 for the treatment of possessive forms when terms like *Inc. and Jr.* are set off by commas.

640 Many organizational names contain words that could be construed as either possessive or descriptive terms.

a. As a rule, use an apostrophe if the term is a singular possessive noun or an irregular plural noun.

McCall's	Children's Hospital
Harper's Bazaar	*Women's Wear Daily*

b. Do not use an apostrophe if the term is a regular plural.

American Bankers Association	Chemical Workers Union
Government Employees Insurance Company	Investors Trust Company

c. In all cases follow the organization's preference when known.

Ladies' Home Journal	Investor's Management Services, Inc.
Reader's Digest	International Ladies' Garment Workers' Union
Barron's	Boys' Clubs of America

Nouns in Apposition

641 Sometimes a noun that ordinarily would be in the possessive is followed by an *appositive,* a closely linked explanatory word or phrase. In such cases add the sign of the possessive to the appositive only.

> Portland, *Oregon's* mayor spoke at our convention. (Note that the comma that would normally follow an appositive is omitted when the possessive ending is added.)
>
> You will need to get Mr. Bartel, *the executor's* signature.

(Continued on page 130.)

NOTE: This kind of construction is usually awkward; whenever possible, use an *of* phrase instead.

> You will need to get the signature *of Mr. Bartel,* the executor.

Separate and Joint Possession

642 To indicate separate possession, add the sign of the possessive to the name of each individual.

> the buyer's and the seller's signatures   the Joneses' and the Browns' houses

NOTE: The repetition of *the* with each name further indicates that separate ownership is intended.

643 To indicate joint (or common) ownership, add the sign of the possessive to the *final* name alone. However, if one of the owners is identified by a pronoun, make each name possessive.

> *Helen* and *Jean's* boat   **BUT:** *Helen's* and *your* boat

Possessives Standing Alone

644 Sometimes the noun that the possessive modifies is merely understood.

> Ask for it at your *grocer's* (store).
> Wear your oldest shirt and *Levi's* (jeans). (The trademark *Levi's* is a singular possessive form.)
> We have been invited to a party at the *Pavlicks'* (house).
> **BUT:** We went to see the *Pavlicks.* (The people themselves are referred to; hence no possessive.)

NOTE: The possessive form must be used in the following construction in order to keep the comparison parallel.

> This month's sales figures are better than last *month's* (sales figures).
> **NOT:** This month's sales figures are better than last *month.* (Incorrectly compares *sales figures* with *month.*)

Inanimate Possessives

645 As a rule, nouns referring to inanimate things should not be in the possessive. Use an *of* phrase instead.

> the hood of the car (**NOT:** the car's hood)
> the terms of the contract (**NOT:** the contract's terms)
> the format of the letter (**NOT:** the letter's format)

646 In many common expressions that refer to time and measurements, however, and in phrases implying personification, the possessive form has come to be accepted usage. (See also ¶817*b*.)

one day's notice	a dollar's worth	a stone's throw
an hour's work	several dollars' worth	for heaven's sake
two years' progress	at arm's length	for conscience' sake
the company's assets	New Year's resolutions	(see ¶631*b*)
the sun's rays	this morning's news	the earth's atmosphere

Possessives Preceding Verbal Nouns

647 When a noun or a pronoun modifies a *gerund* (the *ing* form of a verb used as a noun), the noun or pronoun should be in the possessive form.

> I am concerned about *your* taking the job.
> Was there any record of the *customer's* being notified?

Possessives in *Of* Phrases

648 The object of the preposition *of* should not ordinarily be in the possessive form, since the *of* phrase as a whole expresses possession. However, possessives are used in a few idiomatic expressions.

> He is a friend of *Tom's*. (NOT: of Tom.)
> She is a neighbor of *mine*. (NOT: of me.)

Possessives Modifying Possessives

649 Avoid attaching a possessive form to another possessive. Change the wording if possible.

> AWKWARD: I have not yet seen the *utility company's lawyer's* petition.
> BETTER: I have not yet seen the petition of the *utility company's lawyer*.

Possessives in Holidays

650 Possessives in names of holidays are usually singular.

Mother's Day	Lincoln's Birthday	BUT: Veterans Day
New Year's Eve	Valentine's Day	April Fools' Day

SPELLING

SPELLING GUIDES

When a Final Consonant Is Doubled (¶¶701–702)
When a Final Consonant Is Not Doubled (¶¶703–706)
Final Silent E (¶¶707–709)
When Final Y Is Changed to I (¶¶710–711)
EI and IE Words (¶712)
Words Ending in ABLE and IBLE (¶713)
Words Ending in ANT/ANCE and ENT/ENCE (¶714)
Words Ending in IZE, ISE, and YZE (¶715)
Words Ending in CEDE, CEED, and SEDE (¶716)

WORDS THAT SOUND ALIKE OR LOOK ALIKE (¶717)

TROUBLESOME WORDS (¶718)

In matters of spelling, the most important rule is this: *When in doubt, consult the dictionary.* The next most important rule: *Try to master the principles of spelling so as to avoid frequent trips to the dictionary.*

Section 7 offers three kinds of assistance: ¶¶701–716 present the basic guidelines for correct spelling. ¶717 provides a 12-page list of look-alike and sound-alike words for review and fast reference. ¶718 presents a list of troublesome words—those that are frequently misspelled or that frequently send writers to their dictionaries.

NOTE: The 1976 printing of *Webster's New Collegiate Dictionary* and *Webster's Third New International Dictionary* (both published by the G. & C. Merriam Company, Springfield, Massachusetts) serve as the authority for the spelling in this manual. Whenever two spellings are allowable, only the first form is usually given here.

Spelling Guides

When a Final Consonant Is Doubled

701 When a word of one syllable ends in a single consonant (ba<u>g</u>) preceded by a single vowel (b<u>a</u>g), double the final consonant before a suffix beginning with a vowel (bagg<u>age</u>) or before the suffix y (bagg<u>y</u>).

drop	dropped	swim	swimming	ship	shipper
slip	slippage	glad	gladden	bet	bettor
clan	clannish	skin	skinny	chum	chummy

EXCEPTIONS:

gas	gaseous	saw	sawing	fix	fixed
bus	buses	tow	towed	tax	taxing

- *Compare ¶703.*

702 When a word of more than one syllable ends in a single consonant (refe<u>r</u>) preceded by a single vowel (ref<u>e</u>r) and the accent falls on the last syllable of the root word (re<u>fer</u>), double the final consonant before a suffix beginning with a vowel (referr<u>ed</u>).

regret	regrettable	concur	concurrent
begin	beginning	occur	occurring
control	controller	transfer	transferred (**BUT:** transferable)

NOTE: If the accent *shifts* to the first syllable of a word when a suffix beginning with a vowel is added, the final consonant is not doubled.

refer referred **BUT:** reference   prefer preferred **BUT:** preferable

- *Compare ¶704.*

When a Final Consonant Is Not Doubled

703 When a word of one syllable ends in a single consonant (ba<u>d</u>) preceded by a single vowel (b<u>a</u>d), *do not* double the final consonant before a suffix beginning with a *consonant* (bad<u>ly</u>).

ship shipment   glad gladness   drop droplet

704 When a word of more than one syllable ends in a single consonant (benefi<u>t</u>) preceded by a single vowel (benef<u>i</u>t) and the accent *does not* fall on the last syllable of the root word (<u>ben</u>efit), *do not* double the final consonant before a suffix beginning with a vowel (benefit<u>ed</u>).

differ	differed, differing	total	totaled, totaling
credit	credited, creditor	travel	traveled, traveler
profit	profited, profiting	cancel	canceled, canceling
benefit	benefited, benefiting		(**BUT:** cancellation)
diagram	diagramed, diagraming	worship	worshiped, worshiper

EXCEPTIONS:

program	programmed, programming	kidnap	kidnapped, kidnapping

705 When a word of one or more syllables ends in a single consonant (clou<u>d</u>, repea<u>t</u>) preceded by more than one vowel (cl<u>ou</u>d, rep<u>ea</u>t), do not double the final consonant before any suffix, whether it begins with a consonant (cloud*less*) or a vowel (repeat*ing*).

eat	eaten		deceit	deceitful
look	looking		chief ·	chiefly
bias	biased		wool	woolen **BUT:** woolly

EXCEPTION: equip   equipped   equipping

706   When a word of one or more syllables ends with more than one consonant (wo*rk*, deta*ch*), do not double the final consonant before any suffix (work*day*, detach*ed*).

confirm	confirming		hand	handful
return	returned		warm	warmly

NOTE: Words ending in *ll* usually retain both consonants before a suffix. However, when adding the suffix *ly*, drop one *l* from the root word. When adding the suffixes *less* or *like*, insert a hyphen between the root and the suffix to avoid three *l*'s in a row.

skill	skillful		full	fully	hull	hull-less
install	installment		dull	dully	shell	shell-like

Final Silent *E*

707   Words ending in silent *e* usually *drop* the e before a suffix beginning with a vowel.

use	us*age*		true	tru*ism*	sale	sal*able*
argue	argu*ing*		desire	des*irous*	arrive	arriv*al*

EXCEPTIONS:

agree	agree*ing*		mile	mil*eage*
hoe	hoe*ing*		dye	dye*ing*

NOTE: Words ending in *ce* or *ge* usually retain the e before suffixes beginning with *a*, *o*, or *u*.

enforce*able*, notice*able*, service*able*   **BUT:** forc*ible*
manage*able*, change*able*, knowledge*able*   manag*ing*, chang*ing*, ag*ing*,
advantag*eous*, courag*eous*, outrag*eous*   judg*ing*

708   Words ending in silent *e* usually *retain* the e before a suffix beginning with a consonant.

trouble	trouble*some*		hope	hope*ful*
manage	manage*ment*		sincere	sincere*ly*
like	like*ness*		nine	nine*ty*

EXCEPTIONS:

judge	judgment		acknowledge	acknowledgment
whole	wholly		argue	argument
nine	ninth		true	truly
gentle	gently		due	duly
awe	awful		wise	wisdom

709   Words ending in *ie* change the *ie* to *y* before adding *ing*.

die	dying		lie	lying (**BUT:** liar)
tie	tying		vie	vying (**BUT:** viable)

When Final *Y* Is Changed to *I*

710 Words ending in *y* preceded by a consonant change the *y* to *i* before any suffix except one beginning with *i*.

ordinary	ordinarily	heavy	heaviest	**BUT:**	try	trying
happy	happiness	defy	defiant		thirty	thirtyish
likely	likelihood	hurry	hurried		copy	copyist

711 Words ending in *y* preceded by a vowel usually retain the *y* before any suffix.

delay	delayed	annoy	annoyance	buy	buyer
obey	obeying	betray	betrayal	employ	employable

EXCEPTIONS:

pay	paid	day	daily	gay	gaily
lay	laid	say	said	slay	slain

EI and *IE* Words

712 Put *i* before *e* Or when sounded like *a*
Except after *c* As in *neighbor* and *weigh*.

I Before E

believe	brief	field	niece	**BUT:**	either	height
relieve	chief	wield	piece		neither	leisure
belief	thief	yield	anxiety		seize	foreign
relief	friend	view	variety		weird	forfeit

After C

deceive	receive	conceive	perceive	**BUT:**	ancient	species
deceit	receipt	conceit	ceiling		science	financier

Sounded Like A

freight	their	eight	vein
weight	heir	sleigh	skein

Words Ending in *ABLE* and *IBLE*

713 **a.** The ending *able* is more commonly used.

advisable	dependable	likable	probable	salable
changeable	knowledgeable	payable	receivable	valuable

- *See ¶707 on dropping or retaining silent e before the ending.*

b. However, a number of frequently used words end in *ible*.

compatible	eligible	irrepressible	possible	susceptible
convertible	feasible	irresistible	responsible	terrible
credible	flexible	legible	sensible	visible

Words Ending in *ANT/ANCE* and *ENT/ENCE*

714 Words ending in *ant*, *ance*, *ent*, and *ence* follow no clear-cut pattern. Therefore, consult a dictionary when in doubt.

existent	persistent	defendant	descendant	occurrence
insistent	resistant	dependent	transcendent	recurrence
assistance	maintenance	relevance	surveillance	intelligence

Words Ending in *IZE, ISE,* and *YZE*

715 a. Most words end in *ize.*

apologize	characterize	economize	prize	summarize
authorize	criticize	emphasize	realize	vandalize

b. A number of common words end in *ise.*

advertise	compromise	enterprise	improvise	supervise
advise	devise	exercise	merchandise	surprise
arise	disguise	franchise	revise	televise

c. Only a few words end with *yze.*

analyze	paralyze	catalyze

Words Ending in *CEDE, CEED,* and *SEDE*

716 a. Only *one* word ends in *sede: supersede.*

b. Only *three* words end in *ceed: exceed, proceed, succeed.* (Note, however, that derivatives of these three words are spelled with only one *e: excess, procedure, success.*)

c. All other words ending with the syllable pronounced "seed" are spelled *cede: precede, secede, recede, concede, accede, intercede.*

Words That Sound Alike
or Look Alike

717 The following list contains two types of words: (*a*) words that are pronounced *exactly alike,* though spelled differently (and for which the shorthand outlines are therefore identical); and (*b*) words that look and sound *somewhat alike* (and for which the shorthand outlines may be very nearly the same).

NOTE: A small triangle (▶) marks the start of each group of similar words.

▶**accede**	to comply with
exceed	to surpass
▶**accent**	stress in speech or writing
ascent	act of rising
assent	consent
▶**accept**	to take; to receive
except	(v.) to exclude; (prep.) excluding
▶**access**	admittance
excess	surplus
▶**ad**	short for *advertisement*
add	to join
▶**adapt**	to adjust
adept	proficient
adopt	to choose
▶**addenda**	(see *agenda*)

▶**addition**	something added
edition	one version of a printed work
▶**adherence**	attachment
adherents	followers
▶**adverse**	hostile, unfavorable
averse	disinclined
▶**advice**	(n.) information; recommendation
advise	(v.) to recommend; to give counsel
▶**affect**	to influence; to change; to assume (see ¶1101)
effect	(n.) result; impression; (v.) to bring about

▸**agenda** list of things to be done
addenda additional items

▸**air** atmosphere
heir one who inherits

▸**aisle** (see *isle*)

▸**allowed** permitted
aloud audibly

▸**allusion** an indirect reference
illusion an unreal vision
delusion a false belief
elusion adroit escape

▸**almost** nearly (see ¶1101)
all most all very much

▸**already** previously (see ¶1101)
all ready all prepared

▸**altar** part of a church
alter to change

▸**alternate** (n.) substitute; (v.) to take turns
alternative (n.) one of several things from which to choose

▸**altogether** entirely (see ¶1101)
all together everyone in a group

▸**always** at all times (see ¶1101)
all ways all means or methods

▸**annual** yearly
annul to cancel

▸**ante-** a prefix meaning "before"
anti- a prefix meaning "against"

▸**antecedence** priority
antecedents preceding things; ancestors

▸**anyone** anybody (see ¶1010)
any one any one person in a group

▸**anyway** in any case (see ¶1101)
any way any method

▸**apportion** (see *portion*)

▸**appraise** to set a value on (see ¶1101)
apprise to inform

▸**area** surface; extent
aria a melody
arrears that which is due but unpaid

▸**arrange** to put in order
arraign to call into court

▸**ascent** (see *accent*)

▸**assay** to test, as an ore or a chemical
essay (n.) a treatise; (v.) to attempt

▸**assent** (see *accent*)

▸**assistance** help
assistants those who help

▸**assure** (see *ensure*)

▸**attain** to gain, to achieve
attend to be present at

▸**attendance** presence
attendants escorts; followers; companions; associates

▸**aught** anything (incorrect for *naught,* meaning "ciphcr")
ought should

▸**averse** (see *adverse*)

▸**awhile** (adv.) for a short time (see ¶1101)
a while (phrase) a short period of time

▸**bail** (n.) security; the handle of a pail; (v.) to dip water
bale a bundle

▸**bare** (adj.) naked; empty (v.) to expose
bear (n.) an animal; (v.) to carry; to endure; to produce

▸**base** (n.) foundation; (adj.) mean
bass lower notes in music; a fish

▸**bases** plural of *base* and of *basis*
basis foundation

▸**beat** (n.) throb; tempo; (v.) to strike
beet a vegetable

▸**berry** a fruit
bury to submerge; to cover over

▸**berth** a bed
birth being born

►**beside** by the side of; separate from (see ¶1101)

besides in addition to; also

►**biannual** occurring twice a year

biennial occurring once in two years

►**bibliography** list of writings pertaining to a given subject or author

biography written history of a person's life

►**billed** charged
build to construct

►**birth** (see *berth*)

►**board** a piece of wood; an organized group; meals

bored penetrated; wearied

►**boarder** one who pays for meals and often lodging as well

border edge

►**bolder** more daring
boulder a large rock

►**born** brought into life
borne carried; endured

►**boy** a male child
buoy a float

►**brake** (n.) a retarding device; (v.) to retard

break (n.) an opening; a fracture; (v.) to shatter; to divide

►**bread** food
bred brought up

►**breath** respiration
breathe (v.) to inhale and exhale

breadth width

►**bridal** concerning the bride or the wedding

bridle (n.) means of controlling a horse; (v.) to take offense

►**broach** to open; to introduce

brooch ornamental clasp

►**build** (see *billed*)

►**bullion** uncoined gold or silver

bouillon broth

►**bury** (see *berry*)

►**calendar** a record of time
calender a machine used in finishing paper and cloth

colander a strainer

►**callous** (adj.) hardened
callus (n.) a hardened surface

►**cannot** usual form
can not two words in the phrase *can not only*

►**canvas** (n.) a coarse cloth
canvass (v.) to solicit

►**capital** (n.) city serving as the seat of government; a principal sum of money; a large-sized letter; (adj.) chief; foremost

capitol the building in which a state legislative body meets

Capitol the building in which the U.S. Congress meets

►**carton** a pasteboard box
cartoon a caricature

►**casual** incidental
causal pertaining to a cause

►**cease** to stop
seize to grasp

►**cede** to grant; to give up
seed that from which anything is grown

►**ceiling** top of a room; any overhanging area

sealing closing

►**cell** (see *sell*)

►**cellar** (see *seller*)

►**census** statistics of population

senses mental faculties

►**cent** (see *scent*)

►**cereal** any grain food
serial arranged in a series

► **cession**	a yielding up
session	the sitting of a court or other body
► **choose**	to select
chose	did choose (past tense of *choose*)
chews	masticates
► **chord**	combination of musical tones
cord	string or rope
► **chute**	(see *shoot*)
► **cite**	(v.) to quote; to summon
sight	a view; vision
site	a place
► **clothes**	garments
cloths	fabrics
close	(n.) the end; (v.) to shut
► **coarse**	rough; common
course	direction; action; a way; part of a meal
► **colander**	(see *calendar*)
► **collision**	a clashing
collusion	a scheme to defraud
► **coma**	an unconscious state
comma	a mark of punctuation
► **command**	(n.) an order; (v.) to order
commend	to praise; to entrust
► **commence**	(v.) to begin
comments	(n.) remarks
► **complement**	something that completes
compliment	(n.) a flattering speech; (v.) to praise
► **comprehensible**	understandable
comprehensive	extensive
► **confidant**	a friend; an adviser (feminine form: *confidante*)
confident	sure; positive
► **confidently**	certainly; positively
confidentially	privately
► **conscience**	(n.) the sense of right and wrong
conscious	(adj.) cognizant; sensible; aware

► **conservation**	preservation
conversation	a talk
► **continual**	occurring steadily but with occasional breaks
continuous	uninterrupted; unbroken
► **cooperation**	the art of working together
corporation	a form of business organization
► **cord**	(see *chord*)
► **correspondence**	letters
correspondents	those who write letters; journalists
corespondents	parties in divorce suits
► **costume**	dress
custom	habit
► **council**	an assembly
counsel	(n.) an attorney; advice; (v.) to give advice
consul	a foreign representative
► **councillor**	a member of a council
counselor	one who advises
consular	(adj.) of a consul
► **course**	(see *coarse*)
► **courtesy**	a favor; politeness
curtesy	a husband's life interest in the lands of his deceased wife
curtsy	a gesture of respect
► **credible**	believable
creditable	meritorious, deserving of praise
credulous	ready to believe
► **cue**	a hint
queue	a line of people
► **currant**	a berry
current	(adj.) belonging to the present; (n.) a flow of water or electricity
► **custom**	(see *costume*)
► **dairy**	source of milk products
diary	daily record
► **deceased**	dead
diseased	sick

▶decent   proper; right
descent   going down
dissent   disagreement

▶decree   a law
degree   a grade; a step

▶deduce   to infer
deduct   to subtract

▶defer   to put off
differ   to disagree

▶deference   respect, regard for
               another's wishes
difference   dissimilarity; con-
               troversy

▶delusion   (see *allusion*)

▶deposition   a formal written
               statement
disposition   temper; disposal

▶depraved   morally debased
deprived   taken away from

▶deprecate   to disapprove
depreciate   to lessen in esti-
               mated value

▶desert   (n.) barren land; a
               deserved reward;
               (v.) to abandon
dessert   the last course of
               a meal

▶desolate   lonely; sad
dissolute   loose in morals

▶detract   to take away from
distract   to divert the atten-
               tion of

▶device   (n.) a contrivance
devise   (v.) to plan; to
               convey real estate
               by will

▶dew   (see *do*)

▶die   (n.) mold; (v.) to
               cease living
dye   (n.) that which
               changes the color
               of; (v.) to change
               the color of

▶disapprove   to withhold ap-
               proval
disprove   to prove the falsity
               of

▶disassemble   to take apart
dissemble   to disguise; to
               feign

▶disburse   to pay out
disperse   to scatter

▶discreet   prudent
discrete   distinct; separate

▶disinterested unbiased; impartial
uninterested   bored; unconcerned

▶dissent   (see *decent*)

▶divers   various or sundry;
               plural of *diver*
diverse   different

▶do   to perform
due   owing
dew   moisture

▶done   finished
dun   a demand for pay-
               ment

▶dose   a measured quan-
               tity
doze   to sleep lightly

▶dual   double
duel   a combat

▶due   (see *do*)

▶dying   near death
dyeing   changing the color
               of

▶edition   (see *addition*)

▶effect   (see *affect*)

▶elapse   (see *lapse*)

▶elicit   to draw forth
illicit   unlawful

▶eligible   fitted; qualified
illegible   unreadable

▶elusion   (see *allusion*)

▶elusive   baffling; hard to
               catch
illusive   misleading; unreal

▶emerge   to rise out of
immerge   to plunge into

▶emigrate   to go away from a
               country
immigrate   to come into a
               country

▶eminent   well-known; prom-
               inent
imminent   threatening; im-
               pending
emanate   to originate from;
               to come out of

▶en route   (see *root*)

▶ensure   to make certain
insure   to protect against
               loss
assure   to give confidence
               to someone

▶envelop   (v.) to cover; to
               wrap
envelope   (n.) a wrapper for
               a letter

▶ **equable** even; tranquil
equitable just; right

▶ **erasable** capable of being erased
irascible quick-tempered

▶ **especially** to an exceptional degree
specially particularly, as opposed to generally

▶ **essay** (see *assay*)

▶ **everyday** daily (see ¶1101)
every day each day

▶ **everyone** each one (see ¶1010)
every one each one in a group

▶ **exceed** (see *accede*)

▶ **except** (see *accept*)

▶ **excess** (see *access*)

▶ **expand** to increase in size
expend to spend

▶ **expansive** capable of being extended
expensive costly

▶ **expatiate** to enlarge on
expiate to atone for

▶ **explicit** easily understood
implicit unquestioning

▶ **extant** still existing
extent measure

▶ **facet** aspect
faucet a tap

▶ **facetious** witty
factitious artificial
fictitious imaginary

▶ **facilitate** to make easy
felicitate to congratulate

▶ **facility** ease
felicity joy

▶ **fair** (adj.) favorable; just; (n.) an exhibit
fare (n.) cost of travel; food; (v.) to go forth

▶ **farther** at a greater distance, referring to *actual* distance (see ¶1101)
further to a greater extent or degree, referring to *figurative* distance; moreover; in addition

▶ **faze** to disturb
phase a stage in development

▶ **feet** plural of *foot*
feat an act of skill or strength

▶ **fictitious** (see *facetious*)

▶ **finale** the end
finally at the end
finely in a fine manner

▶ **fineness** delicacy
finesse tact

▶ **fir** a tree
fur skin of an animal

▶ **fiscal** (see *physical*)

▶ **flair** aptitude
flare a light; a signal

▶ **flew** did fly
flue a chimney
flu short for *influenza*

▶ **flour** ground meal
flower blossom

▶ **for** a preposition
fore first; preceding; the front
four numeral

▶ **forbear** to bear with
forebear an ancestor

▶ **forgo** to relinquish; to let pass
forego to go before

▶ **formally** in a formal manner
formerly before

▶ **fort** a fortified place
forte (n.) area where one excels
forte (adj.) loud (musical direction)

▶ **forth** away; forward
fourth next after third

▶ **forward** ahead
foreword preface

▶ **foul** unfavorable; unclean
fowl a bird

▶ **fur** (see *fir*)

▶ **further** (see *farther*)

▶ **genius** talent
genus a classification in botany or zoology

▶gibe   (n.) a sarcastic re-
          mark; (v.) to scoff
          at
jibe   to agree
▶grate   (n.) a frame of
          bars (as in a fire-
          place); (v.) to
          scrape; to irritate
great   large; magnificent
▶guessed   past tense of *guess*
guest   visitor
▶hall   a corridor
haul   to drag
▶heal   to cure
heel   part of the foot or
          a shoe
▶healthful   promoting health
          (e.g., a *healthful*
          food)
healthy   being in good
          health (e.g., a
          healthy person)
▶hear   to perceive by ear
here   in this place
▶heard   past tense of *hear*
herd   a group of ani-
          mals
▶heir   (see *air*)
▶holy   sacred
holey   full of holes
wholly   entirely
holly   a tree
▶human   pertaining to hu-
          manity
humane   kindly
▶hypercritical   overcritical
hypocritical   pretending virtue
▶ideal   a standard of per-
          fection
idle   unoccupied;
          without worth
idol   object of worship
idyll   a description of
          rural life
▶illegible   (see *eligible*)
▶illicit   (see *elicit*)
▶illusion   (see *allusion*)
▶illusive   (see *elusive*)
▶imitate   to resemble; to
          mimic
intimate   (adj.) innermost;
          familiar; (v.) to
          hint; to make
          known

▶immerge   (see *emerge*)
▶immigrate   (see *emigrate*)
▶imminent   (see *eminent*)
▶implicit   (see *explicit*)
▶imply   to suggest (see
          ¶1101)
infer   to deduce
▶inane   senseless
insane   of unsound mind
▶incidence   range of occur-
          rence
incidents   accidental happen-
          ings
▶incinerate   to burn
insinuate   to imply
▶incite   (v.) to arouse
insight   (n.) understanding
▶indict   to charge with a
          crime
indite   to compose and
          write
▶indifferent   without interest
in different   in other (see ¶1101)
▶indigenous   native
indigent   needy
indignant   angry
▶indirect   not direct
in direct   *in* (preposition) +
          direct (adjective)
          (see ¶1101)
▶ingenious   clever
ingenuous   naive
▶insoluble   incapable of being
          dissolved
insolvable   not explainable
insolvent   pertaining to a
          person unable to
          pay his debts
▶instants   short periods of
          time
instance   an example
▶insure   (see *ensure*)
▶intelligent   possessed of un-
          derstanding
intelligible   understandable
▶intense   acute; strong
intents   aims
▶interstate   between states
intrastate   within one state
▶intimate   (see *imitate*)
▶into, in to   (see ¶1101)
▶irascible   (see *erasable*)

▶**isle**   island
aisle   passage between rows

▶**its**   possessive form of *it*
it's   contraction of *it is* (see ¶1056*d*)

▶**jibe**   (see *gibe*)

▶**lapse**   to become void
elapse   to pass
relapse   to slip back into a former condition

▶**last**   final (see ¶1101)
latest   most recent

▶**later**   more recent; after a time
latter   second in a series of two

▶**lath**   a strip of wood
lathe   a wood-turning machine

▶**lay**   to place (see ¶1101)
lie   (n.) a falsehood; (v.) to recline; to tell an untruth
lye   a strong alkaline solution

▶**lead**   (n.) heavy metal; (v.) to guide
led   guided (past tense of *to lead*)

▶**lean**   (adj.) thin; (v.) to incline
lien   a legal claim

▶**leased**   rented
least   smallest

▶**legislator**   a lawmaker
legislature   a body of lawmakers

▶**lend**   to allow the use of temporarily
loan   (n.) something lent; (v.) to lend
lone   solitary

▶**lessee**   a tenant
lesser   smaller
lessor   one who gives a lease

▶**lessen**   (v.) to make smaller
lesson   (n.) an exercise assigned for study

▶**levee**   embankment of a river
levy   (n.) an amount collected by levying; (v.) to raise a collection of money

▶**liable**   responsible
libel   defamatory statement

▶**lie**   (see *lay*)

▶**lien**   (see *lean*)

▶**lightening**   making lighter
lightning   accompaniment of thunder
lighting   illumination

▶**loan, lone**   (see *lend*)

▶**loath**   (adj.) reluctant
loathe   (v.) to detest

▶**local**   pertaining to a particular place
locale   a particular place

▶**loose**   (adj.) free; not bound; (v.) to release
lose   (v.) to suffer the loss of; to part with unintentionally
loss   something lost

▶**lye**   (see *lay*)

▶**made**   constructed
maid   a servant

▶**magnificent**   having splendor
munificent   unusually generous

▶**mail**   correspondence
male   masculine

▶**main**   (adj.) chief; (n.) a conduit
mane   long hair on the neck of certain animals

▶**manner**   a way of acting
manor   an estate

▶**marital**   pertaining to marriage
martial   military
marshal   (n.) an official; (v.) to arrange

▶**maybe**   perhaps
may be   *two words* (see ¶1101)

▶**mean**   (adj.) unpleasant; (n.) the midpoint; (v.) to intend
mien   appearance

▸ **meat**	flesh of animals
meet	to join
mete	to measure
▸ **medal**	a badge of honor
meddle	to interfere
metal	a mineral
mettle	courage; spirit
▸ **miner**	a worker in a mine
minor	(adj.) lesser, as in size, extent, or importance; (n.) a person who is under legal age
▸ **mist**	haze
missed	failed to do
▸ **mite**	a tiny particle
might	(n.) force; (v.) past tense of *may*
▸ **mood**	disposition
mode	fashion; method
▸ **moral**	virtuous
morale	spirit
▸ **morality**	virtue
mortality	death rate
▸ **morning**	before noon
mourning	grief
▸ **munificent**	(see *magnificent*)
▸ **nobody**	no one
no body	no group (see ¶1101)
▸ **none**	not one
no one	nobody (see ¶1013)
▸ **oculist**	an ophthalmologist or an optometrist
opthalmologist	a doctor who treats eyes
optician	one who makes or sells eyeglasses
optometrist	one who measures vision
▸ **official**	authorized
officious	overbold in offering services
▸ **one**	a single thing
won	did win
▸ **ordinance**	a local law
ordnance	arms; munitions
▸ **ought**	(see *aught*)
▸ **overdo**	to do too much
overdue	past due
▸ **packed**	crowded
pact	an agreement

▸ **pail**	a bucket
pale	(adj.) light-colored; (n.) an enclosure
▸ **pain**	suffering
pane	window glass
▸ **pair**	two of a kind
pare	to peel
pear	a fruit
▸ **parameter**	a quantity with an assigned value; a constant
perimeter	the outer boundary
▸ **partition**	division
petition	prayer; a formal written request
▸ **partly**	in part
partially	to some degree
▸ **past**	(n.) time gone by; (adj., adv., or prep.) gone by
passed	moved along; transferred (past tense of *pass*)
▸ **patience**	composure; endurance
patients	sick persons
▸ **peace**	calmness
piece	a portion
▸ **peak**	the top
peek	to look slyly at
pique	(n.) resentment; (v.) to offend; to arouse
piqué	cotton fabric
▸ **peal**	to ring out
peel	to strip off
▸ **pear**	(see *pair*)
▸ **pedal**	(adj.) pertaining to the foot; (n.) a treadle
peddle	to hawk; to sell
▸ **peer**	(n.) one of equal rank; a nobleman; (v.) to look steadily
pier	a wharf
▸ **perfect**	without fault
prefect	an official
▸ **perpetrate**	to be guilty of
perpetuate	to make perpetual
▸ **perquisite**	privilege
prerequisite	a preliminary requirement
▸ **persecute**	to oppress
prosecute	to sue

▸**personal**	private
personnel	the staff
▸**perspective**	a view in correct proportion
prospective	anticipated
▸**peruse**	to read
pursue	to chase
▸**petition**	(see *partition*)
▸**phase**	(see *faze*)
▸**physic**	a medicine
physique	bodily structure
psychic	pertaining to the mind or spirit
▸**physical**	relating to the body
fiscal	pertaining to finances
psychical	mental
▸**piece**	(see *peace*)
▸**pique, piqué**	(see *peak*)
▸**plain**	(adj.) undecorated; (n.) prairie land
plane	(n.) a level surface; (v.) to make level
▸**plaintiff**	party in a lawsuit
plaintive	mournful
▸**pleas**	plural of *plea*
please	to be agreeable
▸**pole**	a long, slender piece of wood or metal
poll	(n.) the casting of votes for a body of persons; (v.) to register the votes of
▸**poor**	(adj.) inadequate; (n.) needy
pore	to study; to gaze intently
pour	to flow
▸**populace**	the common people; the masses
populous	thickly settled
▸**portion**	a part
proportion	a ratio of parts
apportion	to allot
▸**practicable**	workable; feasible
practical	useful
▸**pray**	to beseech
prey	a captured victim
▸**precede**	to go before
proceed	to advance
▸**precedence**	priority
precedents	established rules

▸**preposition**	a part of speech
proposition	an offer
▸**prescribe**	to designate
proscribe	to outlaw
▸**presence**	bearing; being present
presents	gifts
▸**presentiment**	a foreboding
presentment	a proposal
▸**pretend**	to make believe
portend	to foreshadow
▸**principal**	(adj.) chief; leading; (n.) a capital sum of money that draws interest; chief official of a school
principle	a general truth; a rule
▸**profit**	gain
prophet	one who forecasts
▸**prophecy**	a prediction
prophesy	to foretell
▸**propose**	to suggest
purpose	intention
▸**prosecute**	(see *persecute*)
▸**prospective**	(see *perspective*)
▸**psychic**	(see *physic*)
▸**psychical**	(see *physical*)
▸**purpose**	(see *propose*)
▸**pursue**	(see *peruse*)
▸**queue**	(see *cue*)
▸**quiet**	calm; not noisy
quite	entirely; wholly
quit	to stop
▸**rain**	falling water
rein	part of a bridle; a curb
reign	(n.) the term of a ruler's power; (v.) to rule
▸**raise**	to lift something
raze	to destroy
rays	beams
▸**rap**	to knock
wrap	(n.) a garment; (v.) to enclose
▸**read**	to perform the act of reading
reed	a plant; a musical instrument
red	a color

▸ real   actual
reel   (n.) a spool; a dance; (v.) to whirl

▸ reality   actuality
realty   real estate

▸ receipt   an acknowledgment of a thing received
recipe   a formula for mixing ingredients

▸ recent   late
resent   (v.) to be indignant

▸ reference   that which refers to something
reverence   profound respect

▸ relapse   (see *lapse*)

▸ residence   a house
residents   persons who reside in a place

▸ respectably   in a manner worthy of respect
respectfully   in a courteous manner
respectively   in the order indicated

▸ right   (adj.) correct; (n.) a privilege
rite   a ceremony
wright   a worker, a maker (used as a combining form, as in *playwright*)
write   to inscribe

▸ role   a part in a play
roll   (n.) a list; a type of bread; (v.) to revolve

▸ root   (n.) underground part of a plant; (v.) to implant firmly
route   (n.) an established course of travel; (v.) to send by a certain route
en route   on or along the way
rout   (n.) confused flight; (v.) to defeat

▸ rote   repetition
wrote   did write

▸ sail   (n.) part of a ship's rigging; (v.) to travel by water
sale   the act of selling

▸ scene   a setting; an exhibition of strong feeling
seen   past participle of *to see*

▸ scent   odor
sent   did send
cent   penny
sense   meaning

▸ sealing   (see *ceiling*)

▸ seam   a line of junction
seem   to appear

▸ seed   (see *cede*)

▸ seize   (see *cease*)

▸ sell   to transfer for a price
cell   a small compartment

▸ seller   one who sells
cellar   an underground room

▸ senses   (see *census*)

▸ serge   a kind of cloth
surge   (n.) a billow; (v.) to rise in surges

▸ serial   (see *cereal*)

▸ serve   to help (see ¶1101)
service   to keep in good repair

▸ session   (see *cession*)

▸ shear   to cut; to trim
sheer   transparent; unqualified

▸ shoot   to fire
chute   a slide

▸ shown   displayed; revealed; past participle of *show*
shone   gave off light; did shine

▸ sight, site   (see *cite*)

▸ simple   plain, uncomplicated
simplistic   oversimplified

▸ sleight   dexterity, as in "sleight of hand"
slight   (adj.) slender; scanty; (v.) to make light of

▸ so   therefore
sew   to stitch
sow   to scatter seed

▸ soar   (see *sore*)

►soared	did fly
sword	weapon
►sole	one and only
soul	the immortal spirit
►some	a part of
sum	a total
►someone	somebody (see ¶1010)
some one	some person in a group
►sometime	at some unspecified time (see ¶1101)
some time	a period of time
sometimes	now and then
►son	male child
sun	the earth's source of light and heat
►sore	painful
soar	to fly
►spacious	having ample room
specious	outwardly correct but inwardly false
►specially	(see *especially*)
►staid	grave; sedate
stayed	past tense and past participle of *to stay*
►stair	a step
stare	to look at
►stake	(n.) a pointed stick; the prize in a contest; (v.) to wager
steak	a slice of meat or fish
►stationary	fixed
stationery	writing materials
►statue	a carved or molded figure
stature	height
statute	a law
►steal	to take unlawfully
steel	a form of iron
►straight	not crooked; directly
strait	a water passageway; (plural) a distressing situation
►suit	(n.) a legal action; clothing; (v.) to please
suite	a group of things forming a unit
sweet	having an agreeable taste; pleasing

►sum	(see *some*)
►sun	(see *son*)
►superintendence	management
superintendents	supervisors
►surge	(see *serge*)
►sword	(see *soared*)
►tare	allowance for weight
tear	(n.) a rent; (v.) to rip
tear	a drop of secretion from the eye
tier	a row or layer
►taught	did teach
taut	tight; tense
►team	a group
teem	to abound
►tenant	one who rents property
tenet	a principle
►than	conjunction of comparison
then	(adv.) at that time
►their	belonging to them (see ¶1056*d*)
there	in that place
they're	contraction of *they are*
►theirs	possessive form of *they*, used without a following noun (see ¶1056*d*)
there's	contraction of *there is* or *there has*
►therefor	for that thing
therefore	consequently
►through	by means of; from beginning to end; because of
threw	did throw
thorough	carried through to completion
►to	(prep.) toward
too	(adv.) more than enough; also
two	one plus one
►track	a trail
tract	a treatise
►trial	examination; an experiment; hardship
trail	a path

▸**undo**   to open; to render
             ineffective
undue   improper; exces-
             sive

▸**uninterested**   (see *disinterested*)

▸**urban**   pertaining to the
             city
urbane   polished; suave

▸**vain**   proud; conceited
vane   a weathercock
vein   a blood vessel; a
             bed of mineral ma-
             terials

▸**vendee**   purchaser
vendor   seller

▸**veracious** , truthful
voracious   greedy

▸**veracity**   truthfulness
voracity   ravenousness;
             greediness

▸**vice**   wickedness; a
             prefix used with
             nouns to designate
             titles of office
vise   a clamp

▸**waist**   part of the body; a
             garment
waste   (n.) needless de-
             struction; useless
             consumption;
             (v.) to expend use-
             lessly

▸**wait**   to stay
weight   quantity of heavi-
             ness

▸**waive**   (v.) to give up
wave   (n.) a billow; a
             gesture; (v.) to
             swing back and
             forth

▸**waiver**   the giving up of a
             claim
waver   to hesitate

▸**want**   (n.) a need; (v.) to
             lack; to desire
wont   a custom
won't   contraction of *will
             not*

▸**ware**   goods
wear   to have on
were   form of *to be*
where   at the place in
             which

▸**way**   direction; distance;
             manner
weigh   to find the weight
             of

▸**weight**   (see *wait*)

▸**weak**   not strong
week   period of seven
             days

▸**weather**   (n.) state of the at-
             mosphere; (v.) to
             come through
             safely
whether   if (see ¶1101)

▸**whoever**   anyone who
who ever   *two words* (see
             ¶1101)

▸**wholly**   (see *holy*)

▸**whose**   possessive of *who*
who's   contraction of *who
             is* (see ¶1063)

▸**won**   (see *one*)

▸**wrap**   (see *rap*)

▸**wright, write**   (see *right*)

▸**wrote**   (see *rote*)

▸**your**   pronoun (see
             ¶1056*d*)
you're   contraction of *you
             are*

Troublesome Words

718   The following list presents a selection of those words that business
writers often misspell or stop and puzzle over. In some cases, the difficulty results from the inability to apply an established rule; for such
words, references to the rules are given. In many other instances, however, errors result from the peculiar spelling of the words themselves; in
such cases, the only remedy is to master the correct spelling of such
words on an individual basis.

NOTE: For troublesome words that sound alike or look alike, see ¶717. For troublesome compound words, see Section 8.

absence
accidentally (see ¶1101)
accommodate
accompanying
achievement
acknowledgment (see ¶708)
acquaintance
acquiesce
acquisition
across
adjacent
advantageous (see ¶707)
aging (see ¶707)
aisle
Albuquerque
all right (see ¶1101)
alleged
amortize (see ¶715)
analysis
analyze (see ¶715)
answer
apparently
appreciable
approximate
arbitrary
architect
argument (see ¶708)
assistance (see ¶714)
attorney
autumn
auxiliary
bachelor
bankruptcy
basically
beginning (see ¶702)
believe (see ¶712)
beneficiary
benefited (see ¶704)
Berkeley (California)
biased (see ¶705)
boundary
breakfast
buses (see ¶701)
busy
calendar
campaign
canceled (see ¶704)
carriage
catalog
category
cemetery
chaise longue
changeable (see ¶707)
chronological
Cincinnati

coincidence
collateral
colonel
colossal
column
commitment
committee
comparison
concede (see ¶716)
conscience
conscientious
conscious
consensus
continuous
controversy
criticism
debt
debtor
defendant (see ¶714)
defense
deficit
definite
dependent (see ¶714)
Des Moines
descendant (see ¶714)
describe
detrimental
develop
development
dilemma
disappoint
dissatisfied
dissimilar
double
ecstasy
eighth
eligible
eliminate
embarrass
emphasize
empty
enumerate
environment
exaggerate
exceed (see ¶716)
exercise
exhaustible
exhibition
existence (see ¶714)
exorbitant
experience
extension
extraordinary
facsimile
familiar

fascinating
February
forbade
foreign (see ¶712)
foresee
forfeit
forty
fourteen
fourth
fulfill
gauge
government
grammar
grateful
grievous
guarantee
guardian
harass
height (see ¶712)
hemorrhage
hors d'oeuvre
hygiene
hypocrisy
inasmuch as
incidentally
innocuous
innovation
inoculate
insistence (see ¶714)
irrelevant (see ¶714)
itinerary
judgment (see ¶708)
labeled (see ¶704)
laboratory
leisure
liable
liaison
library
license
lieutenant
lightning
likable (see ¶707)
liquefy
lose
maintenance
maneuver
marriage
mileage (see ¶707)
miniature
minutiae (see ¶614)
misapprehension
miscellaneous
mischievous
misspell
mortgage
necessary
negotiate
neither (see ¶712)
nickel

ninety
ninth
noticeable (see ¶707)
occasionally
occurrence (see ¶702)
offense
offered (see ¶704)
omelet
omission
oneself
opinion
pamphlet
panicky
parallel
partially
pastime
patience
permissible (see ¶713)
perseverance
persuade
phase
phenomenal
physician
picnicking
Pittsburgh
plausible (see ¶713)
possessions
practically
preceding (see ¶716)
preferable (see ¶702)
prerogative
presumptuous
pretense
privilege
procedure (see ¶716)
proceed (see ¶716)
programmed (see ¶704)
prohibition
pronunciation
psychiatric
psychological
publicly
pursue
quantity
questionnaire
queue
receipt
receive (see ¶712)
recipient
recommend
recruit
reference (see ¶702)
relevant (see ¶714)
renowned
rescind
resistance (see ¶714)
restaurant
résumé
rhythm

salable (see ¶707)
schedule
seize (see ¶712)
separate
sergeant
siege (see ¶712)
similar
simultaneous
sincerely (see ¶708)
sizable (see ¶707)
skillful
specimen
sponsor
strength
subpoena
subtlety
subtly
suing
San Francisco
summary
superintendent
supersede (see ¶716)
surgeon
surprise
surveillance (see ¶714)
susceptible

technique
temperature
tempt
theater
their (see ¶712)
thoroughly
threshold
through
totaled (see ¶704)
tragedy
transferred (see ¶702)
traveler (see ¶704)
unforgettable (see ¶702)
unmanageable (see ¶707)
unwieldy (see ¶712)
usage (see ¶707)
victim
warehouse
Wednesday
weird (see ¶712)
whether
whiskey
wholly
wield (see ¶712)
woolly (see ¶705)
yield (see ¶712)

COMPOUND WORDS

Some compound words are written as solid words, some are written as separate words, and some are hyphenated. As in other areas of style, authorities do not agree on the rules. Moreover, style is continually changing: many words that used to be hyphenated are now written solid or as separate words. The only complete guide is an up-to-date dictionary. However, a careful reading of the following rules will save you many a trip to the dictionary.

NOTE: The spellings in this section agree with those in the 1976 printing of *Webster's New Collegiate Dictionary* and *Webster's Third New International Dictionary* (published by the G. & C. Merriam Company, Springfield, Massachusetts) unless otherwise indicated.

Compound Nouns

801   Compound nouns follow no regular pattern. Some are written solid, some are spaced, and some are hyphenated.

checkbook	check mark	check-in	airfreight	air force
courtroom	court reporter	court-martial	bankbook	bank draft
crossroad	cross section	cross-reference	bookshelf	book club
eyewitness	eye shadow	eye opener	bylaw	by-product
footstep	foot brake	foot-pound	daylight	day school
goodwill	good sense	good-bye	handshake	hand truck
halfback	half hour	half-truth	homeowner	home rule
lifetime	life cycle	life-style	masterpiece	master plan
lighthouse	light meter	light-year	paperweight	paper clip
nightclub	night owl	night-light	salesclerk	sales slip
timetable	time zone	time-saver	schoolteacher	school board
trademark	trade name	trade-in	standby	stand-in

NOTE: To be sure of the spelling of a compound noun, check a dictionary. If the noun is not listed, treat the components as separate words. For the spelling of compounds in company names, check letterheads for possible variations. (Compare, for example, *American Airlines* with *United Air Lines*.)

802   Some solid and hyphenated compound nouns closely resemble verb phrases. Be sure, however, to treat the elements in a verb phrase as separate words.

Nouns	**Verb Phrases**
a *breakdown* in communications	when communications *break down*
a thorough *follow-up* of the report	to *follow up* the report thoroughly
operate a *drive-in*	*drive in* to your dealer's
a high school *dropout*	don't *drop out* of high school
at the time of *takeoff*	planes cannot *take off* or land
when they give us a *go-ahead*	we can *go ahead* with the plan
come to a *standstill*	we can't *stand still*
let's have a *run-through*	let's *run through* the plan
plan a *get-together*	plan to *get together*
they have the *know-how*	they *know how* to handle it

803 **a.** Many compound nouns ending in *up* are solid, especially if the first part of the compound is one syllable. For example:

> *backup, breakup, brushup, buildup, checkup, cleanup, letup, lineup, lockup, makeup, markup, setup, slipup;* **but:** *follow-up, hang-up, shake-up, tie-up, write-up.*

b. Most compound nouns ending in *in* are hyphenated. For example:

> *break-in, cave-in, check-in, drive-in, lead-in, shoo-in, shut-in, stand-in, tie-in, write-in.*

c. Most compound nouns ending in *out* are solid. For example:

> *blackout, breakout, checkout, cookout, cutout, dropout, handout, hangout, knockout, layout, lockout, printout, shakeout, shutout;* **but:** *fade-out, time-out.*

d. Many compound nouns ending in *off* are now spelled solid, but some still retain the hyphen. For example:

> *castoff, checkoff, cutoff, layoff, leadoff, payoff, runoff, standoff, takeoff.*
> **but:** *brush-off, drop-off, lift-off, play-off, rip-off, send-off, show-off, write-off.*

804 Hyphenate a compound noun when it does not include a noun as one of its elements.

a know-it-all	the well-to-do	the higher-ups
a good-for-nothing	the have-nots	the also-rans
go-betweens	hand-me-downs	do-it-yourselfers

805 Treat compound nouns like *problem solving* as two words, especially when the first word has two or more syllables. (Most words of this pattern are not shown in the dictionary; when they are, follow the dictionary listing.)

problem solving	profit sharing	child rearing
decision making	tape recording	stamp collecting
skill building	word processing	truck driving

> **but:** brainstorming, homeowning, flag-waving, spring-cleaning (as shown in the 1976 printing of *Webster's New Collegiate Dictionary*).

- *See ¶812 for words like* air conditioning, *which are derived from hyphenated infinitives like* air-condition.

806 Always hyphenate two nouns when they signify that one person or one thing has two functions.

secretary-treasurer	dinner-dance
clerk-typist	receptionist-switchboard operator

807 Do not hyphenate civil, military, and naval titles of two or more words.

Chief of Police Potenza	Attorney General Leibowitz
General Manager Werner	Rear Admiral Byrd

a. Hyphenate compound titles containing *ex* and *elect.*

ex-President Ford	Vice President-elect Jordan

- *See ¶¶317 and 362 for the capitalization of titles with* ex *and* elect; *see the entry for* Ex-former *in ¶1101 for the correct usage of* ex.

NOTE: Also use a hyphen when *ex* is attached to a noun (for example, *ex-wife, ex-convict*), but omit the hyphen in Latin phrases (for example, *ex officio, ex cathedra*).

b. The hyphen is being dropped from titles containing *vice*. It is still customary in *vice-chancellor,* but it is rapidly disappearing from *vice president* and it is gone from *vice admiral.*

> Vice-Chancellor Hernandez   Vice President Rockefeller   Vice Admiral Keogh

NOTE: Merriam-Webster dictionaries still show the hyphen in *vice president,* but the hyphen is no longer used by the federal government or by many businesses.

808 Compound nouns containing *man* or *men* as an element have traditionally been used generically to refer to males and females alike.

> not for the average *layman*   the history of *mankind*
> of concern to all *businessmen*   reduce the number of *man-hours*
> write your *congressman*   a new supply of *manpower*

a. The *generic* use of such terms is coming under increasing criticism on the grounds that the masculine bias of these terms makes them unsuitable for reference to women as well as men. The following list suggests appropriate alternatives:

In Place of the Generic Term	Use
businessmen	business owners, business executives, business managers, business people
salesmen	sales representatives, salespersons, salesclerks, sales staff, sales force
foremen	supervisors
policemen	police officers
mailmen	mail carriers
congressmen	members of Congress, representatives
mankind	people, humanity, the human race, human beings
man-hours	worker-hours
manpower	work force, human energy

b. When naming a job or role, avoid the use of compound terms ending in *man* or *woman* unless the term refers to a specific person whose gender is known.

> There are ten candidates seeking election to the City Council. (**NOT:** . . . seeking election as city *councilmen.*)
> **BUT:** *Councilwoman* Walters and *Councilman* Holtz will study the proposal.
>
> Write to your *representative in Congress.* (**NOT:** Write to your *congressman.*)
> **BUT:** I was very much impressed by *Congresswoman Barbara Jordan* of Texas.
>
> Who will be appointed as *head* of the committee?   **OR**   Who will be appointed *to chair* the committee? (**NOT:** . . . appointed *chairman* of the committee?)
> **BUT:** Robert Haas has been appointed *chairman* of the committee.

NOTE: Words like *chairperson* and *spokesperson* have recently been coined as a means of avoiding the generic use of masculine compound nouns. Personal taste will dictate whether to use these terms or not. It should be noted, however, that since such terms often generate as much strong feeling as the words they were intended to replace, alternative constructions (like those shown above) may be the best solution.

809 Terms like *doctor, lawyer,* or *nurse* are generic—that is, they apply equally to women and men. Therefore, do not use compound nouns like *woman lawyer* or *male nurse* unless there is a legitimate reason for making a distinction according to sex.

> Next Wednesday there will be a seminar on the problems facing *women lawyers* in the courtroom.

- *Capitalization of hyphenated compound nouns: see ¶362.*
- *Plurals of compound nouns: see ¶¶611–613.*
- *Possessives of compound nouns: see ¶¶634–635.*

Compound Verbs

810 Compound verbs are usually hyphenated or solid.

to air-condition	to dry-clean	to backstop	to pinpoint
to blue-pencil	to quick-freeze	to downgrade	to proofread
to cross-examine	to spot-check	to handpick	to sidetrack
to double-space	to tape-record	to highlight	to waterproof

NOTE: Do not hyphenate verb-adverb combinations such as *make up, slow down, tie in.* (See also ¶802.)

811 If the infinitive form of a compound verb contains a hyphen, retain the hyphen in the other forms of the verb. (See ¶812 for one exception.)

> Would you like to *air-condition* your entire house?
> The theater was not *air-conditioned.*
> We need an *air-conditioning* expert to advise us.
>
> Please *double-space* this letter.
> This material should not be *double-spaced.*
> **BUT:** Leave a *double space* between paragraphs. (No hyphen in *double space* as a compound noun.)

812 The gerund derived from a hyphenated compound verb requires no hyphen unless it is followed by an object.

> *Dry cleaning* is the best way to clean this garment.
> **BUT:** *Dry-cleaning* this *sweater* will not remove the spot.
>
> *Air conditioning* is no longer as expensive as it used to be.
> **BUT:** In *air-conditioning* an *office,* you must take more than space into account.
>
> *Spot checking* is all we have time for.
> **BUT:** In *spot-checking* the *data,* I found some disturbing errors.

Compound Adjectives

No aspect of style causes greater difficulty than compound adjectives. When a compound adjective is shown hyphenated in the dictionary, you can safely assume only that the expression is hyphenated when it occurs directly *before* a noun. When the same combination of words falls elsewhere in the sentence, the use or omission of hyphens depends on how the words are used.

For the basic rules, see ¶¶813–815. For detailed comments, see the following paragraphs:

- *Adjective + noun (as in* short-term *note): see ¶816.*
- *Number + noun (as in* 40-hour *week): see ¶817.*
- *Compound noun (as in* high school *graduate): see ¶818.*
- *Proper name (as in* Madison Avenue *agencies): see ¶819.*
- *Noun + adjective (as in* tax-free *imports): see ¶820.*
- *Noun + participle (as in* time-consuming *details): see ¶821.*
- *Adjective + participle (as in* nice-looking *receptionist): see ¶822.*
- *Adjective + noun + ed (as in* quick-witted *girl): see ¶823.*
- *Adverb + participle (as in* privately owned *stock): see ¶824a.*
- *Adverb + participle (as in* well-known *facts): see ¶824b.*
- *Adverb + adjective (as in* very exciting *job): see ¶825.*
- *Participle + adverb (as in* warmed-over *ideas): see ¶826.*
- *Adjective + adjective (as in* black leather *notebook): see ¶827.*
- *Phrasal compound (as in* up-to-date *accounts): see ¶828.*

Basic Rules

813 A compound adjective consists of two or more words that function as a unit and express a single thought. These one-thought modifiers are derived from (and take the place of) adjective phrases and clauses. In the following examples the left column shows the original phrase or clause; the right column shows the compound adjective.

Adjective Phrase or Clause	Compound Adjective
imports *that are free of duty*	*duty-free* imports
a woman *who speaks quietly*	a *quiet-spoken* woman
an actor *who is well known*	a *well-known* actor
a conference *held at a high level*	a *high-level* conference
a building *ten stories high*	a *ten-story* building
a report *that is up to date*	an *up-to-date* report

NOTE: In the process of becoming compound adjectives, the adjective phrases and clauses are usually reduced to a few essential words. In addition, these words frequently undergo a change in form (for example, *ten stories high* becomes *ten-story*); sometimes they are put in inverted order (for example, *free of duty* becomes *duty-free*); sometimes they are simply extracted from the phrase or clause without any change in form (for example, *well-known, high-level*).

814 Hyphenate the elements of a compound adjective that occurs *before* a noun. (Reason: The words that make up the compound adjective are not in their normal order or a normal form and require hyphens to hold them together.)

an *old-fashioned* dress (a dress *of an old fashion*)
a *$10,000-a-year* salary (a salary *of $10,000 a year*)
long-range plans (plans *projected over a long range of time*)

(Continued on page 158.)

EXCEPTIONS: A number of compounds like *real estate* and *high school* do not need hyphens when used as adjectives before a noun. (See ¶818.)

815 **a.** When these expressions occur *elsewhere in the sentence*, drop the hyphen if the individual words occur in a normal order and in a normal form. (In such cases the expression no longer functions as a compound adjective.)

Before the Noun	Elsewhere in Sentence
an *X-ray* treatment	It can be treated by X *ray*. (Object of preposition.)
an *up-to-date* report	Please bring the report *up to date*. (Prepositional phrase.)
a *high-level* decision	The decision must be made at a *high level*. (Object of preposition.)
a *never-to-be-forgotten* book	That book is *never to be forgotten*. (Adverb + infinitive phrase.)
an *off-the-record* comment	This comment is *off the record*. (Prepositional phrase.)

b. When these expressions occur elsewhere in the sentence *but are in an inverted word order or an altered form*, retain the hyphen.

Before the Noun	Elsewhere in Sentence
a *tax-exempt* purchase	The purchase was *tax-exempt*. BUT: The purchase was *exempt from taxes*.
government-owned lands	These lands are *government-owned*. BUT: These lands are *owned by the government*.
a *friendly-looking* salesclerk	That salesclerk is *friendly-looking*. BUT: That salesclerk *looks friendly*.
high-priced goods	These goods are *high-priced*. BUT: These goods carry a *high price*.

NOTE: The following kinds of compound adjectives are always hyphenated:

- *Noun + adjective (for example, tax-exempt): see ¶820.*
- *Noun + participle (for example, government-owned): see ¶821.*
- *Adjective + participle (for example, friendly-looking): see ¶822.*
- *Adjective + noun + ed (for example, high-priced): see ¶823.*

Adjective + Noun (see also ¶¶817–819)

816 **a.** Hyphenate this combination of elements *before* a noun. Do not hyphenate these elements when they play a normal function *elsewhere in the sentence* (for example, as the object of a preposition or of a verb). However, if the expression continues to function as a compound adjective, retain the hyphen.

Before the Noun	Elsewhere in Sentence
a *short-term* loan	This loan runs only for a *short term*. (Object of preposition.)
low-risk investments	These investments carry a *low risk*. (Object of verb.)
high-grade ore	This ore is of a *high grade*. (Object of preposition.) BUT: This ore is *high-grade*. (Compound adjective.)
part-time job	This job is *part-time*. (Compound adjective.)

b. Combinations involving comparative or superlative adjectives plus nouns follow the same pattern.

Before the Noun	Elsewhere in Sentence
a *larger-size* shirt	He wears a *larger size.* (Object of verb.)
the *finest-quality* goods	These goods are of the *finest quality.* (Object of preposition.)

Number + Noun

817 a. When a number and a noun form a one-thought modifier *before* a noun (as in *four-story* building), make the noun singular and hyphenate the expression. When the expression has a normal form and a normal function *elsewhere in the sentence,* do not hyphenate it.

Before the Noun	Elsewhere in Sentence
a *50-cent* fee	a fee of *50 cents*
a *two-year* contract	a contract for *two years*
twentieth-century painting	painting of the *twentieth century*
an *8-foot* ceiling	a ceiling *8 feet* high
a *55-mile-an-hour* speed limit	a speed limit of *55 miles an hour*
an *8½- by 11-inch* book (see ¶829)	a book *8½ by 11 inches*
a *5-liter* bottle	a bottle holding *5 liters*
a *100-meter* sprint	a sprint of *100 meters*
a *35-kilogram* limit	a limit of *35 kilograms*

EXCEPTIONS: a *20 percent* increase, a *$12 million* profit

b. A hyphenated compound adjective and an unhyphenated possessive expression often provide *alternative* ways of expressing the same thought. Do not use both styles together.

a *two-week* trip OR a *two weeks'* trip (BUT NOT: a *two-weeks'* trip)

Compound Noun

818 A number of adjective-noun combinations (such as *life insurance* and *real estate*) are actually well-established compound nouns serving as adjectives. Unlike *short-term, low-risk,* and the other examples in ¶816, these expressions refer to well-known concepts or institutions. Because they are easily grasped as a unit, they *do not* require a hyphen.

civil service examination	*income tax* return	*real estate* agent
data processing procedures	*life insurance* policy	*safe deposit* box
mass production techniques	*high school* diploma	*social security* tax

NOTE: When dictionaries and style manuals do not provide guidance on a specific adjective-noun combination, consider whether the expression resembles a well-known compound like *social security* or whether it is more like *short-term.* Then space the combination or hyphenate it accordingly.

Proper Name

819 a. Do not hyphenate the elements in a proper name used as an adjective.

a *Supreme Court* decision	a *Western Union* telegram
a *South American* industrialist	a *Park Avenue* address

(Continued on page 160.)

b. When two or more distinct proper names are combined to form a one-thought modifier, use a hyphen to connect the elements.

a *German-American* restaurant

the *New York-Chicago-Los Angeles* flight (no hyphens within *New York* or *Los Angeles*)

the cuisine is *German-American*

BUT: the flight to New York, Chicago, and Los Angeles

Noun + Adjective

820 **a.** When a compound adjective consists of a noun plus an adjective, hyphenate this combination whether it appears before or after the noun. (See ¶815*b*.)

duty-free	cost-effective	tax-exempt	accident-prone
fire-resistant	labor-intensive	water-repellent	month-long

The income from these bonds is *tax-exempt*.

We import these *water-repellent* fabrics *duty-free*.

b. Through usage a few compound adjectives in this category are now written solid (for example, *carefree, praiseworthy, waterproof*). Moreover, compound adjectives ending in *wide* are now usually written solid (*worldwide, nationwide, statewide, storewide, citywide, countywide, countrywide, industrywide*).

Noun + Participle

821 **a.** When a compound adjective consists of a noun plus a participle, hyphenate this combination whether it appears before or after the noun. (See ¶815*b*.)

air-cooled	interest-bearing	time-consuming
awe-inspiring	law-abiding	tongue-tied
factory-installed	power-driven	wage-earning
government-owned	tailor-made	weather-beaten

The old procedures were all too *time-consuming*.

A number of *city-owned* properties will be auctioned off next week.

b. A few words in this category are now written solid—for example, *handmade, handwoven, handwritten, timesaving, timeworn*.

Adjective + Participle

822 **a.** When a compound adjective consists of an adjective plus a participle, hyphenate this combination whether it appears before or after the noun. (See ¶815*b*.)

smooth-talking	odd-sounding	high-ranking
soft-spoken	sweet-smelling	friendly-looking (see ¶824*a*)

He is a *smooth-talking* operator, who never delivers what he promises.

Betty was anything but *soft-spoken* in arguing against the new procedures.

b. Retain the hyphen even when a comparative or superlative adjective is combined with a participle—for example, *nicer-looking, oddest-sounding, better-tasting, best-looking*.

As the *highest-ranking* official present, Mrs. Egan took charge of the meeting.
This year's brochure is *better-looking* than last year's.

Adjective + Noun + *ED*

823 **a.** When a compound adjective consists of an adjective plus a noun plus
ed, hyphenate this combination whether it appears before or after the
noun. (See ¶815*b*.)

able-bodied	left-handed	short-lived
blue-eyed	light-headed	(pronounced *līvd*)
double-spaced (see ¶811)	middle-aged	small-sized
good-natured	old-fashioned	tough-minded
high-priced	quick-witted	two-fisted

Our success was *short-lived:* the business folded after six months.

These symptoms commonly occur in *middle-aged* executives.

b. Retain the hyphen when a comparative or superlative adjective is
combined with a noun plus *ed*—for example, *smaller-sized, highest-priced, best-natured.*

Our *higher-priced* articles sold well this year.

These goods are *higher-priced* than the samples you showed me.

c. A few compound adjectives in this category are now written solid—for
example, *hardheaded, lighthearted, shortsighted.*

Adverb + Participle (see also ¶825)

824 **a.** Do not hyphenate an adverb-participle combination if the adverb ends
in *ly.*

a *poorly constructed* house	a *privately owned* corporation
a *highly valued* employee	a *newly created* staff

NOTE: Hyphenate adjectives ending in *ly* when they are used with participles. (See ¶822.)

a *friendly-sounding* voice	a *motherly looking* woman

▪ *To distinguish between adjectives and adverbs ending in* ly, *see* ¶¶1069–1070.

b. Other adverb-participle compounds are hyphenated *before* the noun.
When these same combinations occur in the predicate, drop the hyphen if
the participle is part of the verb.

Before the Noun	Elsewhere in Sentence
a *well-known* consultant	This consultant <u>is</u> well <u>known</u>.
much-needed reforms	These reforms <u>were</u> much <u>needed</u>.
the *above-mentioned* facts	These facts <u>were mentioned</u> above.
the *ever-changing* tides	The tides <u>are</u> ever <u>changing</u>.
a *long-remembered* tribute	Today's tribute <u>will be</u> long <u>remembered</u>.

However, if the participle does not become part of the verb and continues to function with the adverb as a one-thought modifier in the predicate, retain the hyphen.

(Continued on page 162.)

Before the Noun	Elsewhere in Sentence
a *well-behaved* child	The child is *well-behaved*.
a decision with *far-reaching* implications	The implications are *far-reaching*.
a *clear-cut* position	Their position was *clear-cut*.

NOTE: You couldn't say, "The child is behaved" or "The implications are reaching" or "Their position was cut." Since the participle is not part of the verb, it must be treated as part of a compound adjective. Compare the use of *fast-moving* in the following examples.

Before the Noun	Elsewhere in Sentence
a *fast-moving* narrative	The narrative is *fast-moving*.
	BUT: The narrative *is* fast <u>moving</u> toward a climax.

c. Hyphenated adverb-participle combinations like those in *b* retain the hyphen even when the adverb is in the comparative or superlative.

a *better-known* brand	the *hardest-working* secretary
the *best-behaved* child	a *faster-moving* stock clerk

Adverb + Adjective

825 **a.** A number of adverb-adjective combinations closely resemble the adverb-participle combinations described in ¶824. However, since an adverb normally modifies an adjective, do not use a hyphen to connect these words.

a *not too interesting* report	a *very moving* story
a *rather irritating* delay	feeling *quite tired*

b. Do not hyphenate comparative or superlative forms where the adverbs *more, most, less,* or *least* are combined with an adjective.

a *more determined* person	a *less complicated* transaction
the *most exciting* event	the *least interesting* lecture

Participle + Adverb

826 Hyphenate a participle-adverb combination *before* the noun but not when it occurs elsewhere in the sentence.

Before the Noun	Elsewhere in Sentence
filled-in forms	These forms should be *filled in*.
worn-out equipment	The equipment was *worn out*.
a *tuned-up* engine	The engine has been *tuned up*.
a *scaled-down* proposal	The proposal must be *scaled down*.
a *turned-on* look	The customers are *turned on*.
unheard-of savings	These savings are *unheard of*.

Adjective + Adjective

827 **a.** Do not hyphenate independent adjectives preceding a noun.

a *distinguished public* orator (*public* modifies *orator; distinguished* modifies *public orator*)

a *long and tiring* trip (*long* and *tiring* each modify *trip*) a *warm, enthusiastic* reception (*warm* and *enthusiastic* each modify *reception;* a comma marks the omission of *and*)

- See ¶¶168–171 for the use of commas with adjectives.

b. In a few special cases, two adjectives joined by *and* are hyphenated because they function as one-thought modifiers. These, however, are rare exceptions to the rule stated in *a.*

a *hard-and-fast* rule   a *cut-and-dried* proposal   a *yes-or-no* answer

Henry views the matter in *black-and-white* terms. (A one-thought modifier.)

BUT: Sue wore a *black and white* dress to the party. (Two independent adjectives.)

c. Hyphenate expressions such as *blue-black, green-gray,* and *red-hot* before and after a noun. However, do not hyphenate expressions such as *bluish green, dark gray,* or *bright red* (where the first word clearly modifies the second).

Always use *blue-black* ink in this office.   Her dress was *bluish green.*

Phrasal Compound

828 **a.** Hyphenate phrases used as compound adjectives *before* a noun. Do not hyphenate such phrases when they occur normally elsewhere in the sentence.

Before the Noun	Elsewhere in Sentence
an *up-to-date* report	The report is *up to date.*
a *change-of-address* notice	This notice shows his *change of address.*
an *out-of-town* visitor	The visitor is from *out of town.*
a *question-and-answer* period	Leave time for *questions and answers.*
a *life-and-death* matter	It is a matter of *life and death.*
a *hit-and-miss* approach	His approach *hits and misses* the mark. **BUT:** His approach is *hit-and-miss.*
a *twelve-year-old* girl	The girl is only *twelve years old.*
a *$100-a-week* job	The job pays *$100 a week.*
a *straight-from-the-shoulder* talk	I spoke *straight from the shoulder.*
a *would-be* authority	He thought he *would be* an authority.
a *pay-as-you-go* plan	This plan lets you *pay as you go.*
a *well-thought-out* plan	The plan was *well thought out.*
a *much-talked-about* party	The party was *much talked about.*

BUT: in the *not too distant* future (see ¶825a)

b. Do not hyphenate foreign phrases used as adjectives before a noun. (See also ¶287.)

an *ad hoc* ruling   an *a la carte* menu
a *bona fide* offer   a *prima facie* case

Suspending Hyphen

829 **a.** When a series of hyphenated adjectives has a common basic element and this element is shown only with the last term, a "suspending" hyphen follows each adjective.

(Continued on page 164.)

long- *and* short-term securities   10- *and* 20-year bonds
8½- *by* 11-inch paper   hard- *and* soft-coal dealers

b. Space once after each suspending hyphen unless a comma is required at that point.

a *six- to eight-week* delay   3-, 5-, *and* 8-gallon buckets

Prefixes and Suffixes

830 In general, do not use a hyphen to set off a prefix at the beginning of a word or a suffix at the end of a word. (See ¶807*a* for two exceptions: *ex-* and *-elect*.)

*after*thought	*mini*bike	king*dom*
*ambi*dextrous	*mis*spell	three*fold*
*ante*date	*mono*syllable	thought*ful*
*anti*climax	*multi*media	neighbor*hood*
*audio*visual	*non*essential	accoun*ting*
*bi*annual	*over*confident	fort*yish*
*by*laws (**BUT**: by-product)	*post*script	heart*less**
*centi*meter	*pre*requisite	child*like**
*counter*productive	*re*organize	careful*ly*
*de*centralize	*retro*active	excite*ment*
*extra*legal	*semi*annual	upper*most*
*fore*most	*step*mother	costli*ness*
*hyper*critical	*sub*division	fire*proof*
*il*legal	*super*abundant	leader*ship*
*im*material	*trans*action	lone*some*
*in*dependent	*ultra*critical	back*ward*
*inter*office	*under*current	nation*wide* (see ¶820*b*)
*kilo*gram	*un*related	edge*wise*
*milli*liter	*up*take	trust*worthy*

* If, in the addition of these suffixes, three *l*'s occur in succession, use a hyphen; for example *bell-like, shell-less.*

831 When the prefix ends with *a* or *i* and the base word begins with the same letter, use a hyphen after the prefix to prevent misreading.

ultra-active   semi-independent   anti-intellectual
intra-abdominal   semi-indirect   anti-inflationary

832 When the prefix ends with *e* or *o* and the base word begins with the same letter, the hyphen is almost always omitted.

coordinate   reeducate   reelect   preempt
cooperative   reemploy   reemphasize   preexisting

BUT: co-op, co-owner, co-worker, de-emphasize, de-escalate

833 Use a hyphen after *self* when it serves as a prefix.

self-confidence   self-addressed   self-evident

Omit the hyphen when *self* serves as the base word and is followed by a suffix.

selfish   selfsame   selfless

834 As a rule, the prefix *re* (meaning "again") should not be followed by a hyphen. A few words require the hyphen so that they can be distinguished from other words with the same spelling but a different meaning.

to *re-form* the class	to *reform* a sinner
to *re-cover* a chair	to *recover* from an illness
to *re-collect* the slips	to *recollect* the mistake
she *re-marked* the ticket	as he *remarked* to me

835 When a prefix is added to a word that begins with a capital, use a hyphen after the prefix.

anti-American	mid-January	pre-Revolutionary War days
non-Asiatic	trans-Canadian	post-World War II period

BUT: transatlantic, transpacific, the Midwest

836 Always hyphenate family terms involving the prefix *great-* or the suffix *-in-law,* but treat terms involving *step-* and *grand-* solid.

her great-grandfather	my grandmother	your brother-in-law
their great-aunt	his grandchild	my stepdaughter

837 Avoid feminine suffixes like *-ess, -ette,* and *-trix.*

She has an established reputation as an *author* and a *poet.* (**NOT:** *authoress* and *poetess.*)

If you have any questions, ask your *flight attendant.* (**NOT:** *steward* or *stewardess.*)

Sometimes One Word, Sometimes Two Words

838 A number of common words may be written either as one solid word or as two separate words, depending on the meaning. See individual entries listed alphabetically in ¶1101 (unless otherwise indicated) for the following words:

Almost–all most	Into–in to (see *In*)
Already–all ready	Maybe–may be
Altogether–all together	Nobody–no body
Always–all ways	None–no one (see ¶1013)
Anyone–any one (see ¶1010, note)	Onto–on to (see *On*)
Anyway–any way	Someone–some one (see ¶1010, note)
Awhile–a while	Sometime–sometimes–some time
Everyday–every day	
Everyone–every one (see ¶1010, note)	Upon–up on (see *On*)
Indifferent–in different	Whoever–who ever
Indirect–in direct	

- *Hyphens in spelled-out numbers: see ¶465.*
- *Hyphens in spelled-out dates: see ¶411.*
- *Hyphens in spelled-out amounts of money: see ¶420.*
- *Hyphens in spelled-out fractions: see ¶427.*
- *Hyphens in numbers representing a continuous sequence: see ¶459.*

WORD DIVISION

Basic Rules (¶¶901–906)
Preferred Practices (¶¶907–918)
Breaks Within Word Groups (¶¶919–920)
Guides to Correct Syllabication (¶¶921–922)

Whenever possible, avoid dividing a word at the end of a line. Word divisions are unattractive, and they may slow down or even confuse the reader. When word division is unavoidable, try to divide at a point that will least disrupt the reader's grasp of the word.

The rules that follow are intended for typists. (Printers may take greater liberties.) The rules fall into two categories: (1) those that a typist must never violate (see ¶¶901–906) and (2) those that a typist should follow whenever space permits a choice (see ¶¶907–920).

NOTE: The 1976 printing of *Webster's New Collegiate Dictionary* (published by the G. & C. Merriam Company, Springfield, Massachusetts) is the authority for the word divisions shown in this manual.

Basic Rules

901 Divide words only between syllables. Whenever you are unsure of the syllabication of a word, consult a dictionary. (See also ¶¶921–922 for some guides to correct syllabication.)

NOTE: Some syllable breaks shown in the dictionary are not acceptable in typewritten material as points of word division. See ¶¶903–904.

902 Do not divide one-syllable words. Even when *ed* is added to some words, they still remain one-syllable words and cannot be divided.

weight	thought	strength	scheme
passed	trimmed	weighed	shipped

903 Do not set off a one-letter syllable at the beginning or the end of a word.

amount (**NOT:** a- mount)	bacteria (**NOT:** bacteri- a)
ideal (**NOT:** i- deal)	piano (**NOT:** pian- o)

NOTE: So as to discourage word division at the beginning or end of a word, some dictionaries no longer mark one-letter syllables at these points.

904 Do not divide a word unless you can leave a syllable of at least three characters (the last of which is the hyphen) on the upper line and you can carry a syllable of at least three characters (the last may be a punctuation mark) to the next line.

ad- joining	*de-* tract	*un-* important	*im-* possible
bluff- *ing*	bet- *ter*	check- *up,*	there- *of.*

NOTE: Whenever possible, avoid dividing any word with fewer than six letters.

905 Do not divide abbreviations.

ILGWU	UNESCO	SUNFED	ASCAP
Ph.D.	admin.	f.o.b.	unasgd.

NOTE: An abbreviation like *AFL-CIO* may be divided after the hyphen.

906 Do not divide contractions.

doesn't	couldn't	can't	o'clock

Preferred Practices

While it is acceptable to divide a word at any syllable break shown in the dictionary, it is often better to divide at some points than at others in order to obtain a more intelligible grouping of syllables. The following rules indicate preferred practices whenever you have sufficient space left in the typed line to permit a choice.

907 Divide a solid compound word between the elements of the compound.

paper- weight	time- table	home- owner	school- teacher

908 Divide a hyphenated compound word at the point of the hyphen.

self- control	brother- in-law	get- together	baby- sitter

909 Divide a word *after* a prefix (rather than within the prefix).

Preferred		Acceptable	
. . . .	intro-	. . . .	in-
duce	inter-	troduce	in-
national. . . .	super-	ternational .	su-
sonic	circum-	personic . . .	cir-
stances	ambi-	cumstances .	am-
dextrous		bidextrous	

However, avoid divisions like the following, which can easily confuse a reader.

Confusing		Better	
. . . .	inter-	. . . .	in-
pret	super-	terpret	su-
fluous	circum-	perfluous . . .	cir-
ference	ambi-	cumference .	am-
tious		bitious	

910 Divide a word *before* a suffix (rather than within the suffix).

> practi- cable (RATHER THAN: practica- ble)
> permis- sible (RATHER THAN: permissi- ble)

911 When a word has both a prefix and a suffix, choose the division point that groups the syllables more intelligibly.

> consign- ment (RATHER THAN: con- signment)

The same principle applies when a word contains a suffix added on to a suffix. Choose the division point that produces the better grouping.

> careless- ness (RATHER THAN: care- lessness)

912 Whenever you have a choice, divide after a prefix or before a suffix (rather than within the root word).

> pre- mature (RATHER THAN: prema- ture)   legal- ize (RATHER THAN: le- galize)

NOTE: Avoid divisions that could confuse a reader.

> re- arrangement (RATHER THAN: rear- rangement)
> re- adjust (RATHER THAN: read- just)

913 When a one-letter syllable occurs within the root of a word, divide *after* it (rather than before it).

> criti- cal   sepa- rate   simi- lar   regu- late

914 When two separately sounded vowels come together in a word, divide between them.

> radi- ator   valu- able   cre- ative   retro- active
> gradu- ation   propri- etary   flu- orescent   physi- ological

915 When necessary, an extremely long number can be divided after a comma; for example, *10,649,-   376,000.*

916 Do not allow more than two consecutive lines to end in hyphens.

917 Try not to divide at the end of the first line or the last full line in a paragraph.

918 Do not divide the last word on a page.

Breaks Within Word Groups

919 Try to keep together certain kinds of word groups that need to be read together—for example, page and number, month and day, month and year, title and surname, surname and abbreviation (or number), number and abbreviation, or number and unit of measure.

> page 63   March 1980   Helen Conti, M.D.   6:05 p.m.
> January 16   Mr. Harris   Joseph Finley II   12 feet

920 When necessary, longer word groups may be broken according to the following rules.

a. *Dates* may be broken between the day and year.

. . . . September 21,   **NOT:** . . . . September
1979 . . . .   21, 1979 . . . .

b. *Street addresses* may be broken between the name of the street and
Street, Avenue, or the like. If the street name consists of two or more
words, the break may come between words in the street name.

. . . . 914 Glen   **NOT:** 914
Avenue . . . .   Glen Avenue . . . .

. . . . 289 East   **NOT:** 289
Mountain Road . . . .   East Mountain Road . . . . . .

c. *Names of places* may be broken between the city and the state or
between the state and the ZIP Code. If the city or state name consists of
two or more words, the break may come between words in the city or state
name.

. . . . Portland,   **OR:** . . . . Portland, Oregon
Oregon 97229, ...   97229, ...

. . . . Grand   **OR:** . . . . Grand Forks, North
Rapids, MI 49505 . . . .   Dakota . . . .

d. *Names of persons* may be broken between the given name (including
middle initial if given) and surname.

. . . . Doris E.   **NOT:** . . . . Doris
Roberts . . . .   E. Roberts . . . .

e. *Names preceded by long titles* may be broken between the title and the
name (preferably) or between words in the title.

. . . . Vice President   **OR:** . . . . Vice
Henry S. Brewster . . . .   President Henry S. Brewster . .

f. *A numbered or lettered list* may be broken before any number or letter.

. . . . these points: **NOT:** . . . . these points: (1)
(1) All cards should . . . .   All cards should . . . .

g. *A sentence with a dash in it* may be broken after the dash.

. . . . Early next year—   **NOT:** . . . . Early next year
say, in March—let's . . . .   —say, in March—let's . . . . .

Guides to Correct Syllabication

921 Syllabication is generally based on pronunciation rather than on roots
and derivations. Careful pronunciation will often aid you in determining
the correct syllabication of a word.

knowl- edge (**NOT:** know- ledge)   prod- uct (**NOT:** pro- duct)
chil- dren (**NOT:** child- ren)   ser- vice (**NOT:** serv- ice)

Note how syllabication changes as pronunciation changes.

Verbs	**Nouns**
pre- sent (to make a gift)	pres- ent (a gift)
re- cord (to make an official copy)	rec- ord (an official copy)
pro- ject (to throw forward)	proj- ect (an undertaking)

922   The following paragraphs offer some guides to syllabication. You are not obliged to divide a word at the points named, but you can safely do so without checking a dictionary.

a. If a word ends in double consonants *before* a suffix is added, you can safely divide *after* the double consonants (so long as the suffix creates an extra syllable).

sell- ers   bless- ing   staff- ing   buzz- ers

BUT: filled, distressed

b. If a final consonant is doubled *because* a suffix is added, you can safely divide *between* the double consonants (so long as the suffix creates an extra syllable).

ship- ping   omit- ted   begin- ner   refer- ral

BUT: shipped, referred

c. When double consonants appear elsewhere *within* the base word (but not as the final consonants), you can safely divide between them.

neces- sary   ter- rible   mil- lion   recom- mend
con- nect   suc- cess   dif- fer   sup- pose

GRAMMAR

Subjects and Verbs

Basic Rule of Agreement

1001 A verb must agree with its subject in number and person.

She is ready to start work on Monday. (Third person singular subject *she* with third person singular verb *is*.)

They are about to move to Utah. (Third person plural subject *they* with third person plural verb *are*.)

I am interested in applying for the job. (First person singular subject *I* with first person singular verb *am*.)

The *invoice was paid* by Check 4712. (Third person singular subject *invoice* with third person singular verb *was paid*.)

Your *chairs were shipped* on the 11th. (Third person plural subject *chairs* with third person plural verb *were shipped*.)

a. A plural verb is always required after *you*, even when *you* is singular, referring to only one person.

You were very kind to me during my illness.

b. Although *s* or *es* added to a *noun* indicates the plural form, *s* or *es* added to a *verb* indicates the third person singular. (See ¶1035.)

The price *seems* reasonable.	The tax *applies* to everyone.
The prices *seem* reasonable.	The taxes *apply* to everyone.

Subjects Joined by *And*

1002 If the subject consists of two or more words connected by *and* or by *both . . . and*, the subject is plural and requires a plural verb.

Ms. Rizzo and *Mr. Bruce have* received promotions.

Both the *collection* and the *delivery* of mail *are* to be curtailed. (The repetition of *the* with the second subject emphasizes that two different items are meant.)

EXCEPTIONS:

a. Use a singular verb when two or more subjects connected by *and* refer to the same person or thing. (See also ¶1028, third example.)

Our *secretary and treasurer is* Frances Eisenberg. (One person.)
Corned beef and cabbage was his favorite dish. (One dish.)

b. Use a singular verb when two or more subjects connected by *and* are preceded by *each, every, many a*, or *many an*. (See also ¶1009b.)

Every jacket, suit, and topcoat *is* marked for reduction.
Many a woman and man *has* responded to our plea for funds.

Subjects Joined by *Or* or Similar Connectives

1003 If the subject consists of two or more *singular* words connected by *or, either . . . or, neither . . . nor*, or *not only . . . but also*, the subject is singular and requires a singular verb.

(Continued on page 174.)

Either *July* or *August is* a good time for the sales conference.
Neither the *Credit Department* nor the *Accounting Department has* the file.
Not only a *typewriter* but also a *stand has* been requisitioned.

1004 If the subject consists of two or more *plural* words connected by *or, either . . . or, neither . . . nor,* or *not only . . . but also,* the subject is plural and requires a plural verb.

Neither the regional *managers* nor the *salesclerks have* the data you want.

1005 If the subject is made up of both singular and plural words connected by *or, either . . . or, neither . . . nor,* or *not only . . . but also,* the verb agrees with the nearer part of the subject. Since sentences with singular and plural subjects usually sound better with plural verbs, try to locate the plural subject closer to the verb whenever this can be done without sacrificing the emphasis desired.

Either *Miss Hertig* or her *assistants have* the data. (The verb *have* agrees with the nearer subject, *assistants*.)

Neither the *buyers* nor the *sales manager is* in favor of the system. (The verb *is* agrees with the nearer subject, *sales manager*.)
BETTER: Neither the *sales manager* nor the *buyers are* in favor of the system. (The sentence reads better with the plural verb *are*. The subjects *sales manager* and *buyers* have been rearranged without changing the emphasis.)

Not only the *teachers* but also the *superintendent is* in favor of the plan. (The verb *is* agrees with the nearer subject, *superintendent*. With the use of *not only . . . but also,* the emphasis falls on the subject following *but also*.)

Not only the *superintendent* but also the *teachers are* in favor of the plan. (When the sentence is rearranged, the nearer subject *teachers* requires the plural verb *are*. However, the emphasis has now changed.)

Not only my *colleagues* but *I am* in favor of the plan. (The first person verb *am* agrees with the nearer subject *I*. Rearranging this sentence will change the emphasis.)

▪ *See the last four examples in ¶1028 for* neither . . . nor *constructions following* there is *or* there are; *see also ¶1049c for examples of subject-verb-pronoun agreement in these constructions.*

Intervening Phrases and Clauses

1006 When establishing agreement between subject and verb, disregard intervening phrases and clauses. (See ¶¶1013, 1025 for exceptions.)

The *purchase order* for new supplies *has* not been found. (Disregard *for new supplies*. *Purchase order* is the subject and takes the singular verb *has*.)

The *prices* shown in our catalog *do* not include sales tax.

Only *one* of the items that I ordered *has* been delivered. (See also ¶1008.)

Her *experience* with banks and brokerage houses *gives* her excellent qualifications for the position.

The *color* of the container, not the contents, *determines* the consumer's initial reaction.

1007 The insertion of phrases introduced by *with, together with, along with, as well as, plus, in addition to, besides, including, accompanied by, followed by, rather than,* etc., between subject and verb does not affect the number of the verb. If the subject is singular, use a singular verb; if the subject is plural, use a plural verb.

> *Mrs. Swenson*, together with her husband and daughter, *is* going to Arizona.
>
> This *study*, as well as many earlier reports, *shows* that the disease can be arrested if detected in time.
>
> The sales *reports*, including the summary, *were* sent to you last week.
>
> *No one*, not even the company officers, *has* been told. (See ¶1010.)

One of . . .

1008 a. Use a singular verb after a phrase beginning with *one of* or *one of the*; the singular verb agrees with the subject *one*. (Disregard any plural that follows *of* or *of the*.)

> *One* of the sales journals *has* been lost.
>
> *One* of the reasons for so many absences *is* poor health.
>
> *One* of us *has* to take the responsibility.
>
> *One* of you *is* to be nominated for the office.

b. The phrases *one of those who* and *one of the things that* are followed by plural verbs because the verbs refer to *those* or *things* (rather than to *one*).

> She is one of *those* who *favor* increasing the staff. (In other words, of *those* who *favor* increasing the staff, she is one. *Favor* is plural to agree with *those*.)
>
> He is one of our *employees* who *are* never late. (Of our *employees* who *are* never late, he is one.)
>
> I ordered one of the *calculators* that *were* advertised. (Of the *calculators* that *were* advertised, I ordered one.)
>
> John is only one of the *staff members* who *are* going to be transferred. (Of the *staff members* who *are* going to be transferred, John is only one.)

EXCEPTION: When the words *the only* precede such phrases, the meaning is singular and a singular verb is required. Note that both words, *the* and *only*, are required to produce a singular meaning.

> John is *the only one* of the staff members who *is* going to be transferred. (Of the staff members, John is *the only one* who *is* going to be transferred. Here the singular verb *is* is required to agree with *one*.)

Indefinite Pronouns Always Singular

1009 a. The words *each, every, either, neither, one, another,* and *much* are always singular. When they are used as subjects or as adjectives modifying subjects, a singular verb is required.

> *Each has* a clear-cut set of responsibilities.
>
> *Each employee is* responsible for maintaining an orderly work station.
>
> *Either* of the women *is* eligible. **OR:** *Either* woman *is* eligible. (See ¶¶1003–1005 for the use of *either . . . or* and *neither . . . nor*.)
>
> *One* shipment *has* already gone out; *another is* to leave the warehouse tomorrow.
>
> *Much remains* to be done. **OR:** *Much* work *remains* to be done.

(Continued on page 176.)

b. When *each, every, many a,* or *many an* precedes two or more subjects joined by *and,* the verb should be singular.

> *Every* teacher and student *has* been notified. (See ¶1002b for other examples.)

EXCEPTION: When *each* follows a plural subject, keep the verb plural. In that position, *each* has no effect on the number of the verb. To test the correctness of such sentences, mentally omit *each.*

> The *members* each *feel* their responsibility.
> *They* each *have* high expectations.
> *Twelve* each of these items *are* required.

1010 The following compound pronouns are always singular and require a singular verb:

anybody	everybody	nobody	somebody
anything	everything	nothing	something
anyone	everyone	no one	someone
OR any one	OR every one		OR some one

> *Everyone is* required to register in order to vote.
> *Something tells* me I'm wrong.

NOTE: Spell *anyone, everyone,* and *someone* as two words when these pronouns are followed by an *of* phrase or are used to mean "one of a number of things."

> *Every one* of us (each person in the group) *likes* to be appreciated.
> BUT: *Everyone* (everybody) *likes* to be appreciated.

1011 Use a singular verb when two compound pronouns joined by *and* are used as subjects.

> *Anyone* and *everyone is* entitled to a fair hearing.

Indefinite Pronouns Always Plural

1012 The words *both, few, many, others,* and *several* are always plural. When they are used as subjects or as adjectives modifying subjects, a plural verb is required.

> *Several* members *were* invited; the *others were* overlooked.
> *Both* books *are* out of print.
> *Many were* asked, but *few were* able to answer.

Indefinite Pronouns Singular or Plural

1013 *All, none, any, some, more,* and *most* may be singular or plural, depending on the noun they refer to. (The noun often occurs in an *of* phrase immediately following.)

> *All* the manuscript *has* been finished.
> *All* the reports *have* been handed in.

> *Some was* acceptable. (Meaning some of the manuscript.)
> *Some were* acceptable. (Meaning some of the reports.)

> *Is* there *any* (money) left?   *Are* there *any* (bills) to be paid?

Do any of you *know* John Ferguson well? (*Any* is plural because it refers to the plural *you*; hence the plural verb *do know*.)

Does any one of you *know* John Ferguson well? (*Any* is singular because it refers to the singular *one*; hence the singular verb *does know*.)

More than one customer *has complained* about that item. (*More* refers to the singular noun *customer*; hence the singular verb *has complained*.)

More than five customers *have complained* . . . (*More* refers to the plural noun *customers*; hence the plural verb *have complained*.)

Most of the stock *has* been sold, but *more* of these suits *are* due.

Some of the food *seems* too high-priced.

Some of the items *seem* too high-priced.

None of the merchandise *was* stolen.

None of the packages *were* properly wrapped.

None were injured. (Meaning none of the passengers.)

NOTE: In formal usage, *none* is still considered a singular pronoun. In general usage, however, *none* is considered singular or plural, depending on the number of the noun to which it refers. *No one* or *not one* is often used in place of *none* to stress the singular idea.

Nouns Ending in *S*

1014 Some nouns appear to be plural but are actually singular. When used as subjects, these nouns require singular verbs.

news (*no plural*)   summons (*plural:* summonses)
measles (*no plural*)   lens (*plural:* lenses)

The *news* from overseas *is* very discouraging.

The *lens has* to be reground.

1015 A number of nouns are always considered plural, even though they each refer to a single thing. As subjects, they require plural verbs.

credentials	goods	premises	riches	thanks
earnings	grounds	proceeds	savings	winnings

The *premises are* now available for inspection.

My *earnings* this year *are* not what I had counted on.

NOTE: The following nouns are considered plural unless preceded by the term *a pair of*.

glasses	scissors	pliers	pants	trousers

The *scissors need* sharpening. **BUT:** A *pair* of scissors *has* been taken.

1016 Some nouns have the same form in the plural as in the singular. When used as subjects, these nouns take singular or plural verbs according to the meaning.

series	means	deer	sheep	moose

The *series* of concerts planned for the spring *looks* very enticing. (One series.)

Three *series* of tickets *are* going to be issued. (Three series.)

One *means* of breaking the impasse *is* to offer more money.

Other *means* of solving the problem *have* not come to mind.

Nouns Ending in *ICS*

1017 Many nouns ending in *ics* (such as *economics, ethics, politics,* and *statistics*) take singular or plural verbs, depending on how they are used. When they refer to a body of knowledge or a course of study, they are *singular.* When they refer to qualities or activities, they are *plural.*

> *Economics* (a course of study) *is* a prerequisite for advanced business courses.
> The *economics* (the economic aspects) of his plan *are* not very sound.

Nouns With Foreign Plurals

1018 Watch for nouns with foreign-plural endings (see ¶614). Such plural nouns, when used as subjects, require plural verbs.

> No *criteria have* been established. (**BUT:** No *criterion has* been established.)
> *Parentheses are* required around such references. (**BUT:** The closing *parenthesis was* omitted.)
> The *media* through which we reach our clients *are* quality magazines and radio broadcasts. (**BUT:** The *medium* we find most effective *is* television.)

NOTE: The noun *data* (which is plural in form) is now commonly followed by a singular verb.

> The *data* obtained after two months of experimentation *is* now being analyzed.
> **BUT:** The *data* assembled by six researchers *are* now being compared. (When the term *data* implies several distinct sets of information, use a plural verb.)

Collective Nouns

1019 The following rules govern the form of verb to be used when a collective noun is the subject. (A *collective noun* is a word that is singular in form but represents a group of persons, animals, or things; for example, *army, audience, board, cabinet, class, committee, company, corporation, council, department, firm, faculty, group, jury, majority, minority, public, society, school.*)

a. If the group is thought of as acting as a unit, the verb should be singular.

> The *Board of Directors meets* Friday.
> The *committee has* agreed to submit *its* report on Monday. (The pronoun *its* is also singular to agree with *committee.*)
> The *firm is* one of the oldest in the field.

b. If the members of the group are thought of as acting separately, the verb should be plural.

> The *committee are* not in agreement on the action *they* should take. (The verb *are* and the pronoun *they* are plural to agree with the plural *committee.*)

NOTE: The use of a collective noun with a plural verb often produces an awkward sentence. Whenever possible, recast the sentence by inserting a phrase like *the members of* before the collective noun.

> The *members* of the committee *are* not in agreement on the action *they* should take.

c. In a number of constructions, the choice of a singular or plural verb often depends on whether you wish to emphasize the group as a unit or as a collection of individuals. However, once the choice has been made, treat the collective noun consistently within the same context.

> I hope your *family is* well. (Emphasizes the family as a whole.)
>
> **OR:** I hope your *family are* all well. (Emphasizes the individuals in the family.)
>
> The *couple was* married (**OR** *were* married) yesterday.
>
> **BUT:** The *couple have* moved into *their* new house. (More idiomatic than "The *couple has* moved into *its* new house.")

NOTE: The expression *a couple of* is plural in meaning.

> A *couple* of customers *have* already reported the error in our ad.

Company Names

1020 Company names may be treated as either singular or plural. Ordinarily, treat the name as singular unless you wish to emphasize the individuals who make up the firm; in that case, use the plural. Once a choice has been made, treat the term consistently within the same context. **NOTE:** If the company is referred to as *they* or *who*, use a plural verb with the company name. If the company is referred to as *it* or *which*, use a singular verb.

> Brooks & Rice *has* lost *its* lease. *It is* now looking for a new location.
>
> **OR:** Brooks & Rice *have* lost *their* lease. *They are* now looking for . . .
>
> (**BUT NOT:** Brooks & Rice *has* lost *its* lease. *They are* now looking for . . .)

Geographical Names

1021 Geographical names that are plural in form are treated as *singular* if they refer to only one thing.

> The *Netherlands is* the first stop on my itinerary.
>
> The *United States has* undertaken a new foreign aid program.
>
> **BUT:** These *United States are* bound together by a common heritage of political and religious liberty.

Titles of Publications

1022 The title of a book or magazine is considered singular, even though it is plural in form.

> *Changing Times* is published every month by Kiplinger.
>
> *U.S. News & World Report* comes out once a week.

The Number; A Number

1023 The expression *the number* has a singular meaning and requires a singular verb; *a number* has a plural meaning and requires a plural verb.

> The *number* of back orders *is* nearly a hundred.
>
> A *number* of our staff *are* going on vacation next week.

Expressions of Time, Money, and Quantities

1024 When subjects expressing periods of time, amounts of money, or quantities represent *a total amount*, singular verbs are used. When these subjects represent *a number of individual units*, plural verbs are used.

> *Three months is* too long a time to wait.
>
> **BUT:** *Three months have* passed since our last exchange of letters.
>
> That *$10,000 was* an inheritance from my uncle.
>
> **BUT:** *Thousands of dollars have* already been spent on the project.
>
> *Ten acres is* considered a small piece of property in this area.
>
> **BUT:** *Ten acres were* plowed last spring.

Fractional Expressions

1025 When the subject is an expression such as *one-half of, two-thirds of, a part of, a majority of,* or *a percentage of:*

a. Use a *singular verb* if a *singular noun* follows *of* or is implied.

> *Three-fourths* of the mailing list *has* been checked.
>
> *Part* of our Norfolk operation *is* being closed down.
>
> A *majority* of 2,000 *signifies* a landslide in this town. (The noun *2,000* is considered singular because it is a total amount. See ¶1024.)

b. Use a *plural verb* when a *plural noun* follows *of* or is implied.

> *Two-thirds* of our customers *live* in the suburbs.
>
> *Part* of the walls *are* to be papered.
>
> A large *percentage* of our students *live* at home.
>
> Over half the *staff have* signed up for the additional benefits. (A collective noun, though singular in form, takes a plural verb when it is plural in meaning.)

Phrases and Clauses as Subjects

1026 When a phrase or clause serves as the subject, the verb should be singular.

> *Analyzing financial reports takes* all my time these days.
>
> *Whether the decision was right or not is* no longer important.
>
> *That they will accept the offer is* far from certain.
>
> *Whomever you support is* likely to be elected.

EXCEPTION: Clauses beginning with *what* may be singular or plural according to the meaning.

> *What we need is* a new statement of policy.
>
> *What we need are* some guidelines.

Subjects in Inverted Sentences

1027 In sentences in which the verb precedes the subject, make sure that the subject and verb agree.

> On the results of this survey *depend the extent* and the *type* of campaign we shall wage.
>
> Attached *are* two carbon *copies.*

What *were* your *reasons* for resigning?
What *is* the *likelihood* of our persuading you to stay?
Where *are* the *reviews* of the Carter book?
NOT: Where *is* (OR *Where's*) the reviews of the Carter book?

1028 In a sentence beginning with *there is, there are, here is,* or *here are,* the real subject follows the verb. Use *is* when the real subject is singular, *are* when it is plural.

There is a vast *difference* between the two plans. (Subject is *difference.*)
There are a great many *angles* to this problem. (Subject is *angles.*)

Here is an old *friend and* former *partner* of mine. (The subject, *friend and partner,* is singular because only one person is referred to. See ¶1002a.)
Here are a *catalog* and an *order blank.* (The subject is *catalog* and *order blank.*)

There is more than one *way* to solve the problem. (See also ¶1013.)
There are more than five *candidates* running for mayor.

There are a *number* of problems to be resolved. (See also ¶1023.)
Here is the number of orders received since Monday.

Here is ten *dollars* as a contribution. (See also ¶1024.)
Here are ten silver *dollars* for your collection.

There is neither a *student* nor a *teacher* who *has* solved that problem. (See ¶1003 for two singular subjects joined by *neither . . . nor.*)
There are neither *staples* nor *paper clips* in the supplies cabinet. (See ¶1004 for two plural subjects joined by *neither . . . nor.*)
There are neither *carbon ribbons* nor *cleaning fluid* left in stock. (*Are* agrees with the nearer subject. See also ¶1005 for singular and plural subjects joined by *neither . . . nor.*)
There is neither *ink eradicator* nor *ink erasers* on hand. (*Is* agrees with the nearer subject, *ink eradicator.* See also ¶1005.)

Subjects and Predicate Complements

1029 Sentences containing a linking verb (such as *become* or some form of *to be*) sometimes have a plural subject and a singular complement or a singular subject and a plural complement. In such cases make sure that the verb agrees with the *subject* (and not with the complement).

Bicycles are the only product we make.
One of the things we have to keep track of *is* entertainment expenses. (Use *is* to agree with *one,* the subject.)
It is they who are at fault. (Use *is* to agree with *it,* the subject.)

NOTE: Do not confuse the last two examples with the *inverted* sentences shown in ¶1028. In a sentence beginning with *here is* or *there is,* the subject follows the linking verb. In a sentence beginning with *it is* or *one . . . is,* the subject precedes the linking verb.

Verbs

This section deals with the correct use of verb tenses and other verb forms. For the rules on agreement of verbs with subjects, see ¶¶1001–1029.

Principal Parts

1030 The principal parts of a verb are the four simple forms upon which all tenses and other modifications of the verb are based.

a. In most verbs, the past and the past participle are formed simply by adding *d* or *ed* to the present form; the present participle is formed by adding *ing* to the present.

Present	Past	Past Participle	Present Participle	
fill	filled	filled	filling	
need	needed	needed	needing	
taxi	taxied	taxied	taxiing	
drop	dropped	dropped	dropping	(see ¶701)
occur	occurred	occurred	occurring	(see ¶702)
offer	offered	offered	offering	(see ¶704)
argue	argued	argued	arguing	(see ¶707)
die	died	died	dying	(see ¶709)
try	tried	tried	trying	(see ¶710)
obey	obeyed	obeyed	obeying	(see ¶711)

b. Many frequently used verbs, however, have principal parts that are irregularly formed.

Present	Past	Past Participle	Present Participle
choose	chose	chosen	choosing
do	did	done	doing
forget	forgot	forgotten OR forgot	forgetting
see	saw	seen	seeing
write	wrote	written	writing
lay (see ¶1101)	laid	laid	laying
lie (see ¶1101)	lay	lain	lying

NOTE: The dictionary shows the principal parts for all *irregular* verbs. If you are in doubt about any form, consult the dictionary. If the principal parts are not shown, the verb is regular (see ¶1030*a* above).

c. The past participle and the present participle, if used as a part of a verb phrase, must *always* be used with one or more auxiliary verbs. The most common auxiliary verbs are:

is	was	can	do	has	have	might	shall	will
are	were	could	did	had	may	must	should	would

Verb Tenses

1031 The first principal part of the verb (the *present tense*) is used:

a. To express *present time.*

We *fill* all orders promptly.   They *do* what is expected of them.

b. To make a statement that is *true at all times.*

Water *seeks* its own level.

c. With *shall* or *will* to express *future time.*

We *will order* (OR *shall order*) new stock next week. (For the use of these auxiliary verbs in the future tense, see the entry for *Shall–will* in ¶1101.)

▪ *See ¶1035 for the third person singular form of the present tense.*

1032 The second principal part of the verb (the *past tense*) is used to express *past time.* (No auxiliary verb is used with this form.)

> We *filled* the order yesterday.   They *did* what was expected of them.

NOTE: Do· not use a past participle form to express the past tense.

> He *drank* his coffee. (**NOT:** He *drunk* it.)
> I *saw* it. (**NOT:** I *seen* it.)
> They *began* it together. (**NOT:** They *begun* it.)
> He was the one who *did* it. (**NOT:** He was the one who *done* it.)

1033 The third principal part of the verb (the *past participle*) is used:

a. To form the *present perfect tense.* This tense indicates action that was started in the past and has recently been completed or is continuing up to the present time. It consists of the verb *have* or *has* plus the past participle.

> We *have filled* the orders. (**NOT:** We *have filled* the orders yesterday.)
> She *has done* what was expected of her.
> The consumer movement *has become* an articulate force in today's business world.

b. To form the *past perfect tense.* This tense indicates action that was completed *before another past action.* It consists of the verb *had* plus the past participle.

> We *had filled* the orders before we saw your letter.
> They *had done* the job before we arrived.

c. To form the *future perfect tense.* This tense indicates action that will be completed *before a certain time in the future.* It consists of the verb *shall have* or *will have* plus the past participle.

> We *will have filled* the orders by that time. (See ¶1101 for the use of *shall* and *will.*)
> They *will have finished* the job by next Friday.

NOTE: Be careful not to use a past tense form (the second principal part) in place of a past participle.

> I have *broken* the racket. (**NOT:** I have *broke* the racket.)
> The dress has *shrunk.* (**NOT:** The dress has *shrank.*)
> Prices have *risen* again. (**NOT:** Prices have *rose* again.)
> He has *worn* his shoes out. (**NOT:** He has *wore* his shoes out.)

1034 The fourth principal part of the verb (the *present participle*) is used:

a. To form the *present progressive tense.* This tense indicates action still in progress. It consists of the verb *am, is,* or *are* plus the present participle.

> We *are filling* all orders as fast as we can.
> They *are doing* all that can be expected of them.

b. To form the *past progressive tense.* This tense indicates action in progress sometime in the past. It consists of the verb *was* or *were* plus the present participle.

(Continued on page 184.)

We *were waiting* for new stock at the time your order came in.

They *were doing* a good job when I last checked on them.

c. To form the *future progressive tense.* This tense indicates action that will be in progress in the future. It consists of the verb *shall be* or *will be* plus the present participle.

We *will be working* overtime for the next two weeks. (See ¶1101 for the use of *shall* and *will.*)

They *will be receiving* additional stock throughout the next two weeks.

d. To form the *present perfect progressive,* the *past perfect progressive,* and the *future perfect progressive* tenses. These tenses are exactly like the simple perfect tenses (see ¶1033) except that the progressive element suggests continuous action. These tenses consist of the verbs *has been, have been, had been, shall have been,* and *will have been* plus the present participle. Compare the following examples with those in ¶1033.

We *have been filling* these orders with Model 212A instead of 212. (Present perfect progressive.)

We *had been filling* these orders with Model 212A until we saw your directive. (Past perfect progressive.)

By next Friday we *will have been working* overtime for two straight weeks. (Future perfect progressive.)

1035 The first principal part of the verb undergoes a change in form to express the third person singular in the present tense.

a. Most verbs simply add *s* in the third person singular.

he feels	**BUT:** I feel, you feel, we feel, they feel
she thinks	I think, you think, we think, they think
it looks	I look, you look, we look, they look

b. Verbs ending in *s, x, z, sh, ch,* or *o* add *es.*

he misses	he wishes
she fixes	she catches
it buzzes	it goes

c. Verbs ending in a vowel plus *y* add *s;* those ending in a consonant plus *y* change *y* to *i* and add *es;* those already ending in *i* simply add *s.*

say: he says	try: it tries	taxi: he taxis
convey: she conveys	apply: she applies	ski: she skis

d. The verb *to be* is irregular since *be,* the first principal part, is not used in the present tense.

I am	we are
you are	you are
he, she, it is	they are

e. A few verbs remain unchanged in the third person singular.

he may	she can	it will
he might	she could	it would

■ *See the entry for* Don't *in* ¶1101.

Passive Forms

1036 The passive forms of a verb consist of some part of the auxiliary verb *to be* plus the past participle of the main verb.

> it is intended (present passive of *intend*)
> we were expected (past passive of *expect*)
> they will be audited (future passive of *audit*)
> she has been notified (present perfect passive of *notify*)
> you had been told (past perfect passive of *tell*)
> he will have been given (future perfect passive of *give*)

1037 A *passive* verb directs the action toward the subject. An *active* verb directs the action toward an object.

> ACTIVE: Melanie (subject) will lead (verb) the discussion (object).
> PASSIVE: The discussion (subject) will be led (verb) by Melanie.

▪ *For additional examples see the entry for* Voice *in the Glossary, page 311.*

a. The passive form of a verb is appropriate (1) when you want to emphasize the *receiver* of the action (by making it the subject) or (2) when the *doer* of the action is not important or is not mentioned.

> I was seriously injured as a result of your negligence. (Emphasizes *I*, the receiver of the action. RATHER THAN: Your negligence seriously injured me.)
> This proposal is based on a careful analysis of all available research studies. (The doer of the action is not mentioned.)

b. In all other cases, use active verb forms to achieve a simpler and more vigorous style. Except in those circumstances cited in *a* above, passive verb forms typically produce awkward or stilted sentences.

> WEAK PASSIVES: It *has been decided* by the Personnel Committee that full pay *should be given* to you for the period of your hospitalization.
> STRONG ACTIVES: The Personnel Committee *has decided* that you *should receive* full pay for the period of your hospitalization.

Verbs Following Clauses of Necessity, Demand, Etc.

1038 Sentences that express *necessity, demand, strong request, urging,* or *resolution* in the main clause require a subjunctive verb in the dependent clause that follows.

▪ *See the entry for* Mood, subjunctive *in the Glossary, pages 305–306.*

a. If the verb in the dependent clause requires the use of the verb *to be*, use the form *be* with all three persons (not *am, is,* or *are*).

> NECESSITY: It is necessary (OR important OR essential) that these questions *be* answered at once. (NOT: are answered.)
> DEMAND: I demand that I *be* given a hearing on this matter. (NOT: am given.)
> REQUEST: They have asked that you *be* notified at once. (NOT: are notified.)
> URGING: We urge (OR suggest) that he *be* given a second chance. (NOT: is given.)
> RESOLUTION: The committee has resolved (OR decided OR ruled) that the decision *be* deferred until the next meeting. (NOT: is deferred.)

(Continued on page 186.)

b. If the verb in the dependent clause is a verb other than *be*, use the ordinary *present tense* form for all three persons. However, do not add *s* for the third person singular.

> NECESSITY: It is essential that he *arrive* on time. (NOT: arrives.)
>
> DEMAND: They insist that he *do* the work over. (NOT: does.)
>
> REQUEST: They have asked that she *remain* on the committee. (NOT: remains.)
>
> URGING: I suggest that she *type* the material triple-spaced. (NOT: types.)
>
> RESOLUTION: They have resolved that Fred *represent* them. (NOT: represents.)

Verbs Following *Wish* Clauses

1039 Sentences that start with *I wish, he wishes,* and so on, require a subjunctive verb in the dependent clause that follows.

a. To express *present* time in the dependent clause, put the verb in the *past tense.*

> I wish I *knew* how to proceed.
>
> I wish I *could attend.*

NOTE: If the verb is *to be*, use *were* (not *was*) for all persons.

> I wish I *were going* to the reception.
>
> I wish he *were going* with me.

b. To express *past* time in the dependent clause, put the verb in the *past perfect tense.*

> I wish that she *had invited* me.
>
> I wish that I *had been* there.
>
> I wish that I *could have attended.*

c. To express *future* time in the dependent clause, use the auxiliary verb *would* instead of *will.*

> I wish he *would arrive* on time.

Verbs in *If* Clauses

1040 When an *if* clause states a condition that is *highly improbable, doubtful,* or *contrary to fact,* the verb in the *if* clause requires special treatment, like that described in ¶1039: *to express present time, use the past tense; to express past time, use the past perfect tense.* (In the following examples note the relationship of tenses between the dependent clause and the main clause.)

> If I *knew* the answer (but I don't), I *would* not *ask* you.
>
> If I *had known* the answer (but I didn't), I *would* not *have asked* you.
>
> If I *were* you (but I am not), I *would take* the job.
>
> If I *had been* in your shoes (but I wasn't), I *would have taken* the job.
>
> If he *were invited* (but he isn't), he *would be* glad to go.
>
> If he *had been invited* (but he wasn't), he *would have been* glad to go.

(NOTE: Do not use *would have* for *had* in an *if* clause. See the entry for *Would have* in ¶1101.)

1041 When an *if* clause states a condition that is *possible* or *likely*, the verb in the *if* clause requires no special treatment. *To express present time, use the present tense; to express past time, use the past tense.* Compare the following pairs of examples. Those labeled "Probable" reflect the verb forms described here in ¶1041. Those labeled "Improbable" reflect the verb forms described in ¶1040.

> PROBABLE: If I *leave* this job (and I may do so), I *will take* a teaching position.
> IMPROBABLE: If I *left* this job (but I probably won't), I *would take* a teaching position.

> PROBABLE: If I *go* to San Francisco (and I may), I *will want* you to go with me.
> IMPROBABLE: If I *were going* to San Francisco (but I probably won't), I *would want* you to go with me.

> PROBABLE: If she *was* in the office yesterday (and she may have been), I *did* not see her.
> IMPROBABLE: If she *had been* in the office yesterday (but she wasn't), I *would have seen* her.

Verbs in *As If* or *As Though* Clauses

1042 When an *as if* or *as though* clause expresses a condition *contrary to fact*, the verb in the clause requires special treatment, like that described in ¶1040.

> She acts as if she *were* the only person who mattered. (But she isn't.)
> He talks as if he *knew* the facts of the situation. (But he doesn't.)
> You act as if you *hadn't* a care in the world. (But you have.)

1043 *As if* or *as though* clauses are now often used to express a condition that is *highly probable*. In such cases do not give the verb special treatment. *Use the present tense to express present time, the future tense to express future time, and the past tense to express past time.*

> It looks as if it *will* rain. (OR: It looks as if it *is going* to rain.)
> She acted as if she *planned* to look for another job.

Infinitives

1044 An infinitive is the form of the verb preceded by *to* (for example, *to write, to do, to be*). When two or more infinitives are used in a parallel construction, the word *to* may be omitted after the first infinitive unless special emphasis is desired.

> Ask Ruth Gonzales *to sign* both copies of the contract, *return* the original to us, and *keep* the carbon copy for her own files. (*Return* and *keep* are infinitives without *to.*)
> I would like you *to explain* the job to Harry, *to give* him help if he needs it, and *to see* that the job is done properly. (For emphasis, *to* is used with all three infinitives—*explain, give,* and *see.*)

NOTE: The word *to* is usually dropped when the infinitive follows such verbs as *see, hear, feel, let, help,* and *need.*

> Will you please help me *prepare* the report? (RATHER THAN: help me *to prepare* the report?)
> You need not *return* the clipping. (OR: You do not need *to return* the clipping.)

1045 Infinitives have two main tense forms: the present infinitive and the perfect infinitive.

a. The perfect infinitive is used to express action that has been completed before the time of the main verb.

> I *am* sorry *to have caused* you so much trouble last week. (The act of causing trouble was completed before the act of expressing regret; therefore, the perfect infinitive is used.)

b. The present infinitive is used in all other cases.

> I planned *to leave* early. (**NOT:** *to have left*. The act of leaving could not have been completed before the act of planning; therefore, the present infinitive is used.)

1046 *Splitting an infinitive* (that is, inserting an adverb between *to* and the verb) should be avoided because (*a*) it typically produces an awkward construction and (*b*) the adverb usually functions more effectively in another location.

> **WEAK:** It was impossible to *even* see a foot ahead.
> **BETTER:** It was impossible to see *even* a foot ahead.
> **WEAK:** He always tries to *carefully* do the work.
> **BETTER:** He always tries to do the work *carefully*.

However, split the infinitive when alternative locations of the adverb produce an awkward or weakly constructed sentence.

a. Before splitting an infinitive, first try to place the adverb *after the object* of the infinitive. In many instances the adverb functions most effectively in that location.

> You ought *to review* these plans *thoroughly*. (**BETTER THAN:** You ought to thoroughly review these plans.)
> I need *to make* the decision *quickly*. (**BETTER THAN:** I need to quickly make the decision.)

b. If step *a* does not produce an effective sentence, try to locate the adverb directly *before* or directly *after* the infinitive. In some cases the adverb functions effectively in this position; in other cases the resulting sentence is awkward.

> **CONFUSING:** I want you *to supervise* the work that is to be done *personally*. (When the object of the infinitive is long or involved, it is difficult to place the adverb after the object without creating confusion. Here *personally* seems to modify *to be done* when in fact it should modify *to supervise*.)
> **AWKWARD:** I want you to supervise *personally* the work that is to be done.
> **GOOD:** I want you *personally* to supervise the work that is to be done.

c. If steps *a* and *b* fail to produce an effective sentence, try splitting the infinitive. If a good sentence results, keep it; if not, try rewording the sentence.

> **CONFUSING:** I want you *to consider* Jenkins' proposal to handle all our deliveries *carefully*. (When *carefully* is located after the complete object, it no longer clearly refers to *to consider*.)

AWKWARD: I want you *carefully* to consider Jenkins' proposal to handle all our deliveries.

AWKWARD: I want you to consider *carefully* Jenkins' proposal to handle all our deliveries.

GOOD: I want you to *carefully* consider Jenkins' proposal to handle all our deliveries.

d. When an infinitive consists of *to be* plus a past participle of another verb, inserting an adverb before the past participle is not considered splitting an infinitive.

These plans need to be *thoroughly* reviewed.

Time appears to be *fast* running out.

NOTE: Nevertheless, in many such sentences the adverb may be located to better advantage elsewhere in the sentence.

▪ *See also ¶1082b for dangling infinitive phrases.*

Sequence of Tenses

1047 When the verb in the main clause is in the past tense, the verb in a subordinate *that* clause should also express past time. Compare the following pairs of examples:

She *says* (present) that she *is* now *working* (present) for CBS.
She *said* (past) that she *was* now *working* (past) for CBS.

He *says* (present) that he *has seen* (present perfect) your résumé.
He *said* (past) that he *had seen* (past perfect) your résumé.

I *think* (present) that he *will see* (future) you tomorrow.
I *thought* (past) that he *would see* (past form of *will see*) you tomorrow.

EXCEPTION: The verb in the subordinate clause should remain in the present tense if it expresses a general truth.

Our legal adviser *pointed out* (past) that all persons under 18 *are* (present) legally considered minors. (General truth.)

Omitting Parts of Verbs

1048 When compound verbs in the same sentence share a common element, that element does not need to be repeated.

We *have* received your letter and forwarded it to our St. Louis office. (The auxiliary verb *have* is shared by the two main verbs, *received* and *forwarded*.)

We can and will *achieve* these goals. (The main verb *achieve* is shared by the two auxiliary verbs, *can* and *will*.)

However, do not omit any element when different parts of the main verb are required.

WRONG: I never have and I never will forget what you have done for me.
RIGHT: I never have *forgotten* and I never will *forget* . . .

WRONG: We have and still are asking for an accounting of the assets.
RIGHT: We have *asked* and still are *asking* for . . .

Troublesome Verbs

■ *See individual entries listed alphabetically in ¶1101 for the following verbs:*

Affect–effect	Graduated–was graduated	Of–have
Appraise–apprise	Imply–infer	Raise–rise
Bring–take	Lay–lie	Serve–service
Come–go	Learn–teach	Set–sit
Done	Leave–let	Shall–will
Don't	May–can	Should–would
Enthused over	Maybe–may be	Would have

Pronouns

Agreement With Antecedents: Basic Rules

1049 a. A pronoun must agree with its *antecedent* (the word for which the pronoun stands) in number, gender, and person.

> *I* must stand by *my* client, just as *you* must stand by *yours*.
>
> *Frank* said that *he* could do the job alone.
>
> *Alice* wants to know whether *her* proposal has been approved.
>
> The *company* has not decided whether to change *its* policy on vacations. (See ¶¶1019–1020.)
>
> The company's *auditors* will issue *their* report tomorrow.
>
> The *Vanderveers* are giving a party at *their* house.
>
> The *grand jury* has completed *its* investigation. (See ¶1019 for collective nouns.)
>
> Why not have *each witness* write *his* or *her* version of the accident? (See ¶1053 for indefinite pronouns as antecedents.)
>
> It is *I* who *am* at fault. (*Who* agrees in person and number with the antecedent *I*; the verb *am* also agrees with *I*.)
>
> It is *they* who *are* behind schedule.
>
> It is *you* who *are* to blame. (*Who* refers to *you*; hence the verb *are* also agrees with *you*.)
>
> **BUT:** You are the *person* who *is* to blame. (*Who* refers to *person*; hence the verb *is* also agrees with *person*.)

b. Use a plural pronoun when the antecedent consists of two nouns joined by *and*.

> *Harry* and *I* think *we* can handle the assignment.
>
> Can *Mary* and *you* give us *your* decision by Monday?
>
> *Sonia* and *Dave* say *they* will attend.
>
> The *Montaignes* and the *Reillys* have sent *their* regrets.

c. Use a singular pronoun when the antecedent consists of two *singular* nouns joined by *or* or *nor*. Use a plural pronoun when the antecedent consists of two *plural* nouns joined by *or* or *nor*. (See also ¶¶1003–1005.)

> Either *Will* or *Ed* will have to give up *his* office. (**NOT:** their.)
>
> Neither *Joan* nor *Helen* wants to do *her* share. (**NOT:** their.)
>
> Either the *Kopecks* or the *Henleys* will bring *their* phonograph.

NOTE: When *or* or *nor* joins a singular noun and a plural noun, a pronoun that refers to this construction should agree in number with the nearer noun. However, a strict application of this rule can lead to problems in sentence structure and meaning. Therefore, always try to make this kind of construction plural.

> Neither Mr. Wing nor his *employees have* reached *their* goal. (The plural pronoun *their* is used to agree with the nearer noun, *employees;* the verb *have* is also in the plural.)

> **NOT:** Neither the employees nor Mr. *Wing has* reached *his* goal. (The sentence follows the rule—*his* agrees with Mr. *Wing*, the nearer noun, and the verb *has* is singular; however, the meaning of the sentence has been distorted.)

Agreement With Common-Gender Antecedents

1050 Nouns that apply both to males and females have a *common* gender.

parent	manager	professor	boss	writer
child	doctor	instructor	supervisor	speaker
customer	lawyer	student	employee	listener

When a singular noun of common gender serves as a *definite* antecedent (one that names a specific person whose gender is known), use *he* or *she* as appropriate.

> My *boss* (previously identified as Robert Hecht) prefers to open *his* own mail.

> Ask your *doctor* (known to be a woman) to sign *her* name on the attached forms.

1051 When a singular noun of common gender serves as an *indefinite* antecedent (*a doctor, any doctor, every doctor*) or as a *generic* antecedent (*the doctor,* meaning "doctors in general"), the traditional practice has been to use *he* as a generic pronoun applying equally to males and females.

> The *writer* should include a table of contents with *his* manuscript.

When an indefinite or generic antecedent names an occupation or a role in which women predominate (for example, *the teacher, the secretary, the nurse*), the traditional practice has been to use *she* as a generic pronoun.

> A *secretary* needs to organize *her* work and set priorities each day.

1052 The traditional use of *he* and *she* as generic pronouns (described in ¶1051 above) has been coming under increasing attack. Critics feel that the masculine bias in the word *he* makes it unsuitable as a pronoun that applies equally to women and men. Moreover, they feel that the generic use of *she* serves to reinforce stereotyped notions about women's occupations or roles. The ideal solution would be a new generic pronoun without masculine or feminine connotations. However, until such a pronoun has been devised and accepted into common usage, here are a number of alternatives to the generic *he* or *she*.

a. Use *he or she, his or her,* or *him or her.* (This solution works well in isolated cases but can become cumbersome if repeated frequently in the same context.)

> An *instructor* should offer *his* or *her* students challenging projects.

> (**RATHER THAN:** An instructor should offer *his* students . . .)

(Continued on page 192.)

b. Change the wording from singular to plural.

> *Parents* of teenage children often *wonder* where *they* went wrong.
>
> (**RATHER THAN:** The *parent* of a teenage child often *wonders* where *he or she* went wrong.)

c. Reword to avoid the generic pronoun.

> When a customer calls, be sure to ask for a phone number.
>
> (**RATHER THAN:** . . . ask *him or her* to leave *his or her* phone number.)
>
> A secretary tries to anticipate the needs of the boss.
>
> (**RATHER THAN:** . . . the needs of *his or her* boss.)

NOTE: If the application of these various alternatives produces wordiness or an unacceptable shift in meaning or emphasis, use the generic *he* or the generic *she* as described in ¶1051. The generic use of these pronouns continues to be acceptable. However, sensitive writers will try, whenever possible, to avoid it.

Agreement With Indefinite-Pronoun Antecedents

1053 a. Use a singular pronoun when the antecedent is a singular indefinite pronoun. The following indefinite pronouns are always singular:

anyone	everyone	someone	no one
anybody	everybody	somebody	nobody
anything	everything	something	nothing
each	every	either	one
each one	many a	neither	another

Every company has *its* own vacation policy. (**NOT:** their.)

NOTE: These singular indefinite pronouns often call for the generic use of *he* or *she* (see ¶¶1051–1052). In the following sentences *he* and *she* are correctly used as generic pronouns. However, alternative wording is shown, wherever possible, to suggest how the generic *he* or *she* can be avoided.

> *Everyone* should submit *his* expense account by Friday.
>
> **BETTER:** All staff *members* should submit *their* expense accounts by Friday.
>
> **OR:** *Everyone* should submit *his or her* expense account by Friday.
>
> If *anyone* should ask for me, tell *him* that I won't return until Monday.
>
> **BETTER:** If anyone should ask for me, say that I won't return . . .
>
> While the conference is in session, does every secretary know how *she* is to handle *her* boss's correspondence?
>
> **BETTER:** . . . do *all the secretaries* know how *they* are to handle *their* bosses' correspondence?
>
> *Nobody* could have helped *himself* in a situation like that.

■ *See also ¶¶1009–1011 for agreement of these indefinite pronouns with verbs; ¶637 for possessive forms of these pronouns.*

b. Use a plural pronoun when the antecedent is a plural indefinite pronoun. The following indefinite pronouns are always plural:

many	few	several	others	both

Many customers prefer to help *themselves; others* like to have someone to wait on *them.*

A *few* of the secretaries have not yet taken *their* vacations.

Several sales representatives made *their* annual goals in nine months.

Both managers have said that *they* want to be considered for Mr. Hall's job when he retires next year.

- See also ¶1012 *for agreement of these indefinite pronouns with verbs.*

c. The following indefinite pronouns may be singular or plural, depending on the noun they refer to.

all   none   any   some   more   most

When these words are used as antecedents, carefully determine whether they are singular or plural. Then make the pronouns that refer to these antecedents agree in number.

Some employees have not yet had *their* annual physical checkup. (*Some* refers to *employees* and is plural; *some* is the antecedent of *their.*)

Some of the manuscript has been typed, but *it* has not been proofread. (*Some* refers to *manuscript* and is singular; *some* is the antecedent of *it* in the second clause.)

- See also ¶1013 *for agreement of these indefinite pronouns with verbs.*

d. Since indefinite pronouns express the third person, pronouns referring to these antecedents should also be in the third person (*he, she, it, they*).

If *anyone* wants a salary advance, *he* or *she* should apply for it in writing.

(**NOT:** If *anyone* wants a salary advance, *you* should apply for it in writing.)

If the indefinite pronoun is modified so that it strongly expresses the first or second person, the personal pronoun must also agree in number. Compare the following examples:

Most parents want *their* children to go to college. (Third person.)

Most of us want *our* children to go to college. (First person.)

A *few* have missed *their* deadlines. (Third person.)

A *few* of you have missed *your* deadlines. (Second person.)

Each employee knows how much *he* or *she* ought to contribute. (Third person.)

BUT: *Each* of us knows how much *he* or *she* ought to contribute. (Third person. In this sentence, *of us* does not shift the meaning to the first person; the emphasis is on what the individual contributes, not on what *we* contribute.)

IMPORTANT NOTE: *Pronouns take different forms, not only to indicate a difference in person (I, you, he), number (he, they), and gender (he, she) but also to indicate a difference in case (nominative, possessive, objective). Although a pronoun must agree with its antecedent in person, number, and gender, it does not necessarily agree with its antecedent in case. The case of a pronoun depends on its own relation to the other words in the sentence. The rules in ¶¶1054–1064 indicate how to choose the right case for pronouns.*

Personal Pronouns

1054 Use the *nominative* forms of personal pronouns (*I, we, you, he, she, it, they*):

a. When the pronoun is the subject of a verb.

> *I* wrote to Eileen McIntyre, but *she* hasn't answered.
> Are *they* planning to follow up?
> Debbie and *I* can handle the job ourselves. (**NOT:** Debbie and me.)
> Either *he* or *I* can work late tonight. (**NOT:** him or me.)

NOTE: In sentences like the last two above, try each subject alone with the verb. You would not say "Me can handle the job" or "Him can work late tonight." Therefore, *I* and *he* must be used.

b. When the pronoun appears in the predicate after some form of the verb *to be* (*am, is, are, was, were*) or after a verb phrase containing some form of *to be* (see the list below). Pronouns that follow these verb forms should be in the nominative.

shall (**OR** will) be	have (**OR** has) been
should (**OR** would) be	had been
shall (**OR** will) have been	may (**OR** might) be
should (**OR** would) have been	may (**OR** might) have been
can (**OR** could) be	must (**OR** ought to) be
could have been	must have (**OR** ought to have) been
It might have been *I.*	Was it *he* or *she* who phoned?
It could have been *they.*	The "culprit" was *she.*
It is *I.*	This is *she.*

NOTE: Sentences like "It is me" and "This is her" are acceptable in colloquial speech but should not be used in writing. Moreover, a sentence like "It could have been they," while grammatically correct, would be better if reworded into idiomatic English: "They could have been the ones."

-   See ¶1064 *for special rules governing pronouns with the infinitive* to be.

1055 Use the objective forms of personal pronouns (*me, us, you, him, her, it, them*):

a. When the pronoun is the direct or indirect object of a verb.

> Larry gave Maris and *us* tickets for the opening.
> They invited my husband and *me* for the weekend.

NOTE: When *my husband and* is mentally omitted, the objective form *me* is clearly the correct pronoun.

> They invited *me* for the weekend.

b. When the pronoun is the object of a preposition.

> This is for *you* and *her.*
> No one knows except *you* and *me.* (**NOT:** except you and I.)
> Between *you* and *me*, that decision is unfair. (**NOT:** between you and I.)
> **EXCEPTION:** He is a friend of *mine* (*yours, his, hers, ours, theirs*). (See also ¶648.)

c. When the pronoun is the subject or the object of an infinitive. (See also ¶1064.)

> The department head asked *him* to resign. (*Him* is the subject of *to resign*.)
> Did you ask Janet to call *me*? (*Me* is the object of *to call*.)

1056 Most personal pronouns have two *possessive* forms.

a. Use *my, your, his, her, its, our,* or *their* when the possessive pronoun immediately precedes the noun it modifies.

> That is *my* book.   It was *their* choice.

b. Use *mine, yours, his, hers, its, ours,* or *theirs* when the possessive pronoun stands apart from the noun it refers to.

> That book is *mine*.   The choice was *theirs*.
> She is a client of *ours*.   George is a neighbor of *hers*.

c. A pronoun that modifies a *gerund* (a verbal noun ending in *ing*) should be in the possessive. (See also ¶647.)

> I appreciated *your* shipping the order so promptly.

d. Do not confuse certain possessive pronouns with contractions that sound like the possessive pronouns.

its (possessive)	it's (it is **or** it has)
their (possessive)	they're (they are)
theirs (possessive)	there's (there is **or** there has)
your (possessive)	you're (you are)

As a test for the correct form, try to substitute *it is* (or *it has, they are, there are, there is, there has,* or *you are,* whichever is appropriate). If the substitution does not make sense, use the corresponding possessive form.

> The firm must protect *its* assets. ("Protect it is assets" makes no sense.)
> **BUT:** *It's* time to take stock of our achievements.
>
> *Their* investing in high-risk stocks was a bad idea.
> **BUT:** *They're* investing in high-risk stocks.
>
> *Theirs* no longer works; that's why they borrow ours.
> **BUT:** *There's* no use expecting him to change.
>
> *Your* thinking is sound, but we lack the funds to underwrite your proposal.
> **BUT:** *You're* thinking of applying for a transfer, I understand.

- *See also ¶¶636–637 for other possessive pronouns.*

1057 When a pronoun follows *than* or *as* in a comparison, determine the correct form of the pronoun by mentally supplying any missing words.

> She types better than *I*. (Than *I do*.)
> I like you better than *him*. (Than *I like him*.)
> You are not as healthy as *she*. (As healthy as *she is*.)

1058 When a pronoun is used to identify a noun or another pronoun, it is either nominative or objective, depending on whether the antecedent is nominative or objective.

(*Continued on page 196.*)

The committee has asked *us*, Ruth and *me*, to present the report. (Since *us* is objective, the identifying pronoun *me* is also objective.)

The explanation was for the *newcomers*, Marie and *me*. (Was for *me*.)

The exceptions were the *newcomers*, Marie and *I*. (Exception was *I*.)

Let's *you* and *me* go to the convention. (*Let's* is a contraction for *let us*. Since *us* is the objective form, the explanatory pronouns *you* and *me* are also objective.)

The company wants *us* employees to work on Saturdays.

We employees need to confer.

NOTE: In sentences like the last two above, mentally omit the noun (*employees*) to determine the correct form.

The company wants *us* to work on Saturdays.

We need to confer.

1059 Some writers consistently use *we* instead of *I* to avoid a seeming over-emphasis on themselves. However, it is preferable to use *we* only when you are speaking on behalf of an organization you represent and to use *I* when speaking for yourself alone.

We shall prepare the necessary forms as soon as you send *us* a signed release. (This writer is speaking on behalf of his firm.)

It is *my* opinion that this patient may be discharged at once. (This writer is speaking only for himself. Under these circumstances it would sound pompous to say, "It is *our* opinion.")

Compound Personal Pronouns

1060 The *self-* or *selves*-ending pronouns (*myself, yourself, himself, herself, itself, ourselves, yourselves, themselves*) should be used:

a. To direct the action expressed by the verb back to the subject.

She found *herself* the only one in favor of the move.

We have satisfied *ourselves* as to the wisdom of the action.

We think that *they* have insured *themselves* against a possible loss.

b. To emphasize or to intensify a noun or pronoun already expressed.

The trainees *themselves* arranged the program.

I myself am bewildered.

I will write her *myself*.

NOTE: Do not use a compound personal pronoun unless the noun or pronoun to which it refers is expressed in the same sentence.

The tickets are for the Wrights and *me*. (**NOT:** myself.)

Henry and *I* can distribute all the mail. (**NOT:** Henry and myself.)

Interrogative and Relative Pronouns

1061 Who and Whom; Whoever and Whomever

a. These pronouns are both *interrogative* pronouns (used in asking questions) and *relative* pronouns (used to refer to a noun in the main clause of a sentence).

Who is going? (Interrogative.)

Mr. Sears is the one *who* is going. (Relative, referring to *one*.)

To *whom* shall I deliver the message? (Interrogative.)

Ms. DeAngelis, *whom* I have never met, is in charge. (Relative, referring to Ms. *DeAngelis*.)

b. These pronouns may be either singular or plural in meaning.

Who is talking? (Singular.)

Who are to be selected? (Plural.)

Whom do you prefer for this job? (Singular.)

Whom do you prefer for these jobs? (Plural.)

c. *Who* (or *whoever*) is the nominative form. Use *who* whenever *he, she, they, I,* or *we* could be substituted in the *who* clause. (If in doubt, mentally rearrange the clause as is done in parentheses after each of the following examples.) (See also ¶1054b.)

Who is at the door? (*She* is at the door.)

Who sang the duet with you? (*He* sang.)

Who shall we say referred us? (We shall say *he* referred us.)

Who did they say was chosen? (They did say *she* was chosen.)

Who could it have been? (It could have been *he*.)

The matter of *who* should pay was not decided. (*He* should pay.)

We want to know *who you think should be appointed*. (You think *she* should be appointed.)

Whoever wins the primary will win the election. (*She* wins the primary.)

I will hire *whoever* meets our minimum qualifications. (*He* meets our minimum qualifications.)

I will speak to *whoever* answers the phone. (*He* answers the phone.)

Please write at once to *whoever you think can supply* the information desired. (You think *she* can supply the information desired.)

Gloria is the one *who can best do the job*. (*She* can best do the job.)

James is the one *who we expect will win*. (We expect *he* will win.)

Please vote for the member *who you believe has done* the most for the class. (You believe *he* has done the most for the class.)

We have referred your claim to our attorney, *who we are sure will reply soon*. (We are sure *she* will reply soon.)

We have sent this order blank to all *who we have reason to believe* are interested in our book. (We have reason to believe *they* are interested in our book.)

d. *Whom* (or *whomever*) is the objective form. Use *whom* whenever *him, her, them, me,* or *us* could be substituted as the object of the verb or as the object of a preposition in the *whom* clause.

Whom did you see today? (You did see *her* today.)

To *whom* were you talking? (You were talking to *him*.)

Whom were you talking about? (You were talking about *him*.)

Whom did you say you wanted to see? (You did say you wanted to see *her*.)

It depends on *whom they mean*. (They mean *him*.)

The question of *whom we should charge* is at issue. (We should charge *her*.)

Whomever you designate will get the promotion. (You designate *him*.)

(*Continued on page 198.*)

I will hire *whomever* I can find. (I can find *her*.)

I will speak to *whomever* you suggest. (You suggest *her*.)

I will give the job to *whomever* you think you can safely recommend. (You think you can safely recommend *him*.)

BUT: I will give the job to *whoever* you think can be safely recommended. (You think *he* can be safely recommended.)

I need a cashier *whom* I can trust. (I can trust *her*.)

The man to *whom* I was referring is Ed Meissen. (I was referring to *him*.)

The person *whom* I was thinking of doesn't have all those qualifications. (I was thinking of *her*.)

The person *whom* we invited to address the committee cannot attend. (We invited *him* to address the committee.)

Jo Olsen is the nominee *whom* they plan to support. (They plan to support *her*.)

Steve Koval is the person *whom* we all thought the committee would nominate. (We all thought the committee would nominate *him*.)

Elaine Gerrity, *whom* I considered to be their most promising representative, resigned this month. (I considered *her* to be their most promising representative.)

1062 *Who, Which,* and *That*

a. *Who* and *that* are used when referring to persons. Select *who* when the individual person or the individuality of a group is meant and *that* when a class, species, or type is meant.

She is the only one of my students *who* can speak French fluently.

He is the kind of student *that* should take advanced math.

b. *Which* and *that* are used when referring to places, objects, and animals. *Which* is always used to introduce nonessential clauses, and *that* is ordinarily used to introduce essential clauses.

Laura's report on personnel benefits, *which* I sent you last week, should be of some help. (*Which* introducing a nonessential clause.)

The report *that* I sent you last week should be of some help. (*That* introducing an essential clause.)

NOTE: Many writers now use either *which* or *that* to introduce an essential clause. Indeed, *which* is to be preferred to *that* (1) when there are two or more parallel essential clauses in the same sentence, (2) when *that* has already been used in the sentence, or (3) when the essential clause is introduced by such expressions as *this . . . which, that . . . which, these . . . which,* or *those . . . which.*

Vivian is taking courses *which* will earn her a higher salary rating in her current job and *which* will qualify her for a number of higher-level jobs.

That is a movie *which* you must not miss.

We need to reinforce *those* ideas *which* were presented in earlier units.

1063 *Whose* and *Who's*

Do not confuse *whose* (the possessive form of *who*) with *who's* (a contraction meaning *who is* or *who has*).

Whose house is it? (It is *his*.)

Who's the owner of that house? (*She* is.)

Pronouns With *To Be*

1064 a. If a pronoun is the subject of *to be,* use the *objective* form.

I want *her* to be successful.
I expected *them* to be late.
Whom do you consider to be the more expert driver? (You do consider *whom* to be the more expert driver?)

b. If *to be* has a subject and is followed by a pronoun, put that pronoun in the *objective* case.

They mistook the *visitors* to be *us.* (*Visitors,* the subject of *to be,* is in the objective; therefore, the predicate pronoun following *to be* is objective, *us.*)
They took *her* to be *me.*
Whom do you take *him* to be? (You do take *him* to be *whom?*)

c. If *to be* has *no* subject and is followed by a pronoun, put that pronoun in the *nominative* case.

The *caller* was thought to be *I.* (*I* agrees with the subject of the sentence, *caller.*)
They were thought to be *we.*
Who was *he* thought to be? (*He* was thought to be *who?*)

Troublesome Pronouns

▪ *See the paragraphs indicated for each of the following pronouns. Entries listed in ¶1101 are in alphabetical order.*

All of
(see ¶1101)
Anyone–any one
(see ¶1010, note)
Between you and me
(see ¶1055*b*)
Both–each
(see ¶1101)
Both alike
(see ¶1101)

Each other–one another
(see ¶1101)
Everyone–every one
(see ¶1010, note)
Most
(see ¶1101)
Nobody–no body
(see ¶1101)
None–no one
(see ¶1013)

Someone–some one
(see ¶1010, note)
That–which–who
(see ¶1062)
These sort–these kind
(see ¶1101)
Who–whom
(see ¶1061)
Whoever–who ever
(see ¶1101)

Adjectives and Adverbs

For definitions of the terms *adjective* and *adverb,* see the appropriate entries in ¶1701, pages 301–302.

1065 Only an adverb can modify an adjective.

Packard's will give you a *really* good buy. (**NOT:** real good.)

1066 When the word following a verb describes the *subject* of the sentence, make sure the word is an *adjective* (not an adverb). Verbs of the *senses* (*feel, look, sound, taste, smell*) and *linking* verbs (the various forms of *be, seem, appear, become*) in most cases are followed by adjectives. A few

other verbs (such as *grow, prove, get, keep, remain,* and *turn*) are sometimes followed by adjectives. (See, however, ¶1067, note.)

I feel *bad* (NOT badly).	He has grown *tall.*
She looked *happy.*	The work proved *hard.*
Your voice sounded *strong.*	I got *lucky.*
He seemed (OR appeared) *shy.*	Let's all keep (OR remain) *calm.*
They became *famous.*	The weather has turned *cold.*

TEST: If *is, are, was, were,* or some other form of *be* can be substituted for
the verb, choose the adjective.

He *looks happy.*   He *is happy.*

1067 When the word following a verb refers to the *action of the verb,* use an
adverb.

He *reads slowly* but he *talks rapidly.*
She *entered* the room *briskly.*
We guarantee *to ship* the goods *promptly.*
They *were injured badly* in the accident.

TEST: If *in a . . . manner* can be substituted for the *ly*-ending word, choose
the adverb.

Read the directions *carefully* (in a careful manner).

NOTE: In the following group of examples, verbs of the senses and linking
verbs (¶1066) are used as verbs of action. Since the modifier refers to the
action of the verb (and does not describe the subject), the modifier must
be an adverb.

She *looked suspiciously* at the visitor in the reception room.
He *felt carefully* along the ledge for the key.
That tree *has grown quickly.*
He *appeared quietly* in the doorway.

1068 Several of the most frequently used adverbs have two forms.

close, closely	fair, fairly	loud, loudly	short, shortly
deep, deeply	hard, hardly	quick, quickly	slow, slowly
direct, directly	late, lately	right, rightly	wide, widely

a. In a number of cases the two forms have different meanings.

Ship the goods *direct.* (Meaning "straight," "without detour.")
They were *directly* responsible. (Meaning "without any intervention.")

They arrived *late.*	The truck stopped *short.*
I haven't seen her *lately.*	You will hear from us *shortly.*
You've been working too *hard.*	Turn *right* at the first traffic light.
I could *hardly* hear him.	I don't *rightly* remember.

b. In some cases the choice is largely a matter of idiom. Some verbs take
the *ly* form; others take the short form.

dig deep	go slow	open wide	come close	play fair
wound deeply	proceed slowly	travel widely	watch closely	treat fairly

c. In still other cases the choice is simply one of formality. The *ly* forms are more formal.

sell cheap **or** sell cheaply   talk loud **or** talk loudly

1069 Although the *ly* ending usually signifies an adverb, a few adjectives also end in *ly*—for example, *costly, orderly, timely, motherly, fatherly, friendly, neighborly.*

Let's look for a less *costly* solution.
Her offer to help you was intended as a *friendly* gesture.

1070 A few common *ly*-ending words are used both as adjectives and adverbs—for example, *early, only, daily, weekly, monthly.*

I always go to bed at an *early* hour. (Adjective.)
The explosion *occurred early* in the day. (Adverb.)

1071 Problems of Comparison

a. The comparative degree of one-syllable adjectives and adverbs is formed by adding *er* to the positive form; the superlative degree, by adding *est*. (See *e* below for a few exceptions.)

thin: thinner, thinnest   soon: sooner, soonest

b. The comparative degree of two-syllable adjectives and adverbs may be formed either by adding *er* to the positive form or by inserting either *more* or *less* before the positive form; the superlative degree, by adding *est* in some cases or by inserting *most* or *least* before the positive form.

happy: happier, more happy   often: oftener, less often
likely: likeliest, most (least) likely   highly: highest, most (least) highly

c. The comparative degree of adjectives and adverbs containing three or more syllables is always formed by inserting *more* or *less* before the positive form; the superlative degree, by inserting *most* or *least* before the positive form.

competent: more competent   adventurous: less adventurous
acceptable: most acceptable   carefully: least carefully

d. Avoid double comparisons.

cheaper (**not:** more cheaper)   unkindest (**not:** most unkindest)

e. A few adjectives have irregular comparisons.

Positive	Comparative	Superlative
good or well (see ¶1101)	better	best
bad or ill	worse	worst
far	farther, further (see ¶717)	farthest, furthest
late	later, latter (see ¶717)	latest, last
little	littler, less, lesser	littlest, least
many, much	more	most
. . . . . .	inner	innermost, inmost
. . . . . .	outer	outermost, outmost

f. Some adjectives and adverbs, from their very meanings, do not logically admit comparison. (Examples: *square, round, unique, completely, universally, correct, perfect, always, never, dead.*) Nevertheless, a number of these words may be modified by *more, less, nearly, hardly,* and similar adverbs to suggest an approach to the absolute.

Next year we hope to do a *more complete* study.

He is looking for a *more universally* acceptable solution.

Craftsmanship of this caliber is *virtually unique* these days.

g. When referring to *two* persons, places, or things, use the comparative form; when referring to *more than two,* use the superlative form.

That is the *finer* piece of linen. (Only two pieces are involved; hence the comparative form.)

This is the *finest* piece of linen I could find. (Many pieces are involved; hence the superlative form.)

Of the two positions open, you have chosen the *more* promising.

Of the three positions open, you have chosen the *most* promising.

That is the *more* efficient of the two methods.

This is the *most* efficient method that could be devised.

I like Evelyn's plan *better* than Joe's or Betty's. (Although three things are involved in this comparison, they are being compared two at a time. Therefore, the comparative is used.)

h. When comparing a person or a thing *within* the group to which it belongs, use the superlative. When comparing a person or a thing with individual members of the group, use the comparative and the words *other* or *else.*

Susan is the *most* conscientious employee on the staff.

Susan is *more* conscientious than any *other* employee on the staff. (Without the word *other,* the sentence would imply that Susan is not on the staff.)

Los Angeles is the *largest* city in California.

Los Angeles is *larger* than any *other* city in California. (Without *other,* the sentence would imply that Los Angeles is not in California.)

Bert's proposal was the *best* of all that were presented to the committee.

Bert's proposal was *better* than anyone *else's.* (**NOT**: anyone's.)

i. Be sure to compare like things. (See also ¶644, note.)

This year's output is lower than last year's. (In other words, "This year's *output* is lower than last year's *output.*")

NOT: This year's output is lower than last year. (Incorrectly compares *this year's output* with *last year.*)

1072 The adverbs *only, nearly, almost, ever, scarcely, merely, too,* and *also* should be placed as close to the word modified—usually before—as possible. Putting the adverb in the wrong position may change the entire meaning of the sentence.

Our list of depositors now numbers *almost* 50,000. (**NOT**: almost numbers.)

Only the Board of Directors can nominate the three new officers. (Cannot be nominated by anyone else.)

The Board of Directors can *only* nominate the three officers. (They cannot elect.)

The Board of Directors can nominate *only* the three officers. (They cannot nominate anyone else.)

> *Only* Robert liked her. (No one else liked her.)
> Robert *only* liked her. (Robert did not love her.)
> Robert liked *only* her. (Robert liked no one else.)

1073 Do not use an adverb to express a meaning already contained in the verb.

return (**NOT:** return back)	cancel (**NOT:** cancel out)
cooperate (**NOT:** cooperate together)	continue (**NOT:** continue on)
repeat (**NOT:** repeat again)	finish (**NOT:** finish up)

Troublesome Adjectives and Adverbs

- *See individual entries listed alphabetically in ¶1101 for the following adjectives and adverbs:*

A-an	Ex-former	More important–
Accidentally	Farther–further	more importantly
All right	Fewer-less	Only
Almost–all most	First–firstly, etc.	Real–really
Already–all ready	Former–first	Said
Altogether–all	Good–well	Same
together	Hardly	Scarcely
Always–all ways	Healthy–healthful	Sometime–
Anxious–eager	Incidentally	sometimes–some time
Anyway–any way	Indifferent–in different	Sure–surely
Awhile–a while	Indirect–in direct	This here
Bad–badly	Last–latest	Unique
Different–differently	Latter-last	Up
Everyday–every day	Maybe–may be	Very

Negatives

1074 To express a negative idea in a simple sentence, use only one negative expression in the sentence. (A *double negative*—two negative expressions in the same sentence—gives a *positive* meaning.)

> We can sit by and do *nothing*.
>
> We can*not* sit by and do *nothing*. (The *not* and *nothing* create a double negative; the sentence now has a positive meaning: "We ought to do something.")
>
> Jim is *unaware* of the facts. (Here the negative element is the prefix *un*.)
>
> Jim is *not unaware* of the facts. (With the double negative, the sentence means "Jim *is* aware of the facts.")

NOTE: A double negative is not wrong in itself. As the examples above indicate, a double negative may offer a more effective way of expressing a *positive thought* than a straightforward positive construction would. However, a double negative *is* wrong if the sentence is intended to have a negative meaning. (**REMEMBER:** Two negatives make a positive.)

1075 A negative expression gives a negative meaning to the *clause* in which it appears. In a simple sentence, where there is only one clause, the negative expression affects the entire sentence (see ¶1074). In a sentence where there are two or more clauses, a negative expression affects only the clause in which it appears. Therefore, each clause may safely contain one negative expression. A double negative results when there are two negative expressions within the *same* clause.

> If Mr. Bogosian can*not* lower his price, there is *no* point in continuing the negotiations. (The *if* clause contains the negative *not;* the main clause contains the negative *no.* Each clause has its own negative meaning.)
>
> I have *not* met Halliday, and I have *no* desire to meet him.
> **or:** I have *not* met Halliday, *nor* do I have *any* desire to meet him. (When the negative conjunction *nor* replaces *and,* the adjective *no* changes to *any* to avoid a double negative.)
>
> We have *never* permitted, *nor* will we permit, any lowering of our standards. (Here the second clause interrupts the first clause. If written out in full, the sentence would read, "We have *never* permitted any lowering of our standards, *nor* will we permit any lowering of our standards.")

NOTE: A second negative expression may be used in a clause simply to repeat or intensify the first negative expression. This construction is not a double negative.

> *No,* I did *not* make that statement.
> I *never, never* said a thing like that.

1076 To preserve the *negative* meaning of a clause, follow these basic principles:

a. If the clause has a *negative verb* (a verb modified by *not* or *never*), do not use any additional negative expressions, such as *nor, neither . . . nor, no, none, no one,* or *nothing.* Instead, use corresponding positive expressions such as *or, either . . . or, any, anyone,* or *anything.*

> I have *not* invited *anyone.* (**WRONG:** I have *not* invited *no one.*)
> She does *not* want *any.* (**WRONG:** She does *not* want *none.*)
> Mary did *not* have *anything* to do yesterday. (**WRONG:** Mary did *not* have *nothing* to do yesterday.)
> I can*not* find *either* the letter *or* the envelope. (**WRONG:** I can*not* find *neither* the letter *nor* the envelope.)
> He did *not* say whether he would mail the money to us *or* whether he would bring it himself. (**WRONG:** He did *not* say whether he would mail the money to us *nor* whether he would bring it himself.)

b. If a clause contains any one of the following expressions—*no, no one, none, nothing,* or *neither . . . nor* (this counts as one expression)—make sure that the verb and all other words are *positive.*

> I see *nothing* wrong with *either* proposal. (**NOT:** neither proposal.)
> *Neither* Paul *nor* Yvonne *can* handle the meeting for me next Thursday. (**NOT:** cannot.)

c. The word *nor* may be used alone as a conjunction (see the third and fourth examples at the top of this page) or together with *neither.* Do not use *nor* in the same clause with any other negative; use *or* instead.

> There are *neither* pens *nor* pencils in the stockroom.
> **BUT:** There are *no* pens *or* pencils in the stockroom. (**WRONG:** no pens *nor* pencils.)
> There are *no* clear-cut rights *or* wrongs in the situation. (**WRONG:** no . . . rights *nor* wrongs.)

Francine has *not* called *or* written us for some time. (**WRONG:** *not* called *nor* written.)

Never try to argue *or* debate with Larry. (**WRONG:** *Never . . .* argue *nor* debate.)

▪ *See individual entries in ¶1101 for Hardly, Only, and Scarcely, which have a negative meaning.*

Prepositions

Words Requiring Certain Prepositions

1077 Usage requires that certain words be followed by certain prepositions. Some of the most frequently used combinations are listed below.

account for something or someone: I find it hard to *account for* his behavior.

account to someone: You will have to *account to* Anne Cuneo for the loss of the key.

agree on or **upon** (reach an understanding): We cannot *agree on* the price.

agree to (accept another person's plan): Will you *agree to* their terms?

agree with (concur with a person or an idea): I *agree with* your objectives.

angry at or **about** something: He was *angry about* the total disorder of the office.

angry with someone: You have every right to be *angry with* me.

apply for a position: You ought to *apply for* Harry's job, now that he has left.

apply to someone or something: You must *apply* yourself *to* the job in order to master it. I am thinking of *applying to* the Field Engineering Company.

argue about something: We *argued about* the terms of the contract.

argue with a person: It doesn't pay to *argue with* Bremer.

compare to (assert a likeness): She *compared* my writing *to* E. B. White's. (She said I wrote like E. B. White.)

compare with (analyze for similarities and differences): When she *compared* my writing *with* E. B. White's, she said that I had a similar kind of humor but that my sentences lacked the clean and easy flow of White's material.

conform to (preferred to *with*): These blueprints do not *conform to* the original plans.

consists in (exists in): Happiness largely *consists in* knowing what it is that will make you happy.

consists of (is made up of): Their new formula for a wage settlement *consists of* the same old terms expressed in different language.

convenient for (suitable): What time will be most *convenient for* you?

convenient to (near at hand): Our plant is *convenient to* all major transportation facilities.

correspond to (agree with): The shipment does not *correspond to* the sample.

correspond with (exchange letters): It may be better to see him in person than to *correspond with* him.

differ about (something): We *differed about* means but not about objectives.

differ from (something else): This job *differs* very little *from* the one that I used to have.

differ with (someone): I *differ with* you over the consequences of our plan.

(Continued on page 206.)

different from: This product is *different from* the one I normally use.

different than: I view the matter in a *different* way *than* you do. (Although *from* is normally preferred, *than* is acceptable in order to avoid sentences like "I view the matter in a different way from the way in which you do.")

identical with (not *to*): This $80 suit is *identical with* one advertised for $135 at other stores.

independent of (not *from*): He wants to be *independent of* his family's money.

interested in: We are *interested in* discussing the matter further with you at the conference in July.

retroactive to (not *from*): This salary adjustment is *retroactive to* May 1.

speak to (tell something to): You must *speak to* them about their frequent absences.

speak with (discuss with): It was good to *speak with* you yesterday.

Superfluous Prepositions

1078 Omit prepositions that add nothing to the meaning—as in the following examples. (See also the entry for *All of* in ¶1101.)

Where is she (at)?
Where did that paper go (to)?
The new applicant seems to be (of) about sixteen years of age.
She could not help (from) laughing.
His house is opposite (to) hers.
The chair is too near (to) the desk.
Why don't we meet at about one o'clock? (Omit either *at* or *about*.)
The carton fell off (of) the truck.

Necessary Prepositions

1079 Conversely, do not omit essential prepositions.

I bought a couple *of* books. (NOT: I bought a couple books.)
Of what use is this gadget? (NOT: What use is this gadget?)
We don't sell that type *of* filter. (NOT: that type filter.)
You seem to have a great interest *in*, as well as a deep respect *for*, fine antiques. (NOT: You seem to have a great interest, as well as a deep respect *for*, fine antiques.)
She frequently appears in movies, *in* plays, and on television. (NOT: in movies, plays, and on television.)

NOTE: The preposition *of* is understood in expressions such as *what color cloth* and *what size shoes*.

Prepositions at the End of Sentences

1080 Whether or not a sentence should end with a preposition depends on the emphasis and effect desired.

INFORMAL: I wish I knew which magazine her article appeared *in*.
FORMAL: I wish I knew the magazine *in which* her article appeared.

STILTED: It is difficult to know *about* what you are thinking.

NATURAL: It is difficult to know what you are thinking *about.*

Short questions frequently end with prepositions.

How many can I count *on?*   What is this good *for?*

Troublesome Prepositions

▪ *See individual entries listed alphabetically in ¶1101 for the following prepositions:*

At about	From–off	On–onto–on to
Beside–besides	In–into–in to	On–upon–up on
Between–among	In regards to	Opposite
Due to–because of– on account of	Like–as, as if	Per–a
	Of–have	Toward–towards
Except	Off	

Sentence Structure

Parallel Structure

1081 Express parallel ideas in parallel form.

a. Adjectives should be paralleled by adjectives, nouns by nouns, infinitives by infinitives, subordinate clauses by subordinate clauses, etc.

WRONG: Our new course is challenging and an inspiration. (Adjective and noun.)

RIGHT: Our new course is *challenging* and *inspiring.* (Two adjectives.)

WRONG: This machine is inexpensive, efficient, and it is easily operated. (Two adjectives and a clause.)

RIGHT: This machine is *inexpensive, efficient,* and *easily operated* (Three adjectives.)

WRONG: The seniors have already started reviewing and to cram. (Participle and infinitive.)

RIGHT: The seniors have already started *reviewing* and *cramming.* (Two participles.)

RIGHT: The seniors have already started *to review* and *cram.* (Two infinitives.)

NOTE: Parallelism is especially important in displayed enumerations.

WRONG: The duties of the hospitality committee are:
1. To greet guests.
2. Ordering refreshments.
3. Arrangement of flowers.

RIGHT: The duties of the hospitality committee are:
1. To greet guests.
2. To order refreshments.
3. To arrange flowers.

b. Correlative conjunctions (*both . . . and, either . . . or, neither . . . nor, not only . . . but also, whether . . . or,* etc.) should be followed by elements in parallel form.

(Continued on page 208.)

WRONG: I am not only proficient in shorthand but also in typing.
RIGHT: I am proficient not only *in shorthand* but also *in typing.*

WRONG: We are flying both to Chicago and San Francisco.
RIGHT: We are flying to both *Chicago* and *San Francisco.*
RIGHT: We are flying both *to Chicago* and *to San Francisco.*

WRONG: He would neither apologize nor would he promise to reform.
RIGHT: He would neither *apologize* nor *promise to reform.*
RIGHT: He would not apologize, nor would he promise to reform.

Dangling Constructions

1082 When a sentence begins with a participial phrase, an infinitive phrase, a gerund phrase, or an elliptical clause (one in which essential words are missing), make sure that the phrase or clause logically agrees with the subject of the sentence; otherwise, the construction will "dangle." To correct a dangling construction, make the subject of the sentence the doer of the action expressed by the opening phrase or clause. If that is not feasible, use an entirely different construction.

a. Participial phrases

WRONG: Having studied your cost estimates, a few questions·occur to me.
RIGHT: Having studied your cost estimates, I would like to ask you a few questions.

WRONG: Putting the matter of costs aside, the matter of production delays remains to be discussed.
RIGHT: Putting the matter of costs aside, we must still discuss the matter of production delays.

b. Infinitive phrases

WRONG: To produce satisfactory carbon copies, unwrinkled carbon paper must be used.
RIGHT: To produce satisfactory carbon copies, the typist must use unwrinkled carbon paper.

WRONG: To obtain the free booklet, this coupon should be mailed at once.
RIGHT: To obtain the free booklet, mail this coupon at once.

c. Prepositional-gerund phrases

WRONG: In passing your store windows, many handsome displays caught my eye.
RIGHT: In passing your store windows, I noticed many handsome displays.

WRONG: In analyzing these specifications, several errors have been found.
RIGHT: In analyzing these specifications, I have found several errors.

d. Elliptical clauses

WRONG: If ordered before May 1, a 5 percent discount will be allowed.
RIGHT: If ordered before May 1, these goods will be sold at a 5 percent discount.

WRONG: When four years old, my family moved to Omaha.
RIGHT: When I was four years old, my family moved to Omaha.

NOTE: *Absolute phrases* (typically involving passive participles) are not considered to "dangle," even though they come at the beginning of a sentence and do not refer to the subject. Such constructions, though grammatically correct, are usually awkward and should be avoided.

WEAK: The speeches having been concluded, we proceeded to take a vote.

BETTER: After the speeches were concluded, we proceeded to take a vote.

1083 When verbal phrases and elliptical clauses fall elsewhere in the sentence, be alert for illogical or confusing relationships. Adjust the wording as necessary.

WRONG: I caught a glimpse of the President, running to the window.

RIGHT: Running to the window, I caught a glimpse of the President.

WRONG: Your desk should be cleared of papers before going out to lunch.

RIGHT: You should clear your desk of papers before going out to lunch.

1084 A prepositional phrase will dangle at the beginning of a sentence if it leads the reader to expect a certain word as the subject and then another word is used instead.

WRONG: As head of the program committee, we think you should make immediate arrangements for another speaker. (The head of the committee is *you*, not *we*.)

RIGHT: We think that as head of the program committee you should make immediate arrangements for another speaker.

11

USAGE

A–An
Accidentally
A.D.–B.C.
Affect–Effect
Age–Aged–At the Age of
All of
All Right
Almost–All Most
Already–All Ready
Altogether–All Together
Always–All Ways
Amount–Number
And
And Etc.
And/Or
Anxious–Eager
Anyone–Any One
Anyway–Any Way
Appraise–Apprise
As
As . . . as–Not so . . . as
At About
Awhile–A While
Bad–Badly
Being That
Beside–Besides
Between–Among
Between You and Me
Both–Each
Both Alike
Bring–Take
But . . . However

But What
Cannot Help But
Class
Come–Go
Come and
Data
Different–Differently
Different From–Different Than
Done
Don't (Do Not)
Doubt That–Doubt Whether
Due to–Because of–On Account of
Each Other–One Another
Enthused Over
Equally as Good
Etc.
Everyday–Every Day
Everyone–Every One
Ex–Former
Except
Farther–Further
Fewer–Less
First–Firstly, etc.
Former–First
From–Off
Good–Well
Graduated–Was Graduated
Hardly
Healthy–Healthful
Help
If–Whether
Imply–Infer

In–Into–In to

In Regards to

Incidentally

Indifferent–In Different

Indirect–In Direct

Irregardless

Its–It's

Kind

Kind of–Sort of

Kind of a

Last–Latest

Latter–Last

Lay–Lie

Learn–Teach

Leave–Let

Like–As, As if

May–Can (Might–Could)

Maybe–May Be

Media

More Important–More Importantly

Most

Nobody–No Body

None–No One

Of–Have

Off

On–Onto–On to

On–Upon–Up on

Only

Opposite

Party

Per–A

Raise–Rise

Real–Really

Reason Is Because

Retroactive to

Said

Same

Scarcely

Serve–Service

Set–Sit

Shall–Will

Should–Would

So–So That

Someone–Some One

Sometime–Sometimes–Some Time

Sort

Such as . . . etc.

Sure–Surely

Sure and

Than–Then

That–Which–Who

These Sort–These Kind

This Here

Toward–Towards

Try and

Type

Unique

Up

Very

Ways

Who–Which–That

Who–Whom

Whoever–Who Ever

Would Have

1101 The following words and phrases are often used incorrectly.

A–an. In choosing *a* or *an*, consider the sound (not the spelling) of the following word. Use the article *a* before all *consonant* sounds, including sounded *h*, long *u*, and *o* with the sound of *w* (as in *one*); for example, *a day, a week, a home, a hotel, a house, a unit, a union, a uniform, a one-week seminar, a CPA, a 60-day note.*

Use *an* before all *vowel* sounds except long *u* and before words beginning with silent *h*; for example, *an army, an evening, an invoice, an outlet, an umbrella, an heir, an hour, an honor, an R* (pronounced "ar"), *an f.o.b. order* (pronounced "ef oh bee"), *an 8-hour day.*

(Continued on page 212.)

NOTE: In speech, both *a historic occasion* and *an historic occasion* are correct, depending on whether the *h* is sounded or left silent. In writing, *a historic occasion* is the form more commonly used.

A-per. See *Per-a*.

Accidentally. Note that this word ends in *ally*. Never spell this word *accidently*.

A.D.-B.C. *A.D.* (abbreviation of *anno Domini*, Latin for "in the year of our Lord") and *B.C.* ("before Christ") are written in all capitals, with a period following each letter.

150 B.C.   465 A.D. (ordinary usage) OR A.D. 465 (formal usage)

NOTE: Do not use a comma to separate *B.C.* or *A.D.* from the year.

Affect-effect. *Affect* is a verb meaning "to influence, change, assume." *Effect* can be either a verb meaning "to bring about" or a noun meaning "result, impression."

The court's decision in this case will not *affect* (influence or change) the established precedent.
She *affects* (assumes) an unsophisticated manner.
It is essential that we *effect* (bring about) an immediate turnaround in our sales performance.
It will be months before we can assess the full *effect* (result) of the new law.

Age-aged-at the age of

I interviewed a man *aged 52* for the job. (NOT: a man age 52.)
You can collect these benefits *at the age of 62*. (NOT: at age 62.)

All of. *Of* is not necessary after *all* unless the following word is a pronoun.

All the staff belong to the softball team. (ALSO: All of the staff . . .)
All of us belong to the softball team.

All right. Like *all wrong*, the expression *all right* should be spelled as two words. (While some dictionaries acknowledge the existence of *alright*, this spelling is not generally accepted as correct.)

Almost-all most. See also *Most*.

The plane was *almost* (nearly) three hours late.
We are *all most* pleased (all very much pleased) with the new schedule.

Already-all ready

The order had *already* (previously) been shipped.
The order is *all ready* (all prepared) to be shipped.

Altogether-all together

He is *altogether* (entirely) too lazy to be a success.
The papers are *all together* (all in a group) on your secretary's desk.

Always-all ways

She has *always* (at all times) done good work.
We have tried in *all ways* (by all methods) to keep our employees satisfied.

Among. See *Between–among*.

Amount–number. Use *amount* for things in bulk, as in "a large amount of lumber." Use *number* for individual items, as in "a large number of students."

And. Retain *and* before the last item in a series, even though that last item consists of two words joined by *and*.

> We need to increase our budgets for advertising, staff training, *and* research and development.
>
> (**NOT:** We need to increase our budgets for advertising, staff training, research and development.)

And etc. Never use *and* before *etc.* (See *Etc.*)

And/or. This is a legalistic term and should be avoided in ordinary writing.

Anxious–eager. Both *anxious* and *eager* mean "desirous," but *anxious* also implies fear or concern.

> I'm *anxious* to hear whether we won the bid or not.
>
> I'm *eager* (**NOT** anxious) to hear about your new house.

Anyone–any one. See ¶1010, note.

Anyway–any way

> *Anyway* (in any case), we can't spare him now.
>
> If we can help in *any way* (by any method), please phone.

Appraise–apprise

> We would like to *appraise* (set a value on) Mrs. Ellsworth's estate.
>
> I will *apprise* (inform) you of any new developments.

As. Do not use for *that* or *whether*; for example, "I do not know *whether* (**NOT** as) I can go." Use *because, since,* or *for* rather than *as* in clauses of reason; for example, "I cannot attend the meeting in Omaha, *because* (**NOT** as) I will be out on the Coast that day."

As . . . as–not so . . .as. The terms *as . . . as* are now commonly used in both positive and negative comparisons. Some writers, however, prefer to use *not so . . . as* for negative comparisons.

> Bob is every bit *as* bright *as* his older sister. (Positive comparison.)
>
> It is not *as* important *as* you think. **OR:** . . . *not so* important *as* you think. (Negative comparison.)

At about. Use either *at* or *about*, but not both words together. For example, "Plan to arrive *at* ten" **OR** "Plan to arrive *about* ten." (**BUT NOT:** Plan to arrive *at about* ten.) (See also ¶1078.)

Awhile–a while. One word as an adverb; two words as a noun.

> You may have to wait *awhile*. (Adverb.)
>
> You may have to wait for *a while*. (Noun; object of *for*.)
>
> I ran into him *a while* back.

Bad–badly. Use the adjective *bad* (not the adverb *badly*) after the verb *feel* or *look.* (See ¶1066.)

> I feel *bad* (**not** badly) about the mistake.
> **BUT:** He was hurt *badly* in the accident.

Because. See *Reason is because.*

Because of. See *Due to–because of–on account of.*

Being that. Do not use for *since* or *because.* For example, "Because (**not** being that) I was late, I could not get a seat."

Beside–besides

> I sat *beside* (next to) Mr. Parrish's father at the meeting.
> *Besides* (in addition), we need your support of the measure.

Between–among. Ordinarily, use *between* when referring to *two* persons or things and *among* when referring to *more than* two persons or things.

> The territory is divided evenly *between* the two sales representatives.
> The profits are to be evenly divided *among* the three partners.

Use *between* with more than two persons or things when they are being considered in pairs as well as in a group.

> There are distinct differences *between* New York, Chicago, and Dallas.
> In packing china, be sure to place paper *between* the plates. (**not:** between *each* of the plates.)

Between you and me (not *I*). (See ¶1055*b.*)

Both–each. *Both* means "the two considered together." *Each* refers to the individual members of a group considered separately.

> *Both* designs are acceptable.   The designs are *each* acceptable.

Both alike. *Both* is unnecessary. For example, "The typewriters are *alike.*" (**not:** both alike.)

Bring–take. *Bring* indicates motion toward the speaker. (**HINT:** Connect the *i* in *bring* with *I*, the speaker.) *Take* indicates motion away from the speaker. (**HINT:** Connect the *a*'s in *take* and in *away.*)

> Please *bring* the research data with you when you next come to the office.
> Please *take* the enclosed letter to Farley when you go to see him.
> You may *take* my copy with you if you will *bring* it back by Friday.

- *See note under* Come–go.

But . . . however. Use one or the other.

> We had hoped to see the show, *but* we couldn't get tickets.
> **or:** We had hoped to see the show; *however,* we couldn't get tickets.
> (**but not:** . . . but we couldn't get tickets, *however.*)

But what. Use *that.* For example, "I do not doubt *that* (**not** but what) he will be elected."

Cannot help but. This expression is a confusion of two others, namely, *can but* and *cannot help.*

I *can but* try.

I *cannot help* feeling sorry for her. (**NOT:** cannot help but feel.)

Class. See *Kind.*

Come–go. The choice between verbs depends on the location of the speaker. *Come* indicates motion *toward;* go, motion *away from.* (See also *Bring–take.*)

> When Bellotti *comes* back, I will *go* to the airport to meet him.
>
> *A secretary speaking over the phone to a customer:* Will it be convenient for you to *come* to our office tomorrow?
>
> *Anyone outside the office speaking:* Will it be convenient for you to *go* to their office tomorrow?

NOTE: When writing about your travel plans to a person at your destination, adopt that person's point of view and use *come.*

> *Midwesterner to Californian:* I am *coming* to California during the week of the 11th. I will *bring* the plans with me if they are ready.

However, if you are telling your travel plans to someone who is *not* at your destination, observe the regular distinction between *come* and *go.*

> *Midwesterner to Midwesterner:* I am *going* to California during the week of the 11th. I will *take* the plans with me if they are ready.

Come and. In formal writing use *come to* instead of the colloquial *come and.* For example, "Come to (**NOT** and) see me."

Data. See ¶1018, note.

Different–differently. When the meaning is "in a different manner," use the adverb *differently.*

> I wish we had done it *differently.*
>
> It came out *differently* than we expected.

After linking verbs and verbs of the senses, the adjective *different* is correct. (See ¶1066.)

> That music sounds completely *different.*
>
> He seems (appears) *different* since his promotion.
>
> Don't believe anything *different.* (Meaning "anything that is different.")

Different from–different than. See ¶1077.

Done. Do not say "I *done* it." Say "I *did* it." (See also ¶1032, note.)

Don't (do not). Do not use *don't* with *he, she,* or *it;* use *doesn't.*

> He *doesn't* talk easily.   **BUT:** I *don't* think so.
> She *doesn't* need any help.   They *don't* want any help.
> It *doesn't* seem right to penalize them.   We *don't* understand.

Doubt that–doubt whether. Use *doubt that* in negative statements and in questions. Use *doubt whether* in all other cases. (See also *If–whether.*)

> We do not *doubt that* she is capable. (Negative statement.)
>
> Does anyone *doubt that* the check was mailed? (Question.)
>
> I *doubt whether* I can go.

Due to–because of–on account of. *Due to* introduces an adjectival phrase and should modify nouns. It is normally used only after some form of the verb *to be* (*is, are, was, were,* etc.)

> Her success is *due to* talent and hard work. (*Due* modifies *success.*)

Because of and *on account of* introduce adverbial phrases and should modify verbs.

> He resigned *because of* ill health. (*Because of* modifies *resigned.*)
> (**NOT:** He resigned *due to* ill health.)

Each–both. See *Both–each.*

Each other–one another. Use *each other* to refer to two persons or things; *one another* for more than two.

> The two partners had great respect for *each other's* abilities.
> The four winners congratulated *one another.*

Eager–anxious. See *Anxious–eager.*

Enthused over. Use *was* or *were enthusiastic about* instead.

> The sales staff *was enthusiastic about* (**NOT** enthused over) next year's styles.

Equally as good. Use either *equally good* or *just as good.*

> This model is newer, but that one is *equally good.* (**NOT:** equally as good.)
> Those are *just as good* as these. (**NOT:** equally as good.)

Etc. This abbreviation of *et cetera* means "and other things." Therefore, do not use *and* before it. A comma both precedes and follows *etc.* (see ¶164). In formal writing, avoid the use of *etc.;* use a phrase such as *and the like* or *and so on* instead.

NOTE: Do not use *etc.* or equivalent expressions at the end of a series introduced by *such as.* The term *such as* implies that only a few selected examples will be given; therefore, it is unnecessary to add *etc.* or *and so on,* which suggests that further examples could be given.

> As part of its employee educational program, the company offers courses in report writing, business correspondence, grammar and style, *and so on.*
> **OR:** . . . the company offers courses *such as* report writing, business correspondence, and grammar and style.
> (**BUT NOT:** . . . the company offers courses *such as* report writing, business correspondence, grammar and style, *and so on.*)

Everyday–every day

> You'll soon master the *everyday* (ordinary or daily) routine of the job.
> He has called *every day* (each day) this week.

Everyone–every one. See ¶1010, note.

Ex–former. Use *ex-* with a title to designate the person who *immediately* preceded the current titleholder in that position; use *former* with a title to designate an earlier titleholder.

Charles Feldman is the *ex-president* of the Harrisburg Chamber of Commerce. (Held office immediately before the current president.)

BUT: . . . is a *former* president of the Harrisburg Chamber of Commerce. (Held office sometime before the current president and that person's immediate predecessor.)

Except. When *except* is a preposition, be sure to use the objective form of a pronoun that follows. For example, "Everyone has been transferred *except* Jean and *me.*" (**NOT:** except Jean and I.) (See also ¶1055*b*.)

Farther–further. *Farther* refers to actual distance; *further* refers to figurative distance and means "to a greater degree" or "to a greater extent."

The drive from the airport to Boone was *farther* (in actual distance) than we expected.

Let's plan to discuss the proposal *further* (to a greater extent).

Fewer–less. *Fewer* refers to a number and is used with *plural* nouns. *Less* refers to degree or amount and is used with *singular* nouns.

Fewer accidents (a smaller number) were reported than was expected.

Less effort (a smaller degree) was put forth by the organizers, and thus *fewer* people (a smaller number) attended.

NOTE: The expression *less than* (rather than *fewer than*) precedes plural nouns referring to periods of time, amounts of money, and quantities.

less than ten years ago   **BUT:** fewer than 60 people

Less than five years ago our sales were under $1 million a year.

First–firstly, etc. In enumerations use the forms *first, second, third* (**NOT** *firstly, secondly, thirdly*).

Former–ex. See *Ex–former.*

Former–first. *Former* refers to the first of two persons or things. When more than two are mentioned, use *first.* (See also *Latter–last.*)

This style is made in wool and in Dacron, but I prefer the *former.*

This style is made in wool, in Dacron, and in Orlon, but I prefer the *first.*

From–off. Use *from* (**NOT** off) with persons.

I got the answer I needed *from* Margaret. (**NOT:** off Margaret.)

Good–well. *Good* is an adjective. *Well* may be used as an adverb or (with reference to health) as an adjective.

Marie got *good* grades in school. (Adjective.)

I will do the job as *well* as I can. (Adverb.)

He admits he does not feel *well* today. (Adjective.)

The security guards look *good* in their new uniforms. (Adjective.)

NOTE: *To feel well* means "to be in good health." *To feel good* means "to be in good spirits."

Graduated–was graduated. Both forms are acceptable.

Hardly. Since *hardly* is negative in meaning, do not use another negative with it.

You *could hardly* (**NOT** couldn't hardly) expect him to agree.

Healthy–healthful. People are *healthy;* a climate or food is *healthful.*

You ought to move to a more *healthful* (**NOT** healthier) climate.

Help. Do not use *from* after the verb *help.* For example, "I couldn't *help* (**NOT** help from) telling her she was wrong."

However. See *But . . . however.*

If–whether. *If* is often used colloquially for *whether* in such sentences as "He doesn't know *whether* he will be able to leave tomorrow." In written material, use *whether,* particularly in such expressions as *see whether, learn whether, know whether,* and *doubt whether.* Also use *whether* when the expression *or not* follows or is implied.

Find out *whether* (**NOT** if) this format is acceptable *or not.*

Imply–infer. *Imply* means "to suggest"; you imply something by *your own* words or actions.

Verna *implied* that we would not be invited.

Infer means "to deduce" or "to arrive at a conclusion"; you infer something from *another person's* words or actions.

I *inferred* from Verna's remarks that we would not be invited.

In–into–in to

The correspondence is *in* the file. (*In* implies position within.)

He walked *into* the outer office. (*Into* implies entry or change of form.)

All sales reports are to be sent *in to* the sales manager. (*In* is an adverb in the verb phrase *are to be sent in; to* is a simple preposition.)

Mr. Boehme came *in to* see me. (*In* is part of the verb phrase *came in; to* is part of the infinitive *to see.*)

In regards to. Substitute *in regard to, with regard to,* or *as regards.*

Incidentally. Note that this word ends in *ally.* Never spell the word *incidently.*

Indifferent–in different

She was *indifferent* (not caring one way or the other) to the offer,

He liked our idea, but he wanted it expressed *in different* (in other) words.

Indirect–in direct

Indirect (not direct) lighting will enhance the appearance of this room.

This order is *in direct* (the preposition *in* plus the adjective *direct*) conflict with the policy of this company.

Irregardless. Use *regardless.*

Its–it's. See ¶1056d.

Kind. *Kind* is singular; therefore, write *this kind, that kind, these kinds, those kinds* (but not *these kind, those kind*). The same distinctions hold for *class, type,* and *sort.*

Kind of–sort of. In formal writing use *somewhat* or *rather* instead of the colloquial expression *kind of* or *sort of.*

I was *somewhat* (**NOT** kind of, sort of) surprised.

She seemed *rather* (**NOT** kind of, sort of) tired.

Kind of a. The *a* is unnecessary. For example, "That *kind of* (**NOT** kind of a) material is very expensive."

Last–latest. *Last* means "after all others"; *latest,* "most recent."

> Mr. Lin's *last* act before leaving was to recommend Ms. Roth's promotion.
>
> Attached is the *latest* bulletin from the Weather Service.

Latter–last. *Latter* refers to the second of two persons or things mentioned. When more than two are mentioned, use *last.* (See also *Former–first.*)

> July and August are good vacation months, but the *latter* is more popular.
>
> June, July, and August are good vacation months, but the *last* is the most popular.

Lay–lie. *Lay* (principal parts: *lay, laid, laid, laying*) means "to put" or "to place." It signifies that someone is placing something in a reclining position. This verb requires an object to complete its meaning.

> Please *lay* the extra file *folders* on the bottom shelf.
>
> I *laid* the *message* right on your desk.
>
> I *had laid* two other *notes* there yesterday.
>
> He is always *laying* the *blame* on his assistants. (Puts the blame.)
>
> The dress *was laid* in the box. (A passive construction implying that someone *laid the dress* in the box.)

Lie (principal parts: *lie, lay, lain, lying*) means "to recline, rest, or stay" or "to take a position of rest." It refers to a person or thing as either assuming or being in a reclining position. This verb cannot take an object.

> Now he *lies* in bed most of the day.
>
> The mountains *lay* before us as we proceeded west.
>
> This letter *has lain* unanswered for two weeks.
>
> Today's mail *is lying* on the receptionist's desk.

TEST: In deciding whether to use *lie* or *lay* in a sentence, substitute the word *place, placed,* or *placing* (as appropriate) for the word in question. If the substitute fits, the corresponding form of *lay* is correct. If it doesn't, use the appropriate form of *lie.*

> I will (*lie* or *lay*?) down now. (You could not say, "I will *place* down now." Therefore, write "I will *lie* down now.")
>
> I (*laid* or *lay*?) the pad on his desk. ("I *placed* the pad on his desk" works. Therefore, write "I *laid* the pad.")
>
> I (*laid* or *lay*?) awake many nights. ("I *placed* awake" doesn't work. Write "I *lay* awake.")
>
> These files have (*laid* or *lain*?) untouched for some time. ("These files have *placed* untouched" doesn't work. Write "These files have *lain* untouched.")
>
> He has been (*laying* or *lying*?) down on the job. ("He has been *placing* down on the job" doesn't work. Write "He has been *lying* down.")

NOTE: When the verb *lie* means "to tell a falsehood," it has regularly formed principal parts (*lie, lied, lied, lying*) and is seldom confused with the verbs just described.

Learn–teach. *Learn* (principal parts: *learn, learned, learned, learning*) means "to acquire knowledge." *Teach* (principal parts: *teach, taught, taught, teaching*) means "to impart knowledge to others."

> I *learned* from a master teacher.
> A first-rate instructor *taught* me how.
> I was *taught* by a first-rate instructor.

Leave–let. *Leave* (principal parts: *leave, left, left, leaving*) means "to move away, abandon, or depart." *Let* (principal parts: *let, let, let, letting*) means "to permit or allow." **TEST:** In deciding whether to use *let* or *leave*, try substituting the appropriate form of *permit*. If *permit* fits, use *let;* if not, use *leave.*

> I now *leave* you to your own devices. (Abandon you.)
> Mr. Morales *left* on the morning train. (Departed.)
> *Let* me see the last page. (Permit me to see.)
> *Leave* me alone. **OR:** *Let* me alone. (Either is acceptable.)

Like–as, as if. *Like* is correctly used as a preposition. Although *like* is also widely used as a conjunction in colloquial speech, use *as* or *as if* in written material.

> We need to hire another person *like* you.
> Kate, *like* her predecessor, will have to cope with the problem.
> Mary looks *like* her mother.
> Mary looks *as* (**NOT** like) her mother did at the same age.
> It looks *like* snow.
> It looks *as if* (**NOT** like) it will snow.
> *As* (**NOT** Like) I told you earlier, we will not reorder for six months.

May–can (might–could). *May* and *might* imply permission or possibility; *can* and *could,* ability or power.

> You *may* send them a dozen cans of paint on trial. (Permission.)
> The report *may* be true. (Possibility.)
> *Can* he present a workable plan? (Has he the ability?)
> Miss Kovacs said I *might* (permission) have the time off if I *could* (power) finish my work in time.

Maybe–may be. *Maybe* is an adverb; *may be* is a verb.

> If we don't receive a letter from them today, *maybe* (an adverb meaning "perhaps") we should call.
> Mr. Boston *may be* (a verb) out of town next week.

Media. *Media,* referring to various channels of communication and advertising, is a plural noun. *Medium* is the singular. (See ¶1018.)

More important–more importantly. *More important* is often used as a short form for "what is more important," especially at the beginning of a sentence. *More importantly* means "in a more important manner."

> *More important,* we need to establish a line of credit very quickly. (What is more important.)
> The incident was treated *more importantly* than it deserved. (In a more important manner.)

Most. Do not use for *almost*. For example, "*Almost all* the money is gone" **or** "*Most* of the money is gone." (**but not:** *Most all* of the money is gone.)

Nobody–no body

> There was *nobody* (no person) at the information desk when I arrived.
>
> *No body* (no group) of employees is more cooperative than yours.

note: Spell *no body* as two words when it is followed by *of*.

None–no one. See ¶1013.

Not so . . . as. See *As . . . as–not so . . . as*.

Number. See *Amount–number*.

Of–have. Do not use *of* instead of *have* in verb forms. The correct forms are *could have, would have, should have, might have, may have, must have, ought to have*, etc.

> What *could have* happened? (**not:** What could *of* happened?)

Off. Do not use *off of* or *off from* in place of *off*. (See also ¶1078.)

> The papers fell *off* the desk. (**not:** off of the desk.)

On–onto–on to

> It's dangerous to drive *on* the highway shoulder. (*On* implies position or movement over.)
>
> He lost control of the car and drove *onto* the sidewalk. (*Onto* implies movement toward and then over.)
>
> Let's go *on to* the next problem. (*On* is an adverb in the verb phrase *go on*; *to* is a preposition.)
>
> She then went *on to* tell about her experiences in Asia. (*On* is part of the verb phrase *went on*; *to* is part of the infinitive *to tell*.)

On–upon–up on

> His statements were based *on* (**or** *upon*) experimental data. (*On* and *upon* are interchangeable.)
>
> Please follow *up on* the Updegraff case. (*Up* is part of the verb phrase *follow up*; *on* is a preposition.)

One another. See *Each other–one another*.

Only. The adverb *only* is negative in meaning. Therefore, do not use another negative with it unless you want a positive meaning. (See ¶1072 for the placement of *only* in a sentence.)

> I use this letterhead *only* for foreign correspondence. (I do not use this letterhead for anything else.)
>
> **but:** I do not use this letterhead *only* for foreign correspondence. (I use it for a number of other things as well.)

Opposite. When used as a noun, *opposite* is followed by *of*.

> Her opinion is the *opposite of* mine.

In other uses, *opposite* is followed by *to* or *from* or by neither.

> Her opinion is *opposite to* (**or** *from*) mine.
>
> She lives *opposite* the school.

Party. Do not use for *person* except in legal work.

Per-a. *Per,* a Latin word, is often used to mean "by the," as in *$5 per hundredweight* or *80 kilometers (50 miles) per hour.* Whenever possible, substitute *a* or *an;* for example, *at the rate of 75 cents an hour, 60 cents a liter.* Do not use *per* in the sense of "according to" or "in accordance with."

> We are sending you samples *as you requested.* (**NOT:** per your request.)

Raise–rise. *Raise* (principal parts: *raise, raised, raised, raising*) means "to cause to lift" or "to lift something." This verb requires an object to complete its meaning.

> Mr. Pinelli *raises* a good *question.*
>
> Most growers *have raised* the *price* of coffee.
>
> We are *raising money* for the United Fund.
>
> Our rent *has been raised.* (A passive construction implying that someone *has raised* the rent.)

Rise (principal parts: *rise, rose, risen, rising*) means "to ascend," "to move upward by itself," or "to get up." This verb cannot be used with an object.

> We will have to *rise* to the demands of the occasion.
>
> The sun *rose* at 6:25 this morning.
>
> The river *has risen* to flood level.
>
> The temperature *has been rising* all day.

TEST: Remember, you cannot "rise" anything.

Real–really. *Real* is an adjective; *really,* an adverb. Do not use *real* to modify another adjective; use *very* or *really.*

> The ring is set with *real* diamonds. (Adjective.)
>
> I was *really* ashamed of myself. (Adverb.)
>
> It was *very* nice of you to call. (**NOT:** real nice.)

Reason is because. Substitute *reason is that.* For example, "The *reason* for such low sales *is that* (**NOT** because) prices are too high."

Retroactive to (**NOT** *from*). For example, "Salaries of all secretaries will be increased $5 a week *retroactive to* January 1." (See also ¶1077.)

Said. The use of *said* in a phrase like "the *said* document" is appropriate only in legal writing. In normal usage write "the document referred to above." (In many cases the document being referred to will be clear to the reader without the additional explanation.)

Same. Do not use for *it.* For example, "We are now processing your order and will have *it* (**NOT** same) ready for you by Saturday."

Scarcely. The adverb *scarcely* is negative in meaning. Therefore, do not use another negative with it. (See ¶1072 for the placement of *scarcely.*)

> I *scarcely* recognized (**NOT** didn't scarcely recognize) you.

Serve–service. Things can be *serviced,* but people are *served.*

> We take great pride in the way we *serve* (**NOT** service) our clients.
>
> For a small additional charge we will *service* the equipment for a full year.

Set–sit. *Set* (principal parts: *set, set, set, setting*) means "to place some-thing somewhere." In this sense, *set* requires an object to complete its meaning. REMEMBER: You cannot "sit" anything.

> It's important to *set* down your *recollections* while they are still fresh.
> I must have lost it when I *set* my *suitcase* down.
> I have *set* my *alarm* for six in the morning.
> The crew *was setting* the *stage* for the evening performance.
> The date *was set* some time ago. (A passive construction implying that someone *set* the date.)

NOTE: *Set* has a few other meanings in which the verb does *not* require an object, but these meanings are seldom confused with *sit*.

> They *set* out on the trip in high spirits.
> The sun *set* at 5:34 p.m. Wednesday.
> Do not disturb the gelatin dessert until it *has set*.

Sit (principal parts: *sit, sat, sat, sitting*) means "to be in a position of rest" or "to be seated." This verb cannot be used with an object.

> So here we *sit*, waiting for a decision from top management.
> I *sat* next to Ebbetsen at the board meeting.
> They *had sat* on the plane a full hour before the flight was canceled.
> They *will be sitting* in the orchestra.

Shall–will. The auxiliary verb *shall* has largely given way to the verb *will* in all but the most formal writing and speech. Some business firms, however, still prefer a formal style and require that the distinction between *shall* and *will* be observed. The following rules reflect both ordinary and formal usage:

a. To express simple future time:

   (1) In *ordinary* circumstances, use *will* with all three persons.

> I (OR *we*) *will* be glad to help you plan the program.
> You *will* want to study these recommendations before the meeting.
> He (OR *she, it, they*) *will* arrive tomorrow morning.

   (2) In *formal* circumstances, use *shall* with the first person (*I, we*) and *will* with the second and third persons (*you, he, she, it, they*).

> I (OR *we*) *shall* be glad to answer all inquiries promptly.
> You *will* meet the McGinnesses at the reception this evening.
> They (OR *he, she*) *will* not find the trip too tiring.

b. To indicate *determination, promise, desire, choice,* or *threat:*

   (1) In *ordinary* circumstances, use *will* with all three persons.

   (2) In *formal* circumstances, use *will* for the first person (*I, we*) and *shall* for the second and third persons (*you, he, she, it, they*).

> In spite of the risk, I *will* go where I please. (Determination.)
> We *will* not be coerced. (Determination.)
> They *shall* not interfere with my department. (Determination.)
> I *will* send my check by the end of the week. (Promise.)

(Continued on page 224.)

We will report you to the authorities if this is true. (Threat.)

You shall regret your answer. (Threat.)

He shall study, or *he shall* leave college. (Threat.)

c. To indicate *willingness* (to be willing, to be agreeable to) in both *ordinary* and *formal* circumstances, use *will* with all persons.

Yes, I *will* meet you at six o'clock.

Should–would. *Should* and *would* follow the same rules as *shall* and *will* (see entry above) in expressions of future time, determination, and willingness. The distinctions concerning ordinary and formal usage also apply here.

ORDINARY: I *would* like to hear from you.

FORMAL: I *should* like to hear from you.

ORDINARY: We *would* be glad to see her.

FORMAL: We *should* be glad to see her.

ORDINARY: I *would* be pleased to serve on that committee.

FORMAL: I should be pleased to serve on that committee.

a. Always use *should* in all persons to indicate "ought to."

I *should* study tonight.

You *should* report his dishonesty to the manager.

He *should* pay his debts.

b. Always use *would* in all persons to indicate customary action.

Every day I *would* swim half a mile.

They *would* only say, "No comment."

She *would* practice day after day.

c. Use *should* in all three persons to express a condition in an *if* clause.

If *I* should win the prize, I will share it with you.

If you *should* miss the train, please call me collect.

d. Use *would* in all three persons to express willingness in an *if* clause.

If he *would* apply himself, he could win top honors easily.

If you *would* consider delaying your decision, I am sure I could offer you a more attractive set of terms.

So–so that. *So* as a conjunction means "therefore"; *so that* means "in order that."

The work is now finished, *so* you can all go home. (See also ¶179.)

Please finish what you are doing *so that* we can all go home.

Someone–some one. See ¶1010, note.

Sometime–sometimes–some time

The order will be shipped *sometime* (at some unspecified time) next week.

Sometimes (now and then) reports are misleading.

It took me *some time* (a period of time) to complete the job.

I saw him *some time* ago.

Sort. See *Kind*.

Sort of. See *Kind of–sort of.*

Such as . . . etc. See *Etc.*

Sure–surely. *Sure* is an adjective; *surely,* an adverb.

> I am *sure* that I did not make that mistake. (Adjective.)
> You can *surely* count on our help. (Adverb.)

Do not use *sure* as an adverb; use *surely* or *very.*

> I was *very* glad to be of help (NOT: sure glad.)

Sure and. In formal writing use *sure to* in place of the colloquial *sure and.* For example, "Be *sure to* turn left at the corner."

Than–then. *Than* is a conjunction introducing a subordinate clause of comparison. *Then* is an adverb meaning "at that time" or "next."

> The compulsory retirement age is considerably lower now *than* it was *then.*
> They *then* asserted that they could handle the account better *than* we. (See ¶1057 for the case of pronouns following *than.*)

NOTE: Remember that *then* (like *when*) refers to time.

That–which–who. See ¶1062.

These sort–these kind. Incorrect; the correct forms are *this* sort, *this* kind. (See also *Kind.*)

This here. Do not use for *this.* For example, "*This* (NOT this here) typewriter is out of order."

Toward–towards. Both forms are correct.

Try and. In written material use *try to* rather than the colloquial *try and.* For example, "Please *try to* be here on time." (NOT: try and be here.)

Type. See *Kind.*

Unique. Do not use in the sense of "unusual." A unique thing is one of a kind (see ¶1071*f*).

Up. Many verbs (for example, *end, rest, lift, connect, join, hurry, settle, burn, drink, eat*) contain the idea of "up"; therefore, the adverb *up* is unnecessary. In the following sentences, *up* should be omitted.

> The electrician will connect (up) the fan.
> Let's divide (up) the sandwiches.
> Can you help me lift (up) this case?
> I will call him (up) tomorrow.

Upon–up on. See *On–upon–up on.*

Very. This adverb can be used to modify an adjective, another adverb, a present participle, or a "descriptive" past participle.

> We are *very happy* with the outcome. (Modifying an adjective.)
> This finish dries *very quickly.* (Modifying an adverb.)
> It is a *very disappointing* showing. (Modifying a present participle.)
> I was *very pleased* with the pictures. (Modifying a descriptive past participle.)

(Continued on page 226.)

When the past participle expresses action rather than description, insert an adverb like *much* after *very*.

> They are *very much opposed* to your plan. (*Opposed* is part of the complete verb *are opposed* and expresses action rather than description.)

Ways. Do not use for *way* in referring to distance. For example, "I live a short way (**NOT** ways) from here."

Whether. See *If–whether.*

Who–which–that. See ¶1062.

Who–whom. See ¶1061.

Whoever–who ever

> *Whoever* (anyone who) is elected secretary should write that letter at once.
> *Who ever* made such a statement? (*Ever* is an adverb.)

Would have. Do not use for *had* in a clause beginning with *if.* For example, "If you *had* (**NOT** would have) come early, you could have seen him."

DICTATION, TRANSCRIPTION, AND TYPING TECHNIQUES

Taking Dictation (¶¶1201–1214)
Transcribing (¶¶1215–1224)
Preparing Carbon Copies (¶¶1225–1229)
Submitting Your Work (¶¶1230–1231)

Taking Dictation

1201 Start each day's dictation on a new notebook page.

1202 Write the date in longhand in the lower left corner of each notebook page that you use during the day; for example, *Jan. 11, 1979.*

1203 Use a ball-point pen with the type of point that allows you the greatest writing fluency. Have several pens at hand for emergency use, and keep a red-ink pen handy for making special notations.

1204 Number the notes for each letter, starting with 1 each day. If your employer hands you a letter or other material related to the dictation, number it to correspond with your notes. This will speed the identification of background material as you transcribe.

1205 Use circled letters to indicate changes in the notes. For example, write Ⓐ at the point in the notes where the first change is to be made; then key the notes for the change in the same way, Ⓐ. If the dictator customarily makes many changes during dictation, keep one notebook column free for writing these changes.

1206 Write the following in longhand:

a. The addressee's name, unless you are familiar with the correct spelling or can easily confirm it; for example, *ec welford.*
b. Street names, unless you know or can easily confirm the spelling.
c. Any unusual words or trade names.

1207 Underscore in your notes as follows:

a. Draw one line under words that are to be underscored in typewritten material or italicized in printed material.
b. Draw two lines under words that are to be typed or printed in all-capital letters.

1208 Use a distinctive mark, such as a double line, to indicate the end of the notes for each dictated item.

1209 Leave a few blank lines between items of dictation so that you will have space to write any special instructions the dictator may give you—for example, *Transcribe first.*

1210 Mark the notes for top-priority items "Rush" (using a colored pen if one is available).

1211 Flag rush dictation by folding back the corner of the notebook page so that it projects beyond the edge of the cover.

1212 Be efficient in turning notebook pages. One method is to keep both hands on the notebook, using your left hand to keep the book steady and your left thumb to move the page gradually upward as you approach the bottom of the page. (If you are left-handed, you naturally will use your right hand and right thumb.)

1213 Watch for subdivisions of thought as you are taking dictation and paragraph accordingly.

1214 Do not interrupt unless the dictator is so far ahead of you that you are losing the meaning of the dictation. Check doubtful words or sentences immediately after the dictator has finished the individual item of dictation. Read back the sentence containing the questioned word. If you are uncertain about an entire sentence, read back the sentence immediately preceding the one in question and as much of the one in question as you can.

NOTE: If you are getting too far behind, call out the last three words you are on. This simple procedure alerts the dictator that you are behind, and it also indicates exactly where you are in your note taking. The dictator will pick up your cue, go back to the words you repeated, and begin dictating again from that point.

Transcribing

1215 Check to see which items, if any, are to receive priority treatment. (See ¶¶1210–1211.)

1216 Check for special instructions from the dictator before you begin to transcribe (see ¶1209). Always make at least one copy of the correspondence (see also ¶¶1225–1229, 1376–1380).

1217 Confirm spellings, numbers, and similar details before you start transcribing.

1218 Transcribe directly from your notes. Develop the ability to read ahead as you transcribe in order to foresee such special problems as errors in grammar, incomplete sentences, and changes in the dictation (see ¶1205).

1219 If possible, do not make a paragraph more than eight to ten lines long. Also avoid dividing the letter into a great many very short (two- or three-line) paragraphs.

1220 Consider the advantages of displaying numbered or lettered items instead of running them together in a paragraph.

1221 Proofread the letter before removing it from the machine. Check carefully for typing accuracy as well as for correct meaning. If you merely scan the copy, you are likely to miss word substitutions (such as *than* for *that* or *now* for *not*) or word repetitions (such as erroneously typing the same word at the end of one line and again at the beginning of the next). You may also miss the accidental omission of a word or a letter (such as *you* instead of *your*). Be sure that you have incorporated all the changes requested by the dictator (see ¶1205).

1222 Cancel the transcribed notes with a diagonal line.

1223 Check your notebook at the end of each day to be sure that you have transcribed all your notes. If any arc left, then the next day give them priority over all new dictation except for rush dictation (which should always be transcribed first).

1224 Keep a rubber band around the notebook at the last page transcribed so that you will know immediately where to resume transcribing or writing during the day or at the beginning of the next day.

Preparing Carbon Copies

1225 a. For carbon copies use *manifold* (an inexpensive, lightweight paper available with either a glazed or an unglazed finish), *onionskin* (a stronger, more expensive paper available with either a smooth or a ripple finish), or *copy letterhead* (lightweight paper with the letterhead and the word *COPY* printed on it).

b. Use carbon paper of the weight and finish most appropriate for the number of copies you must make.

Copies	Weight	Finish
1–4	Standard (8 lb)	Hard
5–8	Medium (6 lb)	Medium*
9+	Light (4 lb)	Soft*

*On electric typewriters, use a hard finish in place of medium and a medium finish in place of soft.

c. Many companies provide preassembled "snap-out" carbon packs in which sheets of carbon paper are interleaved between sheets of copy paper. The sheets of copy paper are often of different colors in order to facilitate the routing of copies.

1226 When assembling a carbon pack:

a. Use carbon paper that has the upper left and lower right corners cut off diagonally. (Reason: It is easier to remove the carbons later on. To do so, grasp the upper left corner of the sheets with one hand and either shake out the carbons or, if the carbons extend below the typed sheets, pull out the carbons from the bottom with your other hand.)

b. Place the *glossy* side of the carbon against the paper on which the copy is to be made.

c. Make sure that a sheet of carbon paper is interleaved between each two sheets of typing paper.

d. Pick up the pack and, holding it loosely, tap the left and top edges against your desk until the sheets are even.

1227 When inserting a carbon pack into the machine:

a. Hold the pack so that the *glossy* side of the carbons is toward you, and roll the pack into the machine. (If necessary, use the ratchet release to prevent slippage when you insert the pack into the machine or when you turn it back to make corrections.)

b. Use an envelope or a sheet of paper to guide a thick carbon pack into the machine. If you use an envelope, place the pack under the flap of a large envelope and then roll them both into the machine far enough to permit removing the envelope from the front of the cylinder. If you use a sheet of paper as a guide, insert the sheet about halfway into the machine. Place the pack between the guide sheet and the cylinder, and then roll them forward until the guide sheet can be removed from the front of the cylinder.

1228 After the carbon pack has been inserted into the machine:

a. Check to be sure that the printed side of the letterhead and the dull side of the carbon sheets are facing you.

b. Be sure that the pack is straight in the machine.

c. Operate the paper release before you start typing in order to release the tension on the papers and to prevent the carbon sheets from making marks on the copies.

1229 When reusing carbon paper, rotate the sheets from the front to the back of carbon packs and turn them from the top to the bottom so that the carbons will wear more evenly.

Submitting Your Work

1230 Check to see that each transcript is clean (no smudges, fingerprints, or obvious erasures) before you submit it to the dictator.

1231 Follow this procedure when you submit transcripts for signature:

a. Place the *unfolded* letter together with any enclosures under the flap of the envelope. Have the address side of the envelope on top.

b. Assemble each carbon copy that is to be signed in the same way you arranged the original letter. Place the carbon copies under the original.

c. Staple the file copy on top of the letter or other correspondence, if any, to which it is related.

d. Put all the transcripts to be signed in a folder (labeled "For Your Signature"), and place the folder on the dictator's desk. If the dictator initials file copies, present them in a separate folder labeled "File Copies."

13 LETTERS AND MEMOS

Section 13 provides guidelines for setting up letters and memos. These guidelines are not intended as inflexible rules; they can—and should—be modified to fit specific occasions as good sense and good taste require.

Parts of Letters

1301 A business letter has the following parts:

	Standard	Optional
Heading:	Letterhead or return address (¶¶1311–1313) Date line (¶1314)	Personal or confidential notation (¶1315) Reference notations (¶¶1316–1317)
Opening:	Inside address (¶¶1318–1344) Salutation (¶¶1346–1351)	Attention line (¶1345)
Body:	Message (¶¶1354–1357)	Subject line (¶¶1352–1353)
Closing:	Complimentary closing (¶¶1358–1360) Writer's identification (¶¶1362–1369) Reference initials (¶¶1370–1372)	Company signature line (¶1361) Enclosure notation (¶¶1373–1374) Mailing notation (¶1375) Carbon copy notation (¶¶1376–1380) Postscript (¶1381)

▪ *Each of these parts is illustrated in the model letters on pages 233–236.*

1302 A business letter is usually arranged in one of the following styles:

a. The Blocked Style. The date line, the complimentary closing, and the writer's identification all begin at center. All other lines begin at the left margin. (This is the style most commonly used.)

b. The Semiblocked Style. This is exactly like the blocked style except for one additional feature: the first line of each paragraph is indented five spaces.

c. The Full-Blocked Style. All lines typically begin at the left margin. Nothing is indented (except for displayed quotations, tables, and similar material).

d. The Simplified Style. As in the full-blocked style, all lines begin at the left margin. However, the simplified style has these additional features: the salutation is replaced by an all-capital subject line; the complimentary closing is omitted; the writer's identification is typed in all-capital letters on one line; and open punctuation (see ¶1309*b*) is always used.

▪ *These four letter styles are illustrated on pages 233–236.*

Blocked Style, Standard Punctuation

Heading

Capitol Products Corporation 250 Lexington Avenue New York, New York 10022

December 12, 1979 →5

Opening

Ms. Susan N. Morales
2839 Clary Street
Fort Worth, Texas 76111 →2

Dear Ms. Morales: →2

Body

We have received and have noted with interest your
letter of application for a sales position with us. →2

At present we do not have a vacancy near Fort Worth,
but we do need a representative who is located in or
near Lubbock and can cover the northwestern part of
the state. If you would like to be considered for
this opening, please fill in the enclosed application
form and mail it back to us. →2

I will be in Fort Worth near the end of the month to
attend a convention. While I am there, I would be
pleased to talk with you. If you are qualified for
the position and are truly interested in joining our
staff, we might be able to settle the matter at that
point and work out the employment details. →2

Sincerely yours, →2

CAPITOL PRODUCTS CORPORATION →4

Kenneth R. Willmott →2

Kenneth R. Willmott
National Sales Manager →2

Closing

bjn
Enclosure
Special delivery
cc Miss A. Rossi

Letterhead: The company's printed name and address.

Date Line: The date (month, day, year) the letter is typed; starts at center on line 15 or three lines below letterhead (whichever is lower).

Inside Address: The name and address of the person you are writing to.

Salutation: An opening greeting like *Dear Ms. Morales.*

Message: The text of the letter; paragraphs are typed single-spaced with no indentations.

Complimentary Closing: A parting phrase like *Sincerely;* starts at center.

Company Signature: Emphasizes that the writer is acting on behalf of the company.

Writer's Identification: The signer's name or title or both.

Reference Initials: The initials of the writer and/or typist.

Enclosure Notation: A reminder that the letter has an enclosure.

Mailing Notation: Indicates that the letter has been sent a special way.

Carbon Copy Notation: The names of those who will receive copies of this letter.

Semiblocked Style, Standard Punctuation

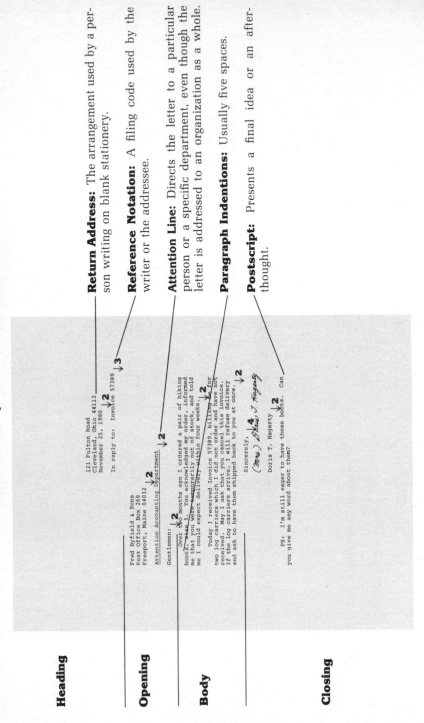

Heading

Opening

Body

Closing

121 Fulton Road
Cleveland, Ohio 44113
November 25, 1980 ↓**2**

In reply to: Invoice 57389 ↓**3**

Fred Byfield & Sons
Post Office Box 268
Freeport, Maine 04032 ↓**2**

Attention Accounting Department ↓**2**

Gentlemen: ↓**2**

Over two months ago I ordered a pair of hiking boots, size 5. You acknowledged my order, informed me that you were temporarily out of stock, and told me I could expect delivery within four weeks. ↓**2**

Today I received Invoice 57389, billing me for two log carriers which I did not order and have not received. May I ask that you cancel this invoice. If the log carriers arrive, I will refuse delivery and ask to have them shipped back to you at once. ↓**2**

Sincerely, ↓**4**

(Mrs.) Doris T. Hagerty

Doris T. Hagerty ↓**2**

PS: I'm still eager to have those boots. Can you give me any word about them?

Return Address: The arrangement used by a person writing on blank stationery.

Reference Notation: A filing code used by the writer or the addressee.

Attention Line: Directs the letter to a particular person or a specific department, even though the letter is addressed to an organization as a whole.

Paragraph Indentions: Usually five spaces.

Postscript: Presents a final idea or an afterthought.

Full-Blocked Style, Open Punctuation

Satellite Traders Inc.
1500 Balboa Street San Francisco, California 94118 (415) 555-6000

April 23, 1979 ↓**2**
CONFIDENTIAL ↓**3**

Mr. Philip Wurlitzer Jr.
Executive Vice President
Satellite Traders Inc.
Apartado Aero 11255
Bogota, D.E.
COLOMBIA ↓**2**

Dear Phil ↓**2**

Subject: Your Request for Early Retirement ↓**2**

I presented your request to the board of directors
last Friday. They were entirely sympathetic to your
reasons for wanting to take early retirement, but
they expressed concern over the timing. Al Barnes,
in particular, raised the following points in a
memo he sent me today: ↓**2**

Ask Phil to identify people in the Bogota
office he considers prospective candidates
for his position. Please ask him to spell
out their present qualifications and estimate the time it would take to groom any
one of these people for his job. ↓**2**

If you and I can identify at least one qualified
candidate acceptable to Al and the other members
of the board, I know they will move quickly to
honor your request. ↓**4**

Best regards ↓**4**

Tom

Thomas P. Gagliardi
President ↓**2**

TPG/np
cc Mr. A. J. Barnes

Heading

Opening

Body

Closing

Confidential Notation: Indicates that the letter should be read only by the person addressed.

Foreign Address: The name of the country is typed in all-capital letters on a line by itself.

Subject Line: Indicates what the letter is about.

Displayed Extract: Copy set off from the rest of the letter for emphasis; indented five spaces from left and right margins.

235

Simplified Style, Open Punctuation

Heading

**Business
Training
Consultants**

5600 Sherwood Avenue
Minneapolis, Minnesota 55424
(612) 555-9300

March 6, 1979 ↓5

Opening

Mrs. Rita Selden
680 Forrest Road, N.E.
Atlanta, GA 30312 ↓3

THE SIMPLIFIED LETTER →3

You will be interested to know, Mrs. Selden, that
a number of years ago the Administrative Management
Society developed a new letter format called the
simplified style. This is a sample. ↓2

1. It makes use of the full-blocked form and open
   punctuation. ↓2

2. It omits the salutation and the complimentary
   closing.

Body

3. It makes use of a subject line, typed in all-
   capital letters and preceded and followed by
   two blank lines. The word Subject is omitted.

4. It identifies the signer by an all-capital line
   that is preceded by four blank lines and followed
   by one—if further notations are used.

5. It tries to achieve a brisk but friendly tone and
   uses the addressee's name at least in the first
   sentence.

Perhaps, Mrs. Selden, for the sake of efficiency,
you ought to give this style a trial. ↓5

(Mrs.) Helen F. Holub

HELEN F. HOLUB - DIRECTOR, SECRETARIAL TRAINING ↓2

jb

Closing

Subject Line: Replaces the salutation; typed in all-capital letters on the third line below inside address.

Complimentary Closing: Omitted.

Writer's Identification: Typed all on one line in all capitals.

236

Stationery Sizes

1303 The following table lists the sizes of stationery most commonly found in current use, as well as the related metric sizes of stationery likely to be introduced in the next few years.

Customary Sizes	Metric Sizes
Standard: $8\frac{1}{2}''$ x $11''$	A4: 210 x 297 mm (approx. $8\frac{1}{4}''$ x $11\frac{3}{4}''$)
Baronial: $5\frac{1}{2}''$ x $8\frac{1}{2}''$	A5: 148 x 210 mm (approx. $5\frac{7}{8}''$ x $8\frac{1}{4}''$)
Monarch: $7\frac{1}{4}''$ x $10\frac{1}{2}''$	(No metric equivalent)
Official: $8''$ x $10\frac{1}{2}''$	(No metric equivalent)

Letter Placement

1304 Top Margin

a. Printed Letterheads. The date line is the first element to be typed. Follow this guideline: Position the date on the third line below the printed letterhead or in a predetermined position (see table below), whichever is lower.

Stationery	Date
Standard ($8\frac{1}{2}''$ x $11''$) and A4 (210 x 297 mm):	Line 15
Monarch ($7\frac{1}{4}''$ x $10\frac{1}{2}''$) and Official ($8''$ x $10\frac{1}{2}''$):	Line 14
Baronial ($5\frac{1}{2}''$ x $8\frac{1}{2}''$) and A5 (148 x 210 mm):	Line 12

b. Unprinted Stationery. The top margin on the first page of a letter depends on whether you type a letterhead address or a return address. (See ¶¶1312–1313 for positioning instructions.) The top margin on each continuation page of a letter is six lines (1 inch or 25 mm).

1305 Side Margins

a. The side margins will depend on the kind of stationery you are using and the size of type your typewriter has—pica or elite.

NOTE: To identify pica or elite type, type a series of periods and compare them with the ones below.

PICA: . . . .   10 strokes to 1 inch (about 25 mm)

ELITE: . . . .   12 strokes to 1 inch (about 25 mm)

b. The following table shows standard margin settings to be used when your stationery is centered at 50 on the carriage scale.

Stationery	Line Length	Margin Settings*
Standard, A4, Monarch, and Official	Pica: 50 spaces Elite: 60 spaces	25–80 20–85
Baronial and A5	Pica: 40 spaces Elite: 50 spaces	30–75 25–80

*An additional five spaces has been added to the right margin setting in order to forestall the frequent use of the margin release key.

■ See ¶1307g *and* ¶1308e *for nonstandard margin settings.*

(Continued on page 238.)

c. To make sure your stationery is centered at 50, follow these tips:

- Position the carriage or carrier so that the printing-point indicator is at 50 on the carriage scale.
- Crease a sheet of paper in half lengthwise; then unfold the sheet and insert it into the typewriter.
- Using the paper release, loosen the paper and slide it right or left until the crease is at the center of the printing-point indicator. Then reset the paper release to its original position.
- Set the paper guide at the left edge of the paper.
- Make a note of the point at which the paper guide appears on the paper-guide scale. Then, when using this size of stationery in the future, simply set the paper guide at the established point and the paper will be automatically centered at 50.

1306 Bottom Margin

a. Leave a bottom margin of at least six lines (1 inch or 25 mm).

b. If the letter is continuing onto a second page, the bottom margin on the first page can be increased up to twelve lines (2 inches or 50 mm).

▪ *See ¶¶1382–1387 on carrying a letter over from one page to the next.*

1307 Lengthening a Short Letter

To spread a short letter (under 75 words) over one page, use any combination of the following techniques:

a. Lower the date by as many as five lines.

b. Allow five or six blank lines between the date and the inside address.

c. Use 1½ blank lines before and after the salutation, between the paragraphs, between the message and the complimentary closing, and between the complimentary closing and the company name.

d. Allow four to six blank lines for the signature.

e. Place the signer's name and title on separate lines.

f. Lower the reference initials one or two lines.

g. On standard, A4, monarch, and official stationery, use a shorter line length. For pica type, set margins at 30–75; for elite, at 25–80.

h. Type the inside address and the message double-spaced, but indent the first line of each paragraph.

1308 Shortening a Long Letter

To *condense* a long letter (over 225 words), use any combination of the following techniques:

a. Raise the date.

b. Allow only two or three blank lines between the date and the inside address.

c. Allow only two blank lines for the signature.

d. Raise the reference initials one or two lines.

e. On standard, official, and A4 stationery, use a longer line length. For pica type, set margins at 20–85; for elite, at 15–90.

Punctuation Patterns

1309 The message in a business letter is always punctuated with normal punctuation (see Sections 1 and 2). The other parts may be punctuated according to one of the following patterns:

a. Standard (Mixed) Pattern. A colon is used after the salutation and a comma after the complimentary closing. (This is the style most commonly used.)

b. Open Pattern. No punctuation is used at the end of any line outside the body of the letter unless that line ends with an abbreviation.

c. Close (Full) Pattern. Each line outside the body of the letter ends with a comma or a period, as shown below. (This style is now rarely used.)

■ *See page 240 for an illustration of all three patterns.*

Spacing

1310 Ordinarily, type all letters single-spaced. (For the use of double spacing in very short letters, see ¶1307h.)

¶¶1311–1317 deal with the heading of a letter. The heading must always include two elements: a letterhead or a return address (¶¶1311–1313) and a date line (¶1314). It may also include a personal or confidential notation (¶1315) and reference notations (¶¶1316–1317). The model letters on pages 233–236 show the relative position of these elements in the heading.

Letterhead or Return Address

1311 Ordinarily, business letters are written on stationery with a *printed letterhead* containing at least these elements: company name, street address, and city, state, and ZIP Code. Some printed letterheads also show area code and telephone number.

1312 If you are using plain paper and are writing on behalf of an organization, create a *typewritten letterhead* as shown below. Center the following information in four double-spaced lines, beginning on the sixth line from the top of the page: (1) the company name; (2) the street address; (3) the city, state, and ZIP Code; (4) the telephone area code and number. (The date then follows on line 15.)

TURPIN AND KELLY INC.   line 6

2550 Mulberry Street   line 8

New York, New York 10012   line 10

(212) 555-3600   line 12

September 28, 1979   line 15

1313 If you are using plain paper and are writing as an individual from your home, type a *return address.* Give the following information on three or

Standard Punctuation

May 3, 1980

Mr. Bernard Kraus Jr.
Purchasing Agent
The Bergen Press Inc.
313 North Street
San Jose, CA 95113

Dear Mr. Kraus:

Sincerely,

HUDSON COMPANY

Lee Brower

Lee Brower
Sales Manager

mr
Enclosure
cc Ms. Loo

Open Punctuation

May 3, 1980

Mr. Bernard Kraus Jr.
Purchasing Agent
The Bergen Press Inc.
313 North Street
San Jose, CA 95113

Dear Mr. Kraus

Sincerely

HUDSON COMPANY

Lee Brower

Lee Brower
Sales Manager

mr
Enclosure
cc Ms. Loo

Close Punctuation

May 3, 1980.

Mr. Bernard Kraus Jr.,
Purchasing Agent,
The Bergen Press Inc.,
313 North Street,
San Jose, CA 95113.

Dear Mr. Kraus:

Sincerely,

HUDSON COMPANY,

Lee Brower

Lee Brower,
Sales Manager.

mr.
Enclosure.
cc Ms. Loo.

more single-spaced lines aligned at the left: (1) the street address; (2) the city, state, and ZIP Code; (3) the date (see ¶1314).

```
238 West 22 Street, Apt. 2B   OR   Apartment 2B
New York, New York 10011             238 West 22 Street
January 24, 1979                     New York, New York 10011
                                     January 24, 1979
```

a. For the *blocked* and the *semiblocked* styles, start each line of the return address at the center of the page (preferred style), or position the return address so that the longest line ends at the right margin.

b. For the *full-blocked* and the *simplified* styles, start each line at the left margin.

c. Position the return address as a block so that the date line falls as follows:

Stationery	Date
Standard (8½″ x 11″) and A4 (210 x 297 mm):	Line 15
Monarch (7¼″ x 10½″) and Official (8″ x 10½″):	Line 14
Baronial (5½″ x 8½″) and A5 (148 x 210 mm):	Line 12

Date Line

1314 a. The date line consists of the *name of the month* (written in full—never abbreviated or represented by figures), the *day* (written in figures and followed by a comma), and the *complete year*.

December 28, 1979 (NOT Dec. 28, 1979 OR December 28th, 1979)

NOTE: Do not use the styles *12/28/79* or *'79* in the date line of a business letter.

b. Some writers prefer to present the date line in this order: day, month, year. This is the style typically used in military correspondence and letters from abroad.

28 December 1979

c. When using letterhead stationery (printed or typewritten), position the date line on the third line below the letterhead or in a predetermined position (see table below), whichever is lower.

Stationery	Date
Standard (8½″ x 11″) and A4 (210 x 297 mm):	Line 15
Monarch (7¼″ x 10½″) and Official (8″ x 10½″):	Line 14
Baronial (5½″ x 8½″) and A5 (148 x 210 mm):	Line 12

NOTE: For the *blocked* and the *semiblocked* styles, you may position the date line as follows: (1) start it at the center of the page (preferred style); (2) position it so that it ends at the right margin; or (3) type it in some other position that is attractive in relation to the letterhead design (so long as it still stands out). For the *full-blocked* and the *simplified* styles, always start the date at the left margin.

d. When using a return address, position the date as shown in ¶1313.

Personal or Confidential Notation

1315 If a letter is of a personal or confidential nature, type the appropriate notation on the second line below the date, at the *left* margin. The notation may be typed in all-capital letters or typed with capital and small letters and underscored.

PERSONAL OR <u>Personal</u>   CONFIDENTIAL OR <u>Confidential</u>

Reference Notations

1316 a. Printed letterheads for large organizations sometimes contain a line reading *When replying, refer to:* in the upper right corner. When using this kind of letterhead, type the appropriate reference number or filing code two spaces after the colon. Align the number or code at the bottom with the printed words.

b. If the guide words *When replying, refer to:* are not printed on the stationery but are desired, type them on the second line below the date (or on the second line below any notation that follows the date). Start typing at the same point as the date.

When replying, refer to: ALG–341

1317 a. When you are replying to a letter that contains a reference number or when you want to emphasize the fact that your letter concerns an insurance policy, an order, or a similar document, type a reference notation on the second line below the date (or on the second line below any notation that follows the date). Start typing at the same point as the date.

In reply to: G241 782 935   Refer to: Policy 234844

b. When there are two reference notations to be given, type your own reference notation first (as indicated in ¶1316). Then type the addressee's reference notation on the second line below.

When replying, refer to: F–17865

Your reference: GAR–X–7

NOTE: Some writers prefer to give the addressee's reference notation in a subject line. (See ¶1353.)

¶¶1318–1351 deal with the opening of a letter. The opening typically includes two elements: the inside address (¶¶1318–1344) and the saluta-tion (¶¶1346–1351). It may also include an attention line (¶1345).

Inside Address

1318 a. For letters going to an individual's home, the inside address should include the following information: (1) the name of the person to whom you are writing, (2) the street address, and (3) the city, state, and ZIP Code. If the person lives in an apartment building, the apartment number should be given after the street address or on the line above.

```
Dr. Margaret P. Vanden Heuvel        Mr. Albert W. Clemons Jr.
615 University Boulevard, N.E.        Meads Creek Road, R.D. 2
Albuquerque, New Mexico 87106        Painted Post, NY 14870

Miss Susan H. Ellington              Mrs. Lorraine Martineau
Apartment 10G                        181 Park Avenue, Apt. 4D
3864 South Kettering Boulevard       West Springfield, MA 01089
Dayton, Ohio 45439
```

NOTE: Sometimes the address for a person living in a small town consists only of (1) the name and (2) the city, state, and ZIP Code. In this case, type the address on two lines. (Do not separate the city from the state to make three lines.)

```
Mrs. Marie S. Allen
Thompson, North Dakota 58278
```

b. For letters going to a business or an organization, the inside address should include the following information: (1) the name of the business or organization, (2) a street address or a post office box number, and (3) the city, state, and ZIP Code. Whenever possible, address the letter to a specific person in the organization and include that person's job title and department (if known). If you do not have the name of a specific person, use a title instead (for example, *Director of Marketing* or *Advertising Manager*).

```
Mr. Arthur L. Quintero               Director of Research
National Sales Manager               Stanton Chemical Company
Paragon Industries                   Post Office Box 21431
211 North Ervay Street               Chattanooga, TN 37421
Dallas, Texas 75201
```

NOTE: When a room number or a suite number is included in the inside address, the following arrangements are acceptable:

```
Ms. Alice G. Alvarez                 James W. Chiverton, M.D.
Woodruff Construction Company        Suite 1200
416 12th Street, Room 12             1111 West Mockingbird Lane
Columbus, Georgia 31901              Dallas, Texas 75247

Mr. Raymond Kermian                  Miss Pauline Leggett
Contemporary Tours Inc.              503 Hanna Building
Room 304, Tower Building             1422 Euclid Avenue
2506 Willowbrook Parkway             Cleveland, OH 44115
Indianapolis, IN 46205
```

c. The inside address should begin on the fifth line below the date. If a notation falls between the date and the inside address (see ¶¶1315–1317), start the inside address on the *third* line below the notation.

d. Single-space the inside address, and align each line at the left. (If the message in a very short letter is to be double-spaced, treat the inside address the same way.)

1319 If a letter is addressed to two or more people at different addresses, the individual address blocks may be typed one under the other (with one blank line between) or attractively positioned side by side. If the inside address blocks take up too much space at the opening of the letter, they may be typed at the end of the letter, two lines below the final notation at the left or, if there are no notations, five lines below the signature block.

1320 If a letter is addressed to two or more people at the same address, list each name on a separate line. Do not show a position title for each person unless it is short and can go on the same line as the name. Moreover, omit the names of departments unless the persons are in the same department. In effect, type only those parts of the address that are common to the people named at the start. (On the respective envelopes for each individual, give the full address for that individual and omit all reference to others named in the inside address.)

```
Dr. Paul J. Rogers
Mr. James A. Dawes
Research Department
Sloan and Hewitt Advertising
700 North Harding Avenue
Chicago, Illinois 60624
```

¶¶1321–1344 *provide additional details concerning the parts of inside addresses. See also Section 16 for special forms of address used for government officials, military personnel, religious dignitaries, and education officials.*

Name of Person and Title

1321 When writing the name of a person in an inside address or elsewhere in the letter, be sure to follow that person's preferences in the spelling, capitalization, and spacing of the name. (See ¶311.) In order to verify the correctness of a name, you may need to consult original correspondence from that person, a mailing list, a card file, or a directory.

NOTE: Do not abbreviate or use initials unless the person to whom you are writing uses an abbreviation or initials; for example, do not write *Wm. B. Sachs* or *W. B. Sachs* if the person to whom you are writing used *William B. Sachs.*

1322 In general, use a title before the name of a person in an inside address. (See ¶517 for appropriate abbreviations of such titles.)

a. If the person has no special title (such as *Dr., Professor,* or *The Honorable*), use the courtesy title *Mr., Miss, Mrs.,* or *Ms.*

b. In selecting *Miss, Mrs.,* or *Ms.,* always respect the individual woman's preference. If her preference is unknown, use the title *Ms.* or omit the courtesy title altogether. (Follow the same practice in the salutation. See ¶1349.)

c. If you do not know whether the person addressed is a man or a woman, do not use any courtesy title. (Follow the same practice in the salutation. See ¶1349.)

NOTE: People who use initials in place of their first and middle names or who have ambiguous names (like *Marion, Leslie, Hilary,* and *Lee*) should always use a courtesy title when they sign their letters so that others may be spared the confusion over which title to use. (See also ¶¶1365–1366.)

1323 a. A letter to a husband and wife is customarily addressed in this form:

Mr. and Mrs. Harold D. Bennisch (**NOT:** Mr. & Mrs.)

b. If the husband has a special title such as *Dr.* or *Professor*, the couple is addressed as follows:

Dr. and Mrs. Thomas P. Geiger

c. If both husband and wife or the wife alone has a special title, list the names on separate lines.

Dean Walter O. Goetz   Dr. Eleanor V. McCormack
Professor Helen F. Goetz   Mr. Joseph L. McCormack

When these special titles are irrelevant to the occasion, use *Mr. and Mrs.*

Mr. and Mrs. Joseph L. McCormack

1324 a. When *Jr., Sr.,* or a roman numeral such as *III* is typed after a name, omit the comma before *Jr., Sr.,* or the roman numeral unless you know that the person addressed prefers the use of a comma. (See also ¶156.)
b. Do not use a title before a name if the term *Esq.* follows the name. (See also ¶518*b*.)

Rita A. Henry, Esq. (**NOT:** Ms. Rita A. Henry, Esq.)

NOTE: A comma separates the last name from the term *Esq.*

c. As a rule, do not use an academic degree with a person's name in an inside address. However, doctors of medicine and divinity often prefer the use of the degree after their names (rather than the title *Dr.* before).

NOTE: If an academic degree does follow the person's name, separate it from the last name with a comma. Also omit the titles *Dr., Miss, Mr., Mrs.,* and *Ms.* before the name. Another title (for example, *Professor, The Reverend, Captain, Dean*) may be used before the name as long as it does not convey the same meaning as the degree that follows. (See ¶519*b*.)

Reva C. Calhoun, M.D.   The Reverend Ernest G. Wyzanski, D.D.

d. Abbreviations of religious orders, such as *S.J.* and *S.N.D.,* are typed after names and preceded by a comma. An appropriate title should precede the name, even though the abbreviation follows the name; for example, *The Reverend John DeMaio, O.P.*

1325 A title of position, such as *Vice President* or *Sales Manager,* should be included in an inside address whenever possible. Ordinarily, type it on the line following the name; if the title runs on to a second line, indent the turnover two spaces. Capitalize every word in the title except prepositions (like *of*) and conjunctions (like *and*) under four letters.

Mrs. Martha Hansen   Mr. Ralph Nielsen
Executive Vice President   Vice President and
                            General Manager

NOTE: If the title is very short, it may be typed on the same line as the person's name in order to balance the length of the lines in the address; in this case the title should be preceded by a comma. As an alternative, a very short title may be typed on the same line as the name of the person's organization (or the name of the department or division within the organization); in this case the title should be followed by a comma.

```
Mr. J. C. Lee, President        Dr. Antoinette H. Marcantonio
Merchants National Bank         President, Haines & Company
```

In Care of . . .

1326 Sometimes a letter cannot be sent to the addressee's home or place of business; it must be directed instead to a third person who will see that the letter reaches the addressee. In such cases, use an "in care of" notation as shown below.

```
Professor Eleanor Marschak     OR  Professor Eleanor Marschak
In care of Henry Wardwell, Esq.    c/o Henry Wardwell, Esq.
```

Name of Organization

1327 Ordinarily, type the organization's name on a line by itself. If the name of a division or a department is needed in the address, it should precede the organization name on a line by itself.

```
Ms. Laura G. Kidd
Assistant Vice President
Department of Consumer Affairs
Holstein, Brooks & Co.
```

NOTE: A very short title may be typed on the same line as the name of the organization. (See ¶1325, note.)

1328 When writing the name of an organization in an inside address, always follow the organization's style for spelling, punctuation, capitalization, spacing, and abbreviations. The letterhead on incoming correspondence is the best source for this information. Note the variations in style in these names:

Time Inc.	Goldman, Sachs & Co.
Newsweek, Inc.	Bass & Company
AMF Incorporated	Halpert, Oberst and Company
Parker Pen Co.	Halsey, Stuart & Co. Inc.
Bee Chemical Company	Shearson Hayden Stone Inc.
Johns-Manville Corp.	Paine, Webber, Jackson & Curtis
Technicon Corporation	Hornblower & Weeks-Hemphill, Noyes
Emersons, Ltd.	Legg Mason/Wood Walker
Fiberglas Canada Ltd.	Post-Keyes-Gardner Inc.
BP Canada Limited	Gulf + Western Industries

1329 If you do not have some way of determining the official form of a company name, follow these rules:

a. Spell out the word *and.* Do not use an ampersand (&).

```
Haber, Curtis, and Hall Inc.        Acme Lead and Tin Company
```

b. Write *Inc.* for *Incorporated* and *Ltd.* for *Limited.* Do not use a comma before the abbreviation.

c. As a rule, spell out *Company* or *Corporation;* if the name is extremely long, however, use the abbreviation *Co.* or *Corp.*

d. Do not use the word *the* at the beginning of a name unless you are reasonably sure it is part of the official name; for example, *The Rand Corporation, The New York Times.*

- *See ¶640 for the use or omission of apostrophes in company names.*

Building Name

1330 If the name of a building is included in the inside address, type it on a line by itself immediately above the street address. A room number or a suite number should accompany the building name.

> Room 118, Acuff Building   1262-1264 Penobscot Building
> 904 Bob Wallace Avenue, S.W.   Griswold Avenue and Fort Street
> Huntsville, Alabama 35801   Detroit, Michigan 48226

- *See ¶1318b, note, for additional examples.*

Street Address

1331 Always type the street address on a line by itself, immediately preceding the city, state, and ZIP Code. (See ¶1318 for examples.)

1332 Use figures for house and building numbers. Do not include the abbreviation *No.* or the symbol **#** before such numbers. EXCEPTION: For clarity, use the word *One* instead of the figure *1* in a house or building number; for example, *One Park Avenue.*

1333 Numbers used as street names are written as follows:

a. Spell out the numbers 1 through 10; for example, *177 Second Avenue.*

b. Use figures for numbers over 10; for example, *27 East 22 Street* or *27 East 22d Street.* The ordinal sign *st, d,* or *th* may be omitted so long as a word such as *East* or *West* separates the street number from the building number. If no such word intervenes, use the ordinal sign for clarity; for example, *144 65th Street.*

1334 Do not abbreviate *North, South, East, West, Northeast, Southwest,* or a similar word when it appears before the street name; for example, *330 West 42 Street.*

1335 Type an abbreviation representing a section of a city after the street name and use a comma before it; for example, *2012 Massachusetts Avenue, N.W.*

1336 Use the word *and,* not an ampersand (&), in a street address; for example, *Tenth and Market Streets.*

1337 Avoid abbreviating such words as *Street* and *Avenue* in inside addresses. (It may be necessary, for reasons of space, to abbreviate in envelope addresses. See ¶1390.)

- *For apartment and room numbers with street addresses, see ¶¶1318, 1330.*

Box Number

1338 a. A post office box number may be used in place of the street address.

```
Post Office Box 1518  OR  P.O. Box 1518  OR  Box 1518
```

b. A station name, if needed, should follow the post office box number (and a comma) on the same line. If very long, the station name may go on the line below.

```
Box 76984, Sanford Station        P.O. Box 11215
Los Angeles, CA 90005             Linda Vista Station
                                  San Diego, CA 92111
```

c. Some companies show both a street address and a post office box number in their mailing address. Whatever information appears in the line preceding the city, state, and ZIP Code determines where the mail is delivered.

```
Henson Supply Corp.
315 South Water Street
Post Office Box 181 ← The mail will be delivered to this address.
Hartford, CT 06101
```

City, State, and ZIP Code

1339 The city, state, and ZIP Code must always be typed on one line, immediately following the street address. Type the name of the city, followed by a comma and one space; the state, followed by one space but no comma; and the ZIP Code.

```
Denver, Colorado 80217  OR  Denver, CO 80217
```

1340 When writing the name of a city in an inside address:

a. Never use an abbreviation (for example, *Chic.* for *Chicago*).

b. Never abbreviate the words *Fort, Mount, Point,* or *Port.* Write the name of the city in full. For example: *Fort Dodge, Mount Vernon, Point Pleasant, Port Huron.*

c. Abbreviate the word *Saint* in the names of American cities; for example, *St. Louis, St. Paul, St. Petersburg.*

NOTE: It may be necessary, for reasons of space, to abbreviate city names in envelope addresses. (See ¶1390.)

1341 In an address, spell out the name of the state or use a two-letter abbreviation of the state name (as shown in the chart on page 249).

NOTE: The two-letter abbreviations (for example, *AL* for *Alabama*) were created by the U.S. Postal Service and should be used only with ZIP Codes in addresses. The more traditional abbreviations of state names (for example, *Ala.* for *Alabama*) should be used in other situations where abbreviations are appropriate. (See ¶¶526–527.)

a. When using the two-letter state abbreviations, type them in capital letters, with no periods after or space between the letters.

b. When giving an address in a sentence, insert a comma after the street address and after the city. Leave one space between the state and the ZIP

Alabama	AL		Missouri	MO
Alaska	AK		Montana	MT
Arizona	AZ		Nebraska	NE
Arkansas	AR		Nevada	NV
California	CA		New Hampshire	NH
Canal Zone	CZ		New Jersey	NJ
Colorado	CO		New Mexico	NM
Connecticut	CT		New York	NY
Delaware	DE		North Carolina	NC
District			North Dakota	ND
of Columbia	DC		Ohio	OH
Florida	FL		Oklahoma	OK
Georgia	GA		Oregon	OR
Guam	GU		Pennsylvania	PA
Hawaii	HI		Puerto Rico	PR
Idaho	ID		Rhode Island	RI
Illinois	IL		South Carolina	SC
Indiana	IN		South Dakota	SD
Iowa	IA		Tennessee	TN
Kansas	KS		Texas	TX
Kentucky	KY		Utah	UT
Louisiana	LA		Vermont	VT
Maine	ME		Virgin Islands	VI
Maryland	MD		Virginia	VA
Massachusetts	MA		Washington	WA
Michigan	MI		West Virginia	WV
Minnesota	MN		Wisconsin	WI
Mississippi	MS		Wyoming	WY

Code. Insert a comma after the ZIP Code unless a stronger mark of punctuation is required at that point.

My address next month will be 501 South 71 Court, Miami, Florida 33144, but mail sent to my office will reach me just as easily.

1342 Omit the name of county or area (such as *Long Island*) in an address.

1343 In a Canadian address, spell out or abbreviate the name of the province or territory.

Alberta	AB	Nova Scotia	NS
British Columbia	BC	Ontario	ON
Labrador	LB	Prince Edward Island	PE
Manitoba	MB	Quebec	PQ
New Brunswick	NB	Saskatchewan	SK
Newfoundland	NF	Yukon Territory	YT
Northwest Territories	NT		

NOTE: The following formats are used for mail going to Canada. (The format on the left is preferred for envelopes.)

```
876 Wolfe Avenue              OR: 876 Wolfe Avenue
Moose Jaw, Saskatchewan           Moose Jaw, Saskatchewan
CANADA                            CANADA  S6H 1J6
S6H 1J6
```

1344 In other foreign addresses, type the name of the country on a separate line in all-capital letters. Do not abbreviate the name of the country. **EXCEPTION:** *U.S.S.R.* (*Union of Soviet Socialist Republics*).

```
Graf–Adolf Strasse 100      Rua Tabapua, 1105
Dusseldorf 4000             Caixa Postal 20689
GERMANY                     Itaim–Bibi, Sao Paulo, S.P.
                            BRAZIL
```

Attention Line

1345 When a letter is addressed directly to a company, an attention line is often used to route the letter to a particular person (by name or title) or to a particular department. For example:

```
Shelton & Warren Industries   Carrolton Labs
6710 Squibb Road              1970 Briarwood Court
Mission, Kansas 66202         Atlanta, GA 30329

Attention Mr. John Ellery     ATTENTION SALES MANAGER
```

NOTE: This form of address emphasizes the fact that the letter deals with a business matter (rather than a personal matter) and may be handled by another person or department than the one named in the attention line. (However, it is simpler to type the name of the person or department above the company name and omit the attention line. Any letter that does not carry a personal or confidential notation will ordinarily be presumed to deal with company business and will be handled by others in the absence of the named addressee.)

a. The attention line should be typed on the second line below the inside address, starting at the left margin.

b. The attention line may be typed in all-capital letters, or it may be typed in capital and small letters, with the complete line underscored. The word *Attention* should not be abbreviated; it need not be followed by the word *of* or a colon. (See the examples above.)

- *See ¶1351 for the salutation to use with an attention line.*

Salutation

1346 Type the salutation, beginning at the left margin, on the second line below the attention line (if used) or on the second line below the inside address. Follow the salutation with a colon unless you are using open punctuation (see ¶1309) or you are typing a social-business letter (see ¶1398b). Omit the salutation if you are using the simplified letter style, and replace it with a subject line (see ¶1352).

NOTE: Be sure that the spelling of the name in the salutation is the same as the spelling in the inside address.

1347 Abbreviate only the titles *Mr., Ms., Mrs., Messrs.,* and *Dr.* All other titles, such as *Professor* and *Father*, should be written out. (See ¶1601 for titles used by officials, dignitaries, and military personnel.)

1348 Capitalize the first word as well as any nouns and titles in the salutation; for example, *Dear Sir, My dear Mrs. Brand, Right Reverend and dear Sir.*

1349 The following are commonly used forms of salutation:

TO ONE PERSON (NAME, GENDER, AND COURTESY TITLE PREFERENCE KNOWN)

Dear Mr. Smith: Dear Ms. Simpson:
Dear Mrs. Gray: Dear Miss Wells:

TO ONE PERSON (NAME KNOWN, GENDER UNKNOWN)

Dear Marion Parker: Dear R. V. Moore:

TO ONE PERSON (NAME UNKNOWN, GENDER KNOWN)

Dear Madam: OR Madam: (more formal)
Dear Sir: OR Sir: (more formal)

TO ONE PERSON (NAME AND GENDER UNKNOWN)

Dear Sir or Madam: OR Sir or Madam: (more formal)
OR Dear Madam or Sir: OR Madam or Sir: (more formal)

TO ONE WOMAN (COURTESY TITLE PREFERENCE UNKNOWN)

Dear Ms. Malloy: OR Dear Ruth Malloy: (see ¶1322*b*)

TO TWO OR MORE MEN

Dear Mr. Gelb and Mr. Harris: OR Gentlemen:
OR Dear Messrs. Gelb and Harris:

TO TWO OR MORE WOMEN

Dear Mrs. Allen, Ms. Ott, and Miss Day:
Dear Mrs. Jordan and Mrs. Kent:*
OR Dear Mesdames Jordan and Kent:
Dear Ms. Scott and Ms. Gomez:*
OR Dear Mses. (OR Mss.) Scott and Gomez:
Dear Miss Winger and Miss Rossi:*
OR Dear Misses Winger and Rossi:

TO A WOMAN AND A MAN

Dear Ms. Kent and Mr. Winston:
Dear Mr. Fong and Miss Landis:
Dear Mr. and Mrs. Green:

TO SEVERAL PERSONS

Dear Mr. Anderson, Mrs. Brodsky, Ms. Carmino, Mr. Dellums, and Miss Eustace:
Dear Friends (Colleagues, Members, *or some other suitable collective term*):

TO AN ORGANIZATION COMPOSED ENTIRELY OF MEN

Gentlemen:

TO AN ORGANIZATION COMPOSED ENTIRELY OF WOMEN

Mesdames: OR Ladies:

TO AN ORGANIZATION COMPOSED OF MEN AND WOMEN

See ¶1350

NOTE: For greater formality, some writers use *My dear* in place of *Dear*.

* See ¶618, note.

1350 For an organization composed of both men and women, the salutation most commonly used is *Gentlemen:*

```
United Services Corporation
100 Kendall Parkway
Somerset, New Jersey 08873

Gentlemen:
```

However, this generic use of *Gentlemen* is coming under increasing attack, on the grounds that the masculine bias of the term makes it unsuitable for reference to a group that includes women as well as men.

a. One alternative is to use *Ladies and Gentlemen* or *Gentlemen and Ladies* in place of *Gentlemen* alone.

b. Another alternative is to address the letter, not to the organization as a whole, but to the head of the organization—by name and title if known, otherwise by title alone. Then the salutation would appear as shown below.

```
Mr. James V. Quillan           President
President                      (OR Chief Executive Officer)
United Services Corporation    United Services Corporation
100 Kendall Parkway            100 Kendall Parkway
Somerset, New Jersey 08873     Somerset, New Jersey 08873

Dear Mr. Quillan:              Dear Sir or Madam:
```

c. Use the simplified letter style and omit the salutation.

1351 When an attention line is used (see ¶1345), the letter is considered to be addressed to the organization rather than to the person named in the attention line. Therefore, use one of the organizational salutations shown in ¶¶1349 and 1350 above. (Whenever possible, omit the attention line and address the letter directly to an individual in the organization—either by name or by title.)

¶¶1352–1357 deal with the body of a letter. The body contains the text of the letter—in other words, the message (see ¶¶1354–1357). The body may also begin with a subject line (see ¶¶1352–1353), which briefly identifies the main idea in the message.

Subject Line

1352 In the simplified letter style, a subject line is used in place of the salutation. Start the subject line on the third line below the inside address. Begin at the left margin and type the subject line in all-capital letters. Do not use a term like *Subject:* to introduce the subject line. (See page 236.)

1353 a. In other letter styles, the subject line (if used) appears on the second line below the salutation. (See page 235.) Ordinarily, the subject line starts at the left margin, but for special emphasis it may be centered. In a semiblocked letter it may be indented the same as the paragraphs. Type it either in all-capital letters or in capital and small letters that are underscored.

MORAN LEASE   <u>Introductory Offer to New Subscribers and</u>
                     <u>Renewal Offer to Present Subscribers</u>

b. The term *Subject:* or (in legal correspondence) *In re:* or *Re:* often precedes the actual subject but is not necessary.

SUBJECT: MORAN LEASE   <u>Subject: Introductory Offer to New</u>
                            <u>Subscribers and Renewal Offer to</u>
In re: Moran Lease   <u>Present Subscribers</u>

c. When replying to a letter that carries a "refer to" notation, put the desired reference number or filing code in a subject line or below the date line (see ¶¶1316–1317).

<u>Refer to: Policy 668485</u>

Message

1354 Begin the message on the second line below the subject line, if used, or on the second line below the salutation. **EXCEPTION:** In the simplified letter style, the message starts on the third line. (See page 236.)

1355 In the semiblocked letter style (see page 234) indent the first line of each paragraph. (Although five spaces is the usual indention, some writers prefer to indent up to ten spaces.) In the other letter styles, start each paragraph at the left margin.

NOTE: Always indent the first line of each paragraph if the letter is double-spaced.

1356 Use single spacing and leave one blank line between paragraphs. (Very short letters may be double-spaced or lengthened by means of other techniques. See ¶1307.)

1357 a. When a quotation or similar material is to be displayed in the body of the letter, indent the material five spaces from each side margin and leave one blank line above and below the material. (See page 235 for an illustration).

■ *See ¶265 for different ways of handling a long quotation.*

b. When a table occurs in the body of a letter, it should be centered between the left and right margins and indented a minimum of five spaces from each side margin. (If the table is very wide, reduce the normal six spaces between columns to as few as two spaces to preserve the indentation of the table on each side.) Leave one to three blank lines above and below the table to set it off from the rest of the text. (See Section 15 for details on setting up a table.)

c. When a list of numbered items appears in the body of a letter, type the list single-spaced with one blank line above and below the list as a whole. Either begin each item at the left margin, or for special display indent the list as a whole five spaces from each side margin. If any item in the list requires more than one line, leave a blank line between all items in the list. Begin each item with a number followed by a period and two spaces. If any item continues onto a second line, indent it so that it begins under the first word in the line above. (See page 236 for an example.)

NOTE: If the list consists entirely of one-line items typed single-spaced, then for appearance' sake the number that begins each item may be followed by a period and only *one* space.

¶¶1358–1381 deal with the closing of a letter. The closing typically includes a complimentary-closing phrase (¶¶1358–1360), the writer's name and title (¶¶1362–1369), and reference initials (¶¶1370–1372). It may also include a company signature line (¶1361), an enclosure notation (¶¶1373–1374), a mailing notation (¶1375), a carbon copy notation (¶¶1376–1380), and a postscript (¶1381).

Complimentary Closing

1358 Type the complimentary closing on the second line below the last line of the body of the letter. In a blocked or semiblocked letter, start the closing at center. In a full-blocked letter, start the closing at the left margin. In a simplified letter, omit the closing.

1359 Capitalize only the first word of a complimentary closing. Place a comma at the end of the line (except when open punctuation is used).

1360 The following complimentary closings are commonly used:

a. Personal in tone: *Sincerely, Cordially, Sincerely yours, Cordially yours.*

b. More formal in tone: *Yours truly, Yours very truly, Very truly yours, Very sincerely yours, Very cordially yours, Respectfully yours.*

c. If an informal closing phrase, such as *Best wishes, Warmest regards,* or *See you in July,* is used instead of a regular complimentary closing, type the phrase in the complimentary-closing position and follow it by a comma. (Stronger punctuation, such as a question mark, an exclamation point, or a dash, may be used if appropriate.) If both a complimentary closing and an informal closing phrase are used, type the complimentary closing in its regular position, and type the informal phrase at the end of the last paragraph or as a separate paragraph with the appropriate terminal punctuation.

NOTE: Once a pattern of personal or informal closings is begun, it should not be discontinued without good reason. Otherwise, if a later letter returns to a more formal closing, the person addressed may wonder what has happened to the established relationship.

Company Signature

1361 A company signature may be used to emphasize the fact that a letter represents the views of the company as a whole (and not merely the individual who has written it). If included, the company signature should be typed in all capitals on the second line below the complimentary closing. Begin the company signature at the same point as the complimentary closing.

```
Very truly yours,

HASKINS & COHEN INC.
```

Writer's Name and Title

1362 Ordinarily, type the writer's name on the fourth line below the company signature, if used, or on the fourth line below the complimentary closing.

NOTE: If the letter is running short, you can leave up to six blank lines for the signature. If the letter is running long, you can reduce the signature space to two blank lines. (See also ¶¶1307–1308.)

a. Start typing at the same point as the company signature or the complimentary closing. **EXCEPTION:** In the simplified letter style, type the writer's name and title on the *fifth* line below the body, in all-capital letters starting at the left margin. (See ¶1363.)

b. Although some writers prefer to give only their title and department name in the signature block, a typewritten signature should also be included so that the carbons will clearly show who sent the letter. If the writer prefers to omit the name from the signature block, then it should be spelled out in the reference initials. (See ¶1370*b*.)

1363 Arrange the writer's name, title, and department to achieve good visual balance. (See the five variations below.) If a title takes two or more lines, block all the lines at the left.

```
Janice Mahoney, Manager        Ernest L. Welhoelter
Data Processing Division       Head, Sales Department

Charles Saunders               Franklin Browning
Assistant Manager              Vice President and
Credit Department              General Manager

CHARLES SAUNDERS — ASSISTANT MANAGER, CREDIT DEPARTMENT (sim-
plified style)
```

1364 A person who has a special title should observe the following style in the signature block.

a. A person who wants to be addressed as *Dr.* should use an appropriate academic degree after his or her name (not *Dr.* before it).

Jane Bishop, M.D.   Morris Finley, D.D.   Nancy Buckwalter, Ph.D.

b. A person who wishes to be addressed by a title of academic or military rank (*Dean, Professor, Major*) should type this title *after* the name or on the next line, not before it.

Edwin C. Powell   Joseph F. Corey
Dean of Students   Major, USAF

(**NOT** Dean Edwin C. Powell)   (**NOT** Major Joseph F. Corey)

(Continued on page 256.)

c. In cases where a title of address cannot be placed after a surname or suggested by the initials of an academic degree, then it may precede the name.

> Rev. Joseph W. Dowd   Mother Ellen Marie O'Brien

1365 Ordinarily, a man should not include *Mr.* in his signature. However, if he has a name that could also be a woman's name (*Kay, Adrian, Beverly, Lynn*) or if he uses initials (*J. G. Eberle*), he should use *Mr.* in either his handwritten or typewritten signature when writing to people who do not know him. If given in the handwritten signature, *Mr.* should be enclosed in parentheses. If given in the typewritten signature, *Mr.* should appear without parentheses.

> Sincerely,   Sincerely,
>
> *(Mr.) Lynn Treadway*   *Lynn Treadway*
>
> Lynn Treadway   Mr. Lynn Treadway

1366 A woman should include a courtesy title (*Ms., Miss,* or *Mrs.*) in her signature unless she is called by a special title (see ¶1364). If she gives her name without any title at all, the reader of the letter is put in the awkward position of having to decide which title to use in a letter of reply.

NOTE: In the following examples, note that the courtesy title is enclosed in parentheses when it appears in the handwritten signature but not when it appears in the typewritten signature.

a. A woman who does not want to indicate whether she is married or single should use *Ms.* in either her handwritten or her typewritten signature.

> Sincerely yours,   Sincerely yours,
>
> *(Ms.) Constance G. Booth*   *Constance G. Booth*
>
> Constance G. Booth   Ms. Constance G. Booth

b. A single woman who wants to indicate that she is a single woman should include *Miss* in either her handwritten or her typewritten signature.

> Cordially,   Cordially,
>
> *(Miss) Margaret L. Galloway*   *Margaret L. Galloway*
>
> Margaret L. Galloway   Miss Margaret L. Galloway

c. A married woman who wants to retain her unmarried name for career purposes may use either *Ms.* or *Miss,* as illustrated in *a* and *b* above.

d. A married woman or a widow who prefers to be addressed as *Mrs.* has many variations to choose from. The following examples show the possible styles for a woman whose maiden name was Nancy O. Ross and whose husband's name is John A. Wells.

Cordially yours,

(Mrs.) Nancy O. Wells

Nancy O. Wells

Cordially yours,

Nancy O. Wells

Mrs. Nancy O. Wells

Cordially yours,

(Mrs.) Nancy R. Wells

Nancy R. Wells

Cordially yours,

Nancy R. Wells

Mrs. Nancy R. Wells

Cordially yours,

(Mrs) Nancy Ross Wells

Nancy Ross Wells

Cordially yours,

Nancy Ross Wells

Mrs. Nancy Ross Wells

Cordially yours,

(Mrs.) Nancy O. Ross-Wells

Nancy O. Ross—Wells

Cordially yours,

Nancy O. Ross-Wells

Mrs. Nancy O. Ross—Wells

NOTE: Giving the husband's name in the typewritten signature (as in the example below) is a style often used for social purposes. It should not be used in business.

Cordially yours,

Nancy O. Wells

Mrs. John A. Wells

e. A divorced woman who has resumed her maiden name may use *Ms.* or *Miss* in any of the styles shown in *a* and *b* on page 256. If she retains her ex-husband's surname, she may use *Ms.* or *Mrs.* in any of the styles shown in *a* and *d* above. (**EXCEPTION:** The style which uses the husband's name in the typewritten signature would be inappropriate for a divorcée.)

1367 A secretary who signs a letter at the boss's request may use either of the following styles, depending on the boss's preference and the circumstances involved.

Sincerely yours,

Dorothy Kozinski

Ms. Dorothy Kozinski
Secretary to Mr. Benedict

Sincerely yours,

Robert H. Benedict
  DK

Robert H. Benedict
Production Manager

1368 If the person who signs for another is not actually the secretary, either of the following forms may be used:

Sincerely yours,

(Miss) Alice R. Brentano

For Robert H. Benedict
Production Manager

Sincerely yours,

Robert H. Benedict
  ARB

Robert H. Benedict
Production Manager

1369 When two people have to sign a letter, arrange the two signature blocks side by side or one beneath the other.

a. If they are placed side by side, start the first signature block at the left margin and the second block at center. If this arrangement is used, the complimentary closing should also begin at the left margin. (This arrangement is appropriate for all letter styles.)

b. If the signature blocks are positioned one beneath the other, start typing the second block on the fourth line below the end of the first block. Align the signature blocks at the left. (In the blocked and semiblocked styles, start typing at center; in the full-blocked and simplified styles, start typing at the left margin.)

Reference Initials

1370 a. The initials of the typist (or those of the writer and the typist) are typed at the left margin, on the second line below the writer's name and title. When used, the initials of the writer precede those of the typist. The following are commonly used styles:

```
L:C            lba            t
APB/mm         MFF:CCR        STG:ebh
```

RBMJr:jb (use *Jr.* or *Sr.* only if both persons work for the same firm)

■ *See ¶516c for initials with names like* McFarland *and* O'Leary.

b. If the writer's name is typed in the signature block, the writer's initials can be omitted. If the writer's name is not typed in the signature line, type the writer's initials and surname before the initials of the typist; for example, *BSDixon/rp.*

1371 When the letter is written by someone other than the person who signs it, this fact may be indicated by showing the writer's and the typist's initials (not the signer's and the typist's).

Sincerely yours,

Herbert Heymann

Herbert Heymann
President

PBR/jb

1372 Do not include reference initials in a personal letter.

Enclosure Notation

1373 If one or more items are to be included in the envelope with the letter, indicate that fact by typing the word *Enclosure* (or an appropriate substitute) at the left margin, on the line below the reference initials.

NOTE: Be sure that the number of enclosures shown in the enclosure notation agrees with the number cited in the body of the letter and also with the number of items actually enclosed.

a. The styles illustrated below are commonly used.

```
Enclosure              2 Enclosures           Enclosures:
Enc.                   2 Enc. (see ¶504)      1. Check for $500
1 Enc.                 Enc. 2                  2. Invoice A37512
1 Enclosure            Enclosures 2
Check enclosed         Enclosures (2)
```

b. Some writers use the term *Attachment* or *Att.*

1374 If material is to be sent separately instead of being enclosed with the letter, indicate this fact by typing *Separate cover* or *Under separate cover* on the line below the enclosure notation (if any) or on the line directly below the reference initials. The following styles may be used:

```
Separate cover 1       Under separate cover:
                       1. Annual report
                       2. Product catalog
                       3. Price list
```

Mailing Notation

1375 If a letter is to be delivered in a special way, type an appropriate notation on the line below the enclosure notation (if used) or on the line below the reference initials.

```
crj                    HWM/ldb                tpg
Enc. 2                 Special delivery       Enclosures 4
Certified              cc Mr. Fry             By messenger
```

Carbon Copy Notation

1376 A carbon copy (cc) notation lets the addressee know that one or more other persons will be sent a copy of the letter. The initials *cc* are used, even if the copy has been made by some other process (like photocopying).

a. Type *cc* at the left margin, on the line below the mailing notation, the enclosure notation, or the reference initials, whichever comes last. If several persons are to receive carbon copies, the names should be listed according to the rank of the persons or, if there is no difference in rank, alphabetically.

```
AMH:HT                 WFG/mf                 LBW:ncy
Enclosure              Enc. 4                 cc Contract File
Registered             cc Mrs. A. C. Case        Houston Office
cc Ms. Hoey               Mr. R. G. Flynn        Sales Department
```

b. The initials *cc* may be typed in small letters or capitals, with or without a colon following. When there are two or more names to be listed, the initials *cc* may be typed only with the first name or repeated with each name.

```
cc Miss Fox  OR  cc:  Miss Fox        cc Ms. Rae  OR  cc Ms. Rae
CC Miss Fox  OR  CC:  Miss Fox           Mr. Poe      cc Mr. Poe
```

1377 If the addressee is not intended to know that one or more other persons are being sent a copy of the letter, use a *bcc* (blind carbon copy) notation. First remove the original letter and any copies on which the *bcc* notation is not to appear. Then on each of the remaining copies, type a *bcc* notation in the upper left corner (starting at the left margin on the seventh line from the top). The file copy should show all the *bcc* notations, even though the individual copies do not.

NOTE: Any of the forms used for a regular *cc* notation may be used for a *bcc* notation.

```
bcc Mrs. Hope        bcc:  Ms. Ruiz
```

1378 Courtesy titles may be omitted from *cc* notations if a first name is used with the surname; for example, *cc George Glover.*

1379 When a letter carries both an enclosure notation and a *cc* notation, it is assumed that the enclosures accompany only the original letter. If a copy of the enclosures is also to accompany a copy of the letter, this fact may be indicated as follows:

```
cc:      Mr. D. R. Wellak    (received only the letter)
cc/enc:  Mr. J. Baldwin      (received the letter and the enclosures)
         Mrs. G. Conger      (received the letter and the enclosures)
```

1380 A copy is not usually signed unless the letter is addressed to several people and the copy is intended for one of the people named in the salutation. However, a check mark is usually made on each copy next to the name of the person or department for whom that copy is intended.

```
cc Ms. A. M. Starr ✔      cc Ms. A. M. Starr
   Mr. H. W. Fried           Mr. H. W. Fried ✔
```

NOTE: When an unsigned carbon copy is likely to strike the recipient as cold and impersonal, it is appropriate for the writer to add a brief handwritten note at the bottom of the copy and sign or initial it.

Postscript

1381 A postscript can be effectively used to express an idea that has been deliberately withheld from the body of a letter; stating this idea at the very end gives it strong emphasis. A postscript may also be used to express an afterthought; however, if the afterthought contains something central to the meaning of the letter, this usage of the postscript may suggest that the letter was badly organized. When a postscript is used:

a. Start the postscript on the second line below the *cc* notation (or whatever was typed last). If the paragraphs are indented, indent the first line of the postscript; otherwise, begin it at the left margin (see page 234).

b. Type *PS:* or *PS.* before the first word of the postscript, or omit the abbreviation altogether. (If *PS* is used, leave two spaces between the colon or period and the first word.)

c. Use *PPS:* or *PPS.* (or no abbreviation at all) at the beginning of an additional postscript, and treat the additional postscript as a separate paragraph.

Continuation Pages

1382 Use plain paper of the same quality as the letterhead (but never a letterhead) for the second and each succeeding page of a long letter.

1383 Use the same left and right margins that you used on the first page.

1384 On the seventh line from the top of the page, type a continuation-page heading consisting of the following: the name of the addressee, the page number, and the date. Either of the following styles is acceptable:

```
        Mrs. Laura R. Austin          2          September 30, 1980
    OR: Mrs. Laura R. Austin
        Page 2
        September 30, 1980
```

1385 Space down three lines from the last line of the continuation-page heading, and resume typing the message.

a. Do not divide a paragraph that contains three or fewer lines.

b. For a paragraph of four or more lines, always leave at least two lines of the paragraph at the bottom of the previous page, and carry over at least two lines to the continuation page.

c. Never use a continuation page to type only the closing section of a business letter. (The complimentary closing should always be preceded by at least two lines of the message.)

1386 Leave a margin of 6 to 12 lines at the foot of each page of a letter (except the last page). Try to keep the bottom margin as uniform as possible on all pages except the last.

1387 Do not divide the last word on a page.

Addressing Envelopes

1388 The following table indicates which envelopes may be used, depending on the size of the stationery and the way in which it is folded.

Stationery	Fold*	Envelope
Standard (8½″ x 11″) and Official (8″ x 10½″)	In thirds	No. 10 (9½″ x 4⅛″)
	In half, then in thirds	No. 6¾ (6½″ x 3⅝″)
Monarch (7¼″ x 10½″)	In thirds	No. 7 (7½″ x 3⅞″)
Baronial (5½″ x 8½″)	In thirds	No. 6¾ (6½″ x 3⅝″)
	In half	No. 5⅜ (5¹⁵⁄₁₆″ x 4⅝″)
A4 (210 x 297 mm) (approx. 8¼″ x 11¾″)	In thirds	DL (220 x 110 mm)
	In half, then in thirds	C7/6 (162 x 81 mm)
	In half, then in half	C6 (162 x 114 mm)
A5 (148 x 210 mm) (approx. 5⅞″ x 8¼″)	In thirds	C7/6 (162 x 81 mm)
	In half	C6 (162 x 114 mm)

* See ¶¶1392–1396 for detailed instructions on folding.

1389 When typing an address on an envelope:

a. Always use single spacing and blocked style. Capitalize the first letter of every word except prepositions (like *of* and *for*) and conjunctions (like *and*) under four letters.

NOTE: See the examples on page 263. For specific details on the handling of elements within the address block, see ¶¶1318–1344.

b. Always type the city, state, and ZIP Code on the last line. Leave one space between the state and the ZIP Code. The state name may be spelled out or given as a two-letter abbreviation. (See ¶1341.)

c. The next-to-last line in the address block should contain a street address or post office box number. (See ¶1338c.)

```
Mr. Christopher Schreiber        Elvera Agresta, M.D.
Director of Manufacturing        218 Oregon Pioneer's Building
Colby Electronics Inc.           320 Southwest Stark Street
P.O. Box 6524                    Portland, Oregon 97204
Raleigh, NC 27628
```

d. When using a large envelope (No. 10 or DL), start the address on line 14 about 4 inches (100 millimeters) from the left edge. When using a small envelope (No. 7, 6¾, 5⅜, C6, or C7/6) or a postcard, start the address on line 12 about 2 inches (50 millimeters) from the left edge.

e. When the envelope contains a printed return address for a company or an organization, type the name of the writer on the line above the return address, aligned at the left. (See the second illustration on page 263.)

f. If a printed return address does not appear on the envelope, type a return address in the upper left corner, beginning on line 3 about five spaces in from the left edge. The return address should contain the following information, arranged on separate lines: (1) the name of the writer; (2) the name of the company (if appropriate); (3) a street address or post office box number; and (4) the city, state, and ZIP Code. (See the first illustration on page 263.)

g. A notation such as *Personal, Confidential, Please Forward,* or *Hold for Arrival* goes below the return address. It should begin on line 9 or on the third line below the return address, whichever is lower. Begin each main word with a capital letter, and use underscoring. The notation should align at the left with the return address.

h. If an attention line was used within the letter itself, it should appear on the envelope as well. Treat the attention line exactly like a personal or confidential notation, as described in g above. (See the note to ¶1345 on avoiding the use of attention lines.)

i. If a special mailing procedure is used, type the appropriate notation (such as *SPECIAL DELIVERY* or *REGISTERED*) in all-capital letters in the upper right corner of the envelope, beginning on line 9. The notation should end about five spaces from the right margin.

j. Make sure that the spelling of the name and address on the envelope agrees with the spelling shown in the inside address (and with the spelling shown on the file card or the incoming document).

▪ See ¶1320 *concerning letters being sent to two or more people at the same address.*

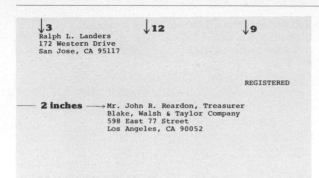

↓3
Ralph L. Landers
172 Western Drive
San Jose, CA 95117

↓12

↓9

No. 6¾ envelope with
mailing notation.

REGISTERED

—— **2 inches** ——→ Mr. John R. Reardon, Treasurer
Blake, Walsh & Taylor Company
598 East 77 Street
Los Angeles, CA 90052

No. 10 envelope with confidential notation.

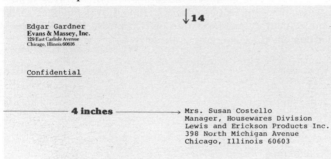

↓14

Edgar Gardner
Evans & Massey, Inc.
129 East Carlisle Avenue
Chicago, Illinois 60616

Confidential

——————— **4 inches** ——————→ Mrs. Susan Costello
Manager, Housewares Division
Lewis and Erickson Products Inc.
398 North Michigan Avenue
Chicago, Illinois 60603

1390 When preparing an address that will be imprinted by means of an address plate or computerized equipment:

a. Keep in mind the maximum number of strokes you can get in any one line (typically, 26 to 28 strokes).

b. Use the two-letter state abbreviations (see ¶1341). If necessary to save space, use other abbreviations freely and omit punctuation.

NOTE: To help keep the line length down, the U.S. Postal Service has provided three special sets of abbreviations: one for state names; another for long names of cities, towns, and places; a third for names of streets and roads and general terms like *University* or *Institute*. By means of these abbreviations (see Postal Service Publication 59), it is possible to limit the last line of any domestic address to 22 strokes; for example, *Bloomfield Hills, Michigan 48013* can be written *BLOOMFLD HLS MI 48013*.

c. Type the lines in all-capital letters, single-spaced and aligned at the left. Omit punctuation.

MR HENRY T POLING JR
CAMPING ENTERPRISES INC
412 HIGH ST ROOM 980
WASHINGTON DC 20017

(*Continued on page 264.*)

d. When imprinting the address on an envelope, leave a bottom margin of at least ⅝ inch (15 millimeters) and a left margin of at least 1 inch (25 millimeters). Nothing should be written or printed below the address block or to the right of it.

e. The last line in the address block should contain the city, state, and ZIP Code. Leave one space between the state and the ZIP Code.

f. The next-to-last line in the address block should contain a street address or post office box number. (See ¶1338c.)

g. If a room number or a suite number is part of the address, it should appear immediately after the street address on the same line. (See examples in c and h.) When it is impossible to fit this information on the same line as the street address, it may go on the line above but never on the line below.

h. If special information is to be imprinted along with the address, it may appear on any line above the last two lines in the address block. A serial number, if used, typically appears a line or two above the addressee's name. An attention line, if used, comes directly below the name of the organization.

```
H 048469 1078 AT5

BROCK & WILSON CORP
ATTN MRS M R TURKEVICH
79 WALL ST SUITE 1212
NEW YORK NY 10005
```

1391 To chain-feed envelopes:

a. After addressing the first envelope, roll it back until only about ⅝ inch (15 millimeters) shows in front of the cylinder.

b. Insert the next envelope from the front, placing its bottom edge between the first envelope and the cylinder.

c. Turn the cylinder toward you to remove the first envelope and to bring the second one into typing position.

Chain-feeding envelopes. Each new envelope is inserted from the front, with its bottom edge placed between the previous envelope and the cylinder.

Courtesy International Business Machines Corporation

Folding and Inserting Letters

The following rules give several methods for folding and inserting letters into envelopes. See the table in ¶1388 to determine which method is appropriate for the stationery and envelope you are using.

1392 To fold a letter in thirds:

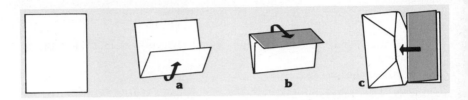

a. Bring the bottom third of the letter up and make a crease.

b. Fold the top of the letter down to within $\frac{3}{8}$ inch (10 millimeters) of the crease you made in step *a*. Then make the second crease.

c. The creased edge you made in step *b* should go into the envelope first.

NOTE: Use this method for $8\frac{1}{2}''$ x 11'' and 8'' x $10\frac{1}{2}''$ stationery with a No. 10 envelope; $7\frac{1}{4}''$ x $10\frac{1}{2}''$ stationery with a No. 7 envelope; $5\frac{1}{2}''$ x $8\frac{1}{2}''$ stationery with a No. $6\frac{3}{4}$ envelope; A4 stationery with a DL envelope; A5 stationery with a C7/6 envelope. See also ¶1388.

1393 To fold a letter in half and then in thirds:

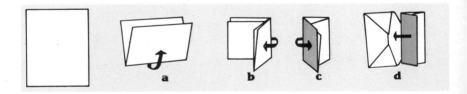

a. Bring the bottom edge to within $\frac{3}{8}$ inch (10 millimeters) of the top edge and make a crease.

b. Fold from the right edge, making the fold a little less than one-third the width of the sheet before you crease it.

c. Fold from the left edge, bringing it to within $\frac{3}{8}$ inch (10 millimeters) of the crease you made in step *b* before you crease the sheet again.

d. Insert the left creased edge into the envelope first. This will leave the crease you made in step *b* near the flap of the envelope.

NOTE: Use this method for $8\frac{1}{2}''$ x 11'' and 8'' x $10\frac{1}{2}''$ stationery with a No. $6\frac{3}{4}$ envelope; also for A4 stationery with a C7/6 envelope. See also ¶1388.

1394 To fold a letter in half:

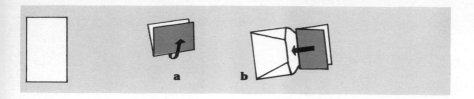

a. Bring the bottom edge to within $\frac{3}{8}$ inch (10 millimeters) of the top edge and make a crease.

b. Insert the creased edge into the envelope first.

NOTE: Use this method for $5\frac{1}{2}''$ x $8\frac{1}{2}''$ stationery with a No. $5\frac{3}{8}$ envelope; also for A5 stationery with a C6 envelope. See also ¶1388.

1395 To fold a letter in half and then in half again:

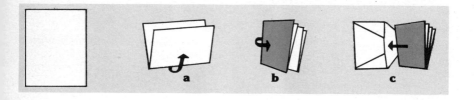

a. Bring the bottom edge to within $\frac{3}{8}$ inch (10 millimeters) of the top edge and make a crease.

b. Bring the left edge to within $\frac{3}{8}$ inch (10 millimeters) of the right edge and make a crease.

c. Insert the left creased edge into the envelope first.

NOTE: Use this method for A4 stationery with a C6 envelope. See also ¶1388.

1396 To fold a letter for insertion into a window envelope:

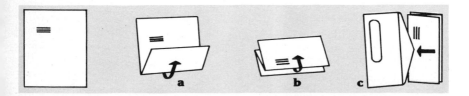

a. Bring the bottom third of the letter up and make a crease.

b. Fold the top of the letter *back* to the crease you made in step *a.* (The inside address should now be facing you.)

c. Insert the letter with the inside address toward the *front* of the envelope. The inside address should now be fully readable through the window of the envelope. There should be at least $\frac{1}{4}$ inch (7 millimeters) between the address and the left, right, and bottom edges of the window, no matter how much the letter slides around in the envelope.

Memos

1397 When typing a memo on a printed form:

a. Set the left margin stop at a point two or three spaces after the longest guide word in the left half of the printed heading (for example, after DEPARTMENT).

NOTE: Some writers prefer to set the left margin stop at the point where the printed guide words begin. In this case it is necessary to set a tab stop two or three spaces after the longest guide word in the left half of the printed heading.

Interoffice Memorandum

Tab ↓

To	Secretarial Staff	From	Robert C. Nelson
Department	All Divisions	Department	Office Training
Subject	Form for Memorandums	Date	January 17, 1979 ↓3

Here are our updated guidelines for setting up a typewritten interoffice memo. ↓2

Set the left margin stop either at a point two or three spaces after the longest printed guide word in the left half of the heading or at the point where the printed guide words begin. The right margin should be the same width as the left margin. ↓2

Set a tab stop two or three spaces after the longest printed guide word in the right half of the heading. ↓2

Type the writer's name, initials, or title on the second line below the body of the memo. Begin typing at the tab stop that has been set for the right half of the heading. ↓2

Handle reference initials, enclosure notations, and carbon copy notations just as you would in a letter. ↓2

RCN ↓2

CS
cc Mr. Kendrick

b. Set a tab stop two or three spaces after the longest guide word in the right half of the printed heading (for example, after DEPARTMENT).

c. Set the right margin stop to leave a right margin equal to the left margin.

d. Type in the appropriate information after each printed guide word. Make sure that the typewritten fill-ins align at the left. They should also align at the bottom with the printed guide words.

(*Continued on page 268.*)

e. Begin typing the message on the third or fourth line below the last fill-in line in the heading.

NOTE: An interoffice memorandum ordinarily does not require a salutation, especially if the memo is an impersonal announcement being sent to a number of people or the staff at large. However, when a memo is directed to one person, many writers use a salutation—such as *Dear Andy:* or *Andy:* alone—to keep the memo from seeming cold or impersonal. (If a salutation is used, begin typing the body of the memo on the second line below.)

f. Use single spacing, and either block or indent the paragraphs.

g. Type the writer's name or initials on the second line below the last line of the message, beginning at the tab stop you set in step *b.* Add the writer's title (if desired) on the following line.

NOTE: Although memos do not require a signature, many writers prefer to sign or initial their memos. In such cases, type the writer's name or initials on the *fourth* line below the end of the message.

h. Type the reference initials (see ¶1370) on the second line below the writer's name, initials, or title; block them at the left margin.

i. Type an enclosure (or attachment) notation, if needed, on the line below the reference initials, beginning at the left margin.

j. Type a carbon copy notation, if needed, on the line below the enclosure notation, if used, or on the line below the reference initials.

k. If the memo continues beyond the first page, type a continuation heading on a fresh sheet of paper. (Use the same style as shown in ¶1384 for a letter.) Then continue typing the message on the third line below the last line of the continuation-page heading. (See ¶1385 for additional details on continuing the message from one page to another.)

Social-Business Correspondence

1398 Social-business correspondence usually differs from that of regular business correspondence in such details as these:

a. The inside address may be typed at the bottom of the letter, beginning at the left margin on the fifth line below the typewritten signature.

b. The salutation is usually very informal (for example, *Dear Betty* or *Dear Jack*) and is followed by a comma or with no punctuation at all.

c. Numbers are often written according to the "word style" (see ¶¶404–406).

d. The complimentary closing is usually very informal (for example, *Best regards* or *Yours*).

e. The writer's typewritten signature may be omitted if the writer knows the addressee well.

f. The reference initials are omitted, and even though an enclosure may be mentioned in the letter, the enclosure notation is usually omitted.

g. Carbon copy and other notations rarely appear in social-business letters.

NOTE: This social-business style is also used when writing formal letters to high officials and dignitaries.

Postcards

1399 When typing on a standard-size postcard ($5\frac{1}{2}$ by $3\frac{1}{4}$ inches):

a. Set margins five or six spaces in from the left and right sides.

b. Type the date on the third line from the top of the card, beginning at the center.

c. Omit the name and address of the person to whom the card is being sent.

d. Type the salutation (for example, *Dear Mrs. Davis:*) on the second line below the date, beginning at the left margin. If it is necessary to conserve space, omit the salutation.

e. Begin typing the message, using single spacing, on the second line below the salutation.

f. Type the closing lines starting on the second line below the last line of the message; begin each line at the center. In order to leave a bottom margin of three lines, omit the following elements if necessary: the complimentary closing (for example, *Sincerely*), the handwritten signature, and reference initials.

NOTE: When typing on a stiff or smooth card, advance the card at the end of each typed line by using the cylinder knob instead of the carriage-return lever or key. It may also be necessary to hold the card with one hand as you turn the cylinder knob in order to ensure even line spacing.

■ *See ¶¶1388–1390 for the procedure in addressing envelopes; ¶1391 for the procedure in chain-feeding envelopes. The same procedures are used for postcards.*

14 REPORTS AND MANUSCRIPTS

TYPING THE MANUSCRIPT

FOOTNOTES

Elements of Footnotes (¶¶1419–1424)
> *Footnote Number* (¶1419)
> *Names of Authors* (¶1420)
> *Publisher's Name* (¶1421)
> *Place of Publication* (¶1422)
> *Date of Publication* (¶1423)
> *Page Numbers* (¶1424)

Subsequent Footnote References (¶¶1425–1426)

BIBLIOGRAPHIES (¶¶1427–1433)

Typing the Manuscript

Paper, Copies, and Ribbon

1401 Use a good-quality bond paper. Type on only one side of the paper.

1402 Always make one file copy (photocopy or carbon copy) in case the original is lost or mislaid. Prepare additional copies as necessary for distribution.

- *See ¶¶1225–1229 for details on preparing carbon copies.*

1403 Use a black record ribbon so that the copy will be clear and permanent.

Margins

1404 Top Margin of First Page

a. Leave twelve blank lines at the top.

b. If the report or manuscript consists of only one major section or chapter, center the title of the work on line 13 and type it in all-capital letters. Center the author's name on the second line below the title. (If a subtitle is to be included in the heading, center it on the second line below the main title; then type the author's name on the second line below the subtitle.) On the third line below the author's name, begin typing the first line of the body of the manuscript.

c. If the report or manuscript consists of several major sections or chapters, then the title of the overall work as well as the author's name should go on a special title page (see ¶1412a). Start each major section or chapter on a fresh page. Type the title of that section or chapter on line 13, centered and in all-capital letters. Then begin typing the first line of text on the third line below.

1405 Top Margin of Other Pages

a. Leave six blank lines at the top.

b. Type the page number on the seventh line from the top, and begin typing the text on the third line below the page number. (See ¶1410.)

1406 Side Margins

Insert the paper so that it is centered horizontally at 50. (See ¶1305c for this procedure.) Then set left and right margins as shown in the table below. NOTE: If the report is to remain unbound or will simply be stapled in the upper left corner, use the margin settings in the Unbound column. If the report is to be inserted in a binder or is to be stapled at several points along the left edge of the paper, use the margin settings in the Bound column.

	Spaces	Margins (Unbound)*	Margins (Bound)*
Pica:	60	20–85	23–88
Elite:	70	15–90	18–93

* An additional five spaces has been added to the right margin setting in order to forestall the frequent use of the margin release key.

1407 Bottom Margin

a. Leave six to nine blank lines at the bottom. When a report or a manuscript runs to several pages, try to maintain a consistent bottom margin.

b. To better control the bottom margin, draw a light pencil mark six lines above the point at which you want the last line to be typed. (Draw the line before inserting the paper into the machine; then erase the pencil mark later on.)

c. Another way to control the bottom margin is to prepare a page line guide as follows: Simply type a column of numbers—from 66 to 1—down the right edge of a fresh sheet of paper. Insert this sheet behind the paper on which you type; position it so that the column of numbers appears beyond the right edge of the top sheet. Then as you type and advance the paper, the column of numbers at the right will tell you how many lines away you are from the bottom edge of the paper.

1408 Backing Sheet

To keep margins uniform on all pages, prepare a *backing sheet* as follows:

a. Take a blank sheet of paper and draw a light pencil mark six lines above the point at which you want the last line to be typed. Then insert the paper in the typewriter and center it horizontally at 50. Set the left and right margins as shown in ¶1406.

b. Space down to the seventh line from the top and type a full row of Xs—60 for pica, 70 for elite. (Do not type in the extra five spaces added to the right margin setting.)

c. Space down to the light pencil mark and type another full row of Xs. (This will represent an early warning signal that the bottom of the page is near.)

d. Space down six lines and type another full row of Xs. (This will represent the last line on the page.)

e. Draw a rectangle with heavy black lines to enclose the top and bottom rows of Xs and mark off the left and right margins. (The vertical line drawn for the right margin will represent the ideal line endings, even though the right margin setting permits an extra five spaces.)

f. Place this sheet between the original copy and the back of the first carbon sheet; the rulings will show through the original copy to serve as a guide.

NOTE: Backing sheets may be purchased ready-made at many stationery stores.

Spacing and Indentions

1409 Observe these rules of spacing and indention:

a. Leave two blank lines between the last line in the title block and the first line of text. (See also ¶1404b, c.)

b. Ordinarily, double-space all text matter. However, single-space the text in business reports when the costs of paper, reproduction, file space, and mailing are important considerations. (When single-spacing the text, leave one blank line between text paragraphs.)

NOTE: Manuscripts or drafts to be submitted for editing or evaluation should be double-spaced.

c. Indent text paragraphs five spaces.

d. Quoted material that will make four or more typewritten lines should be typed as a single-spaced extract. Indent the extract five spaces from each side margin, and leave one blank line above and below the extract. If the quoted matter represents the start of a paragraph in the original, indent the first word an additional five spaces. (See ¶265a.)

e. Items in a list are typed single-spaced with one blank line above and below the list as a whole. Indent the list five spaces from each side margin. If any item in the list requires more than one line, leave a blank line between all items in the list. If the item begins with a number or letter, a period and two spaces should follow. If the item continues onto a second line, indent it so that it begins under the first word in the line above.

```
    9.   Capitalize the first word of each item
         displayed in a list or an outline.

   10.   Capitalize the first word of each line
         in a poem.
```

NOTE: If the list consists entirely of one-line items typed single-spaced, then for appearance' sake the number or letter that begins each item should be followed by a period and only *one* space.

f. Table text is usually single-spaced but may be double-spaced if desired. (Establish one style of spacing for all tables within the same report or manuscript and follow it.) Leave one or more blank lines above and below the table. (See Section 15 for details on setting up tables.)

g. A centered heading displayed on a line by itself should be preceded by two blank lines and followed by one blank line. Type the centered heading in capital and small letters, and underscore it. (See ¶1409h, note.)

h. A side heading displayed on a line by itself should be preceded by two blank lines and followed by one blank line. When a side heading comes directly below a centered heading, leave only one blank line above the side heading. Type the side heading in all-capital letters without under-scoring.

NOTE: Many writers prefer to use a different style of capitalization for centered and side headings. They use all-capital letters (without under-scoring) for *centered* headings and capital and small letters (with under-scoring) for *side* headings. (See ¶108*b* for an example of this style.)

i. A run-in heading (one that begins a paragraph and is immediately followed by text matter on the same line) should be indented five spaces from the left. Like all new paragraphs, a paragraph that begins with a run-in heading should be preceded by one blank line (whether the text is typed single-spaced or double-spaced). The run-in heading should be typed in capital and small letters, underscored, and followed by a period (unless some other mark of punctuation, such as a question mark, is required). The text then begins two spaces after the punctuation. (See also ¶108*a* and the example in ¶108*b*.)

▪ *See page 275 for illustrations of these spacing and indention guidelines. See ¶¶1385a–b and 1387 on the breaking of paragraphs and the division of words between one page and the next. See ¶¶1413–1417 for the positioning of footnotes.*

Page Numbering

1410 Number the pages as follows:

a. When the first page contains the title of the manuscript or the report, it is counted as page 1 but the number is not typed on the page.

b. Type all page numbers (except those on chapter-opening pages) on the seventh line from the top. Place the number at the right margin (ignore the five spaces added on to the right margin setting). The word *Page* may precede the number.

▪ *See ¶1411 for the positioning of page numbers on chapter-opening pages.*

c. After typing the page number, begin the first line of text on the third line below (on line 10).

d. To save space, type the page number on line 4 (instead of line 7) and the first line of text on line 6.

NOTE: An acceptable variation is to type all page numbers at the bottom of the page. In this case, (1) begin the text on the seventh line from the top of the page, (2) type the last line of text on the ninth line from the bottom of the page, and (3) leaving two blank lines, type the page number (without the word *Page*) centered on the sixth line from the bottom.

1411 Start each chapter of a report or manuscript on a fresh page. When the chapter title appears at the top of a page, type the page number at the foot of the page. (See steps 2 and 3 in the note directly above.)

NOTE: As an alternative, type the page number in the upper right corner (as indicated in ¶1410*b*).

HOW TO TYPE A TERM PAPER ↓2

A Special Report ↓2

By Gordon McCrea ↓3

Introduction ↓2

Many people learn to type so that they may use this skill in typing term papers and other reports that are assigned to them in high school and college. The purpose of this report is to review how such papers should be typed. ↓3

SOURCES OF INFORMATION ↓narrower ↓2

The information in this report was gathered from two sources: interviews and readings.

Investigation ↓2

Interviews. The subject was discussed with a number of people, including a free-lance typist, two college students, two high school teachers, and a college instructor.

Readings. Ideas and details were also drawn from two typing textbooks, a magazine article, and a booklet published by the English department of a college. ↓3

ORGANIZATION OF FINDINGS ↓2

The findings deal with four major topics: the use of a clear outline, the arrangement of pages, the treatment of tables, and the treatment of quotations and footnotes. The four topics are discussed in the following sections.

The first page of a properly typed manuscript will look like this. Notice the margins and the spacing above and below the headings.

↓7

5↓3

A quote that would fill three or fewer full lines when it is typed is shown in quotation marks, but a longer quote should be given special display; it is single-spaced and indented five spaces from each side margin, as shown below. ↓2

Footnotes. The credits in a report are numbered in the order in which they occur. Each is typically explained in a footnote at the bottom of the same page.

Each footnote is arranged as a "separate paragraph." It is indented. It is single-spaced. It is numbered."[3] The footnotes must be kept apart from the body of the report: ↓2

Separate a footnote from the text above it by a 2-inch line of underscores--that would be 20 pica spaces long or 24 elite spaces long. Be sure, also, to double-space after typing the line, so that one blank space will be left between the typed line and the first footnote below the line.[4] ↓3

Summary ↓2

The rules for typing a term paper may vary from school to school, but in most respects the rules are standard.

As long as the typist remembers to display headings so that they stress the outline of the report, to arrange pages with proper margins, to set up tables with care, and to give full credit for borrowed thoughts and words, typing the term paper will be easy to manage. ↓1
↓2

[3]Alan C. Lloyd and Russell J. Hosier, Personal Typing, 3d ed., McGraw-Hill Book Company, New York, 1969, p. 115. ↓2

[4]Ibid., p. 116.

The top margin on the other pages of the manuscript is much narrower. Two properly typed quotations and two footnotes are also shown.

Front Matter

1412 When a report or manuscript consists of two or more major sections or chapters, it usually contains one or more pages of front matter, such as a title page, a table of contents, and a preface or foreword.

a. The title page should contain the title in all-capital letters and the subtitle, if any, in capital and small letters on the second line below the title. The author should be identified by name and also, if appropriate, by title or organizational affiliation. The title page may also show the date on which the report or manuscript was submitted and the person or group to which it was submitted. For an academic report, include the name of the course and the instructor.

NOTE: There is no one correct arrangement of these items. The title and the author identification (as well as other information such as the date) may be treated as one block of copy or broken into two or more blocks for display. However arranged, the copy on the title page as a whole should appear centered horizontally and vertically. (See the first illustration on page 277 for an example.)

b. The table of contents should be typed on a fresh page. Type *CONTENTS* (or *TABLE OF CONTENTS*) in all-capital letters and center it on line 13. On the third line below, begin typing the first line of the table. (See the second illustration on page 277.)

NOTE: As an alternative, center the table of contents vertically on the page.

c. The preface should start on a fresh page. Use the same side margins as for the rest of the report or manuscript. (See ¶1406.) Type *PREFACE*, *FOREWORD*, or some other appropriate heading in all-capital letters, centered on line 13. Then begin typing the first line of the text on the third line below. If the preface or foreword continues beyond the first page, use a top margin of six blank lines on all continuation pages.

d. On all pages of front matter except the title page, type a page number centered on the sixth line from the bottom of the page. Leave two blank lines above the page number, more if the text above runs short. Type the page number in small roman numerals (for example, *ii, iii, iv,* and so on). Count the title page as page i, even though no number is typed on that page.

Footnotes

Functions of Footnotes

1413 a. Footnotes serve two functions: (1) they convey subordinate ideas which the writer feels might be distracting if incorporated within the main text; (2) they serve as references, identifying the source of a statement quoted or cited in the text. (The second kind of footnote is often called a *reference footnote*. See also ¶1418.)

b. Footnotes are ordinarily keyed by number to a word, phrase, or sentence in the text.

c. Footnotes have traditionally appeared at the foot of the same page as

↓13

CONTENTS ↓3

ii

MARKET TRENDS IN VOCATIONAL EDUCATION ↓2

An Analysis of Enrollment and Expenditure Projections
From 1975 to 1985

Prepared by

Jonathan H. Stier
Market Planning and Analysis Department
Cummings and Hall Inc.

January 12, 1980

277

the textual matter to which they refer. However, an alternative is to place all these notes in a section at the end of the manuscript or report. (This style is becoming increasingly popular because it is much easier to type than the foot-of-the-page style. See ¶1416.)

Footnote References in the Text

1414 a. To indicate the presence of a comment or reference at the bottom of the page or in a special section at the end, type a superior (raised) figure immediately following the appropriate word, phrase, or sentence in the text. Do not leave any space between the superior figure and the preceding word. If a punctuation mark follows the word, place the superior figure immediately after the punctuation mark. (**EXCEPTION:** The superior figure should precede, not follow, a dash.)

> Her latest article, "Everyone Loses,"[1] was published about three months ago.

NOTE: To type a superior number, turn the cylinder back slightly with one hand and type the number with the other hand.

b. The numbering of footnotes may (1) run consecutively throughout, (2) begin again with each new chapter, or (3) begin again with each new page. The third method should not be used for materials to be set in type, since the pagination will differ.

c. Footnotes are sometimes keyed by symbol rather than by number, particularly in tables where there are only a few footnotes and the tabular matter itself consists of numbers. In such cases footnotes may be identified by the following sequence of symbols: *, **, ***.

Placement of Footnotes

1415 When footnotes appear at the foot of the page:

a. Type a long underscore line (about 20 to 24 strokes) to separate footnotes from the text above. Type the underscore one line below the last line of text, starting at the left margin. (See illustration at the right on page 275.)

b. Start the first footnote on the second line below the underscore line.

c. Type each footnote single-spaced, and leave a blank line between footnotes.

d. Indent the first line of each footnote five spaces. Additional lines within the same footnote should begin at the left margin.

NOTE: When typing a page on which footnotes are to appear, you will need to estimate—ahead of time or as you go along—the number of lines to be reserved at the bottom of the page. Allow three to four lines for each reference footnote; this estimate allows for space above and below each footnote.

1416 When footnotes are placed in a special section at the end of a report or manuscript:

a. Type a centered heading *NOTES* on line 13 of a fresh page.

b. On the third line below, begin typing the first note. Use the same side margins as on other pages.

c. Indent the first line of each note five spaces. Additional lines within the same note should begin at the left margin.

d. Type the identifying number on the line (not as a superior figure). See ¶1419*b*.

e. Type each note single-spaced, and leave one blank line between notes.

f. For the placement of page numbers, follow the directions in ¶1411.

1417 Footnotes to a table should go directly beneath the table. See the illustration on page 291.

Patterns for Reference Footnotes

1418 The following patterns (and examples) provide guidelines for constructing the kinds of reference footnotes that most commonly occur. These patterns can be modified as necessary to fit the varying needs of individual circumstances. For detailed information about specific elements within footnotes, see the following paragraphs:

- *Footnote number: see ¶1419.*
- *Names of authors: see ¶1420.*
- *Underscoring titles of complete works: see ¶289.*
- *Quoting titles of parts of complete works: see ¶242.*
- *Quoting titles of unpublished works: see ¶243.*
- *Capitalization in titles: see ¶¶360–361.*
- *Publisher's name: see ¶1421.*
- *Place of publication: see ¶1422.*
- *Date of publication: see ¶1423.*
- *Page numbers: see ¶1424.*
- *Subsequent references in footnotes: see ¶¶1425–1426.*

a. Book Title: Basic Pattern

[1]Author, <u>book title</u>, publisher, place of publication, year of publication, page number [if reference is being made to a specific page].

[1]John Kenneth Galbraith, <u>The Affluent Society</u>, Houghton Mifflin Company, Boston, 1958, p. 101.

NOTE: If any of these elements have already been identified in the text (for example, the author's name and the book title), they need not be repeated in the footnote. Moreover, if reference is made to the book as a whole rather than to a particular page, omit the page number.

According to Professor J. K. Galbraith, in his widely acclaimed book <u>The Affluent Society</u>, "It falls within the power of the modern large corporation to mitigate or eliminate (with one exception) every important risk to which business enterprises have anciently been subject."[1]

---

[1]Houghton Mifflin Company, Boston, 1958, p. 101.

(*Continued on page 280.*)

b. Book Title: With Subtitle

[1]Author, <u>book title: subtitle</u>, publisher, place, year, page number.

[1]Arthur M. Okun, <u>Equality and Efficiency: The Big Tradeoff</u>, The Brookings Institution, Washington, 1975, pp. 32–64.

NOTE: Do not show the subtitle of a book unless it is significant in identifying the book or in explaining its basic nature. If a subtitle is shown, separate it from the main title with a colon and extend the underscore (without a break) to the end of the subtitle.

c. Book Title: With Edition Number

[1]Author, <u>book title</u>, edition number [if not the first edition], publisher, place, year, page number.

[1]Lois Irene Hutchinson, <u>Standard Handbook for Secretaries</u>, 8th ed., McGraw–Hill Book Company, New York, 1975, p. 440.

NOTE: Use an edition number only when the book is not in the first edition. If included, the edition number follows the main title and any related elements, such as the subtitle or the volume number and title. (For examples see ¶1418d below.) The following abbreviated forms are commonly used: *2d ed., 3d ed., 4th ed.,* or *rev. ed.* (for "revised edition").

d. Book Title: With Volume Number and Volume Title

[1]Author, <u>book title</u>, volume number, <u>volume title</u>, edition number [if not the first edition], publisher, place, year, page number.

[1]E. Lipson, <u>The Economic History of England</u>, Vol. 1, <u>The Middle Ages</u>, 12th ed., Adam & Charles Black, London, 1959, pp. 511–594.

NOTE: As a rule, do not show the volume title in a footnote unless it is significant in identifying the book. When the volume title is included, both the volume number and the volume title follow the book title (and subtitle, if any) but precede the edition number. The volume number is usually preceded by the abbreviation *Vol.* or by the word *Book* or *Part* (depending on the actual designation). The volume number may be arabic or roman, depending on the style used in the actual book.

- See also ¶1418e.

e. Book Title: With Volume Number Alone

[1]Author, <u>book title</u>, edition number [if not the first edition], publisher, place, year, volume number, page number.

[1]Robert E. Spiller et al. (eds.), <u>Literary History of the United States</u>, The Macmillan Company, New York, 1948, Vol. II, pp. 639–651. OR: . . . II, 639–651.

NOTE: When the volume number is shown without the volume title, it follows the date of publication. When the volume number and page number occur one after the other, they may be styled as follows:

Style for Roman Volume Number	Style for Arabic Volume Number
Vol. III, p. 197 OR III, 197	Vol. 5, pp. 681–684 OR 5:681–684

Do not use the latter forms (with figures alone) if there is a chance your reader will not understand them.

f. Book Title: With Chapter Reference

[1]Author, book title, publisher, place, year, chapter number, "chapter title" [if significant], page number.

[1]Will Durant and Ariel Durant, The Age of Napoleon, Simon and Schuster, New York, 1975, Chap. XII, "Napoleon and the Arts," pp. 278–285.

NOTE: When a footnote refers primarily to the title of a book, a chapter number and a chapter title are not usually included. If considered significant, however, these details can be inserted just before the page numbers. The word *chapter* is usually abbreviated as *Chap.*, the chapter number is arabic or roman (depending on the original), and the chapter title is enclosed in quotation marks.

g. Selection in Anthology

[1]Author of selection, "title of selection," **in** editor of anthology **(ed.),** book title, publisher, place, year, page number.

[1]Lisa Getman, "From Conestoga to Career," in W. Todd Furniss and Patricia Albjerg Graham (eds.), Women in Higher Education, American Council on Education, Washington, 1974, pp. 63–66.

h. Selection From Collected Works of One Author

[1]Author, "title of selection," book title, publisher, place, year, page number.

[1]Sylvia Plath, "The Courage of Shutting Up," Winter Trees, Harper & Row, New York, 1972, pp. 8–9.

i. Article in Newspaper

[1]Author [if known], "article title," name of newspaper, date, page number, column number.

[1]Albert Karr and Richard Janssen, "SST's Destiny," The Wall Street Journal, October 16, 1975, p. 1, col. 6.

NOTE: If a particular issue of a newspaper is published in several sections and the page numbering begins anew with each section, include the section number before the page number.

[2]Tom Wicker, "On the Fifth of July," The New York Times, July 7, 1976, Sec. A, p. A27, cols. 1–3.

- See ¶1422 on including the place of publication.

j. Article in Magazine

[1]Author [if known], "article title," name of magazine, date, page number.

[1]"The Office of the Future," Business Week, June 30, 1975, pp. 48–84.

[2]Trudy Slaughter, "Vision Care for the Elderly," Modern Healthcare, November 1975, pp. 47–49.

(Continued on page 282.)

k. Article in Technical or Scholarly Journal

[1]Author, "article title," title of journal [often abbreviated], series number [if given], volume number, issue number [if given], page number, date.

[1]Glen G. Eye, "Many Researchers but Few Synthesizers," The Journal of Educational Research, Vol. 68, No. 8, p. 294, April 1975.

OR: [1]Glen G. Eye, "Many Researchers but Few Synthesizers," JER, 68(8):294, April 1975.

NOTE: Titles of journals are often abbreviated in footnotes whenever these abbreviations are likely to be familiar to the intended readership or are clearly identified in a bibliography at the end. Moreover, volume numbers and page numbers may be expressed in a short form so long as this style will be clearly understood by the reader. For example:

Style for Roman Volume Number

Vol. IX, pp. 217–243 (full form)   OR   IX, 217–243 (short form)

Style for Arabic Volume Number

Vol. 3, pp. 381–392 (full form)   OR   3:381–392 (short form)

If a series number or an issue number is also included, use the following style:

Ser. 8, Vol. 5, pp. 213–219   OR   (8)5:213–219
Vol. 59, No. 5, pp. 765–769   OR   59(5):765–769

l. Bulletin, Pamphlet, or Monograph

[1]Author [if given], "article title" [if appropriate], title of bulletin, series title and series number [if appropriate], sponsoring organization, place, date, page number.

[1]"The Pause That Won't Refresh," Monthly Economic Letter, First National City Bank, New York, September 1975, pp. 5–6.

[1]Environmental Health Planning Guide, U.S. Public Health Service Publication No. 823, Washington, 1967, pp. 21–22. (Here the name of the sponsoring organization is incorporated in the series designation.)

[2]Author [if given], "article title" [if appropriate], title of bulletin, volume number and issue number, page number, sponsoring organization, place, date.

[2]"Economics for Young Americans," Washington Report, Vol. 14, No. 19, p. 3, Chamber of Commerce of the United States, Washington, September 22, 1975.

OR: [2]"Economics for Young Americans," Washington Report, 14(19):3, Chamber of Commerce of the United States, Washington, September 22, 1975. (See note to ¶1418k above.)

NOTE: Because the pertinent data used to identify bulletins, pamphlets, and monographs varies widely, adapt either of the two patterns shown above as necessary to fit each particular situation.

m. Unpublished Dissertation or Thesis

[1]Author, "title of thesis," **doctoral dissertation OR master's thesis** [identifying phrase to be inserted], name of academic institution, place, date, page number.

[1]David Harry Weaver, "An Experimental Study of the Relative Impact of Controllable Factors of Difficulty in Typewriting Practice Material," doctoral dissertation, Syracuse University, Syracuse, N.Y., 1966, p. 121.

Elements of Footnotes

1419 Footnote Number

a. Make sure that the number at the start of a footnote corresponds to the appropriate superior number in the text above.

b. Indent the footnote number five spaces, and (1) type it as a superior figure without any space following it or (2) type it on the line (like an ordinary number) followed by a period and two spaces. The second style is gaining in popularity because it is easier to type.

[1]Caroline Bird, The Case Against College, David McKay Company, Inc., New York, 1975, pp. 83 ff.

OR: 1.   Caroline Bird, The Case Against College, David McKay Company, Inc., New York, 1975, pp. 83 ff.

- *See 1414b on numbering footnotes consecutively; 1414c on the use of symbols in place of numbers.*

1420 Names of Authors

a. Type an author's name (first name first) exactly as it appears on the title page of a book or in the heading of an article. (See ¶1418a, note.)

[1]Arthur M. Schlesinger, Jr., A Thousand Days, Houghton Mifflin Company, Boston, 1965, p. 31.

b. When two authors share a common surname, show the surname with each author's listing.

[2]John W. Wyatt and Madie B. Wyatt, Business Law, 5th ed., McGraw–Hill Book Company, New York, 1975, pp. 98 ff.

c. When there are three or more authors, list only the first author's name followed by *et al.* (meaning "and others"). Do not underscore *et al.*

[3]Horace R. Brock et al., Accounting: Principles and Applications, 3d ed., McGraw–Hill Book Company, New York, 1974, p. 695.

NOTE: If desired, the names of all the authors may be given. This style, if adopted for a given manuscript, should be used consistently throughout.

d. When an organization (rather than an individual) is the author of the material, show the organization's name in the author's position.

(*Continued on page 284.*)

[4]Committee for Economic Development, <u>The Schools and the Challenge of Innovation</u>, McGraw–Hill Book Company, New York, 1969, p. 28.

However, if the organization is both the author and the publisher, show the organization's name only once—as the publisher.

[5]<u>Patterson's American Education, 1979</u>, Educational Directories Inc., Mount Prospect, Ill., 1978, Vol. LXXV.

e. When a work such as an anthology carries an editor's name rather than an author's name, list the editor's name in the author's position, followed by the abbreviation *ed.* in parentheses. (If the names of two or more editors are listed, use the abbreviation *eds.* in parentheses.)

[6]John A. Myers, Jr. (ed.), <u>Predicting Managerial Success</u>, Foundation for Research on Human Behavior, Ann Arbor, Mich., 1968, p. 13.

If a *reference work* carries the name of an editor rather than an author, the editor's name is usually omitted.

[7]<u>Webster's Third New International Dictionary</u>, G. & C. Merriam Company, Springfield, Mass., 1966, pp. 30a–31a.

1421 Publisher's Name

a. List the publisher's name as it appears on the title page (*McGraw-Hill Book Company*) or in a shortened form (*McGraw-Hill*); use one form consistently throughout. If a division of the publishing company is also listed on the title page, it is not necessary to include this information in the footnote. Publishers, however, often do so in references to their own materials.

b. Omit the publisher's name from footnote references to magazines, newspapers, and journals.

1422 Place of Publication

a. As a rule, list only the city of publication (for example, *New York, Cleveland, Washington, Toronto*). If the city is not well known or is likely to be confused with another city of the same name, add the state or the country (for example, *Cambridge, Mass.; Cambridge, England*). If the title page lists several cities in which the publisher has offices, use only the first city named.

b. Omit the place of publication from footnote references to magazines and journals.

c. Incorporate the city name in the name of a newspaper that might otherwise be unrecognized. For example, *The Star-Ledger* (published in Newark, New Jersey) should be referred to in a footnote as *The Newark (N.J.) Star-Ledger*.

1423 Date of Publication

a. For books, show the year of publication. (If this date does not appear on the title page, use the most recent year shown in the copyright notice.)

b. For monthly periodicals, show both the month and the year. (See ¶1418*j* for an example.)

c. For weekly or daily periodicals, show the month, day, and year. (See ¶1418*i, j, k* for examples.)

1424 Page Numbers

a. Page references in footnotes occur in the following forms:

p. 3	p. v	pp. 301 f. (meaning "page 301 and the following page")
pp. 3–4	pp. v–vi	pp. 301 ff. (meaning "page 301 and the following pages")

b. In a range of page numbers the second number is sometimes abbreviated; for example, *pp. 981–983* may be expressed as *pp. 981–83.* (See ¶460.)

Subsequent Footnote References

1425 When a footnote refers to a work that was fully identified in the footnote *immediately preceding,* it may be shortened by use of the abbreviation *ibid.* (meaning "in the same place"). *Ibid.* replaces all those elements that would otherwise be carried over intact from the previous footnote.

[1]Nancy J. Weiss, The National Urban League, 1910–1940, Oxford University Press, New York, 1974, pp. 47–60.

[2]Ibid., p. 63. (*Ibid.* represents all of the elements in the previous footnote except the page number.)

[3]Ibid. (Referring to page 63 in the same work. Here *ibid.* represents everything in the preceding footnote, including the page number.)

NOTE: Do not underscore *ibid.*

1426 a. When a footnote refers to a work fully identified in an earlier footnote but *not the one immediately preceding,* it may be shortened as follows:

[1]Author's surname, page number.

[8]Weiss, p. 79. (Referring to the work fully identified before; see footnote 1 in ¶1425 above.)

b. When previous reference has been made to different authors with the same surname, the use of a surname alone in a subsequent reference would be confusing. Therefore, the basic pattern in ¶1426*a* must be modified as follows:

[1]Author's initial(s) plus surname, page number.

OR: [2]Author's full name, page number.

[1]Cecil Williams, The Foundations of Intelligence, Comet Press Books, New York, 1953, p. 86.

[2]John K. Williams, The Wisdom of Your Subconscious Mind, Prentice–Hall, Inc., Englewood Cliffs, N.J., 1964, pp. 137–139.

[3]C. Williams, p. 88.

[4]J. K. Williams, p. 145.

(*Continued on page 286.*)

c. If previous reference has been made to different works by the same author, any subsequent reference should contain the title of the specific work now being referred to. When feasible, this title may be shortened to a key word or phrase; the word or phrase should be sufficiently clear, however, so that the full title can be readily identified in the bibliography or in an earlier footnote.

> [1]Author's surname, book title [shortened if feasible], page number.

> [1]Clinton Rossiter, Seedtime of the Republic, Harcourt, Brace and Company, New York, 1953, p. 70.
> [2]Clinton Rossiter, 1787: The Grand Convention, The Macmillan Company, New York, 1966, p. 163.
> [3]Rossiter, Seedtime, p. 73.

If referring to an article in a periodical, refer to the periodical title rather than the article title.

> [1]Author's surname, periodical title [shortened if feasible], page number.

> [4]Daniel P. Moynihan, "A Diplomat's Rhetoric," Harper's, January 1976, p. 40.
> [5]V. S. Pritchett, . . .
> [6]Moynihan, Harper's, p. 43. (Referring to the work identified in footnote 4 above.)

d. A more formal style in subsequent references uses the abbreviations *loc. cit.* ("in the place cited") and *op. cit.* ("in the work cited").

> [1]Author's surname, **loc. cit.** (This pattern is used when reference is made to the *very same page* in the work previously identified.)

> [2]Author's surname, **op. cit.**, page number. (This pattern is used when reference is made to a *different page* in the work previously identified.)

> [1]John Kenneth Galbraith, The Great Crash: 1929, 2d ed., Houghton Mifflin Company, Boston, 1961, p. 65.
> [2]Jan Tinbergen and J. J. Polak, The Dynamics of Business Cycles, The University of Chicago Press, Chicago, 1950, p. 83.
> [3]Galbraith, op. cit., p. 67. (Referring to a different page in *The Great Crash.*)
> [4]Tinbergen and Polak, loc. cit. (Referring to the same page in *The Dynamics of Business Cycles.*)
> [5]Ibid. (Referring to exactly the same page as shown in footnote 4. *Ibid.* may be used only to refer to the footnote immediately preceding. See ¶1425.)

NOTE: Do not underscore *loc. cit.* or *op. cit.* in footnotes.

Bibliographies

1427 A bibliography at the end of a manuscript or a report typically lists all the works consulted in the preparation of the material as well as all the works that were previously cited in the footnotes. The format of a

↓13

BIBLIOGRAPHY ↓3

Auerbach, Jerold S., Jr., Labor and Liberty, The Bobbs-Merrill
        Company, Inc., Indianapolis, 1966. ↓2

Brock, Horace R., et al., Accounting: Principles and Appli-
        cations, 3d ed., McGraw-Hill Book Company, New York,
        1974.

Burchell, Robert W., and David Listokin (eds.), Future Land
        Use: Energy, Environmental, and Legal Constraints,
        Center for Urban Policy Research, Rutgers Univer-
        sity, 1975.

Committee for Economic Development, The Schools and the
        Challenge of Innovation, McGraw-Hill Book Company,
        New York, 1969.

Galbraith, John Kenneth, The Affluent Society, Houghton
        Mifflin Company, Boston, 1958.

------, The Great Crash: 1929, 2d ed., Houghton Mifflin
        Company, Boston, 1961.

------, "How to Control the Military," Harper's, June 1969,
        pp. 31-46.

------, Money: Whence It Came, Where It Went, Houghton
        Mifflin Company, Boston, 1975.

------ and Molinder S. Randhawa, The New Industrial State,
        Houghton Mifflin Company, Boston, 1968.

A Guide to Graduate Study: Programs Leading to the Ph.D.
        Degree, 3d ed., American Council on Education,
        Washington, 1965.

bibliography is also used for any list of titles, such as a list of recommended readings or a list of new publications.

1428 **a.** A bibliography should begin on a fresh sheet under the centered
heading *BIBLIOGRAPHY* (or some other title, if appropriate).

b. Start with the heading on line 13, or center the bibliography vertically
on the page.

c. Use the same left and right margins as on other pages in the manuscript. (See also ¶1406.)

d. For the placement of page numbers, follow the directions in ¶1411.

1429 Each entry should be typed single-spaced. Leave two blank lines between
the heading and the first entry. Leave one blank line between each of the
other entries.

1430 Each entry within the bibliography should begin at the left margin. Use a
uniform indentation of ten spaces for additional lines within each entry.

1431 Entries in bibliographies contain the same elements and follow the same style as footnotes except that:

a. Entries are not numbered.

b. The name of the author is listed in inverted order (last name first). When an entry includes two or more authors' names, only the first author's name is inverted. When an organization is listed as the author, do not invert the name. (For examples, see the first four entries in the illustration on page 287.)

c. Page numbers are included in bibliographic entries only when the material being cited is part of a larger work. In such cases show the range of pages (for example, *pp. 215–232*) on which the material appears. (For an example, see the seventh entry in the illustration on page 287.)

1432 **a.** Entries in a bibliography are listed alphabetically by author.

b. Entries lacking an author are alphabetized by title. Disregard the words *The* or *A* at the beginning of a title in determining alphabetical sequence. (For an example, see the last entry in the illustration on page 287. Note that this entry is alphabetized on the basis of *Guide*, following *Galbraith*.)

1433 When a bibliography contains more than one work by the same author, replace the author's name with a long dash (six hyphens) in all of the entries after the first. List the works alphabetically by title. (For examples, see the fifth, sixth, seventh, and eighth entries in the illustration on page 287. Note that these titles are alphabetized on the key words *Affluent*, *Great*, *How*, and *Money*. The ninth entry involves a coauthor and therefore follows the works written by the first author alone.)

TABLES

General Guidelines

1501 Before typing any tabular material, plan the horizontal and vertical placement carefully.

a. If the table is to appear on the same page with straight copy, it should be centered horizontally within the established margins and should be set off by one to three blank lines from the straight text above or below, as follows:

Kind of Table	Spacing in Table Text	Blank Lines Above and Below Table
Without column heads or table title	Single	1
Without column heads or table title	Double	2
With column heads	Single or double	2
With table title	Single or double	3

b. If the table is to appear on a page by itself, it should be centered horizontally within the established margins and also centered vertically on the page. To determine vertical placement on a full page, see ¶¶1508–1509. To determine horizontal placement, use the backspace method (see ¶1510).

1502 The elements in a table should be styled as described below and as illustrated on page 291.

a. Title of Table. Type in all-capital letters and center.

b. Subtitle of Table. Type in capital and small letters and center.

c. Column Heads. Type in capital and small letters; center over the column text (see ¶¶1512–1513), or block left on the column text. Underscore each line of the column head in unruled tables. (See examples 1 and 2 on page 291.)

(Continued on page 290.)

d. Spacing of Title, Subtitle, and Column Heads.   If the title, subtitle, or column head requires more than one line, use single spacing for each additional line.

e. Table Text.   Use single or double spacing in the table text, but treat all tables in the same context consistently. Since the proportions of any table will vary depending on whether the table text is single- or double-spaced, use the spacing that will produce the more attractive appearance in the space available. If column heads are used, center the text in each column under the head or block the column head and the text at the left. As a rule, leave six spaces between columns.

NOTE: If any item in the table text requires more than one line, use single spacing and indent the extra line two spaces. (See example 6 on page 291.)

f. Table Footnote.   Type a short line of underscores (10 to 12 strokes) one line below the last line of table text. Then leave a blank line before typing the footnote. (See example 5 on page 291.)

NOTE: Begin the table footnote flush left. Type an asterisk (*) and then the first word (with no space intervening). If the table footnote requires more than one line, use single spacing and indent the extra line one space to align with the first word above. If there are two or more footnotes in a table, use the following sequence of symbols: *, **, ***, and so on. In this case indent the first line of each footnote five spaces and align turnovers at the left margin.

1503 For the proper spacing between elements in a table, see page 291.

1504 If the table requires rules, any of these methods may be used:

a. Insert all rules on the typewriter, using the underscore. Place a horizontal rule above and below the column heads and at the bottom of the table; do not underscore the column heads. These rules should extend to the full width of the table. As shown in examples 3 and 4 on page 291, type each rule on the line immediately following the preceding copy. This creates the appearance of a blank line above the underscore. Leave one blank line between an internal rule and any table copy that follows; leave two or three blank lines between the bottom rule and any straight copy that follows. If vertical rules are to be used to separate the columns, insert the page sideways after you have finished typing the table text and type the vertical rules, using the underscore. Do not type rules at the left and right sides of the table; the sides should remain open.

b. Insert all rules with a ball-point pen and a ruler after the typing has been completed. Be sure to leave adequate space for these rules when typing the table.

c. Insert all horizontal rules on the typewriter, as described in *a* above. Insert all vertical rules by ball-point pen.

1505 a. In columns of dollar amounts, insert a dollar sign only before the first amount at the head of the column and before the total amount. The dollar signs should align in the first space to the left of the longest amount in the column (see illustration on page 295).

b. If all the amounts in a column are whole dollar amounts, omit the decimal and zeros; for example, type $656 rather than $656.00. However,

1

```
LIFE EXPECTANCY AT BIRTH↓2

   From 1930 to 1972↓3


Year    Male    Female↓2

1930    58.1    61.6
1940    60.8    65.2
1950    65.6    71.1
1960    66.6    73.1
1970    67.1    74.8
1972    67.4    75.2
```

2

```
COMPULSORY SCHOOL ATTENDANCE
LAWS FOR SELECTED STATES↓3

                Year        Age
State           Enacted     Limits↓2

Idaho           1887        7-16
Iowa            1902        7-16
Maine           1875        7-16
Ohio            1877        6-18
Texas           1915        7-17
Utah            1890        6-18
```

3

```
LIFE INSURANCE IN FORCE↓2

   ($000,000 Omitted)↓1
                                    ↓2
Year     Ordinary      Group↓1
                                    ↓2
1910     11,783         ---
1940     79,346         14,938
1960     341,881        175,903
1973     928,192        708,322↓1
```

4

```
MEDIAN FAMILY INCOME↓1
                                    ↓2
           Median
           Family       Annual
Year       Income       Gain↓1
                                    ↓2
1970       $ 9,867      4.6%
1971       10,285       4.2%
1972       11,116       8.1%
1973       12,051       8.4%↓1
```

5

```
MOTOR VEHICLE PRODUCTION, 1972*↓2

    (In Thousands)↓3

United States ........ 11,270.7
Japan ................  6,300.0
West Germany .........  3,816.9
France ...............  3,337.8↓1

            ↓2
*Source:  Information Please
Almanac, 1975, page 35.
```

6

```
ESTIMATED ENROLLMENTS IN
VOCATIONAL EDUCATION, 1978↓3

Stenographic and
  Secretarial . . . . . 796,000
Typing  . . . . . . . . 790,000
Filing  . . . . . . . . 501,000
Accounting  . . . . . . 497,000
Auto Mechanics  . . . . 497,000
Metalworking  . . . . . 449,000
Family Relations  . . . 331,000
Child Development . . . 296,000
```

if any amount in a column includes cents, use the decimal and zeros with all whole dollar amounts for consistent appearance (see ¶415).

c. If the column of dollar amounts has a *total* line, type a line of underscores after the last amount as wide as the longest number in the column (including the dollar sign). Then type the dollar sign and total amount below. Leave one blank line (if desired) before typing the totals (see illustration on page 295), or type the totals on the line directly below the underscores.

1506 If all the numbers in a column represent percentages and the column heading clearly indicates this fact, do not use the percent sign with the numbers. However, if the column heading does not make this point clear, type a percent sign (%) after each number. (See example 4 on page 291.)

1507 Whenever the items in the first column of a table vary widely in length, you may use leaders (rows of periods that lead the eye across the page). The shortest line of leaders should have at least three periods. A line of leaders should be preceded and followed by one blank space. Leaders may be formed by typing periods in solid sequence, without spacing, or by alternately typing periods and spaces. The first method is faster, but the second is neater. If spaces are used, all the periods in the leader lines must align. Illustrations of closed and spaced leaders are shown in examples 5 and 6 on page 291.

Vertical Placement

1508 To center a table vertically on a full 8½- by 11-inch sheet:

a. Count the number of lines in the table. (Be sure to include the blank lines.)

b. Subtract the number of lines in the table from the total number of lines available on the page. (There are 6 standard typewriter lines to an inch; there are 66 lines on an 8½- by 11-inch sheet of paper.)

c. Divide the difference by 2 to find the number of the line on which to start typing the table; if there is a fraction in your answer, count the fraction as the next whole number (for example, if your answer is 12½, start typing on line 13).

NOTE: The bottom margin will be one or two lines deeper than the top margin. However, the table will appear to be centered on the page.

▪ See ¶1514a for an example.

1509 To center a table vertically on a full sheet of A4 paper (210 by 297 mm), use the same procedure described in ¶1508. However, there are 70 lines on an A4 sheet (compared to 66 on an 8½- by 11-inch sheet).

Horizontal Placement

1510 a. Establish a key line as follows. First, select the key item (longest item) in each column, whether it occurs in the column head or in one of the items below the column head. Next, determine the number of spaces to be left between columns. (Normally leave six spaces; however, in financial statements two blank spaces between adjacent columns of dollar amounts is sufficient.) This combination of letters and spaces makes up the key line.

- *For an example of a key line, see ¶1514b and the illustration on page 295.*

b. Determine the centering point on the page. If the left and right margins have been established in advance, the centering point will fall halfway between these margins. If the left and right margins have not been established and are to be equal, use the exact center of the page as the centering point.

c. Clear all tab stops and the margin stops on the typewriter.

d. From the centering point, backspace once for each pair of strokes in the key line. Do not backspace for an odd stroke left over at the end. Set the left margin stop at the point to which you backspaced; this will be the left margin of the first column in the table.

NOTE: If the left margin is less than 1 inch (25 mm) wide, you may reduce the width of the table by leaving three, four, or five blank spaces between columns instead of the usual six blank spaces. If you decide to use fewer than six spaces between columns, repeat step *d* so that the table will appear centered within the new margins.

e. From the left margin of the table, space forward once for each stroke in the first column plus once for each of the spaces between columns and set a tab stop at this point (the beginning of the second column).

f. Repeat step *e* until the tab stops have been set for each of the remaining columns.

Column Heads

1511 A long column head should be broken into no more than two or three lines. Clear abbreviations are permissible in long column heads.

1512 To center a *narrow* column head (narrower than the column text):

a. Take the number of strokes in the longest line in the column head and subtract it from the number of strokes in the longest line in the body of the column.

b. Divide the difference by 2 (drop any fraction) to find the number of spaces to indent the longest line in the column head. Center the other lines in the column head in relation to the longest line.

- *For an example, see the head in the first column of the table on page 295; see also the analysis in ¶1514d (1).*

NOTE: If all the column heads are short, you may align each line in the column head at the left with the column text (instead of centering the column head over the column text).

1513 To center a *wide* column head (wider than the column text):

a. Type the longest line in the column head six spaces following the preceding column. Center any other lines in the column head in relation to the longest line.

(Continued on page 294.)

b. Take the number of strokes in the longest line of the column text, and subtract it from the number of strokes in the longest line in the column head.

c. Divide the difference by 2 (drop any fraction) to find the number of spaces to indent the column text. Set a tab stop here so that you can begin all lines in the body of the column at this point.

▪ *For an example, see the head in the last column of the table on page 295; see also the analysis in ¶1514d (3).*

Example of Table Placement

1514 The table on page 295 has been used to illustrate how to plan the placement of a table on an 8½- by 11-inch sheet of paper.

a. Vertical Placement

Number of lines available on sheet	66
Total number of lines in table (typed and blank)	18
Lines available for top and bottom margins (66 − 18 = 48)	48
Line on which to start typing (48 ÷ 2 = 24)	24*

b. Horizontal Placement

Establish the key line.

    San Francisco123456Last Year123456This Year123456Increase in

c. Setting Margins and Tab Stops

(1) Clear all tab stops and the margin stops on the typewriter.

(2) Move the carriage or carrier to the centering point.

(3) To find the left margin, backspace once for each two strokes in the key line. (Do not backspace for a single stroke left over at the end.) In this case you would backspace 30 times (there are exactly 60 letters and spaces in the key line) and then set the left margin stop.

(4) To set the tab stop for the second column, space once from the margin stop for each stroke in the first column (13) plus 6 spaces for the area between the first and second columns, or 19 times (13 + 6); set the tab stop

(5) To set the tab stop for the third column, space once from the second column tab stop for each stroke in the second column (9) plus 6 spaces for the area between the second and third columns, or 15 times (9 + 6); set the tab stop.

(6) To set the tab stop for the fourth column, space once for each stroke in the third column (9) plus 6 spaces for the area between the third and fourth columns, or 15 times (9 + 6); set the tab stop.

d. Making Adjustments for Column Heads

(1) The head for the first column is 7 spaces narrower than the column text (13 − 6). Indent 3 spaces (7 ÷ 2; drop the fraction) from the left margin stop before typing the head.

---

* If A4 paper is used, the calculations for vertical spacing will differ as follows: There are 70 lines on A4 paper. Therefore, the lines available for top and bottom margins will equal 52 (70 − 18). Typing should begin on line 26 (52 ÷ 2).

ANALYSIS OF SALES QUOTAS

From January 1 Through March 31

Branch	Last Year	This Year	Increase in Sales
Chicago	$ 78,000	$ 84,000	$ 6,000
Cincinnati	57,000	65,000	8,000
Los Angeles	83,000	91,000	8,000
Memphis	48,000	53,000	5,000
New Orleans	45,000	51,000	6,000
New York	89,000	96,000	7,000
Philadelphia	83,000	88,000	5,000
San Francisco	76,000	85,000	9,000
Seattle	62,000	69,000	7,000
TOTALS	$621,000	$682,000	$61,000

(2) Heads for the second and third columns are 1 space wider than the column text (9 − 8). In this case do not indent the column text since the amount of indention would be less than 1 space (1 ÷ 2).

(3) The fourth column has a two-line head. The first line is 6 spaces wider than the second line (11 − 5). First type the wider line of the column head. Then center the narrower line under it by indenting 3 spaces (6 ÷ 2). Also, the first line in the column head is 4 spaces wider than the column text (11 − 7). To center the column text below the head, indent 2 spaces (4 ÷ 2) to the right and reset the tab stop.

16 FORMS OF ADDRESS

1601 The following forms of address are correct for government officials; members of the armed services; Roman Catholic, Protestant, and Jewish dignitaries; and education officials. In the salutations that follow the forms of address, the most formal one is listed first.

NOTE: For the sake of simplicity, the masculine forms of address have been given throughout. When an office is held by a woman, make the following substitutions:

For *Sir*, use *Madam*.

For *Mr*. followed by a name (for example, *Mr. Brandt*), use *Miss, Mrs.*, or *Ms*. as appropriate.

For *Mr*. followed by a title (for example, *Mr. President, Mr. Secretary, Mr. Mayor*), use *Madam*.

Government Officials

PRESIDENT OF THE UNITED STATES
The President
The White House
Washington, DC 20500

Mr. President:
Dear Mr. President:

VICE PRESIDENT OF THE UNITED STATES
The Vice President
United States Senate
Washington, DC 20510

OR: The Honorable . . . (*full name*)
Vice President of the United States
Washington, DC 20501

Sir:
Dear Mr. Vice President:

CHIEF JUSTICE OF THE UNITED STATES
The Chief Justice of the
United States
Washington, DC 20543

OR: The Chief Justice
The Supreme Court
Washington, DC 20543

Sir:
Dear Mr. Chief Justice:

CABINET MEMBER
The Honorable . . . (*full name*)
Secretary of . . . (*department*)
Washington, DC   ZIP Code

OR: The Secretary of . . . (*department*)
Washington, DC   ZIP Code

Sir:
Dear Mr. Secretary:

UNITED STATES SENATOR
The Honorable . . . (*full name*)
United States Senate
Washington, DC 20510

OR: The Honorable . . . (*full name*)
United States Senator
(*local address and ZIP Code*)

Sir:
Dear Senator . . . :

UNITED STATES REPRESENTATIVE
The Honorable . . . (*full name*)
House of Representatives
Washington, DC 20515

OR: The Honorable . . . (*full name*)
Representative in Congress
(*local address and ZIP Code*)

Sir:
Dear Mr. . . . :

GOVERNOR

In Massachusetts, New Hampshire, and by courtesy in some other states:

His Excellency the Governor
of . . .
State Capital, State ZIP Code

In other states:
The Honorable . . . (*full name*)
Governor of . . .
State Capital, State ZIP Code

Sir:
Dear Governor . . . :

STATE SENATOR
The Honorable . . . (*full name*)
The State Senate
State Capital, State ZIP Code

Sir:
Dear Senator . . . :

STATE REPRESENTATIVE OR ASSEMBLY
MEMBER
The Honorable . . . (*full name*)
House of Representatives
(OR The State Assembly)
State Capital, State ZIP Code

Sir:
Dear Mr. . . . :

MAYOR
The Honorable . . . (*full name*)
Mayor of . . . (*city*)
City, State ZIP Code

OR: The Mayor of the City of . . .
City, State ZIP Code

Sir
Dear Mr. Mayor:
Dear Mayor . . . :

Members of the Armed Services

The addresses of both officers and enlisted men in the armed services should include title of rank, full name followed by a comma and the initials USA, USN, USAF, USMC, or USCG. Below are some specific examples together with the appropriate salutations.

ARMY, AIR FORCE, AND MARINE CORPS
OFFICERS
Lieutenant General . . . (*full name*), USA
Address

Sir:
Dear General . . . :
(NOT: Dear Lieutenant General . . . :)

For first and second lieutenants, use:

Dear Lieutenant . . . :

NAVY AND COAST GUARD OFFICERS
Rear Admiral . . . (*full name*), USN
Address

Sir:
Dear Admiral . . . :

For officers below the rank of Commander, use:

Dear Mr. . . . :

ENLISTED MEN
Sergeant . . . (*full name*), USA
Address

Seaman . . . (*full name*), USN
Address

Dear Sergeant (OR Seaman) . . . :

Roman Catholic Dignitaries

CARDINAL
His Eminence . . . (*given name*)
Cardinal . . . (*surname*)
Archbishop of . . . (*place*)
Address

Your Eminence:
Dear Cardinal . . . :

(*Continued on page 298.*)

ARCHBISHOP AND BISHOP
The Most Reverend . . . (*full name*)
Archbishop (**or** Bishop) of
. . . (*place*)
Address

Your Excellency:
Dear Archbishop (**or** Bishop) . . . :

MONSIGNOR
The Right Reverend Monsignor
. . . (*full name*)
Address

Right Reverend Monsignor:
Dear Monsignor . . . :

PRIEST
The Reverend . . . (*full name,
followed by comma and initials
of order*)
Address

Reverend Father:
Dear Father . . . :

MOTHER SUPERIOR
The Reverend Mother Superior
Address

or: Reverend Mother . . . (*name,
followed by comma and initials
of order*)
Address

Reverend Mother:
Dear Reverend Mother:
Dear Mother . . . :

SISTER
Sister . . . (*name, followed by
comma and initials of order*)
Address

Dear Sister:
Dear Sister . . . :

Protestant Dignitaries

PROTESTANT EPISCOPAL BISHOP
The Right Reverend . . . (*full name*)
Bishop of . . . (*place*)
Address

Right Reverend Sir:
Dear Bishop . . . :

PROTESTANT EPISCOPAL DEAN
The Very Reverend . . . (*full name*)
Dean of . . .
Address

Very Reverend Sir:
Dear Dean . . . :

METHODIST BISHOP
The Reverend . . . (*full name*)
Bishop of . . .
Address

Reverend Sir:
Dear Bishop . . . :

CLERGYMAN WITH DOCTOR'S DEGREE
The Reverend Dr. . . . (*full name*)
Address

or: The Reverend . . . (*full name*), D.D.
Address

Reverend Sir:
Dear Dr. . . . :

CLERGYMAN WITHOUT DOCTOR'S DEGREE
The Reverend . . . (*full name*)
Address

Reverend Sir:
Dear Mr. . . . :

Jewish Dignitaries

RABBI WITH DOCTOR'S DEGREE
Rabbi . . . (*full name*), D.D.
Address

or: Dr. . . . (*full name*)
Address

Dear Rabbi (**or** Dr.) . . . :

RABBI WITHOUT DOCTOR'S DEGREE
Rabbi . . . (*full name*)
Address

Dear Rabbi . . . :

Education Officials

PRESIDENT OF A COLLEGE OR UNIVERSITY
. . . (*full name, followed by comma
and highest degree*)
President, . . . (*name of college*)
Address

OR: Dr. . . . *(full name)*
President, . . . *(name of college)*
Address

Dear President . . . :
Dear Dr. . . . :

PROFESSOR
Professor . . . *(full name)*
Department of . . .
. . . *(name of college)*
Address

OR: . . . *(full name, followed by comma
and highest degree)*
Department of . . .
. . . *(name of college)*
Address

OR: Dr. . . . *(full name)*
Professor of . . . *(subject)*
. . . *(name of college)*
Address

Dear Professor (OR Dr.) . . . :
Dear Mr. . . . :

SUPERINTENDENT OF SCHOOLS
Mr. (OR Dr.) . . . *(full name)*
Superintendent of . . . Schools
Address

Dear Mr. (OR Dr.) . . . :

MEMBER OF BOARD OF EDUCATION
Mr. . . . *(full name)*
Member, . . . *(name of city)*
Board of Education
Address

Dear Mr. . . . :

PRINCIPAL
Mr. (OR Dr.) . . . *(full name)*
Principal, . . . *(name of school)*
Address

Dear Mr. (OR Dr.) . . . :

TEACHER
Mr. (OR Dr.) . . . *(full name)*
. . . *(name of school)*
Address

Dear Mr. (OR Dr.) . . . :

GLOSSARY OF GRAMMATICAL TERMS

Adjective
Adverb
Adverbial Conjunctive (or
  Connective)
Antecedent
Appositive
Article
Case
  Nominative Case
  Objective Case
  Possessive Case
Clause
  Adjective Clause
  Adverbial Clause
  Coordinate Clauses
  Elliptical Clause
  Essential (or Restrictive) Clause
  Nonessential (or Nonrestrictive)
    Clause
  Noun Clause
Comparison
  Positive
  Comparative
  Superlative
Complement
  Object
  Predicate Noun
  Predicate Adjective
Conjunction
  Coordinating Conjunction
  Correlative Conjunctions
  Subordinating Conjunction
Connective
Consonants
Contraction

Dangling Modifier
Direct Address
Elliptical Expressions
Essential Elements
Gender
Gerund
Infinitive
Interjection
Modifier
Mood (Mode)
  Indicative
  Imperative
  Subjunctive
Nonessential Elements
Noun
  Abstract Noun
  Collective Noun
  Common Noun
  Proper Noun
Number
Object
  Direct Object
  Indirect Object
Ordinal Number
Parallel Structure
Parenthetical Elements
Participle
  Present Participle
  Past Participle
  Perfect Participle
  Dangling Participle
Parts of Speech
Person

Phrase
   Adjective Phrase
   Adverbial Phrase
   Essential (or Restrictive) Phrase
   Gerund Phrase
   Infinitive Phrase
   Nonessential (or Nonrestrictive)
     Phrase
   Noun Phrase
   Participial Phrase
   Prepositional Phrase
   Prepositional-Gerund Phrase
   Verb Phrase

Predicate
   Complete Predicate
   Simple Predicate
   Compound Predicate

Prefix

Preposition

Principal Parts

Pronoun

Punctuation
   Terminal (or End) Punctuation
   Internal Punctuation

Question
   Direct Question
   Indirect Question
   Independent Question

Quotation
   Direct Quotation
   Indirect Quotation

Sentence
   Simple Sentence
   Compound Sentence
   Complex Sentence
   Compound-Complex Sentence
   Declarative Sentence
   Elliptical Sentence
   Exclamatory Sentence
   Imperative Sentence
   Interrogative Sentence
   Sentence Fragment
   Statement

Subject

Suffix

Syllable

Tense

Transitional Expressions

Verb
   Auxiliary (Helping) Verb
   Intransitive Verb
   Linking Verb
   Transitive Verb

Verbal
   Active Voice
   Passive Voice

Vowels

1701 This glossary provides brief definitions of all the grammatical terms that have been used elsewhere in this manual.

Adjective. A word that answers the question *what kind* (*excellent* results), *how many* (*four* acres), or *which one* (the *latest* data). An adjective may be a single word (a *wealthy* man), a phrase (a man *of great wealth*), or a clause (a man *who possesses great wealth*). An adjective modifies the meaning of a noun (fresh *fish*) or a pronoun (unlucky *me*, *I* was wrong).

Adjective, predicate. See *Complement.*

Adjective clause, phrase. See *Clause; Phrase.*

Adjectives, comparison of. See *Comparison.*

Adverb. A word that answers the question *when, where, why, in what manner,* or *to what extent.* An adverb may be a single word (speak *clearly*), a phrase (speak *in a clear voice*), or a clause (speak *as clearly as* *you can*). An adverb modifies the meaning of a verb, an adjective, or another adverb.

> He signed the note *slowly*. (Modifies the verb *signed*.)
> We moved to a *rapidly* growing suburb. (Modifies the adjective *growing*.)
> She agreed *most* reluctantly. (Modifies the adverb *reluctantly*.)

Adverbial clause, phrase. See *Clause; Phrase.*

Adverbial conjunctive (or **connective**). An adverb that connects the main clauses of a compound sentence; for example, *however, therefore, nevertheless, hence, moreover, otherwise, consequently*. (See also ¶178.)

Adverbs, comparison of. See *Comparison.*

Antecedent. A noun or a noun phrase to which a pronoun refers.

> She is the *person who* wrote the letter. (*Person* is the antecedent of *who*.)
> *Owning your own home* has *its* advantages. (*Owning your own home* is the antecedent of *its*.)

Appositive. A noun or a noun phrase that identifies another noun or pronoun that immediately precedes it. (See ¶¶148–150.)

> Mr. S. Mancuso, *our purchasing agent,* would like to meet you.

Article. Classed as an adjective. The *definite* article is *the;* the *indefinite, a* or *an.* (See ¶1101.)

Case. The form of a noun or of a pronoun that indicates its relation to other words in the sentence. There are three cases: nominative, objective, and possessive. *Nouns* have the same form in the nominative and objective cases but a special ending for the possessive. The forms for *pronouns* are:

Nominative	Objective	Possessive
I, we	me, us	my, mine, our, ours
you	you	your, yours
he, she, it	him, her, it	his, hers, its
they	them	their, theirs
who	whom	whose

Nominative case. Used for the subject or the complement of a verb.

> *She* sings well. (Subject.)   It is *I*. (Complement.)

Objective case. Used for (1) the object of a verb, (2) the object of a preposition, (3) the subject of an infinitive, (4) the object of an infinitive, or (5) the complement of the infinitive *to be.*

> Tom hit *him*. (Object of the verb *hit*.)
> Brenda has not written to *me*. (Object of the preposition *to*.)
> The president encouraged *her* to run for office. (Subject of the infinitive *to run*.)
> You ought to see *him* today. (Object of the infinitive *to see*.)
> They believed me to be *her*. (Complement of the infinitive *to be*.)

Possessive case. Used to show ownership. See ¶¶627–650 for the formation of the possessives of nouns.

Clause. A group of related words that contains a subject and a predicate. An *independent* clause (also known as a *main clause* or *principal clause*) expresses a complete thought and can stand alone as a sentence. A *dependent* clause (also known as a *subordinate clause*) does not express a complete thought and cannot stand alone as a sentence.

I will go (independent clause) if I am invited (dependent clause).

Adjective clause. A dependent clause that modifies a noun or a pronoun in the main clause. Adjective clauses are joined to the main clause by relative pronouns (*which, that, who, whose, whom*).

The charge, *which includes painting,* seems reasonable. (Modifies *charge.*)

Adverbial clause. A dependent clause that functions as an adverb in its relation to the main clause. Adverbial clauses indicate time, place, manner, cause, purpose, condition, result, reason, or contrast.

These orders can be filled *as soon as stock is received.* (Time.)
I was advised to move to a locality *where the climate is dry.* (Place.)
She worked *as though her life depended on it.* (Manner.)
Please write me at once *if you have any suggestions.* (Condition.)
Because our plant is closed in August, we cannot accept your order. (Reason.)
The first batch was too thin, *whereas this batch is too thick.* (Contrast.)

Coordinate clauses. Clauses of the same rank. They may be independent or dependent clauses.

Carl will oversee the day-to-day operations, and Sheila will be responsible for the finances. (Coordinate independent clauses.)
When you have read the chapter and *you can answer all the questions correctly,* you ought to try these special problems. (Coordinate dependent clauses.)

Elliptical clause. A clause from which key words have been omitted. (See ¶¶102, 111, 130*b*, 1082*d*.)

Now, for the next topic.   *Really?*   *If possible,* arrive at one.

Essential (or **restrictive**) **clause.** A dependent clause that cannot be omitted without changing the meaning of the main clause. Essential clauses are *not* set off by commas.

The magazine *that came yesterday* contains some beautiful illustrations.

Nonessential (or **nonrestrictive**) **clause.** A dependent clause that adds descriptive information but could be omitted without changing the meaning of the main clause. Such clauses are separated from the main clause by commas.

Her latest book, *which is set in the Far East,* has sold quite well.

Noun clause. A dependent clause that functions as a noun in the main clause.

Whether the proposal will be accepted remains to be seen. (Noun clause as subject.)
They thought *that the plan was a failure.* (Noun clause as object.)

Comparison. The forms of an adjective or adverb that indicate degrees in quality, quantity, or manner. There are three degrees: positive, comparative, and superlative. (See ¶1071.)

(Continued on page 304.)

Positive. The simple form; for example, *old, beautiful* (adjectives); *soon, quietly* (adverbs).

Comparative. Indicates a higher or lower degree of quality or manner than is expressed by the positive degree. It is used when two things are compared. It is regularly formed by adding *er* to the positive degree (*older, sooner*). In longer words, it is formed by adding *more* or *less* to the positive (*more beautiful, less beautiful; more quietly, less quietly*).

Superlative. Denotes the highest or lowest degree of quality or manner and is used when more than two things are compared. It is regularly formed by adding *est* to the positive degree (*oldest, soonest*). In longer words, it is formed by adding *most* or *least* (*most beautiful, least beautiful; most quietly, least quietly*).

Complement. A word or phrase that completes the sense of the verb. It may be an object, a predicate noun, or a predicate adjective.

Object. Follows a transitive verb. (See *Verb*.)

I have already mailed the *letter*.

Predicate noun. Follows a linking verb. It explains the subject and is identical with it. (Also called a *predicate complement, subject complement*, and *predicate nominative*.)

Miss Kwong is our *accountant*. (*Accountant* refers to Miss Kwong.)

Predicate adjective. Completes the sense of a linking verb. (Also called a *predicate complement*.)

The charge is *excessive*. (The adjective *excessive* refers to *charge*.)

NOTE: In this manual, *complement* is used to refer only to a predicate noun or adjective following a linking verb. The term *object* is used to denote the complement of a transitive verb.

Conjunction. A word or phrase that connects words, phrases, or clauses.

Coordinating conjunction. Connects words, phrases, or clauses of equal rank. The coordinating conjunctions are *and, but, or*, and *nor*.

Correlative conjunctions. Coordinating conjunctions used in pairs; for example, *both . . . and, not only . . . but (also), either . . . or, neither . . . nor, whether . . . or (not)*.

Subordinating conjunction. Used to join subordinate clauses to main clauses. A few common ones are *when, where, after, before, if, whether, since*, and *though*. (See also ¶132.)

Conjunctive adverb. See *Adverbial conjunctive*.

Connective. A word that joins words, phrases, or clauses. The chief connectives are conjunctions, adverbial conjunctives, prepositions, and relative pronouns.

Consonants. The letters *b, c, d, f, g, h, j, k, l, m, n, p, q, r, s, t, v, w, x, y, z*. The letters *w* and *y* sometimes serve as vowels (as in *saw* and *rhyme*).

Contraction. A shortened form of a word or phrase in which an apostrophe indicates the omitted letters or words; for example, *don't* for *do not; o'clock* for *of the clock*. (See ¶505.)

Dangling modifier. A modifier that is attached to no word in a sentence or to the wrong word. (See ¶1082.)

Direct address. A construction in which a speaker or a writer addresses another person directly. For example, "What do you think, Sylvia?"

Elliptical expressions. Condensed expressions from which key words have been omitted. (See also *Clause; Sentence.*)

Essential elements. Words, phrases, or clauses that are necessary to the completeness of the structure or the meaning of a sentence. (See also *Clause; Phrase.*)

Gender. The characteristic of nouns and pronouns that indicates whether the thing named is *masculine* (*man, boy, stallion, he*), *feminine* (*woman, girl, mare, she*), or *neuter* (*book, concept, it*). Nouns that refer to either males or females have *common* gender (*person, child, horse*).

Gerund. A verb form ending in *ing* and used as a *noun.*

> Selling is fun. (Subject.)   I enjoy *selling.* (Direct object of *enjoy.*)
> She is experienced in *selling.* (Object of preposition *in.*)

Dangling gerund. A prepositional-gerund phrase that is attached to no word in a sentence or to the wrong word. (See ¶1082c.)

Imperative. See *Mood.*

Indicative. See *Mood.*

Infinitive. The form of the verb usually introduced by *to* (see ¶¶1044–1046). An infinitive may be used as a noun, an adjective, or an adverb.

> NOUN: *To do her a favor* is a pleasure. (Subject.)
>   She asked *to see the book.* (Object.)
> ADJECTIVE: I still have two more contracts *to draft.* (Modifies *contracts.*)
> ADVERB: He resigned *to take another position.* (Modifies *resigned.*)

Interjection. A word that shows emotion; usually without grammatical connection to other parts of a sentence.

> *Oh,* so that's what he meant.   *Hooray!* We win.

Modifier. A word, phrase, or clause that qualifies, limits, or restricts the meaning of a word. (See *Adjective; Adverb; Dangling modifier.*)

Mood (mode). The form of the verb that shows the manner of the action. There are three moods: indicative, imperative, and subjunctive.

Indicative. States a fact or asks a question.

> The lease has expired.   When does the lease expire?

Imperative. Expresses a command or makes a request.

> Call me next week.   Please send me a catalog.

Subjunctive. Used following clauses of necessity, demand, or wishing (see ¶¶1038–1039); also used in *if, as if,* and *as though* clauses that state conditions which are improbable, doubtful, or contrary to fact (see ¶¶1040–1043).

(*Continued on page 306.*)

I demand that we *be* heard.　　　　We urge that she *be* elected.
It is imperative that he *be* notified.　　I wish I *were* going.
If he *were* appointed head of the department, I would quit.

Nonessential elements. Words, phrases, or clauses that are not necessary to the completeness of the structure or the meaning of a sentence. (See also *Clause; Phrase.*)

Noun. The name of a person, place, object, idea, quality, or activity.

> **Abstract noun.** The name of a quality or a general idea; for example, *courage, freedom.*
>
> **Collective noun.** A noun that represents a group of persons, animals, or things; for example, *audience, company, flock.* (See ¶1019.)
>
> **Common noun.** The name of a class of persons or things; for example, *child, house.* (See ¶¶307–310.)
>
> **Predicate noun.** See *Complement.*
>
> **Proper noun.** The official name of a particular person, place, or thing; for example, *Ellen, San Diego, Wednesday.* Proper nouns are capitalized. (See ¶¶303–306.)

Number. The characteristic of a noun, pronoun, or verb that indicates whether one person or thing (singular) or more than one (plural) is meant.

> NOUN: girl, girls　　　PRONOUN: she, they　　　VERB: he *works*, they *work*

Object. The person or thing that receives the action of the verb. An object may be a word, a phrase, or a clause.

> I bought a *calculator.* (Word.)
> She likes *to sculpt.* (Infinitive phrase.)
> I did not realize *that it was so late.* (Clause.)

> **Direct object.** The person or thing that is directly affected by the action of the verb. (The object in each of the three sentences above is a *direct* object.)
>
> **Indirect object.** The person or thing indirectly affected by the action of the verb. The indirect object can usually be made the object of the preposition *to* or *for.*
>
> He gave (to) *me* the book.

Ordinal number. The form of a number that indicates order or succession; for example, *first, second, twelfth.* (See ¶¶424–426.)

Parallel structure. See ¶1081.

Parenthetical elements. Words, phrases, or clauses that are not necessary to the completeness of the structure or the meaning of a sentence.

Participle. A word that may stand alone as an adjective or may be combined with helping verbs to form different tenses (see ¶¶1033–1034). There are three forms: present, past, and perfect.

> **Present participle.** Ends in *ing;* for example, *making, advertising.*
>
> **Past participle.** Regularly ends in *ed* (as in *asked* or *filed*) but may be irregularly formed (as in *lost, seen,* and *sung*). (See ¶1030*a,b.*)

Perfect participle. Consists of *having* plus the past participle; for example, *having asked, having lost.*

When a participle functions as an *adjective,* it modifies a noun or a pronoun.

A *leaking* pipe caused all the trouble. (Modifies *pipe.*)
Having retired last year, I now do volunteer work. (Modifies *I.*)

Because a participle has many of the characteristics of a verb, it may take an object and be modified by an adverb. The participle and its object and modifiers make up a *participial phrase.*

Waving his hand, he drove quickly away. (Object is *hand.*)
Speaking quickly, she described the project in detail. (*Quickly* modifies *speaking.*)

Dangling participle. A participial phrase attached to no word in a sentence or to the wrong word. (See ¶1082*a.*)

Parts of speech. The eight classes into which words are grouped according to their uses in a sentence: verb, noun, pronoun, adjective, adverb, conjunction, preposition, and interjection.

Person. The characteristic of a word that indicates whether a person is speaking (*first person*), is spoken to (*second person*), or is spoken about (*third person*). Only personal pronouns and verbs change their forms to show person. All nouns are considered third person.

FIRST PERSON: *I* liked this book.   *We* liked this book.
SECOND PERSON: *You* liked this book.   *You* liked this book.
THIRD PERSON: *She* liked this book.   *They* liked this book.

Phrase. A group of two or more words not having a subject and a predicate, used as a noun, an adjective, or an adverb.

Adjective phrase. A phrase that functions as an adjective (such as an infinitive phrase, a participial phrase, or a prepositional phrase).

Adverbial phrase. A phrase that functions as an adverb (such as an infinitive phrase or a prepositional phrase).

Essential (or **restrictive**) **phrase.** A phrase that limits, defines, or identifies something; cannot be omitted without changing the meaning of the main clause.

The chapter *explaining that law* appears at the end of the book.

Gerund phrase. A gerund plus its object and modifiers; used as a noun.

Running your own business is not as easy as it looks.

Infinitive phrase. An infinitive plus its subject, object, and modifiers; may be used as a noun, an adjective, or an adverb. An infinitive phrase that is attached to no word in a sentence or to the wrong word is called a *dangling infinitive* (see ¶1082*b*).

To pass this subject requires conscientious study. (As a noun.)
We still have more checking *to do.* (An adjective modifying *checking.*)
He resigned *to enlist.* (An adverb modifying *resigned.*)

(*Continued on page 308.*)

Nonessential (or **nonrestrictive**) **phrase.** A phrase that can be omitted without changing the meaning of the sentence.

Joan, *wishing to improve her typing skill,* registered for a second course.

Noun phrase. A phrase that functions as a noun (such as a gerund phrase, an infinitive phrase, or a prepositional phrase).

Participial phrase. A participle and its object and modifiers; used as an adjective.

We heard the rain *splashing on the window.*
The old man, *confused by the bright lights,* stepped in the path of the car.
I can now relax, *having finished the assignment.*

Prepositional phrase. A preposition and its object and modifiers; may be used as a noun, an adjective, or an adverb.

From New York to Denver is a long way to drive. (Noun.)
The package *on the large desk* is ready to be sent. (Adjective.)
They have gone *to Cleveland.* (Adverb.)

Prepositional-gerund phrase. A phrase that begins with a preposition and has a gerund as the object. (See ¶1082c.)

By rechecking the material before it is set in type, you avoid expensive corrections later on. (*By* is the preposition; *rechecking,* a gerund, is the object of *by.*)

Verb phrase. A phrase that functions as a verb.

You *should work together* with Nora on the report. (The verb phrase consists of the verb form *should work* plus the adverb *together.*)

Positive degree. See *Comparison.*

Predicate. That part of a sentence that tells what the subject does or what is done to the subject or what state of being the subject is in.

Complete predicate. The complete predicate consists of a verb and its complement along with any modifiers.

Barbara *has handled the job well.*

Simple predicate. The simple predicate is the verb alone, without regard for any complement or modifiers that may accompany it.

Barbara *has handled* the job well.

Compound predicate. Two or more predicates in the same sentence.

Barbara *has handled the job well* and *ought to be commended.*

Predicate adjective, complement, nominative, noun, object. See *Complement.*

Prefix. A letter, syllable, or word added to the beginning of a word to change its meaning; for example, *a*float, *re*upholster, *under*nourished.

Preposition. A connective that shows the relation of a noun or pronoun to some other word in the sentence. The noun or pronoun following a preposition is in the objective case. (See ¶¶1077–1080.)

He has left the sales figures *with me.*

Principal parts. The forms of a verb from which all other forms are derived: the *present,* the *past,* the *past participle,* and the *present participle.* (See ¶¶1030–1035.)

Pronoun. A word used in place of a noun. (See ¶¶1049–1064.)

DEMONSTRATIVE: *this, that, these, those*

INDEFINITE: *each, either, any, anyone, someone, everyone, few, all,* etc.

INTENSIVE: *myself, yourself,* etc.

INTERROGATIVE: *who, which, what,* etc.

PERSONAL: *I, you, he, she, it, we, they*

RELATIVE: *who, whose, whom, which, that,* and compounds with *ever* (such as *whoever*)

Punctuation. Marks used to indicate relationships between words, phrases, and clauses.

Terminal (or **end**) **punctuation.** The period, the question mark, and the exclamation point—the three marks that may indicate the end of a sentence.

Internal punctuation. The comma, the semicolon, the colon, the dash, parentheses, quotation marks, the underscore, the apostrophe, ellipsis marks, the asterisk, the diagonal, and brackets.

Question, direct. A question in its original form, as spoken or written.

He then asked me, "What is your opinion?"

Indirect question. A statement of the substance of a question without the use of the exact words of the speaker.

He then asked me what my opinion was.

Independent question. A question that represents a complete sentence but is incorporated in a larger sentence.

The main question is, Who will translate this idea into a clear plan of action?

Quotation, direct. A quotation of words exactly as spoken or written.

Ruth said, "I plan to take a 10 o'clock flight."

Indirect quotation. A statement of the substance of a quotation without using the exact words.

Ruth said that *she planned to take a 10 o'clock flight.*

Sentence. A group of words representing a complete thought and containing a subject and a verb (predicate) along with any complements and modifiers.

Simple sentence. A sentence consisting of one independent clause.

I have no recollection of the meeting.

Compound sentence. A sentence consisting of two or more independent clauses.

Our Boston office will be closed, and our Dallas office will be relocated.

(*Continued on page 310.*)

Complex sentence. A sentence consisting of one independent clause and one or more dependent clauses.

We will make an exception to the rule if circumstances warrant.

Compound-complex sentence. A sentence consisting of two independent clauses and one or more dependent clauses.

I tried to handle the monthly report alone, but when I began to analyze the data, I realized that I needed your help.

Declarative sentence. A sentence that makes a statement.

All the newspapers were sold.

Elliptical sentence. A word or phrase that is treated as a complete sentence, even though the subject and the verb are only understood but not expressed.

Enough on that subject.   Why not?

Exclamatory sentence. A sentence that expresses strong feeling.

Don't remove these files!

Imperative sentence. A sentence that expresses a command or a request. (The subject *you* is understood if it is not expressed.)

Send a check at once.   Please close the door.

Interrogative sentence. A sentence that asks a question.

When does the conference begin?

Sentence fragment. A phrase or clause that is incorrectly treated as a sentence. (See ¶102, note.)

Statement. A sentence that asserts a fact. (See also the entry for *Declarative sentence* above.)

Subject. A word, phrase, or clause that names the person, place, or thing about which something is said.

The book was printed in Chicago.
That the work will be completed by the first of the month is doubtful.

Compound subject. A subject consisting of two or more simple subjects joined by conjunctions.

Glazer and *Little* are planning to establish a partnership.

Subjunctive. See *Mood.*

Suffix. A letter, syllable, or word added to the end of a word to modify its meaning; for example, friend*ly*, count*less*, receiver*ship*, lone*some*.

Superlative degree. See *Comparison.*

Syllable. A single letter or a group of letters that form one sound.

Tense. The property of a verb that expresses *time.* (See ¶¶1031–1035.)

The three primary tenses correspond to the three time divisions: *present (they think), past (they thought),* and *future (they will think).*

There are three *perfect* tenses, corresponding to the primary tenses: *present perfect* (*they have thought*), *past perfect* (*they had thought*), and *future perfect* (*they will have thought*).

There are six *progressive* tenses, corresponding to each of the primary and perfect tenses: *present progressive* (*they are thinking*), *past progressive* (*they were thinking*), *future progressive* (*they will be thinking*), *present perfect progressive* (*they have been thinking*), *past perfect progressive* (*they had been thinking*), *future perfect progressive* (*they will have been thinking*).

There are two *emphatic* tenses: *present emphatic* (*they do think*) and *past emphatic* (*they did think*).

Transitional expressions. Expressions that link independent clauses or sentences; for example, *as a result, therefore, on the other hand, nevertheless.* (See also ¶138a.)

Verb. A word used to express action or state of being. (See also *Mood.*)

The phone *rang.* (Action.)   The job *is* exciting. (State of being.)

Auxiliary (helping) verb. A verb that helps in the formation of the particular form of another verb. The chief auxiliaries are *be, can, could, do, have, may, might, must, ought, shall, should, will, would.*

Intransitive verb. A verb that does not require an object to complete its meaning.

My watch *stopped.*

Linking verb. A verb that connects a subject with a predicate adjective or noun. The various forms of *to be* are the most commonly used linking verbs. *Become, look, seem, appear,* and *grow* are often used as linking verbs. (See ¶1066.)

He *became* a mining engineer.

Principal parts of verbs. See *Principal parts.*

Transitive verb. A verb that requires an object to complete its meaning. (See also *Object.*)

I *wrote* that letter.

Verbal. A word that partakes of the nature of a verb but functions in some other way. (See *Gerund; Infinitive; Participle.*)

Voice. The property of a verb that indicates whether the subject acts or is acted upon.

Active voice. A verb is in the active voice when its subject is the doer of the act.

Norman *wrote* the report.

Passive voice. A verb is in the passive voice when its subject is acted upon.

The report *was written* by Norman.

Vowels. The letters *a, e, i, o,* and *u.* The letters *w* and *y* sometimes act like vowels (as in *awl* or in *cry*). (See also *Consonants.*)

REFERENCE
BOOKS

1801 Certain basic reference books are a must in almost any business office. These include a desk-sized dictionary, a secretarial handbook, and a telephone directory. In addition, each type of business has its own special reference sources. The public library also is a good source of information.

Almanacs
Information Please Almanac, Atlas and Yearbook, Simon and Schuster, New York. (Published annually.)
The Official Associated Press Almanac, Hammond Almanac, Inc., Maplewood, N.J. (Published annually.)
Reader's Digest Almanac and Yearbook, W. W. Norton & Company Inc., New York. (Published annually.)
The World Almanac & Book of Facts, Newspaper Enterprise Association, Inc., New York. (Published annually.)

Biographical Information
Webster's Biographical Dictionary, G. & C. Merriam Company, Springfield, Mass., 1974.
Who's Who, St. Martin's Press, New York. (A biographical dictionary of notable persons, mostly British; published annually.)
Who's Who in America, Marquis Who's Who, Inc., Chicago. (A biographical dictionary of notable living Americans; published biennially. Similar biographical dictionaries are *Who's Who in American Politics, Who's Who in Finance and Industry, Who's Who in the Midwest,* etc.)

Book and Periodical Directories
Ayer Directory of Publications, Ayer Press, Philadelphia. (Published annually.)
Books in Print, R. R. Bowker Company, New York. (An author-title-subject index to *The Publishers' Trade List Annual;* published annually.)
Cumulative Book Index, The H. W. Wilson Company, New York. (A listing of currently published books in the English language; published monthly.)
The New York Times Index, The New York Times Company, New York. (Published semimonthly.)
The Publishers' Trade List Annual, R. R. Bowker Company, New York. (Published annually.)
Readers' Guide to Periodical Literature, The H. W. Wilson Company, New York. (Published semimonthly, September–June; monthly, July–August.)

Business and Government Directories

Encyclopedia of Associations, 9th ed., Gale Research Co., Detroit, 1975. (Updated by quarterly reports.)

The Martindale-Hubbell Law Directory, Martindale-Hubbell, Inc., Summit, N.J. (Published annually.)

Polk's World Bank Directory, North American Edition, R. L. Polk & Co., Nashville. (Published semiannually.)

Poor's Register of Corporations, Directors and Executives, Standard & Poor's Corporation, New York. (Published annually.)

Rand McNally International Bankers Directory, Rand McNally & Company, Chicago. (Published semiannually.)

Thomas Register of American Manufacturers, Thomas Publishing Company, New York. (Published annually.)

Also consult local telephone directories (both alphabetic and classified) as well as local city directories and lists of city officials.

Dictionaries and Wordbooks

The American Heritage Dictionary of the English Language, American Heritage Publishing Co., Inc., and Houghton Mifflin Company, Boston, 1973.

Byers, Edward E., *10,000 Medical Words,* Gregg Division, McGraw-Hill Book Company, 1972.

Funk & Wagnalls New Standard Dictionary of the English Language, Funk & Wagnalls Publishing Company, New York, 1963. (Unabridged.)

Funk & Wagnalls Standard College Dictionary, Funk & Wagnalls Publishing Company, New York, 1963. (Desk-sized.)

Kurtz, Margaret A., *10,000 Legal Words,* Gregg Division, McGraw-Hill Book Company, 1971.

Leslie, Louis A., *20,000 Words,* 7th ed., Gregg Division, McGraw-Hill Book Company, New York, 1977. (A pocket-sized book for checking spelling and word division.)

The Oxford English Dictionary, Oxford University Press, New York, 1933.

The Random House Dictionary of the English Language, Random House, Inc., New York, 1966.

Roget's International Thesaurus, 3d ed., Thomas Y. Crowell Company, New York, 1962. (A word book for finding a word to fit an idea.)

Webster's Collegiate Thesaurus, G. & C. Merriam Company, Springfield, Mass., 1976.

Webster's New Collegiate Dictionary, G. & C. Merriam Company, Springfield, Mass., 1976. (Eighth edition; desk-sized.)

Webster's New World Dictionary of the American Language, Second College Edition, William Collins + World Publishing Co., Inc., Cleveland, 1976.

Webster's Third New International Dictionary, G. & C. Merriam Company, Springfield, Mass. (Unabridged.)

Encyclopedias

The Encyclopedia Americana, Americana Corporation, New York, 1974.

The New Columbia Encyclopedia, Columbia University Press, New York, 1975.

The New Encyclopaedia Britannica, Encyclopaedia Britannica, Inc., Chicago, 1974.

Etiquette and Personal Development

Amy Vanderbilt's New Complete Book of Etiquette, Doubleday & Company, Inc., Garden City, N.Y., 1967.

Post, Elizabeth L., *The New Emily Post's Etiquette,* Funk & Wagnalls, New York, 1975.

Whitcomb, Helen, and Laura S. Cochran, *The Modern Ms.,* Gregg Division, McGraw-Hill Book Company, New York, 1975.

———— and Rosalind Lang, *Today's Woman,* 3d ed., Gregg Division, McGraw-Hill Book Company, New York, 1976.

Financial and Credit Information

Corporation Records, Standard & Poor's Corporation, New York. (Published semimonthly.)

Dun & Bradstreet Reference Book, Dun & Bradstreet, Inc., New York. (By subscription only; published bimonthly.)

Moody's manuals, Moody's Investors Service, Inc., New York. (There are six separate manuals: *Moody's Bank & Finance Manual, Moody's Industrial Manual, Moody's Municipal & Government Manual, Moody's OTC Industrial Manual, Moody's Public Utility Manual,* and *Moody's Transportation Manual.* Published annually; updated by news reports published twice a week.)

Geographical and Travel Information

Commercial Atlas & Marketing Guide, Rand McNally & Company, Chicago. (Published annually.)

Hotel & Motel Red Book, American Hotel Association Directory Corporation, New York. (Published annually.)

Travel information and road maps may be obtained from various automobile associations, oil companies, and map publishers.

Grammar and Style Books

Bernstein, Theodore M., *The Careful Writer: A Modern Guide to English Usage,* Atheneum, New York, 1965.

Follett, Wilson, *Modern American Usage,* Hill & Wang, New York, 1966.

Fowler, H. W., *A Dictionary of Modern English Usage,* 2d ed., revised by Sir Ernest Gowers, Oxford University Press, New York, 1965.

Hutchinson, Lois Irene, *Standard Handbook for Secretaries,* 8th ed., McGraw-Hill Book Company, New York, 1973.

A Manual of Style, 12 ed., rev., The University of Chicago Press, Chicago, 1969. (A standard reference for anyone who prepares typewritten copy for the printer.)

Perrin, Porter G., *Writer's Guide and Index to English,* 4th ed., Scott, Foresman and Company, Chicago, 1965. (Consists of two parts: a writer's guide, which discusses general English topics, and an index to English, which gives details on grammar and usage arranged alphabetically.)

U.S. Government Printing Office Style Manual, rev. ed., U.S. Government Printing Office, Washington, 1973.

Words Into Type, 3d ed., Prentice-Hall, Inc., 1974.

Postal and Shipping Information
Address Abbreviations, U.S. Postal Service Publication No. 59, Washington.

Bullinger's Postal and Shippers Guide for the United States and Canada, Bullinger's Guides, Inc., Westwood, N.J. (Published annually.)

Directory of Post Offices, U.S. Postal Service, Washington.

Dun & Bradstreet Exporters' Encyclopaedia, Dun & Bradstreet, Inc., New York. (Published annually.)

International Mail, U.S. Government Printing Office, Washington.

National ZIP Code Directory, U.S. Postal Service, Washington. (Revised periodically.)

Postal Service Manual, U.S. Government Printing Office, Washington.

Quotations
Bartlett's Familiar Quotations, 14th ed., Little, Brown and Company, Boston, 1968.

The Oxford Dictionary of Quotations, 2d ed., Oxford University Press, New York, 1953.

Secretarial and Clerical Handbooks
Anderson, Ruth I., et al., *The Administrative Secretary,* 2d ed., Gregg Division, McGraw-Hill Book Company, New York, 1976.

Archer, Fred C., et al., *General Office Procedures,* 4th ed., Gregg Division, McGraw-Hill Book Company, 1975.

Bate, Marjorie Dunlap, and Mary C. Casey, *Legal Office Procedures,* Gregg Division, McGraw-Hill Book Company, 1975.

Bredow, Miriam, *Medical Office Procedures,* Gregg Division, McGraw-Hill Book Company, New York, 1974.

Dallas, Richard J., and James M. Thompson, *Clerical and Secretarial Systems for the Office,* Prentice-Hall, Inc., Englewood Cliffs, N.J., 1975.

Fries, Albert C., et al., *Applied Secretarial Practice,* 7th ed., Gregg Division, McGraw-Hill Book Company, New York, 1974.

Hanna, J Marshall, et al., *Secretarial Procedures and Administration,* 6th ed., South-Western Publishing Co., Cincinnati, 1973.

Hutchinson, Lois Irene, *Standard Handbook for Secretaries,* 8th ed., McGraw-Hill Book Company, New York, 1973.

Lee, Dorothy E., and Walter A. Brower, Jr., *Secretarial Office Procedures, College Series,* Gregg Division, McGraw-Hill Book Company, 1976.

Meehan, James R., et al., *Clerical Office Procedures,* 5th ed., South-Western Publishing Co., Cincinnati, 1973.

———, *Secretarial Office Procedures,* 8th ed., South-Western Publishing Co., Cincinnati, 1972.

Place, Irene, et al., *College Secretarial Procedures,* 4th ed., Gregg Division, McGraw-Hill Book Company, New York, 1972.

Statistics
Statistical Abstract of the United States, U.S. Bureau of the Census, Washington. (Statistics on social, political, and economic organization; published annually.)

The GREGG REFERENCE MANUAL

INDEX

This index contains many entries for individual words. If you are looking for a specific word that is not listed, refer to ¶717, which contains a 12-page guide to words that are frequently confused because they sound alike or look alike (for example, *capital–capitol–Capitol* or *stationary–stationery*).

NOTE: The boldface numbers in this index refer to paragraph numbers; the lightface numbers refer to page numbers.